Interfaith Marketing

Religious affiliation and religiosity of consumers can give rise to a differentiation of marketing strategy and marketing mix. They influence the values, habits and attitudes of consumers as well as their decision-making and consumption behavior. This book presents a comprehensive overview of the current state of knowledge of comparative religious research.

The authors discuss the basic concepts and approaches of this interdisciplinary field. They describe central concepts of religious studies (e.g. intrinsic vs. extrinsic religiosity) and the various world religions. Then, they analyze how religiosity and religious affiliation influence consumer behavior, and what consequences this has for companies that operate across borders. How can or should they take into account the religious characteristics of their target groups?

This original book will be a valuable resource for scholars of international marketing and business, consumer behavior and religious studies.

Frank G. Cabano is an Assistant Professor of Marketing at Kansas State University. He previously was an Assistant Professor of Marketing at the University of Texas at El Paso. His major fields of research are religion's influence on consumer behavior, identity-based consumption, and judgment and decision making. He has published articles in scientific journals such as *Journal of Service Research, European Journal of Marketing, Information & Management, Journal of Business Research, Journal of Behavioral Decision Making, Psychology & Marketing,* and *Marketing Letters.*

Stefan Müller was Full Professor of Business Administration and Marketing at Dresden University of Technology. His major fields of research are customer behavior, cross-cultural marketing, international marketing and interfaith marketing. He has published articles in scientific journals such as *Journal of International Business Studies, Management International Review, Journal of Business Research, Marketing Letters* and *Journal of Euromarketing.*

Katja Gelbrich is Full Professor of Business Administration and International Management at Catholic University of Eichstaett-Ingolstadt, Germany. Her major fields of research are automated agents, digital services, cross-cultural marketing & management and service recovery. She has published articles in scientific journals such as *Journal of the Academy of Marketing Science*, *Journal of Service Research*, *Journal of Retailing*, *Journal of Business Research*, *Marketing Letters*, *Business Ethics Quarterly*, *Journal of Retailing and Consumer Services* and *Journal of Services Marketing*.

Routledge Studies in Marketing

This series welcomes proposals for original research projects that are either single- or multi-authored or an edited collection from both established and emerging scholars working on any aspect of marketing theory and practice and provides an outlet for studies dealing with elements of marketing theory, thought, pedagogy and practice.

It aims to reflect the evolving role of marketing and bring together the most innovative work across all aspects of the marketing 'mix' – from product development, consumer behaviour, marketing analysis, branding, and customer relationships, to sustainability, ethics and the new opportunities and challenges presented by digital and online marketing.

44 **Marketing in Developing Nations**
Contemporary Developments, Cases and Problems in Africa Asia and the Middle East
Edited by Ayodele C. Oniku

45 **Money and Marketing in the Art World**
Henrik Hagtvedt

46 **Interfaith Marketing**
A Cross-Religious Approach
Frank G. Cabano, Stefan Müller and Katja Gelbrich

47 **Decolonizing Marketing Theory and Practice**
Beyond Inclusivity and Sustainability Debates
Edited by Hasan Gilani

48 **The Future of Charity Marketing**
Edited by Sarah-Louise Mitchell and Fran Hyde

For more information about this series, please visit: www.routledge.com/Routledge-Studies-in-Marketing/book-series/RMKT

Interfaith Marketing

A Cross-Religious Approach

Frank G. Cabano, Stefan Müller and Katja Gelbrich

Routledge
Taylor & Francis Group
LONDON AND NEW YORK

First published 2025
by Routledge
4 Park Square, Milton Park, Abingdon, Oxon OX14 4RN

and by Routledge
605 Third Avenue, New York, NY 10158

Routledge is an imprint of the Taylor & Francis Group, an informa business

British Library Cataloguing-in-Publication Data
A catalogue record for this book is available from the British Library

ISBN: 9781032827476 (hbk)
ISBN: 9781032827483 (pbk)
ISBN: 9781003506010 (ebk)

DOI: 10.4324/9781003506010

Typeset in Sabon
by codeMantra

Contents

Lists of figures *xi*
List of tables *xiii*
Preface *xv*

PART I
Introduction to interfaith marketing 1

1 Interfaith marketing: a neglected field of research 3
2 Religion as a subject of social science research 6
3 Religion as a subject of business and economic research 10
4 Methodological problems of comparative religion research 21

PART II
Religion and religiosity 27

1 Main concepts of religious studies 29
2 Old and new religions 40
3 World religions: an overview 44

PART III
Basics of consumer behavior 49

1 Introduction 51
2 Religion, religiosity and personality 52
3 Religion, religiosity and consumer behavior 64

4 Purchase motives and buyer types 66
5 Purchase decisions 70
6 Customer satisfaction and likelihood of complaint 81
7 Customer loyalty 82

PART IV
Strategic marketing 85

1 Marketing goals 87
2 Standardization vs. differentiation 91
3 Target groups 96

PART V
Product policy 105

1 Types of benefits 107
2 Product innovation 109
3 Product design 118
4 Branding 135
5 Product types 142

PART VI
Service policy 149

1 Forms and characteristics of services 151
2 Service businesses 153
3 Perceived service quality 161
4 Managing service failures 164

PART VII
Pricing policy 177

1 Attitudes toward money and possessions 179
2 Price fairness 183

3 Price consciousness 185

4 Willingness to pay 189

PART VIII
Distribution policy 199

1 Fundamentals 201

2 Market entry barriers 202

3 Negotiations 209

4 Market entry strategies 211

5 Distribution channels 216

6 Store management 223

7 Shopping place preference 227

PART IX
Communication policy 233

1 Communication goals 235

2 Target groups of communication 240

3 Time and subject of communication 243

4 Media usage 244

5 Personal communication 249

6 Advertising 251

Notes *267*
Bibliography *271*
Index *325*

Figures

1	Structural model of interfaith marketing	5
2	Attitudes toward socially controversial issues	8
3	Religious affiliation, religiosity and consumer behavior	19
4	From religious behavioral imperatives to secular consumer behavior	19
5	Religiosity and the desire for friendly sales staff	25
6	Religious and spiritual beliefs	36
7	Denominational structure of societies	45
8	Causes or correlates of ethnocentrism	56
9	Religiosity and national pride	58
10	Sociopolitical map	62
11	Structural model of research on interfaith consumer behavior	65
12	Intention to buy halal products according to the "Theory of Reasoned Action"	78
13	Confessionally homogeneous country groups as the starting point for the Differentiated Standardization strategy	94
14	Religiosity and willingness to buy innovative technical products	111
15	Religious affiliation-specific innovation diffusion curve	114
16	Attitudes of religious people toward artificial intelligence	115
17	Influence of God/human/nature understanding on support for environmental protection organizations	125
18	Animosity of Israeli consumers toward Arab products	132
19	Structure of value-based satisfaction research in the service sector	152
20	Basic structure of the confirmation/disconfirmation model of satisfaction research in conjunction with the SERVQUAL approach to service research	162
21	Materialism in selected countries	181
22	Willingness to pay as a function of religious affiliation	190
23	Percentage willingness to pay more as a function of product benefit	193

24 Willingness to pay for fair trade coffee as a function of the presence of religion 196
25 Structural equation model of willingness to engage in corruption 205
26 Influence of different distance measures on market entry 208
27 Image profile of smaller neighborhood stores 219
28 Religiosity and ethnocentrism as a function of religious affiliation 221
29 Influence of religiosity and religious centrism on customer behavior: Results of a path analysis 232
30 Personality and risk perception 242
31 Typology of American online users 247

Tables

1	Basic structure of an ideal study design	23
2	Two-dimensional operationalization of religiosity	33
3	Religion-specific scales for measuring religiosity	35
4	New religions that emerged in opposition to a world religion	42
5	New religions that emerged in opposition to established political power	43
6	Distribution and development of world religions (in millions)	44
7	World religions at a glance	46
8	Scale for measuring fatalism	58
9	Factor structure of purchasing behavior	69
10	Willingness to pay of brand-conscious German consumers	71
11	Extract from Muncy-Vitell consumer ethics scale	74
12	Attitude/behavior discrepancy in the purchase of ethical products as a function of religious denomination	80
13	Confessionally homogeneous countries	93
14	Religious diversity in the US, in %	95
15	Influence of religious affiliation on attitudes toward genetically modified foods	116
16	Religion-specific color associations	127
17	Animosity research at a glance	132
18	Willingness to pay more depending on religious affiliation	191
19	Religious freedom ranking in 2019	212
20	Importance of shopping place characteristics	229

Preface

More than 30 years ago, Cutler (1991) published an analysis of the literature on *Religion and Marketing* with a telling subtitle: *Important Research Area or a Footnote in the Literature?* A decade later, the answer to this rhetorical question was no different. The research field was still considered under-researched (cf. Lindridge 2005). Above all, there was a lack of systematic comparative studies. Meanwhile, while some high-quality review articles are available (e.g. Agarwala et al. 2019), no comprehensive account of interfaith marketing has yet been published in book form. In the English-language literature, one searches in vain for titles such as *Interfaith Marketing.*

Denomination-specific treatises are also rare and, moreover, do not offer a comprehensive account of the field of knowledge. Rather, readers will find more general reflections on the significance of Buddhist (cf. Williams-Oerberg 2021), Hindu (cf. Vinod 2013), Jewish (cf. Friedman 2001) or Confucian values (cf. Fam et al. 2009) for business activity. The closest to the claim of a comprehensive monograph is Sandıkcı/Rice (2011) with their *Handbook of Islamic Marketing*, albeit limited to the Islamic faith. Minton/Kahle (2016), in turn, have provided a book well worth reading on the influence of religions on a specific area of this research field: consumer behavior.

Interfaith marketing has two main focuses. On the one hand, it is of interest whether and in which way companies should adapt their strategies and marketing mix to the respective religious environment (e.g. their product policy to the numerous religion-specific taboos and rules of conduct). On the other hand, interfaith marketing deals with the influence of the type and strength of religiosity of the respective target group on the marketing mix (e.g. intrinsically religious consumers make ethical purchasing decisions to a greater extent than extrinsically religious consumers). Not addressed, however, are topics such as "church marketing" (i.e. marketing to a faith community, for example, to keep believers from leaving the church; e.g. Tscheulin/Dietrich 2001; Webb et al. 1998; Shawchuck et al., 1992) or what different faith groups think about marketing (e.g. Cutler/Winans, 1998).

At the first level of outline, the structure of this book is that of a traditional marketing textbook.

- Strategic decisions (e.g. Are managers who believe in a forgiving God more likely to make unethical decisions than managers whose God is a punitive God?).
- Product policies (e.g. Jews and Muslims are more interested in innovation than Catholics).
- Service policy (e.g. With religious complainants, an apology promises more success than material compensation for the service failure that they complained about).
- Distribution policy (e.g. The good reputation of a shopping place is even more important to Buddhists than its priceworthiness).
- Communication policy (e.g. In Muslim societies, comparative advertising is considered manipulative and therefore immoral).

However, differences also emerge at the second and third levels of classification. On the one hand, this is because the relevant research has so far not been as diverse and differentiated as traditional marketing research, and there are therefore still numerous "blanks." Second, this occurs because marketing textbooks do not usually address topics such as religious commitment and consumers' religious beliefs. While, to give an example, dissatisfied customers have three response options according to traditional readings (complaining, word of mouth, and switching providers), this book discusses in detail a fourth option typical of religion: forgiveness.

Furthermore, we regularly use some technical terms of marketing research and statistics that we cannot assume to be used by the target audience of this book and therefore briefly explain them here (priming, framing, operationalization, moderation, mediation):

- **Priming** refers to a process that occurs mostly unconsciously, but can also be used purposefully to achieve certain effects. Literally, priming means preparation. In terms of content, it is about the fact that emotions and cognitions usually do not arise "out of nowhere" but are initiated by the actualization of certain schemata. Schemata are mental structures in which our knowledge about the world is stored. Especially in ambiguous situations, activated schemas control the perception, mental processing and memorability of stimuli (cf. Aronson et al. 2020). For example, someone standing in front of a restaurant is more likely to think about food than if they were standing in a soccer stadium. A lily of the valley scent makes us think of spring, and the smell of lubricating oil makes us think of a car repair. Experiments show that people can easily be misled and also manipulated by priming. A well-known example is that if you ask study participants to say the word "refrigerator" ten times and then ask them, "What does a cow drink?", then a strikingly large number answer "milk" instead of "water" because of the association thus formed (refrigerator → milk). Both social science and comparative religion research exploit this phenomenon for the operationalization of independent variables (cf. Watanabe/Laurent 2018). Instead of asking, for example, the type and strength of individual religiosity, this is "primed" (i.e. the study participants are specifically placed in a corresponding state). In principle, all sensory organs can be used; however, visual and semantic priming are most frequently used.

A simple variant of semantic priming is to have study participants read some Bible texts or other religious writings before the actual investigation begins (cf. Carpenter/Marshall 2009). An even simpler way was chosen by Casidy et al. (2021). Their participants were made to think about religion in their lives by asking questions such as, "How much are you thinking about God right now?" Much more sophisticated is the Scrambled Sentences method (see, e.g. Zhang et al. 2020). In this method, sentences (e.g. religious texts such as the Islamic creed) are "scrambled" (i.e. put into a random order). An example of this would be, "And there is Muhammad, the Messenger of God, but God is no God." In order to be able to put this currently meaningless sentence back into its original meaningful form ("There is no God but God, and Muhammad is the Messenger of God"), the study participants have to deal with it intensively. As such, without being aware of the manipulation, they internalize the content of this sentence.

- **Framing**: Social information is mostly ambiguous. It acquires its concrete meaning, valid for a specific situation, only through additional information, such as the context (or "frame") in which it is presented. Framing research has repeatedly demonstrated, among other things, that decisions are decisively influenced solely by the way in which information is presented. For example, Thaler and Sunstein (2008) showed that more patients agree to undergo a difficult operation if they are told in the educational talk: "Of 100 patients who have this operation, 90 are alive after five years" (= gain frame). In contrast, the loss frame ("... 10 are dead") deters comparatively many, although the objective information is identical in both cases: 10% mortality rate.
- **Operationalization:** Constructs play an important role in social science research. These are social phenomena that cannot be observed directly, but from whose effects one can conclude that there must be "such a thing." Probably the best known construct is intelligence. Because obviously some people regularly perform better than others (at school, at work, or in everyday life), it is plausible that there must be something that the successful possess to a greater degree than the less successful. Science has agreed to call this something intelligence. To make it useful for empirical research, constructs must be made measurable. The technical term for the

measurement specification to be developed for this purpose is operationalization. Intelligence, for example, is often operationalized as learning progress in a defined task, as speed of problem-solving or as performance on a standardized intelligence test.

For comparative religion research, religiosity is an extremely important construct. It is mostly operationalized by behavioral indicators such as frequency of attendance at religious services, self-assessment ("How religious do you think you are?") or agreement or disagreement with important religious beliefs.

- **Moderation:** This term states that the influence of a variable A on a variable B is strengthened or weakened by a variable C: the moderator. In interfaith marketing research, religious affiliation and religiosity are the most important moderators. Thus, it has been shown that the perceived price worthiness of a shopping place (= A) has a stronger influence on the shopping place preference (B) of very religious consumers than on that of less religious consumers (= C).

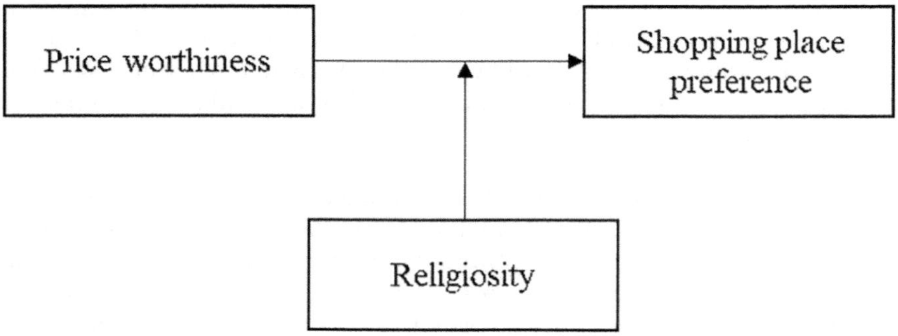

- **Mediation:** This term states that variable A does not directly affect variable B, but rather variable C affects variable B and variable A affects C. Thus, religious people (= A) are more convinced than average of the credibility of advertising messages (= B). If, however, the variable "trust in other people" (= C) is included in the analysis, this correlation dissolves. Now the picture shown in the graphic emerges: religiousness strengthens trust in other people, and those who trust other people in principle consider advertising to be credible.

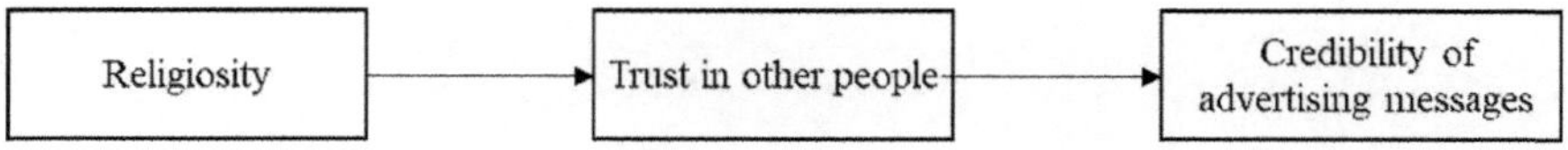

We would be pleased to receive feedback and suggestions for improvement. Lecturers can also request a PowerPoint file with the illustrations used in this book.

Frank G. Cabano, Stefan Müller,
Katja Gelbrich, April 2024

Part I

Introduction to interfaith marketing

1 Interfaith marketing

A neglected field of research

Religions influence almost all areas of life in a society, including consumption. This is because they determine the overarching value system in many respects, from which taboos, social norms, cultural standards and ultimately economically relevant behavior can be derived (cf. Fam et al. 2004, p. 552).

> For many people religion is about far more than a mere belief or opinion about God; it serves as the source of their morals and functions as a guide for the right course of action, including in the sphere of business and management.
>
> (Richardson/Ariffin 2019, p. 279)

In contrast to religious affiliation, the formal membership in a religious community, religiosity describes people's individual attitude toward "their" religion. As such, it is generally more concrete and behaviorally relevant than religious affiliation (cf. Essoo/Dibb 2004; Delener 1990a; Delener 1990b). The majority of the empirical studies we report on in this book, therefore, use individual differences in religiosity as an independent variable to explain the variance of the dependent variables, such as the willingness of consumers to follow religion-specific dietary laws or the acceptance of sexualized advertising messages.

Interfaith marketing (IFM) provides an answer to the question of whether and in what way companies in different country markets should adapt their marketing strategy and marketing tools to the respective religious environment. More than 80% of the world's population identifies as being religious (see Pew Research Forum 2017). Nevertheless, the keywords "religion" and "religiosity" are rarely found in recent marketing textbooks or academic articles. The reasons why scholars have thus far generally neglected this topic are manifold:

- Religion is often subsumed under the broader construct of culture (cf. Müller/Gelbrich 2021, p. 66).
- Nowadays, religion plays only a peripheral role in the public life of many societies (cf. Richardson/Ariffin 2019, p. 278). This sometimes results in certain ignorance.

DOI: 10.4324/9781003506010-2

- Another possible explanation is the conviction that other scientific disciplines are responsible for this area of inquiry (e.g., anthropologists, sociologists, psychologists).
- Hirschman (1983, p. 132) speculated that "religion may be viewed as a taboo subject, being too sensitive to submit to investigation." Others argued with the special sensitivity of this subject (cf. Bailey/Sood 1993).
- Paradoxically, however, the ubiquity of religion may be the problem. This is because the analytical understanding of science that prevails in marketing presupposes clearly identifiable variables. But if religion permeates all levels of our lives, regardless of whether we are believers or not, it is difficult to clearly identify cause and effect (cf. Delener 1994).
- The inner contradiction between the prevailing mostly materialistic understanding of science and the transcendence of the phenomenon of religion may also play a role.

Indeed, the warning by the author of a fundamental work on Islamic humanism in the 10th century is still relevant. He considered it "dangerous cultural illiteracy if we measure the importance of an area only by its economic strength and no longer by its spiritual-cultural wealth" (Arkoŭn 1982). For in fact, hardly anything has contributed so much to the differentiation of cultural areas as the various religions and moral teachings that have emerged worldwide in the course of human history (cf. Lavoie/Chamlee-Wright 2001). In the words of Harrison (2011, p. 26), "Religion may not be the only fount of cultural values, beliefs, and attitudes ... [but] it is surely one of the most influential."

It should be added, however, that to no lesser extent different language structures (cf. Huntington 1993) and climatic conditions[1] (cf. Landes 1998) have given rise to the national cultural diversity we know today. Together, they have each created a unique combination of social norms and values on the one hand, and attitudes and lifestyles on the other. Taken together, these influence consumer behavior and, consequently, marketing in a manner as presented below (cf. Figure 1). For this reason, some studies do not measure national culture directly, but indirectly, with religion and language as proxy variables (e.g., Stulz/Williamson 2003; Baldauf et al. 2000).

Everyday life offers numerous examples of the relevance of the religious environment for IFM. One needs only think of the production and distribution of alcoholic beverages or of revealing clothing. The sensitivity required in the use of colors is often underestimated, since in many societies they fulfill a liturgical function and are therefore conditioned by religion (cf. V-3.5). But what about the purchase or use of seemingly value-free services or products? That religious beliefs also play a significant role in this process may not be assumed at first glance, but it has been shown to be the case empirically many times before.

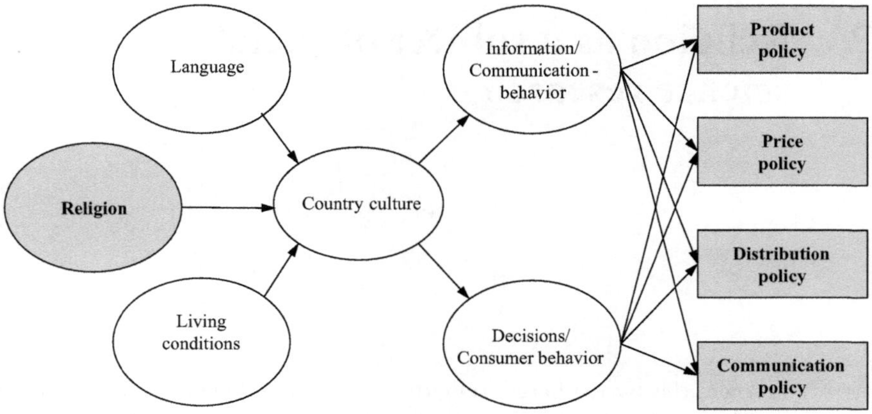

Figure 1 Structural model of interfaith marketing.
Source: Own representation.

Beginning with, for example, Bailey/Sood (1993) and Hirschman (1983), an independent field of research "Religion & Consumption" has gradually developed (Casidy/Arli 2018; see Part III, Chapter 3). Apart from this, religion has been a subject of research in social sciences and business/economic sciences, providing important insights that can be used for IFM.

2 Religion as a subject of social science research

At first glance, the two spheres, religion and science, seem to have little in common. Many are even convinced that faith and science are mutually exclusive. In fact, however, the distance is smaller than one might think. Religions influence human behavior in two ways:

- Directly, by creating highly specific and binding rules of conduct.
- Indirectly, by shaping or justifying values and attitudes that influence economically relevant behaviors, such as attitudes toward and use of luxury products.

2.1 Theoretical basis

Marketing research attempts to explain, forecast and influence human behavior. Why do some people always buy the cheapest product, while others mainly purchase prestigious brands? Who prefers to listen to the advice of friends and acquaintances, and who trusts trade journals and other neutral sources?

According to expected utility theory preferred by economists, consumers generally choose the option or product that promises them the greatest utility (cf. Dubé 2019; Chintagunta/Nair 2011). However, the theory of social identity has greater explanatory power for Interfaith Marketing (IFM) (cf. Tajfel/Turner 1986). According to this theory, people prefer to make decisions like other people who belong to the same social category as they do. One of the most important, and for many the most important, social category is religious affiliation. This is why people with similar religious beliefs often develop similar preferences, make similar decisions and behave in similar ways.

2.2 Food laws and other rules of behavior

Apart from Buddhism, most religions provide believers with more or less detailed rules of conduct. What may be consumed and when? How are certain foods to be prepared (cf. Heiman et al. 2019)? Jews and Muslims,

DOI: 10.4324/9781003506010-3

for example, should not eat pork, while Hindus should not eat beef. In general, Jews should eat kosher ("pure"). This also applies to Muslims (halal). But for no religious community are the dietary laws (Kashrut) as elementary as for Judaism (cf. Spiegel 2010; Regenstein et al. 2003). However, the halal concept is much broader and regulates not only the type and preparation of food but almost all areas of life (see Muhamad/Mizerski 2013).

Jews may only eat meat from animals that are both ruminants and have cloven hooves (e.g., sheep, cows). Conversely, the meat of pigs, horses, camels or rabbits is unclean. Because the consumption of blood is strictly forbidden, as little blood as possible should remain in the carcass when the animals are slaughtered. For this reason, animals are slaughtered by making an incision through the carotid artery and, to remove any remaining blood, they are then cleaned ("butchered") with salt and water. Since most foods contain flavor enhancers, emulsifiers, preservatives and the like, some of which are made from animal substances, orthodox believers are not allowed to consume many foods. As such, the product packaging must clearly state the composition of the product. Believers are also forbidden to visit non-Jewish restaurants.

Commandments, prohibitions and taboos are one thing. However, the willingness of individuals to actually abide by them is another. If one follows the results of a small, exploratory study (16–107 subjects in the various subsamples), then only Muslims (=80%) and Jews (=62%) are willing to observe the dietary rules of their religion (cf. Bailey/Sood 1993). Of the Hindus surveyed, 47% were willing, while this seems to be of secondary importance for Buddhists (=30%) and for adherents of Christian denominations (Protestants = 11%, Catholics = 10%).

In the course of secularization, many of these religious rules of conduct have become obsolete. As a result, although non-religious members of a society may also observe them, they ultimately perform social rather than religious rituals, often during major holidays (e.g., attendance at Christmas mass). However, this should not be underestimated. After all, festivals (e.g., Easter) and rituals (e.g., burial) are meaningful for the social order of the respective society (see Renfrew et al. 2016). They also make the places where they are celebrated (e.g., temples, cemeteries) culturally meaningful places.

2.3 Values, attitudes and individual behavior

If one understands religion as a canon of fundamental values and religiosity as the extent to which a person adheres to these values, the behavioral relevance is evident (cf. Batson et al. 1993; Hirschman 1982). For example, those who have internalized the eighth commandment, "Thou shalt not bear false witness against thy neighbor," are likely to make more effort than others to be tax honest (cf. Stack/Kposowa 2006). Although there have long been indications and empirical evidence of a close link between religious affiliation and economically relevant behavior (e.g., Weber 1905), other disciplines besides marketing have initially addressed this field of research. The majority of sociologists, psychologists, religious scientists and anthropologists have analyzed the influence of religiosity on:

i Infidelity and divorce rates (e.g., Tuttle/Davis 2015)
ii Gender roles (e.g., Höpflinger et al. 2008) and sexual behavior (e.g., Vasilenko et al. 2013)
iii Attitudes toward family life (e.g., Sabatier et al. 2011) and politics (e.g., Deitelhoff et al. 2019)
iv Identity formation (e.g., Mendl et al. 2020)
v Personality structure (e.g., Henningsgaard/Arnau 2008)

In addition, what people think about gender roles, abortion, homosexuality and other controversial issues can be predicted quite well if one knows their religious affiliation (cf. Figure 2). While only a minority – or a slight majority – of Muslims accept gender equality, divorce, abortion and homosexuality (12–55%), the approval ratings of members of other faith communities are significantly higher at 48–82% (cf. Inglehart/Norris 2003). Another consequence of religiosity that is not insignificant for society concerns family planning. Religious families have an average of 2.1 children, irrespective of their religious affiliation, while non-religious families have only 1.6 children on average.

Last but not least, religious values contribute to one's self- as well as social identity. They unite people with similar convictions in a faith community and distinguish it from other groups (cf. Mavor/Ysseldyk 2020; Ysseldyk et al. 2010). This leads to greater cohesion and cooperation within the religious in-group.

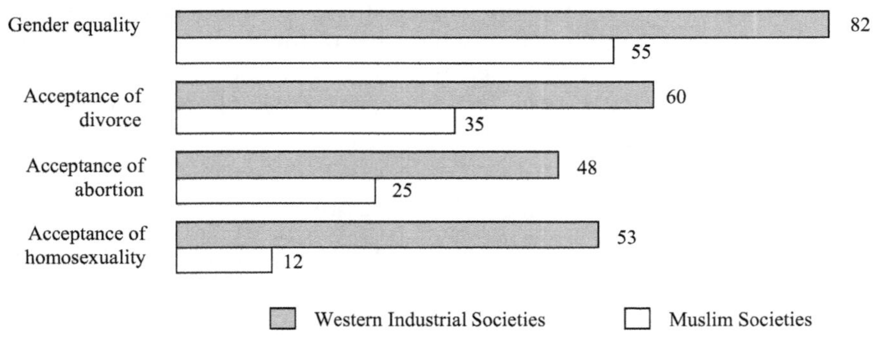

Figure 2 Attitudes toward socially controversial issues.
Source: Inglehart/Norris (2003, p. 69).

2.4 Institutional and organizational behavior

When non-governmental organizations such as Transfair call on politicians and companies not to trade with certain countries because human rights are being violated there, the call for a boycott is rooted not least in Christian ethics. For at the center of these ethics is human dignity. The dignity of the individual was first established by the story of creation (Genesis, 1st Book of Moses): As made in the image and likeness of God, every single human being possesses inalienable dignity. With the Enlightenment, humanistic justifications were added (cf. Pinto de Oliveira 1980, p. 420ff.). Finally, the ideals of the French Revolution ("liberty, equality, fraternity") paved the way for a secularized worldview and humanity characterized by rationality. As a result, the individual human being changed from object to subject (cf. Ratzinger 2000, p. 63).

Like the family, religion can be seen as an institution that "produces trust and values" and, thus, ensures that many transactions can be carried out far more efficiently than if the actors behaved opportunistically (cf. Berger 1986). Under the influence of Buddhism, Hinduism and Confucianism, the question of whom one can trust and with whom one can consequently maintain (business) relations is answered very concretely and rigidly in collectivist societies: "the members of one's family." For individualistic, Christian societies, however, the answer to this question is rather abstract: All people who share one's values and convictions are trustworthy (e.g., because they are of the same faith).

Furthermore, it has been shown that religion and religiosity play a constructive role in many decision-making fields of corporate management:

- Designing succession in family businesses (cf. Shen/Su 2017)
- Credit financing of corporate activity (see Cai/Shi 2019)
- Revenue management and tax avoidance (cf. Hofmann/Schwaiger 2020)

3 Religion as a subject of business and economic research

Many years after the pioneering sociological studies of religion by Weber (1905), Mayer/Sharp (1962) were the first to empirically analyze the relationship between religious affiliation and economic success. By means of personal interviews, they found that Jews and Orthodox Christians were significantly more successful than Catholics in particular. However, the authors acknowledged that their study was biased. This is because certain religious communities are conspicuously more likely to practice certain professions, which in turn promise economic success to varying degrees. Thus, it is not clear whether economic success is influenced by religious affiliation or by occupational status. The lasting merit of this study, however, is to have placed the influence of religious beliefs on economic activity on the agenda of empirical research. In the course of research in the sociology and economics of religion, however, it became increasingly clear that religiosity is often a better predictor of socioeconomic behavior than religious affiliation (see I-4.1).

3.1 Business ethics

As an "economic theory of morality," business ethics deals with the consequences of ethical principles (e.g., responsibility, justice) on economic behaviors. The current environmental crisis provides an example of this: What prevents or induces acting persons and institutions to behave in an environmentally friendly way? As another example, is it fair when executives receive many times more than ordinary employees are paid (cf. Holzmann 2019; Lütge/Uhl 2017)? Indeed, it is undisputed that religions encourage or oblige people to act morally in one way or another (cf. Gokcekus/Ekici 2020, p. 566).

3.1.1 Jewish business ethics

The guiding principle of Jewish business ethics is egalitarian and aimed at enabling the individual, as made in the image of God, to live a dignified,

DOI: 10.4324/9781003506010-4

autonomous life. Two overriding principles serve this goal: Mercy and Justice. They are emphasized in the:

- Sabbatical year: Man should always be free from economic constraints.
- Debt relief: In the seventh year, debtors are to have their debts cancelled so that they can lead a free life again.
- Jubilee year: After 50 years, the original ownership conditions are to be restored (e.g., through land restitution).
- Treating the poor fairly, without regard to person, and granting them interest-free loans.

Ch. 62 of the Halacha is also committed to human dignity:[2]

> Whoever takes advantage of his neighbor, whether the seller takes advantage of the buyer or the buyer takes advantage of the seller, transgresses a prohibition, it says: If you sell one to another or buy from another's hand, do not take advantage of your brother.
>
> (Leviticus 25:14)

As in all agrarian societies with limited value creation that can hardly be increased, charity played an important role in Judaism. Donations are not voluntary, but a religious duty. Jews must give alms, a total of at least 10% of net earnings per year (ch. 34: Charity). Even poor people who receive alms or welfare themselves must give a portion to others. Nevertheless, the religious scriptures do not glorify poverty. Priority is given to work that, carried out according to divine law, brings long life, peace and prosperity (cf. Albertini 2022). In business, honesty should prevail and create mutual trust. As in Islam, the prohibition of interest plays an important role in Jewish ethics. However, it is disputed whether this applies only to Jews or also to non-Jews.

3.1.2 Catholic business ethics

Catholic business ethics has gone through various phases and transformations, starting with a phase critical of the economy. It is symbolized by a scene from the New Testament in which Jesus expels the merchants from the temple. It can be understood as the central theme of the relationship between economic life and early Christianity (cf. Kaufer 1998, p. 16). Initially, Christians explicitly rejected the city and urban culture as a creation of Cain (Genesis 4:17) and thus implicitly rejected the world of consumption. Only those who shun the worldly and repent can escape both and tread the "path of salvation." Their need for earthly goods was covered by the church at that time with the help of the "giving economy" (cf. Maus 1990) – in exchange for the spiritual treasures that the church acquired with its prayers and penitential practices. Merchants, however, were to be expelled from the church because of their profession, since they could hardly or never please God (Canon Ejiciens Dominus). Paradoxically, nationalism, communism and other totalitarian systems of rule seamlessly adopted the anti-merchant ideology of Christianity, from which they were otherwise so distant.

In the course of the 13th century, a fundamental change took place that increasingly reconciled the economy and religion (i.e., phase of coexistence). Since the increasingly numerous inhabitants of the cities could obviously only obtain the necessities of life through barter, the thesis of the "hinge function of the merchants" found increasing acceptance (cf. Kaufer 1998, p. 55). At the same time, however, their actions were increasingly subject to moral and ethical evaluation (e.g., prohibition of usury, function and legitimacy of property, problem of the fair price).

Another characteristic of the Christian doctrine of salvation is the idealization of poverty. The fact that those who renounce earthly possessions in this world or live in poverty for other reasons will be rewarded in the afterlife is a central component of the Catholic value system. As a counterbalance, sharing and charity are heavily emphasized. These values ensure social solidarity and maintain a lasting balance in an environment characterized by scarce resources. At the same time, however, they prevent social change in general, and economic accumulation and entrepreneurial behavior in particular.

The phase of acceptance found visible expression in Catholic social teaching. Now, the free-market economic order is advocated in the form of a social market economy with a focus on balance. The economy should serve people and not subject them to the sheer pursuit of profit. The goal is the broadest possible distribution of wealth (cf. Ockenfels 1992). Recent studies on the sociology of religion show that this is the case: Of all the religious groups studied, Catholics show the strongest positive correlation between religious convictions and acceptance of economic goals such as economic growth, while negative attitudes predominate among Muslims (cf. Guiso et al. 2003).

3.1.3 Protestant business ethics

Protestant business ethics is a consequence of the Reformation, which revolutionized the hitherto dominant Christian medieval worldview. It initially enabled Protestant societies to achieve above-average economic success, for which above all the appreciation of an ascetic and rational way of life is held responsible. It emphasizes the willingness to work hard and to exercise strict self-control (cf. III-2.8).

Ascetic Protestantism permanently changed the worldview of the Christian world. It displaced some of the anti-achievement norms established by Catholicism and, in contrast, strengthened the achievement-oriented norms that were essential for the modernization of Europe. The Protestants' ascetic lifestyle also enabled them to accumulate significant capital in the course of the 19th century, thus laying the foundation for industrialization. Their financial resources enabled them to invest more heavily in industrial plants and increase productivity.

Unlike Catholics, the people in Protestant areas increasingly accepted the capitalist economic system. They no longer considered the accumulation of economic goods to be reprehensible, as Catholic doctrine tended to do, but rather as evidence of God's favor. The so-called doctrine of predestination can also explain why Calvinist, Pietist and Puritan societies tolerate class and welfare differences much more than Catholic societies.

3.1.4 *Orthodox business ethics*

The Orthodox Church rejects the driving force of the capitalist economic system: the pursuit of profit and the possession of economic goods (cf. Rothlauf 2012, p. 595 f.). Unlike unproductive capital and God-given land ownership, labor is accepted as an indispensable factor of production. However, it is not, as in Protestantism, in the service of an individualistic work ethic but is necessary so that the individual can fulfill his or her duties to the authorities. Priority is given to spiritual tasks.

3.1.5 *Islamic business ethics*

Arabia used to be equated with wealth and happiness: Arabia Felix.[3] Today, despite or because of the oil wealth of some states, this cultural region is threatened by economic stagnation and, in some places, impoverishment of broad sections of the population (see Koopmans 2020). Religion is repeatedly cited as one of the causes of this undesirable development. One argument against the thesis that Islamic economic ethics inhibit economic development is that the Koran – interpreted in modern terms – describes a form of social market economy (see Nienhaus 2004). Allah, the ultimate owner of all goods, makes them available to people. In this respect, Islam recognizes the right to private property, even in the means of production, except in the case of mineral resources and other natural resources, which are collectively owned.

However, all private-sector activities are subject to the primacy of the common good, justice, stability and solidarity. Entrepreneurs should pay their employees a fair wage, demand reasonable local prices from their customers, use honest weights and measures and strive for reasonable profits (see Leipold 2022, p. 736). Monetary policy is not intended to pursue expansionary goals (economic growth) but to ensure monetary stability. However, the prohibition of interest (riba) has proven to be a structural problem. Originally, it was intended to prevent the usury that was common in the past when emergency loans were granted after bad harvests, as this practice had forced many people into financial hardship. In a modern economy based on the division of labor, however, credit-financed investments are common and necessary. Consequently, financing instruments had to be developed that do not require interest payments (e.g., profit-sharing). These instruments became known as Islamic banking (see VI-2.4).

In summary, it is not Islam per se that is responsible for the pronounced hostility to innovation and weak growth in many Islamic countries (see Abdel-Samad 2019; Landes 1998), but rather it is certain personality traits that often go hand in hand with strong religiosity. Specifically, these are dogmatism, fatalism, belief in authority and an extreme sense of tradition (cf. III-2). These and also the extensive exclusion of women – that is, half the population – from public life and the economic process are causal factors in the struggles of this region. Islamic culture differs from Christian culture not only in its attitude toward equality but also toward democracy (Inglehart/Norris 2003, p. 68).

3.1.6 Confucian business ethics

Confucianism favors similar attitudes toward achievement and wealth as Protestantism. For this reason, among others, the ambivalent relationship of Catholic occidental culture to success and wealth is alien to the Chinese cultural sphere. Unlike in European literature, where the poor and poverty usually embody the good, in Chinese sagas only the bad are ever poor (cf. Doyle/Doyle 2001).

The rapid economic growth in East Asia since the 1990s has often been explained by the renewed influence of Confucian moral teachings on this region (cf. Lee 1995). According to the neo-Confucianism thesis, a new Confucian economic ethics has emerged from the traditional Eastern collective-oriented values on the one hand, and the modern individualistic economic values of the West on the other. Drivers of the "Asian miracle" include (see Terry 2015):

- Good governance
- Successful industrial policy
- Overcoming the rigid social hierarchy of professions and developing modern job profiles (e.g., entrepreneur, manager, engineer)
- High overall economic investment ratio
- A culturally conditioned willingness to perform and save (due to family obligation) as well as other Confucian virtues

For Confucian societies, reverence for ancestors and parents is a moral duty and establishes close ties within the family. Not dishonoring them is one of the primary goals one tries to achieve through "hard work." The goal of preparing people for the future is one of the highest goals, which one tries to achieve through "hard work" (cf. Baumann/Winzar 2017). Achievement orientation is considered a value in itself, and social advancement succeeds through lifelong learning. Individuals should also take their fate into their own hands. Those who thereby attain wealth and prestige have obviously been given a gift from heaven. Furthermore:

- Public demonstration of wealth and prosperity is not an antisocial display, but an expression of the lived Confucian order.
- A profit motive is desired.
- It is right to strive for a better life by "all" means.
- Status symbols can be put on display.

On the whole, Confucianism promotes a pro-business attitude: values such as work, obedience, hierarchy and the pursuit of profit are clearly positive in East Asia. The flip side of Confucianism, however, has been the development of an exuberant bureaucracy and, in its wake, corruption. In ancient China, officials were highly respected but were only paid a very modest regular salary, which is why "courtesy gifts to officials, bribes, taxes diverted into one's own pocket, extorted fees and other extra income were commonplace and turned practically all offices into gold mines" (Klaschka 2000, p. 72). Consequently, there was nothing more important in life in the Ming period (1368–1644) than the usually ten-year preparation for the extremely strict three-stage civil service examination. However, only a few were lucky enough to obtain 1 of the approximately 20,000 offices in the Chinese empire. "The goal of the studies and the examinations was not to acquire any kind of specialized knowledge, but to become a cultivated individual educated in the spirit of Confucian ethics" (Klaschka 2000, p. 72).

Despite the burden of omnipresent corruption, Confucian-style bureaucracy was initially quite positive. Many centuries ago, it contributed to the replacement of the mostly incompetent hereditary nobility (i.e., the aristocracy by a "meritocracy": the aristocracy of merit).

The decisive disadvantage of Confucianism, which had stabilized China socially and in terms of power politics over a long period of time, became apparent only in the 19th century, when the excessive bureaucracy prevented the modernization of the country. Worried about losing their privileges, civil servants thwarted all attempts to emulate the industrial revolution of the West. China's elite, whom had only been trained ethically and morally, but not professionally, failed at that time. Its further decline was determined by the fact that the traditional bureaucratic state was forcibly dissolved in 1911, but bureaucracy and corruption remained in Chinese society.

3.1.7 *Hindu business ethics*

Hindu business ethics are characterized by the fulfillment of duty, renunciation and adaptation to nature. Man should not subjugate nature but rather respect and revere it. Instead of striving for comprehensive satisfaction of needs, as in the capitalist economic model, an "economy of renunciation" is propagated (cf. Uppal 1986). Individual interests should take a back seat to the collective interests of the family and caste, and greed is to be combated through yoga and asceticism. Last but not least, the pronounced ethics of responsibility purports that every action has consequences that no one can escape.

In addition to the idealization of renunciation and physical labor, the concentration on self-sufficient farming communities and small artisanal production units has proved to be an obstacle to the economy and growth. The same applies to the disregard for individual performance, performance-related pay and division of labor. Another obstacle is the caste system, which has drastically curtailed the freedom to choose an occupation (see Weber 1988, p. 109 ff.).

Nevertheless, India was and is successful in various economic sectors – first with diamond cutting, then with the production of ready-made clothing and finally in the IT sector (e.g., call centers, payroll accounting, software development). This can be explained, on the one hand, by the widely accepted ethics of renunciation in this society (for example, with regard to wage levels and working conditions) and, on the other hand, by the mathematical and logical thinking fostered in India.

3.1.8 Buddhist business ethics

Central to Buddhism is the idea of suffering as the essence of human existence. Suffering is often caused by mental poisons such as greed and egoism. The human being, who is trapped in a double illusion (e.g., ego-illusion), can overcome it by a "noble eight-part path of truth" (cf. II-4.1) and renounces the ultimately illusory world. This reveals a large difference between Buddhist business ethics and the Western economic model. The Western economic model's homo economicus, the equally rational and egoistic maximizer of benefits who exploits his or her environment, is opposed by Buddhist business ethics[12] that proposes an altruistic understanding of the economy in every respect, based on "pratityasamutpada," the mutual dependence of people on each other and on the environment (cf. Drechsler 2019). Accordingly, companies care about the well-being of their employees, customers, shareholders, the community and the environment. The goal of this "compassionate economy" is prosperity for all in a sustainable world with minimal suffering (cf. Brown/Zsolnai 2018).

It is true that the pursuit of possessions and material wealth is seen as the main cause of human suffering and that consumption is not a source of individual happiness (cf. Daniels 2005). However, economic activity is considered "good" *if* it helps to overcome suffering. Therefore, contrary to what is sometimes assumed, secular Buddhists are not forbidden to acquire greater possessions, as long as greed is not the driving force and they give it away to others. As a prerequisite for the ability to donate, which is very important in these societies, economic success is even quite desirable. For donations secure the livelihood of the countless temples and monks. However, the commandment of modesty is likely to promote passivity and reduce motivation to perform. Satisfying the material needs of the people is primarily the task of agriculture and handicrafts. Trade and its service providers are not considered to have a value-creating function. Profits are seldom reinvested; instead, they are mostly invested in real estate, spent on "good works" or used for other purposes (e.g., the construction of a temple) or contributed to foundations.

Sometimes economic transactions are linked to religious practices in a way that seems naïve from a Western perspective. One pays ("sacrifices") for an upcoming transaction and expects a positive result in return. Because of the direct connection with honor and sacrifice, economic activity is shaped as a kind of religious obligation with sometimes serious consequences. For example, the conviction that the gods have agreed to a project can encourage unjustified confidence. If the project fails, however, situational disturbances are usually blamed for it, rather than the individual. After all, the latter had assured himself or herself of the divine benevolence through his or her sacrifice.

The Buddha gave a "sixfold explanation" about the relationship between people. Besides the teaching about the relationship between teachers and students, the teaching about hierarchical relationships (between master and servant, king and people, etc.) is especially important for management. They are similar to the Confucian relationships of duty. According to this, subordinates have, among other things, the duty to fulfill tasks assigned to them and to help colleagues. Those higher up in the hierarchy, however, are obligated to show care and a cooperative style of leadership. In view of a reality that is perceived as extremely complex, decisions are predominantly made intuitively.

And how can this skeptical attitude toward the economy be reconciled with Japan's rise as a major economic power in the 1970s and 1980s? There, Buddhism entered into a symbiotic relationship with Shintoism. Shintoism's strong orientation toward this world and its positive view of humanity favor performance-oriented work and leadership behavior. This means, for example, that no precise distinction is made between work and leisure time. Since the concept of the family has been transferred to companies, Buddhist rituals (e.g., ancestor veneration) are also significant in one's work life.

3.2 Consumption and behavioral regulation

Religiously based norms and taboos have given rise to numerous regulations and rules of conduct that companies still have to take into account today. One need only think of the purchase of alcoholic beverages or clothing (see Migdalis et al. 2014). A good example of this are the Islamic clothing regulations, which require women to cover up to a large extent, including headgear and, in some cases, veils (cf. Binark/Kılıçbay 2002). According to

Lord/Putrevu (2005), 54% of Muslims are aware of these regulations while shopping.

In this context, it is worth recalling the case of the famous Barbie doll from Mattel. Since 1959, it has delighted children's hearts worldwide. However, the "Committee for the Promotion of Virtue and the Prevention of Vice" in Saudi Arabia considered the classic (i.e., "Western") Barbie to be un-Islamic because of her revealing clothing and overly feminine body proportions and finally banned her in 2003. The alternative is called Fulla and corresponds far more to the Islamic ideal. She hides her black hair under a headscarf, while Barbie wears her long blonde hair free. Also, "Fulla is honest, kind, loving and respects her father and mother. These are qualities that are particularly welcome in countries like Saudi Arabia, a market with the strongest consumers in the Middle East" (Hackensberger 2005).

No less well known are the rules that relate to eating habits. Muslims observe the fasting month of Ramadan, Jews eat kosher (i.e., "pure"), and Hindus avoid beef. Christians, however, are supposed to abstain from meat on Fridays and especially on Good Friday[4] and also moderate themselves in other ways.

Many of these patterns of consumption, which can be explained in terms of religious history, have become detached from their original meaning over the course of time. As a result, only strict believers consider it a sin to violate such commandments (cf. Shatenstein et al. 1993). However, if non-religious people obey the commandments, ultimately they "only" perform religious rituals (e.g., when Catholics observe Lent and Muslims Ramadan), preferably on the occasion of major holidays (e.g., baptism, communion, confirmation, wedding, funeral). From an anthropological perspective, this is done in order to demonstrate or strengthen their social, cultural or religious identity.

3.3 An interfaith attitudinal/behavioral model

It is true that the values prevailing in a society do not last forever, as numerous studies have shown (cf. Inglehart 1998). But a change in values, such as that experienced by Germany and Japan after World War II, lasts decades or longer. In Rokeach's (1968; 1969) theory of values, religiosity has the status of a terminal value: striving for inner harmony and redemption. Following the value typology of Vinson et al. (1977, p. 46), religiosity can be defined as a domain-specific value that is less centrally anchored than a global value and directly influences people's behavior.

Religious affiliation and religiosity are both relatively stable over time and influence attitudes and behavior in a more or less predictable way (cf. Delener 1990a, p. 27). However, numerous analyses have shown that the various forms of religiosity contribute more to explaining attitudes and behaviors than does religious affiliation (cf. Hardy et al. 2019; McDaniel/Burnett 1990). Figure 3 shows a simplified behavioral model of Interfaith Marketing (IFM).

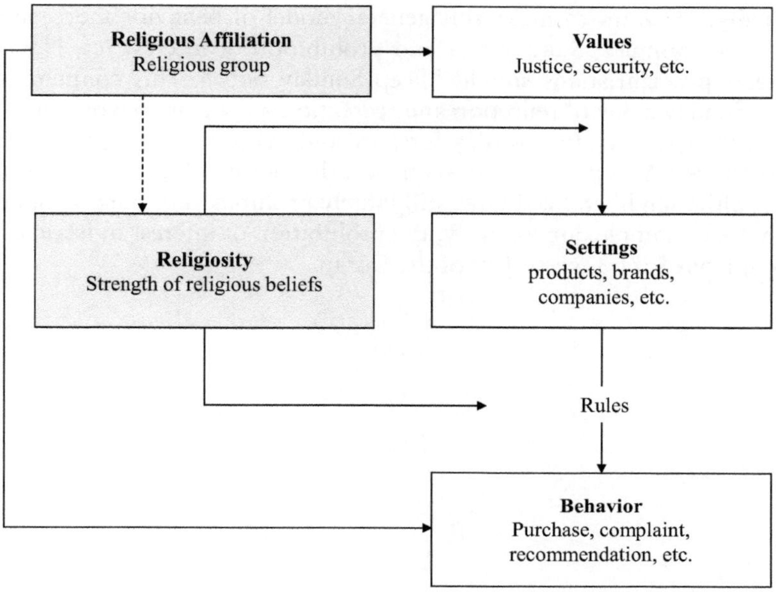

Figure 3 Religious affiliation, religiosity and consumer behavior.
Source: Own illustration.

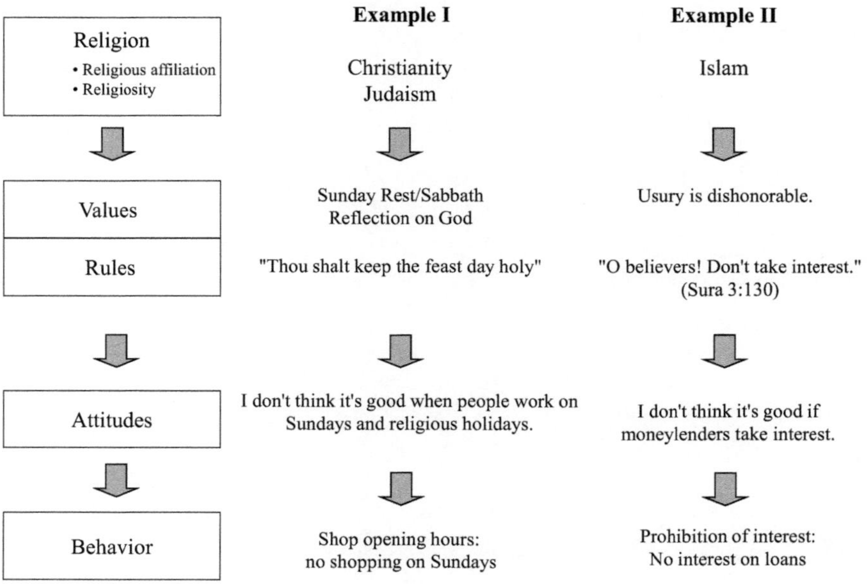

Figure 4 From religious behavioral imperatives to secular consumer behavior.
Source: Own representation.jn

Finally, we want to make this general model of behavior more tangible with two examples: Sunday rest and prohibition of interest (cf. Figure 4). For example, Christians should "keep Sunday holy." This commandment makes Sunday a day of reflection and recreation on which no work should be done (corresponding to Saturday for Jews and, with some exceptions, Friday for Muslims). As a practical consequence, the German law on the closing of stores, although liberalized now, still largely prohibits shopping on Sundays. As another example, analogously, the prohibition of interest in Islam can be derived from Sura 3, verse 130 of the Koran.

4 Methodological problems of comparative religion research

In the recent past, a number of articles have been published on the influence of religion and religiosity on marketing-relevant issues that meet the highest methodological standards (e.g., Casidy et al. 2021; Hyodo/Bolton 2021; Kurt et al. 2018). However, the majority of papers are not yet at the methodological level that general marketing research has now reached. Thus, correlational studies are often still the norm and so are the epistemological problems associated with this type of research (e.g., lack of causality, generalizability). The Journal of Islamic Marketing and other comparable journals publish, in addition to many conceptual articles, primarily papers that use structure-discovering methods based on correlational relationships (especially factor analysis, structural equation modeling) but often (over)interpret their findings causally (e.g., Effendi et al. 2020). Controlled experimental research (e.g., leveraging priming techniques) is still not very common.[5]

4.1 Experimental design

By experimental design, we mean the planning, execution and evaluation of experimental studies. Of central importance are the numerous confounding factors that can distort the results of such studies and the measures that can be taken to control these confounding factors.

4.1.1 Religion and/or religiosity?

Does membership in a particular religious community provide a sufficient predictor of behavior? Or is individual religiosity (i.e., a person's individual attitude toward his or her religion) a better predictor, as suggested by the results of numerous studies (e.g., Agarwala et al. 2019; Choi et al. 2013; Essoo/Dibb 2004; McDaniel/Burnett 1990)? There are several reasons for the larger explanatory contribution of religiosity. Undoubtedly, religious affiliation directly influences certain behaviors. For the most part, however, religious values and norms are behaviorally relevant only to the extent that they are important to the individual. The more religious a person is (i.e., the more

DOI: 10.4324/9781003506010-5

important his religion is to him), the more likely he is to behave according to its principles. For example, only orthodox Jews observe the strict dietary rules of Judaism without any exceptions.

Most relevant empirical studies focus on either religious affiliation or religiosity. Only rarely are both considered simultaneously. Among the exceptions are Heiman et al. (2019). Their analysis of the acceptance of time-saving products found that in this case, there is no clear correlation between religious affiliation and religiosity. They found that for Jews,[6] religiosity moderates this relationship, but neither for Christians nor Muslims. This finding may not be generalizable to other product categories or behaviors, but it does suggest that a distinction should be made between religious affiliation and religiosity in empirical studies (i.e., that they should be considered different, simultaneous independent variables).

4.1.2 Religion and/or culture?

The empirical basis of the majority of comparative religion studies is members of different religious affiliations within a country, region or city. For example, Bailey/Sood (1993) surveyed Buddhists, Hindus, Jews, Catholics, Muslims and Protestants living in Washington, DC about their purchasing behavior. Mathras et al. (2016) describe this approach (i.e., limiting the study to one country) as a good way to separate the influence of religious affiliation on consumer behavior from that of the country's culture. Given the close theoretical and empirical relationship that exists between religions and culture (see Moschis/Ong 2011 and I-1.2), this distinction is imperative. But this also means that no statements can be made about the consumer behavior of Buddhists, Hindus, Catholics, etc. in general, but only about Buddhists, Hindus, Catholics, etc. living in Washington, DC (or at best in the US), for instance.

It is possible that they did not find any significant differences in the purchasing behavior of Buddhists, Jews and Muslims because all study participants lived in an urban environment with an individualistic national culture, which may have overrode the expected differentiating influence of the various religious affiliations. Furthermore, the most important sects within the religious affiliation should be taken into account. For example, liberal Jews lead a fundamentally different life than Orthodox Jews and are guided by different attitudes, values, beliefs, etc. Since religiosity is usually the more informative predictor in comparative religion consumer research, this variable should also be considered in experimental design. For the purpose of comparing members of the three monotheistic religions, an ideal study design can be derived from approach, consisting of 24 cells (cf. Table 1). Assuming 50 participants per cell, the sample size would then have to be at least n = 1,200.

In order to be able to formulate basic statements such as "Catholics are the XY type of buyer while Hindus are the YZ type," Bailey/Sood (1993)

Table 1 Basic structure of an ideal study design

	Jews				*Christians*				*Muslims*			
	Liberal		*Orthodox*		*Catholics*		*Protestants*		*Shiites*		*Sunnis*	
	a	*b*	*a*	*b*	*a*	*b*	*a*	*b*	*a*	*b*	*a*	*b*
Individualists	1	2	3	4	5	6	7	8	9	10	11	12
Collectivists	13	14	15	16	17	18	19	20	21	22	23	24

Notes: a = not, different or few believers, b = strong believers; 1–24 = cells or study units.

Source: Own representation.

should have additionally surveyed not only members of the various religious affiliations in an urban region, but also their brothers and sisters in a rural setting, which would require a duplication of the research design. It is obvious that this is desirable but utopian in view of the effort involved. We know of no study that leverages a design that even remotely approaches this.

4.1.3 *Majority or minority religion?*

Bailey/Sood (1993, p. 348) have found empirical evidence that Buddhists in a diaspora situation (i.e., when they belong to the religious minority) tend to abandon important religious beliefs and to adapt to the prevailing cultural norms at the behavioral level. Hindus and Muslims, however, did not adapt. For this reason, Catholics and Protestants living in Washington, DC, for example, where they acquired their attitudes and values as members of the majority religion there, are not comparable with Catholics and Protestants living in Singapore, where they are in the minority. The reverse is true for Buddhists. Hindus, Jews and Muslims are, however, living in a clearly Christian environment in Washington, DC and in a more Buddhist environment in Singapore.

Scientific statements are only reliable if they are based on comparable study conditions. Let's say a study found that Catholics buy luxury brands more often than Protestants. The researchers cite the different religious socialization as the reason: the baroque splendor of Catholic houses of worship on the one hand and the ascetic simplicity of Protestant houses of worship on the other. This quite plausible explanation, however, was undermined when a critical reanalysis of the study revealed that the selected Catholics had significantly more disposable income than the selected Protestants and failed to control for this confounding variable. The above examples (possible influence of national culture, urban environment, religiosity, majority/minority situation) should illustrate how complex it can be to ensure comparability of study conditions in comparative religion research.

4.2 Operationalization problems

Like other empirical social sciences, comparative religion behavioral research also uses various constructs to gain knowledge. These are variables that cannot be observed directly (e.g., religiosity) but can be inferred from indices (e.g., regular church attendance, observance of the fasting period). A central problem of this type of research is the validity of the constructs used. Do the scales developed to operationalize them ("make them measurable") actually measure what they claim to measure?

A concrete example that this is often not guaranteed is provided by Rehman/Shabbir (2010). They claim to investigate the relationship between religiosity and the adoption of innovative products. However, their dependent variable "New Product Adoption (NPA)" was operationalized completely inadequately. Cronbach's alpha, a measure of the internal consistency of the scale, is not "satisfactory" at 0.56, as the two authors claim, but must be rated as "poor" (= 0.5) to "questionable" (= 0.6), according to the usual criteria.

The operationalization chosen for this study, however, lacks not only internal consistency but also apparent validity. As a look at the six items used reveals, the NPA scale measures all sorts of things but certainly not the willingness or intention to purchase or use new (i.e., innovative) products. Items 1, 3, 4 and 5 can be interpreted in terms of influenceability (i.e., receptiveness to social influence and recommendations), item 2 is related to thriftiness, and item 6 is related to thriftiness as well but also with a tendency toward sustainability and environmental protection.

- "I prefer to buy products recommended by friends and neighbors."
- "It is important to reduce expenses and put money in my savings account."
- "I never care about other people's opinions on the products I buy."
- "I will buy products I love despite negative opinions from friends and family members."
- "I will buy what I feel good about and never care about other's opinions."
- "If things can still function, I will not buy new ones to replace them."

Religiosity is often operationalized one dimensionally: by self-assessment. However, this is problematic insofar as it can obscure something essential: the fundamental difference between extrinsic and intrinsic religiosity (see II-1.2). In the case of the Indonesian consumers surveyed by Arli/Tjiptono (2017), for example, only intrinsic religiosity favored environmentally protective attitudes and purchase intentions, regardless of religious affiliation (i.e., among both Christians and Muslims). Extrinsically religious people, however, expressed different views on the subject of environmental protection depending on which religious group they belonged to: Muslims tended to be negative, while Christians were more positive. This study is just one example that highlights the need to consider the multiple dimensions of religiosity in studying the influence of religiosity on consumption.

4.3 Response bias

Religious people in general tend to self-aggrandize and in particular to give socially desirable answers in surveys (cf. III-5.3). It is true that many people strive to present as positive an image of themselves as possible, whether in front of others (i.e., impression management) or in front of themselves (i.e., self-deception or self-protection). In the case of religious people, however, this response tendency is usually particularly pronounced (cf. Burris/Navara 2002; Sedikides/Gebauer 2010). This is because they are under strong pressure to behave morally in the way their religion prescribes them to do. It follows that the self-reports of very religious people should be taken with a certain skepticism or, even better, corrected for their social desirability bias. Models for this are survey research (cf. Gittelman et al. 2015) and comparative cultural research (cf. Johnson/Van de Vijver 2003).

4.4 Confusion of significance with relevance

McDaniel/Burnett (1990) wanted to know which criteria consumers use to select a retail outlet. They found that friendly, supportive sales staff is most important to them.[7] A look at the group averages (see Figure 5) reveals, however, that although this statement is plausible, it is hardly supported by the survey findings. Rather, friendly sales personnel is only "somewhat important" to all respondents. This is true for the very religious participants somewhat more than for the less religious people. But the difference in mean values is minor (0.3 scale units on the seven-point response scale) and of little practical relevance. Retailers will certainly not deduce from this finding that they should treat very religious customers in a particularly friendly manner and that they can deal with the less religious in a somewhat less friendly manner.

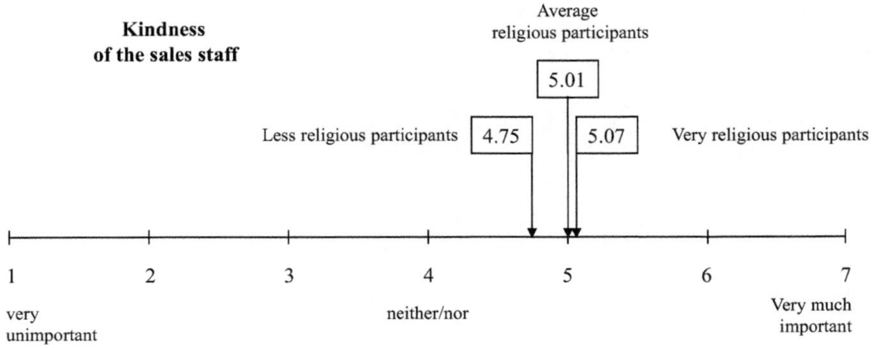

Figure 5 Religiosity and the desire for friendly sales staff.

Source: Own representation based on data from McDaniel/Burnett (1990, p. 108).

Part II
Religion and religiosity

1 Main concepts of religious studies

What are the differences between religion, religiosity, mysticism, spirituality and superstition, to name only a few of the concepts of religious studies that are essential for our further considerations?

1.1 Religion

Colloquially, religion is understood to be the belief shared and professed by a community of people. Apart from such a commonly held understanding, however, this term is neither uniformly nor unambiguously defined.

1.1.1 An overview

Tylor (1871), a renowned social philosopher and ethnologist of his time, equated religion with belief in spiritual beings. La Barre (1970, p. 12 f.) recognized in it, from a psychological point of view, a collective dream or nightmare in which people learn the "right attitude" toward the divine represented by their parents. For the anthropologist Spiro (1966, p. 96), religion is a system of knowledge or a collection of explicitly and implicitly formulated views about the relations of people with the (superhuman) world. The most well-known, however, were probably the theses critical of religion by Marx ("Opium for the People") and Freud. The founder of classical psychoanalysis criticized religion as a "universal obsessive neurosis" and as an expression of a "childish expectation of an omnipotent being."

Despite all the differences, there are important commonalities, which all explanations and definitions address more or less explicitly.

- Religions develop characteristic rituals.
- Religious actions can change the state of consciousness or perception.
- Unexplainable or surprising events are attributed to non- or superhuman forces.
- Religions formulate norms or rules of conduct that enable believers to live together in harmony.

DOI: 10.4324/9781003506010-7

1.1.2 *Definitions*

The manifestations of religion are too diverse to be adequately captured by a single definition (cf. McKinnon 2002). Therefore, a differentiation is made: Institutional definitions describe and systematize religions according to the nature and intensity of their attachment to certain organizational forms. There are:

- Institutionally bound religions (e.g., Christianity, Judaism)
- Unaffiliated "religions" (e.g., New Age movement, Human Potential Movement)

Substantive definitions conceive of religions as a system of beliefs, symbols and ritualistic behavior. This system of beliefs (= faith) explicitly refers to one or more supernatural entities (= God). Consequently, Confucianism, for example, is not considered a religion, since it "merely" gives advice on how to create and maintain a certain social order that is considered desirable (cf. II-6).

According to the functional definitions, the "essence" of a religion is not decisive. What is decisive are the tasks it fulfills (i.e., its functions):

- Identity function: By creating common sacred beliefs and practices, religions integrate the individual into society (cf. Durkheim 1912/1994). From the perspective of evolutionary theory, religion is a "social invention" that helps to organize the respective society efficiently. It is irrelevant whether the contents of belief are true or false. What is important is the social benefit that religions create. It is often assumed that this benefit consists of taking away the believers' fear of death. In fact, however, only a few religions (Islam, Christianity) promise believers a life after death. The crucial function of religion can be explained by the example of the African Mbona cult. Its members repeatedly erect a shrine. If it falls apart, which happens regularly, a new shrine must be built – but only after the believers have settled their disputes. When "progressive" Europeans offered to build the shrine out of durable material, the Mbona refused. The shrine was ultimately of secondary importance. What mattered was its social function: to resolve conflicts (cf. Wilson 2002).
- Meaning function: One of the fundamental tasks of religion is to provide meaning. People who have to cope with critical life events want to give them meaning by placing the event in an overarching worldview. Fundamental is the human need for orientation and insight into the meaning of life (cf. Steger et al. 2008).
- Structural function: Believers follow the "path of salvation" by fulfilling certain ethical requirements and cultic obligations (prayer, sacrifice, etc.). Thanks to the norms and values thus conveyed, religions provide not only social identity but also social stability.
- Sociocultural function: Religions contribute to coping with life by linking central issues (e.g., health, poverty) with the help of moral doctrines

from the respective religion (cf. Baucal/Zittoun 2013). Thus, negative events (e.g., illness, poverty) can be interpreted as the direct consequence of behavior that is incompatible with the commandments of one's own religion (= sins).

- Psychological function: Religions legitimize the values that are dominant in a society and thus also provide believers with individual stability and security (cf. Vail et al. 2010).

1.1.3 Operationalization problems

A problem for comparative religion research is that the commitment to a particular faith community is sometimes less clear than it seems. For example, Vietnamese who call themselves Buddhists rarely mean concrete beliefs or ritual acts. Rather, they want to signal that they are neither Christians nor Muslims nor atheists.

For the most part, the Japanese also do not see religion as an exclusive and norm-setting creed, but as a means to an end – namely, to ensure social identity and societal stability. For this reason, only about one-third of Japanese feel that they belong exclusively to one religion (cf. Sasaki/Suzuku 1996, p. 588). According to a representative study by the Japanese Office of Religious Affairs, most of them profess both Shintoism (= 92 million) and Buddhism (= 87 million). Together with 2 million Japanese Christians and 9 million others, this adds up to 225 million religious denominations, with a total population of about 130 million, as of 2015. The multi-confessionalism of the Japanese is favored by the fact that their two main religions fulfill different functions. While Shintoism primarily influences extra-familial behavior, Buddhism is responsible for the private sphere (see Hendry 2019). In addition, Confucianism is an ethical, non-religious concept of behavior and morality (see II-6.2), which ensures that Japanese are generally extremely loyal to hierarchically superior individuals.

1.2 Religiosity

As a rule, the variable religiosity is more predictive of socioeconomic behavior than the variable religious affiliation. But even in the case of religiosity, it is not easy to answer exactly what is meant by it (= definition) and how this variable can be measured reliably and validly (= measurement concepts). However, it is indisputable that most people believe in God or a god-like force and that religious people are an important target group of Interfaith Marketing (IFM) (cf. IV-3.1). In the US, for example, 75–80% believe in God (cf. Hrynowski 2019).

1.2.1 Definitions

Religiosity is usually described as the "transformation of religion into an individual system of meaning and action," as an individual attitude toward one's own religion, and as the extent to which the individual aligns his or her values, norms or actions with the commandments and prohibitions of his or her religion (cf. Reutter/Bigatti 2014, p. 56). Some also speak of religious commitment in this context. But ultimately they mean something else: "Religious commitment indicates the degree to which a person adheres to his or her religious values, beliefs, and practices, and uses them in daily living" (Ma et al. 2021, p. 246). Remarkably, the majority of the religious locate their ego in their heart, but the majority of the non-religious or less religious locate their ego in their head. This corresponds to different problem-solving strategies: some are more analytical, while others are more intuitive (cf. Evans/Fetterman 2021).

Sometimes, religious affiliation is confused with religiosity, such as when the growing number of people leaving the church in many European countries is interpreted as evidence of the loss of significance of religiosity in contemporary culture. However, the number of people who classify themselves as religious has remained largely the same.

1.2.2 Measurement concepts

In the course of research in the sociology of religion, three different approaches have been developed to capture religiosity (cf. Alston 1975):

- Subjective measures (self-assessment of the intensity of inner attachment to a particular religion)
- Behavioral measures (frequency and regularity of religious practice, such as attendance at religious services)
- Quasi-institutional measures (e.g., acceptance of church authority)

However, the proposals for quantifying religiosity documented in the literature differ not only in content but also by their dimensionality. For example, Glock/Stark (1965) described religiosity as a five-dimensional construct:

- Ritual dimension: participation in religious festivals and rituals (e.g., attendance at religious services, prayer, confession, Holy Communion)
- Ideological dimension: belief in the doctrine (especially God) propagated by a religion and in life after death
- Intellectual dimension: knowledge about one's own religion and foreign creeds (e.g., content of the Bible or the Koran)
- Social dimension: behavior in accordance with the norms and values of a religion (such as following the Ten Commandments)
- Dimension of religious experience: feelings (e.g., fear, security, happiness or comfort) and beliefs (e.g., significance of faith for one's life) associated with practicing a religion

Faulkner/De Jong (1966) developed five Guttmann scales on the basis of information from 362 college students, each consisting of several statements of ascending or descending intensity, which could be agreed with ("yes") or disagreed with ("no"). This finally resulted in the five-dimensional scale of the sociology of religion. Contrary to what the term dimension suggests, the five dimensions were not really independent, according to the intercorrelation matrix. In particular, the ideological dimension showed strong overlaps with three of the four other dimensions.[8] Although this operationalization problem was repeatedly criticized in the following period (e.g., Gibbs/Crader 1970), many scholars adopted this scale.

Based on a reassessment of relevant empirical studies, Batson et al. (1993) then proposed an alternative three-dimensional operationalization:

- Intrinsic religiosity: Religion is central to the conduct of life and manifests itself in a firm belief and conviction of control. Intrinsically religious people subordinate everything to their faith, perceive their lives as meaningful and suffer less than others from fears and doubts.
- Extrinsic religiosity: People belong to a religious community and practice its rites in order to achieve certain worldly goals (e.g., social recognition or a sense of community due to regular attendance at religious services). The relationship between the extrinsically religious and their religion is primarily utilitarian. They find religion confining, have less self-confidence and are more intolerant and prejudiced than intrinsically religious people.
- Religiosity as a search: The focus of this form of religiosity is on dealing with existential questions. "Seekers" are more open to other forms of religiosity than intrinsically religious people and are generally more flexible and tolerant. Many of them strive for mystical experiences, want to gain insight into cosmic laws and see the "real," the non-terrestrial reality.

In research practice, however, a distinction is usually made only between intrinsic and extrinsic religiosity. Not only conceptually are these two independent constructs, but also empirically. For example, Vitell et al. (2009) found a slightly negative but not significant correlation ($r = -0.18$) among 110 students at an American university.

According to another two-dimensional approach (cf. Table 2), religiosity manifests itself on the one hand in the extent to which someone believes (= cognitive dimension) and on the other hand in visible behaviors (= conative

Table 2 Two-dimensional operationalization of religiosity

Cognitive dimension (thoughts)	*Conative dimension (behavior)*
How religious do you consider yourself to be? My religion is very important to me. I believe in God.	How often do you go to church? How much do you donate to the church or to church organizations?

Source: McDaniel/Burnett (1990, p. 106).

dimension). Others define cognitive religiosity not as intensity of belief, but content (= what one believes), and conative religiosity as how one believes (cf. Richardson/Ariffin 2019).

However, this operationalization is only suitable to a limited extent for interreligious comparisons. Statements such as "I believe in God" do not allow us to capture the religiosity of Buddhists and others who do not worship a personal God. It should also be remembered that in the course of secularization, the ritual (e.g., regular church attendance) has become increasingly detached from the spiritual (individual belief). For example, 49% of Greeks surveyed in 2018 classified themselves as "very religious," and 59% stated that they are "absolutely certain to believe in God," but only 38% attend a church service at least once a month and only 29% pray daily. Among Poles, too, there is a discrepancy between ritual and spiritual behavior, albeit with the opposite sign. The fact that 61% are regular churchgoers, but only 45% believe in God with certainty, 40% are very religious and 27% pray daily speaks to strong social pressure, especially in the rural regions of Poland.

A global comparison based on data from the World Values Survey-6 reveals: Muslim societies are the most religious, led by Jordan, Libya and Pakistan. In contrast, only a few individualistic societies largely agree with statements such as, "Religion is very important in my life," "I believe in God" or "I pray several times a day," with the rarest being Swedes, Dutch and Australians. Comparably low levels of agreement were registered in China and, with some reservations, also in Germany (see Allison et al. 2021). Remarkably, Poland and the US occupy places in the indifference range of the scale: neither religious nor atheist. This is remarkable because both are perceived by the public as distinctly religious societies.

In order to be able to analyze the influence of the religiosity of Americans and Japanese on their consumer behavior, Sood/Nasu (1995) divided the religiosity scale they used into a general and a religion-specific section (see Table 3). The religion-specific section takes into account the Buddhist doctrine of rebirth ("Man has an infinite number of lives") as well as the idea of individual responsibility typical of Protestantism. Both scales show relatively satisfying reliability values (Cronbach's alpha = 0.82 for the American and 0.65 for the Japanese sample). The degree of religiosity is calculated as the mean value of the nine items in each case (four = universal, five = religion-specific).

Using a median split, the sample was divided into strict believers and occasional religionists. While this characteristic appears to be gender-unspecific (52% of women and 44% of men were classified as strict believers), a striking country effect emerged: 81% of Americans but only 33% of Japanese described themselves as strict believers. The reason for this could be the extensive secularity of Japanese society. However, it is also possible that different response tendencies play a role (e.g., the "tendency toward the middle," which is very pronounced among the Japanese, i.e., the preference for the center of the scale (cf. Müller/Gelbrich 2021, p. 136).

Table 3 Religion-specific scales for measuring religiosity

Japanese Buddhists	*American Protestants*
Universal part	
I regularly attend a church service. Spiritual values are more important than material things. Religious people are better citizens. How do you characterize yourself (not religious – very religious)?	
Religion-specific part	
The highest reality is beyond the imagination of the human mind. Religion is self-education, with which pain, sorrow and suffering can be overcome. Man has an infinite number of lives. The individual human being is not important in itself. One should strive for inner purity through contemplation and following ceremonies.	Jesus Christ is the Son of God. Everyone is free to choose for himself to approach God. The Bible is the Word of God. Man is responsible for using his free will for good. The soul of man is immortal.

Note: Five-point Likert scale: "completely disagree" to "completely agree."

Source: Sood/Nasu (1995).

In research dealing with this topic at the corporate level, completely different operationalizations of religiosity are used (cf. Leventis et al. 2018):

- Number of churches, mosques and other places of worship
- Proportion of the religious population in the total population
- Extent of population participation in religious activities

These indicators are based on the country or region in which the company's headquarters are located.

1.2.3 *Religious affiliation and religiosity*

Around 82% of the world's population classify themselves as religious (see Pew Research Forum 2017). If we follow the results of a reanalysis of various waves of the WVS, Muslims are significantly more religious than other religious groups. The fact that belief in the existence of hell is even more widespread among them than belief in heaven indicates a negative image of God (see Toprakyaran 2019). Conversely, among Protestants and, surprisingly, also among the Orthodox, secularization seems to be far advanced (cf. I-1.5).

Cohen/Hill (2007) surveyed 1,364 students at an American university (Berkeley) on the topic of religiosity and religious affiliation. According to this, Protestants are predominantly intrinsically religious, while Jews and Catholics are more often extrinsically religious. For them, it is not the personal relationship with God that creates identity, as it does for Protestants, but the social community and rituals that create community.

1.3 Spirituality and mysticism

Based on the root of the word (Latin: spiritus = spirit), spirituality can also be understood in distinction to materiality or as the search for meaning of life in God. This ultimately ambiguous term is often equated with religiosity. This is not unjustified insofar as numerous studies suggest that both religiosity and spirituality promote mental and physical health (cf. Reutter/Bigatti 2014).

Polls show that 84% of the world's population feel that they belong to a particular religion. However, this does not mean that the rest are unbelievers. Of the unaffiliated Americans, for example, 27% are "absolutely sure" and 22% are "fairly sure" that they believe in God (cf. Waller/Casidy 2021).

Germans, like the French and British, seem to be less devout than Italians and especially than Americans and Mexicans ("I know that God really exists and have no doubts."). Germans can often be described as being spiritual: 33% of them "do not believe in a personal God, but in a higher power" (cf. Figure 6).

There is a growing body of work in consumer research that has specifically examined how spirituality influences consumption behavior. For example, it has been shown that the emotion of awe increases consumers' spirituality, which then decreases conspicuous consumption (Hu et al. 2018). In addition, research has demonstrated that spirituality increases ethical consumer behavior, such as recycling more, due to a heightened moral identity (Rodriguez-Rad/Ramos-Hidalgo 2018). This finding has also been demonstrated in a cross-cultural context across five different countries (the United

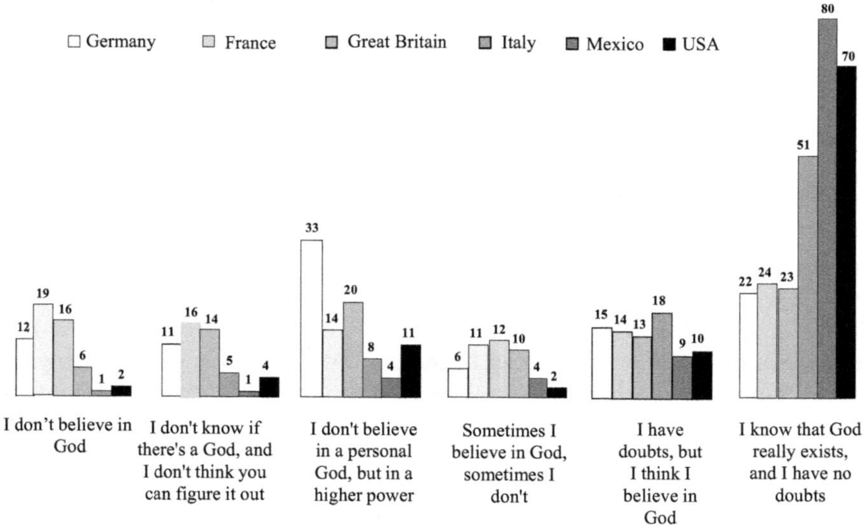

Figure 6 Religious and spiritual beliefs.

Source: AP-Ipsos (2005).

States, France, Spain, India and Egypt), where the researchers showed that the more spiritual a consumer is, the more likely that individual is to be ethically predisposed (Vitell et al. 2016). Research has also explored the influence of spirituality on the consumer behavior of older adults specifically, given that older adults reach spiritual maturity or experience significant spiritual growth near the end of their life (Ulvoas-Moal 2010). For instance, qualitative research has investigated how older adults may meet their spiritual needs through travel, and this travel consumption further enhances their spiritual development (Moal-Ulvoas/Taylor 2014).

As a manifestation of spirituality, mysticism is one of the special forms of religious behavior. This form of religiosity, which was important worldwide before the Enlightenment and is still important in some societies, is characterized by the fact that believers strive for inner union with the deity who is at the center of the respective faith (Unio Mystica). On the one hand, mystics tread the path of purification with the help of contemplation, meditation and asceticism. On the other hand, they strive with religious fervor for extraordinary sensuality, in extreme cases up to ecstasy and visions, combined with personal revelations. Among the precursors are the mystery cults in ancient Greece.

The goal of Christian mystics is direct unity with Jesus Christ (e.g., in Passion mysticism through "co-suffering" with God's Son). The prophetic mysticism of Hildegard von Bingen and the speculative mysticism of Meister Eckehart, a Dominican monk, have become well-known. Well-known mystical currents of Judaism are Hasidism, Kabbalah and Sabbatianism. In Islam, Sufism plays a corresponding role, and in Hinduism the teachings of Advaita-Vedanta are related to mysticism. According to Buddhists, mystics can attain a higher level of knowledge through the four stages of right immersion and recognize the "non-being," the full emptiness. Today, this philosophy is especially widespread in Japanese Zen.

1.4 Secularization and sacralization

As a result of the Enlightenment, the scientific paradigm replaced the mythological explanation of the world. There was a "disenchantment of the world" (Weber 1920, p. 54), and the logical style of thinking took the place of the partly magical, partly normative thinking that had prevailed for so long previously. This was accompanied by secularization: the suppression or revaluation of religion and a secularization of public as well as private life (cf. Lehmann 2004). One indication among many is the growing number of people leaving the church. In Germany, for example, the proportion of Catholic and Protestant church members in the population fell from 93.7 to 52.1% between 1960 and 2019. The proportion of people of other faiths and, above all, of non-believers rose accordingly. Indeed, in virtually all high-income countries, there are declining levels of religiosity (Inglehart 2020). However, it is important to note that in Muslim-majority countries, religion remains strong, while in most former communist nations, religiosity has increased since communism's collapse (Inglehart 2020).

The process of change in declining levels of religiosity, which can also be described as a change in values and is accompanied by de-institutionalization, has significantly changed the social position of churches in large parts of the industrialized world. Especially in wealthy industrialized countries, only a minority is still convinced that one must believe in God to be a "good person." According to an evaluation of the Global Attitudes Survey (spring 2019) by the Pew Research Center, there is an almost perfect negative correlation ($r = -0.86$) between this "privatization of morality" and gross national product (per capita). Specifically, this means: In countries with an annual per capita income of less than $15,000 (e.g., Kenya, India, Nigeria, Philippines), about 90% hold this belief, but only 10–20% of Australians, Dutch, Swedes, etc. do ($60,000–70,000).

In most prosperous countries, churches have largely lost their centuries-old monopoly on satisfying people's longing for orientation and meaning in life, except for exceptional situations such as birth, marriage and death, as well as major holidays. They now compete for this monopoly of interpretation with state, economic and family institutions (cf. Arnoldi 2001).

Using the example of a representative sample of German consumers, another consequence of secularization can be demonstrated, as there is generally extensive convergence of opinions and attitudes among members of the various religious groups within a country. In Germany, for example, thrift and consumer restraint are no longer typical Calvinist virtues but are just as widespread among Catholics as among Protestants.

As a countermovement to secularization, two things have occurred in post-materialist societies:

- Appreciation of alternative places and forms of religion or search for religious substitutes (e.g., esotericism)
- Sacralization of everyday life

As more and more consumers have "sacralized" certain luxury items (e.g., jewelry, high-end cars and clothing) and brands (i.e., revering them as something special and divine-like (cf. Belk et al. 1989, p. 11)), the world of consumption has now also been divided into a sacred and a profane sphere. The function, originally incumbent only on religions, of integrating individuals socially by means of shared sacred beliefs and practices, is now increasingly being assigned to the world of consumption as well – through "institutions" such as fan clubs and fitness clubs (cf. V-4.2 and VIII-6.6).

Montgomery (2003) has examined whether increased interdenominational competition could stop or even reverse the trend toward secularization. The starting point of his considerations is an economic axiom. According to this axiom, the intensity of competition correlates with the quality of service. If, so the reasoning goes, the various religious groups were to make more effort and respond better to the needs and wishes of the faithful, then they would not have to lament such a large number of church departures as in the recent past, and the faithful would again participate more in religious life. However, this thesis cannot be confirmed on the basis of historical data. In 1900, the participation of believers in the highly competitive districts of the United States was lower than in areas where there was less religious diversity.

1.5 Atheism

Atheism refers to either the lack of belief in the existence of a god or the belief in the non-existence of a god or gods (Blackburn 1996). Atheists can be distinguished as either passive or active atheists (Bechert 2021). Passive atheists may or may not refer to themselves as atheists, as they are generally indifferent toward religion (Bechert 2021). Indeed, they can be described as not anti-religious but rather areligious (Lüchau 2010). Conversely, active atheists are much more likely to describe themselves as atheists as they directly reject religion and often negatively react against religion in public settings (Bechert 2021).

There has been limited consumer research that has investigated the influence of atheism on consumer behavior. As one of the few exceptions, there is recent research that has examined how atheism affects consumer ethics (Arli et al. 2021). In this work, the authors found that atheism negatively influences consumers' unethical beliefs. As such, the authors conclude that religious consumers are not necessarily more ethical, and atheist consumers are not necessarily less ethical as many people biasedly assume (Brown-Iannuzzi et al. 2018; Xygalatas 2017; Gervais et al. 2011). In addition, other research has investigated how atheism influences consumers' sustainable behaviors. In this vein, previous work has shown that atheists tend to be highly environmental conscious consumers and that they engage in more sustainable behaviors than people low in religiosity (Minton et al., 2015).

1.6 Agnosticism

It is important to note that non-religious people are not always atheists (Arli et al. 2021). Indeed, non-religious individuals could be agnostic rather than atheist. Agnosticism refers to individuals who are neither religious believers nor atheists (Draper 2017). Agnostics argue that it is not possible to find reliable evidence that either proves there is or there is no God (Dockrill 1971), while atheists specifically do not believe in a god or gods. Similar to aforementioned research that showed that atheists are no less ethical consumers than are religious individuals, there is work that suggests that agnostics do not behave less morally than religious people, even if their ethical behavior is driven by different motivations (Hauser/Singer 2005). Further, other research has shown that agnostics, in addition to atheists, are more likely to hold biodiversity conservationist views in Europe than are religious individuals (Recio-Román et al. 2023).

2 Old and new religions

The religious life of primitive peoples was and is determined by animism, ancestor worship and magic. Numerous spiritual beings, who embody the forces of nature and natural phenomena, fulfill this world of belief. These beings can be reached and influenced through ritual ceremonies.

2.1 Natural religion

The beliefs or religious ideas of primitive peoples are called natural religion. With the help of myths, they pass on their moral norms to subsequent generations. Central is magic: the "experience with power and the acting with this power." Magic works mostly by means of a medium, an artificially created or processed object. Essential is also the dynamism (i.e., the belief in a power (= mana)), which has taken possession of certain objects, persons, beings or places. This power cannot be explained rationally and is closely related to magic. The places, persons or objects seized by mana are taboo for the believers.

Animism is a primitive form of human religiosity that is still influential today in Africa and Latin America and can be seen as a precursor of deism or theism. Characteristic is the idea of an "animate" world in which objects, spirits and ancestors play an important role. Animists worship souls and spirits. One must live up to their expectations at all times in order to be able to obtain protection from them or not to become their victim. From the belief in spirit beings (personalism), the belief in an animated universe is to be distinguished (animatism). The earth, personalized as the nurturing "mother of mankind," is usually worshiped as a deity. She is directly responsible for the fertility of the soil and indirectly responsible for the survival and well-being of the people. In the understanding of time of animistic societies, the past and the present dominate, while the orientation toward the future is weak.

The ancestor cult, which is practiced above all in past-oriented societies (cf. Figure 7), together with the fertility cult, forms the ideological foundation of natural religions. The deceased, who are granted a pre-divine status, can directly intervene in the fate of the living (e.g., by giving fertility to women and manhood to men). For this reason, sacrificial rituals and ritual

DOI: 10.4324/9781003506010-8

acts are performed in order to show favor to the ancestors, whose life outside the earth does not differ fundamentally from their earthly existence. For although the followers of the ancestor cult, who live mainly in China and Japan as well as in West Africa, Polynesia and Melanesia, the deceased are viewed as powerful spiritual and sometimes even god-like beings. At the same time, they are convinced that their ancestors are interested in their lives and destinies and use their power to protect their family in the long run. Viewed as mediators between humans and the gods, the ancestors are both revered and feared. While they speak to the living through dreams (and in extreme cases even take possession of their bodies), the living can contact them through supplications, sacrifices, humble offerings and atonement.

2.2 Superstition

Belief in the existence of supernatural forces is considered the "flip side of religious convictions" (cf. Martin 2009). In religious history, superstition refers to other beliefs that deviate from one's own. In ethnological terms, it refers to orally transmitted folk beliefs that incorporate religious beliefs from the past and outdated scientific knowledge in the form of legends, mythical creatures, folk medicine, fortune-telling, etc. The Enlightenment, however, understood superstition to mean beliefs that deviate from one's own faith. It was understood as the belief in phenomena that can neither be explained by natural science nor by orthodox religious doctrine.

Superstition is often accompanied by a number of personality traits: rigidity, dogmatism, intolerance of dissent, racism and ethnocentrism (cf. III-2). Especially those societies in which uncertainty avoidance is important are open to superstitious belief systems. For the superstition offers simple explanatory patterns for a complex world experienced by many as threatening (cf. Müller/Gelbrich 2015, p. 106 ff.).

People are often superstitious if they do not have a positive image of God (i.e., if they do not understand God as a rational, principally calculable and above all benevolent authority). Therefore, nontheistic religions, such as Buddhism, also provide a breeding ground for superstitious belief systems. The same applies to natural religions, which believe that the divine manifests itself in natural phenomena and for which totems and magic are significant.

2.3 Popular belief

Folklorists refer to the religious beliefs and rituals of the "common people" as folk piety. Together with superstitious ideas and practices, they make up folk beliefs. Important is the conviction or hope that curses and blessing formulas are as effective as religious symbols (e.g., images of saints).

Popular Buddhism, which is widespread in many parts of Asia, emerged from the blending of the original animistic beliefs with elements of the Buddhist, Confucian and Taoist teachings that later penetrated this region.

Animistic rituals still characterize daily life there (especially ancestor worship). This also applies to the popular belief of the Japanese: Shintoism. This term, which is commonly used in the West, is the generic term for the various Japanese natural religions.

2.4 New religions

Around 1900, about 1,800 religious denominations were counted worldwide; a century later, there were far more, namely about 33,000. This growth can essentially be explained by the phenomenon of the New Religions or New Religious Movements: spiritual groups or faith communities that cannot be counted among the classical world religions.

Numerous crises, be they primarily social or economic, have strengthened the need for spiritual orientation worldwide, which the established religions are often not (or no longer) able to satisfy. The growing pluralization of societies, the renaissance of East Asian doctrines and esoteric concepts of the world continued to provide support. In terms of religious systems, a New Religion is formed when a community of believers has been created that lives out the principles promoted by the new doctrine. Many New Religions have developed and present themselves as a counter-model to one of the established religions (cf. Table 4).

Others present themselves as a counter-model to the established political order. The characteristic feature of syncretic religions is the return to the teachings and traditions of one's own, usually idealized, people or tribe (see Table 5).

The New Religions have in common the conviction that they possess and proclaim the ultimate (or contemporary) truth as revelation, knowledge or world law, which is often understood as the original, now restored truth. Often they are carried by the idea of the near end of the world – or the transformation of this world into a higher and better world – and are elitist and/or authoritarian. Their founders or their original congregation also refer to religious experiences. Mostly the New Religions show a strong practical reference with emphasis on meditation, community experience and mental health. In Latin America and Africa, they are characterized by the blending of

Table 4 New religions that emerged in opposition to a world religion

Sphere of Christianity	*Sphere of Islam*	*Sphere of Hinduism*	*Sphere of Buddhism*
• Adventists • Mormons • Jehovah's Witnesses	• Ahmadija • Bahai	• Bhagwan Movement • Hare Krishna Movement • Transcendental Meditation	• Nichiren-shoshu • Soka-gakkai • Rissho-koseikai

Source: o.V. (2004, p. 463).

Table 5 New religions that emerged in opposition to established political power

Latin America	*North America*	*Oceania*	*Central Europe*
• Wodu (Voodoo) • Candomblé • Umbanda	• Black Muslims • Peyote Cult	• Cargo Cults • New Polynesian Religions	• German Believers • New Paganism

Source: o.V. (2004, p. 463).

traditional cults and magical practices of popular belief with Christianity and Islam. They are mostly healing cults in which dance and trance experience play a role. They are also often associated with social-revolutionary ideas of redemption (o.V. 2004, p. 462 f.).

3 World religions

An overview

The various religions can first be described quantitatively (i.e., in terms of their degree of prevalence) (cf. II-3.1). Furthermore, they can also be distinguished qualitatively in the sense of a religious phenomenology: according to their idea content (cf. II-3.2).

3.1 Diffusion of religions

The religions that are widespread worldwide include, in order of quantitative importance (cf. Table 6):

- Christianity (with the various Catholic and Orthodox denominations as well as the Protestant denominations)
- Islam (with its various denominations)

Table 6 Distribution and development of world religions (in millions)

	1990	*2000*	*2025 (forecast)*
World population	5,266.4	6,055.0	7,823.7
Christians (all denominations)	1,747.4	1,999.5	2,616.7
Roman Catholics	929.4	1,056.9	1,362.0
Protestants	296.3	342.0	468.6
Orthodox	203.7	215.1	252.7
Anglican	68.1	79.6	113.7
Catholics (non-Roman)	5.2	6.6	9.6
Muslims	962.3	1,188.2	1,784.9
Hindus	685.9	811.3	1,049.2
Buddhists	323.1	359.9	418.3
Tribal Religions	200.0	228.3	277.2
Sikh	19.3	23.5	31.4
Jews	14.1	14.4	16.1
Atheists (professed)	145.7	150.0	159.5
Religious	707.1	768.1	875.1
New Religions	92.3	102.3	114.7

Source: www.fides.org/German/2001/g20011019e.html;15.3.2003Gelbrich/Müller(2023, p. 49f.).

DOI: 10.4324/9781003506010-9

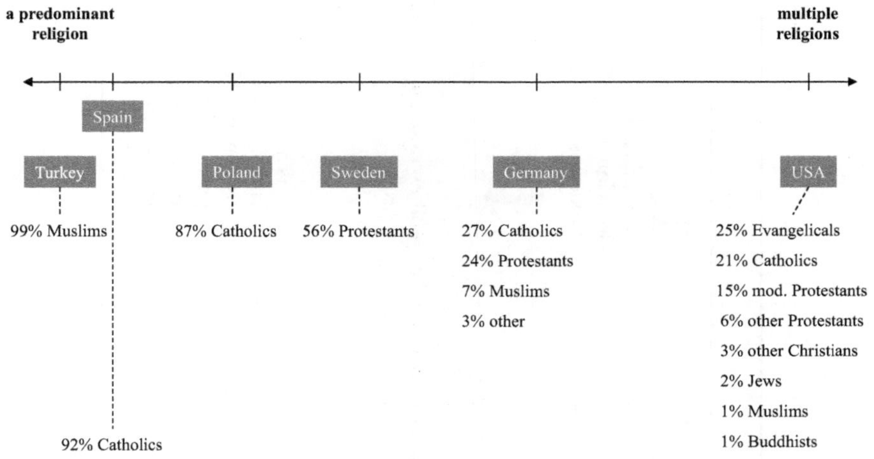

Figure 7 Denominational structure of societies.

Source: Own representation.

- Hinduism
- Buddhism (including the teachings of Confucianism, Shintoism and Taoism influenced by it)
- Judaism

As reported by the International Bulletin of Missionary Research, the number of Christians increased by 14.4% between 1990 and 2000, almost in line with the growth of the world population during this period (= 14.9%). At the same time, however, the Muslim community grew by 23.5%.

Mono-confessional societies such as Turkey can be distinguished from multi-confessional societies on the basis of the proportion of the population that professes a particular religion (see Figure 7). The latter include the United States, where freedom of religion is guaranteed by the First Amendment to the Constitution of the US.

3.2 Phenomenology of religions

There are countless attempts to draw up a comprehensive typology of religions. As heterogeneous and incompatible as they may be, all religions are united by the conviction that God or the gods, in the tension between justice and freedom, have committed man primarily to justice, at least toward the members of his or her own society or religious community. But man always had to fight for his freedom from his gods. Further commonalities are the belief in the immortality of the soul and the Last Judgment (see Table 7).

Number of deities: In the Western Middle Ages, the number of gods worshipped by a religious community was the decisive distinguishing criterion.

Table 7 World religions at a glance

	Hinduism	*Buddhism*	*Catholicism*	*Islam*	*Protestantism*
Approx. Beginnings	2,000 BC	530 BC	1 century AD	610 AD	16 century AD
Holy Writings	Vedas	None	Bible	Koran	Bible
Mono/Polytheistic	Polytheistic	Polytheistic	Monotheistic	Monotheistic	Monotheistic
Locus of Control	Individual	Individual	Church hierarchy	God's Will	Individual
Reliance on Supernatural	Weak	Weak	Strong	Moderate	Moderate
Immortality of Soul	Yes	Yes	Yes	Yes	Yes
Reward and Retribution after Death	Yes	Yes	Yes	Yes	Yes
Idealized Life Directives	Pursue self-control, charity, detachment, nonviolence and compassion	Pursue tolerance, respect for individual and unimportance of self	Follow example of Jesus	Submit to will of God at all times	Follow example of Jesus
Other Major Beliefs/ Practices	Reincarnation, caste system; taboo: meat	Reincarnation, control appetites and passions, follow middle path	Jesus is Son of God, Trinity of God, His Son and Holy Spirit, confession and pennace, infallibility of pope	Muhammad is Prophet, prayer five times a day, fasting during Ramadan, pilgrimage to Mecca; taboo: alcohol and pork	Jesus is Son of God, Trinity of God, His Son and Holy Spirit, individuals can approach God directly, strong work ethic

Source: Bailey/Sood (1993, p. 337).

This resulted in the well-known classification: monotheistic (Judaism, Christianity, Islam), polytheistic (Hinduism) and nontheistic religions (Buddhism).

Monotheistic Western religions (Christianity, Judaism and Islam) follow a monotheistic perspective by viewing their key person as a prophet, with obeying this prophet the key to achieving the goal of heavenly life. Further, Western religious scriptures teach that God created nature and, therefore, God and man hold a superior position to nature. In contrast, Eastern religions (Hinduism, Buddhism, Taoism and Confucianism; Schmidt et al. 2014) follow a pantheistic (i.e., many gods) perspective, viewing their key person as an awakened one. Eastern teachings view life as a process of seeking, with an end-life goal of enlightenment, and that God is in and through all elements of nature (Minton et al. 2018a).

Type of ethics: Some, such as Christianity or Confucianism, call for selfless service in family and state. Others, like (early) Hinduism and especially Buddhism, propagate a more egocentric goal in life: self-redemption from this world.

Nature vs. culture religions: For a number of primitive peoples, the divine manifests itself primarily in natural phenomena, and magic continues to be important. In a cultural religion, however, which is carried by a society that has matured from a tribe or clan to a people, the religious consciousness is characterized by divine figures with human-like individual personalities and differentiated functions.

Dynamistic vs. theistic religions: Another typology makes the type of experience of God the distinguishing criterion: the respective path to God. For the theistic religion, the archetype in the history of religion, the divine is concretized in the experience of power, while in the various manifestations of popular belief, magic establishes the connection to divine power. The divine is grasped free of material ties (i.e., as purely spiritual). Animism, however, for which the belief in spirits, ancestors and demons is phenomenologically characteristic, understands everything (e.g., mountain, tree and forest; river, lake and sea; house, village and city) as the dwelling place of spirits. While the materially bound divine power works undirected in dynamism, the animist understands it as demonic, and thus as unpredictable, but nevertheless as related to the believer: establishing an individual relationship between the individual and the divine. Conversely, at the center of theistic religions is the belief in God or gods. Believers do not perceive divine power as demonic, but as rational and predictable in principle. Thanks to this constructive conception of the divine, human existence and the (surrounding) world were no longer subject to chaos. This created an important prerequisite for a rational view of the self and the world, and ultimately for the emergence of modern meritocracy.

Demanding vs. giving religions: Demanding religions, such as Judaism and Islam, are law religions. Their deity has fixed his will in writing (e.g., in laws), which is to be obeyed. Decisive for the type of giving religion, which can only be found among the folk religions, is the idea of grace. It is a gift of God and cannot, on the way to salvation, be acquired individually by righteousness, law-abidingness, etc.

Revelation religions: Judaism is one of those religions that abolish the "four secrets" of God. According to their teachings, the being of God, which is hidden to the non-believer, is revealed to the believer through religious experience. In natural religions, the divine reveals itself in natural phenomena (e.g., thunderstorms, drought). Conversely, in cultural religions, the divine reveals itself through instructions, which are handed down both verbally and in writing in religious texts.

Evolved vs. endowed religions: The origin of evolved religions such as animism or dynamism lies in the darkness of prehistory. However, the founders of religions, who are known by name and as historical figures, proclaim spiritual experiences of particular depth and uniqueness.

Mystical vs. prophetic religions: Mystics are concerned with regaining the individual relationship with the eternal. This union is threatened or already lost by the vanity and superficiality of the world. However, the negation of the will to live is foreign to the prophetic religions. Their God is worldly, a God of will and deed. Mystical religions are considered tolerant, since foreign gods appear to them merely as other designations or manifestations of the same one divine, while prophetic religions are often intolerant. This is because they exclude the existence of other deities or fight against them. By asking people to seek their own way to union with God, mystical religions are "asocial." In contrast, the "neighbor," the "fellow human being," is at the center of many reflections of prophetic religions.

Part III

Basics of consumer behavior

1 Introduction

It is well known that consumers prefer products and services that correspond to the behavioral patterns of the social groups to which they themselves belong or would like to belong. Since religious people in general and members of certain religious groups in particular can also be understood as social groups, it can be assumed that religious beliefs have a significant influence on consumer behavior.

Nevertheless, of the more than 7,000 articles published in the leading American marketing journals between 1959 and 1989, only 6 were devoted to this topic (cf. Cutler 1991, p. 155). In the early 1980s, a researcher founded the research field of "religion/religiosity and consumer behavior" when she first interviewed Jewish, Catholic and Protestant New Yorkers about their information and purchasing behavior (cf. Hirschman 1982) and a little later published a programmatic article that gave consumer research on the influence of religion a theoretical and conceptual foundation (cf. Hirschman 1983). In the following period, this field of research received more attention. But we are still far from being able to form a comprehensive picture.

Based on the empirical studies available to date, three impact paths can be assumed:

- Religion and religiosity directly influence consumer behavior by providing a more or less comprehensive and binding code of conduct: How religious consumers should behave. This is most obvious in the case of monotheistic religions, for which orthodoxy is important. Judaism, Christianity and Islam are normative in that they unequivocally prescribe to believers what behaviors are expected of them which ones are not acceptable. The religious norm of consuming kosher (Jews) or halal (Muslims) plays an important role here (cf. Siala 2013).
- Religion and religiosity have an indirect effect in that, on the one hand, they influence the personality of believers and, on the other, they shape attitudes and values that are reflected in consumer behavior. For example, the above-average brand loyalty of many religious people can be linked to their risk aversion.
- Religious beliefs and practices do not influence consumer behavior.

DOI: 10.4324/9781003506010-11

2 Religion, religiosity and personality

Religions influence the personalities of believers in many ways, and these influence consumer behavior. This happens partly directly and obviously, and partly indirectly and not recognizable at first glance.

2.1 Overview

As various studies have shown, members of certain religious groups are more prone than others to authoritarianism, materialism, national pride or racism. Catholics, for example, are more authoritarian than Jews, more traditionalist and more willing to obey orders. Furthermore, Catholics are less self-determined, less interested in material possessions and less flexible and rational. In this respect, Protestants resemble Jews more than Catholics or occupy a middle position (cf. McDaniel/Burnett 1990).

However, it has been shown consistently that it is less a matter of religious affiliation than of the intensity and type of individual religiosity. According to findings from the sociology of religion and personality psychology, religious people are more likely than average to display the following characteristics, regardless of the religious community to which they belong: authoritarian (cf. Frenkel-Brunswik 1954), dogmatic (cf. Rokeach 1969) and conservative (cf. Donahue 1985).

In addition, they are considered tradition-conscious, sentimental, dependent, insecure, rather intolerant and not very flexible. As Inglehart (1998, p. 122) reported, societies in which a large part of the population considers God or religion to be "important" place great value on obedience and respect for authority. Family and abundance of children as well as work and national pride remain central (see III-2.7).

2.2 Authoritarianism

The worldview of the authoritarian personality type is pessimistic and prejudiced, characterized by conformist thinking and obedience to authorities.

DOI: 10.4324/9781003506010-12

In addition, there are racist tendencies (see III-2.5) and pronounced ethnocentrism (see III-2.6). Authoritarianism:

- Paralyzes the willingness to investigate cause-effect relationships independently and with confidence in one's own ability to judge
- Promotes the tendency to avoid unknown, novel or ambivalent behaviors or situations (e.g., innovative products and services) out of fear of uncertainty

The authoritarianism construct is based on the theories of Reich (1933) and Fromm (1936). According to their observations, authoritarian individuals often grew up in families in which a dominant, status-conscious father and a restrictive mother suppressed any form of disobedience. This style of upbringing promotes submissiveness and identification with the powerful, in this case the parents. Besides submissiveness, conventionalism is common (cf. Adorno et al. 1950). Authoritarian people:

- Rigidly adhere to the traditional values of their social class and react aggressively when others question them
- Idealize the moral authority of the existing and tend to follow the judgment of older or higher ranking people
- Believe in the predetermination of individual destiny and are prone to superstition, mysticism and stereotypical judgments
- Prefer to think in terms of opposites (such as dominance-submission, strong-weak, leader-follower) and identify with power
- Are convinced that the world is a dangerous place

The authoritarian personality type is more widespread among Catholics than among young people (cf. Jones 1958). It is also found with above-average frequency in Islamic societies (cf. Brown 1996). Hinduism, however, does not provide a breeding ground for authoritarian tendencies. As a polytheistic religion, it knows no ultimate authority, unlike Christianity or Islam. Indians, for example, most of whom are Hindus, are considered tolerant and have a pronounced tolerance for ambiguity. The ability to tolerate contradictions, which is meant by this, is incompatible with authoritarian aspirations (cf. Duriez et al. 2003). According to Ramanujan (1989), Indians combine opposites without any problems in their thinking and behavior and do not clearly separate "I" from "others."

2.3 Dogmatism

The conviction that there are certain, undoubtedly "true" statements (i.e., dogmas) is called dogmatism. Sometimes dogmatism is also understood as the intensity with which one's own views and opinions are held: resolutely and unyieldingly. Dogmatic persons tend to engage in self-righteousness. They avoid new kinds of information, tend to be less empathetic, resistant to change and unwilling to question their fundamental beliefs or have them questioned. Dogmatism correlates with numerous other psychological constructs, such as:

- Conservatism (= adherence to traditional values and ideas)
- Animosity (= hostile attitude toward members of other nations)
- Xenophobia (= generalized fear of strangers)
- Ethnocentrism (= conviction of being fundamentally superior to members of other ethnic groups)

Comparative cultural research indicates that members of uncertainty-avoidant societies are more prone to dogmatism (Müller/Gelbrich 2021, p. 226 f.). In this context, too, it is primarily not religious affiliation but the extent of religiosity that is decisive. Irrespective of their religious affiliation, religious people are more dogmatic than average. They are also considered tradition-conscious, dependent, insecure, rather intolerant and rigid.

2.4 Materialism

People also differ in the intensity with which they value the material aspects of life. Possessions fill materialists with satisfaction and serve as a measure of personal success for them (cf. Richins/Dawson 1992). A generational effect should be noted here: American members of Generation Y (i.e., those born between 1980 and the end of 1990) are more materialistically minded and less religious than the baby boomer generation (cf. Loroz/Helgeson 2013).

The various religions regard materialism as an obstacle on the path to spirituality and salvation (cf. Belk et al. 2003), above all Buddhism (cf. Pace 2013). However, Calvinist Protestantism values material possessions as a symbol or indication of being chosen by God. Taken together, this speaks for an ambiguous relationship between religion and materialism (cf. Burroughs/Rindfleisch 2002). A recent survey of 232 Turkish Muslims, however, allows quite clear statements to be made about the influence of religiosity: very religious people are generally not materialists, are clearly opposed to excessive consumption and are nevertheless – or because of this – more satisfied with their lives than others (cf. Balikcioglu/Kiyak 2022). For members of Generation Y from Malaysia, Rahman et al. (2017) found a negative moderation effect. In their case, religiosity weakened the link between materialism and interest in fashion or the purchase of fashionable clothing.

2.5 Racism

Racism is a special form of bias and manifests itself in prejudice against other ethnic groups. Religious and racist people place equal value on social conformity and tradition (cf. Hall et al. 2010).

All over the world, religions propagate the peaceful coexistence of people. Nevertheless, history shows that crimes against members of other creeds, cultures or ethnic groups were often religiously motivated. This is less contradictory than it seems. To be sure, there is no compelling relationship between religiosity and intolerance. But many people interpret their religion in a highly narrow way, which fosters not only racism but also intolerance, for example, toward women (see Guiso et al. 2003). In a survey of 214 German Protestants, Catholics and non-believers, Duriez et al. (2003, p. 221) operationalized racism with statements such as "We must keep our race pure and fight mixing with other races" or "In general, immigrants should not be trusted." Religiosity was distinguished in:

- The belief in the supernatural ("inclusion vs. exclusion of transcendence")
- The strictness with which someone interprets the Word of God ("literal vs. symbolic")

Correlationally, it was found that strict believers are more intolerant toward other ethnic groups than persons who understand their faith more symbolically ($r = 0.43$; $p < 0.0001$). Further, and as expected, older, less educated individuals expressed more racism. The second dimension of religiosity ("inclusion vs. exclusion of transcendence") exerts no influence ($r = -0.03$). Thus, it is not faith per se that favors racism, but the way it is interpreted.

2.6 Ethnocentrism

This term is used in research to describe the tendency of people to regard their own group (e.g., family, sports team, nation) as the "measure of all things," superior to others in every respect. Foreign groups are judged negatively in principle and usually without reason (cf. Shimp/Sharma 1987). There is a close connection between ethnocentrism and authoritarianism (cf. Perreault/Bourhis 1999). Furthermore, it has been shown that in some societies, there are strong links to patriotism (e.g., Turkey) and in others to nationalism (e.g., Czech Republic) (cf. Balabanis et al. 2001 and III-2.7).

Eisinga et al. (1990) discussed the connection between authoritarian attitudes, local patriotism and Christian faith on the one hand and ethnocentrism on the other. Local patriotism, operationalized, among other things, as participation in community work, correlates with religiosity. Religious people are more likely than average to be involved in their community and to identify with it. It can therefore be assumed that local patriots generally have a positive attitude toward their own group and a negative attitude toward others. Authoritarianism or authoritarian attitudes can be described by two components. First, authoritarian aggression indicates the extent to which individuals condemn or affirm the violation of accepted norms and values. Second, authoritarian submission describes the tendency not to question authority.

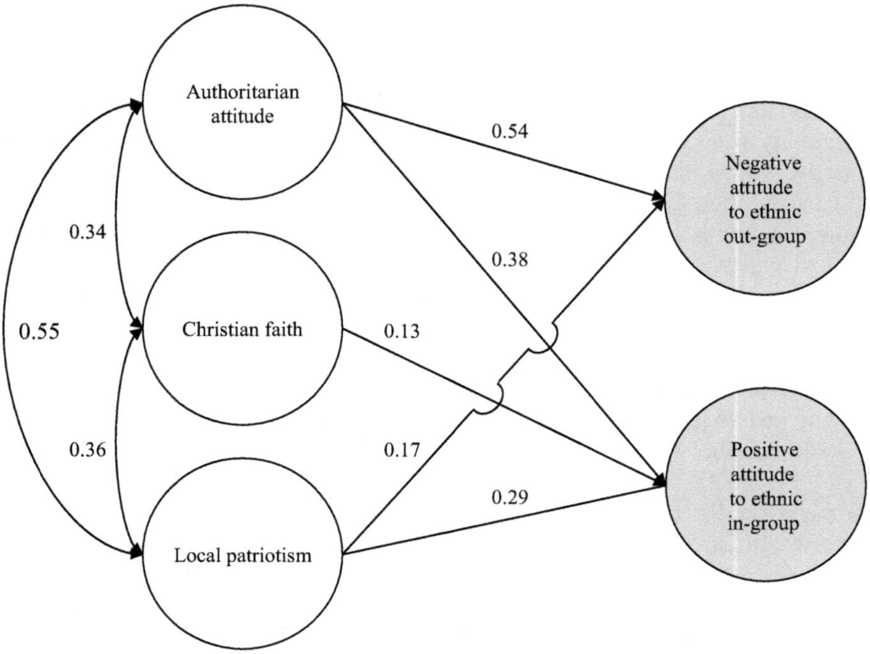

Figure 8 Causes or correlates of ethnocentrism.
Source: based on Eisinga et al. (1991, p. 314).

Do Christians tend to have more authoritarian attitudes because, as members of a strictly hierarchically organized church, they have learned not to question the dogmas of their religion (e.g., infallibility of the pope)? To be able to test this thesis, Eisinga et al. (1991) interviewed a total of 1,224 representatively selected Dutch adults. The type and intensity of individual faith were recorded on the basis of ten questions (e.g., "There is a God whom we can know through Jesus Christ"). As expected, Christian faith correlates positively with authoritarian attitudes and local patriotism. In addition, it influences the attitude toward one's own group (positively), but not toward foreign groups (see Figure 8).

The religious also articulate more ethnocentric attitudes than atheists (cf. Kusumawardani/Yolanda 2021; Tabassi et al. 2012). This is particularly true for extrinsically religious people and somewhat less so for intrinsically religious people (cf. Arli et al. 2021b).

2.7 Nationalism, patriotism and national pride

By patriotism we refer to the "love of one's own country" and by nationalism the "conviction that one's own country is fundamentally superior to other countries." With a view to economic contexts, we sometimes also speak of economic patriotism: This refers to the conviction that one should buy domestic products and not those produced abroad. In an online survey of 10,049 Americans, Byrne et al. (2021) found, as expected, high correlations between:

- Patriotism (e.g., "I am proud to be an American") and economic patriotism (e.g., "Consumption of local products helps the US economy") ($r = 0.452$)
- Nationalism (e.g., "In view of America's moral and material superiority, it is only right that we should have the biggest say in deciding United Nations policy") and patriotism ($r = 0.540$)
- Xenophobia (e.g., "Some groups of people are simply not the equals of others") and nationalism ($r = 0.492$)

On the one hand, the high correlations indicate that these constructs capture similarities to an appreciable extent. However, if we calculate the proportion of common variance,[9] we see that the two constructs overlap only partially.

There is a close connection between these constructs and religiosity, which has already been empirically shown many times (cf. Schmitt et al. 2008). According to Bechert (2021), atheists are outsiders in strictly religious societies, where they are rejected as "unpatriotic" and alienated from their societies of origin. In addition, Gervais et al. (2017) found that anti-atheist attitudes are common across religiously diverse societies, including in countries with Buddhist, Christian, Hindu and non-religious majorities, showing that such attitudes are not exclusive to countries with Abrahamic religious majorities.

According to the World Values Survey 1990/1993, in countries such as Brazil, Ireland, Nigeria, Poland and the US, 70–80% of the population are proud of their own nationality. They also believe that God plays an important role in their lives (see Figure 9). Conversely, in Germany, Japan, Russia and the Netherlands, only a minority tends toward national pride and intense religious convictions. On the whole, however, the variables correlate strongly ($r = 0.71$).

Remarkably, among the societies whose populations are both very proud of their nation and very religious, there are surprisingly many with comparatively dysfunctional governments (e.g., India, Nigeria, Turkey, South Africa, Brazil). The reason for this could be the associated uncertainties, even crisis-like living situations. According to Kay et al. (2010b), these factors compensate for a pronounced need for control and security, which can be satisfied by both national pride and belief in God.

2.8 Fatalism

In the world as experienced by fatalists, many events are predetermined by an external power: providence, fate or an omnipotent God (cf. Fiori et al. 2006). This explains why many religious people are fatalists (cf. Carey/Paulhus

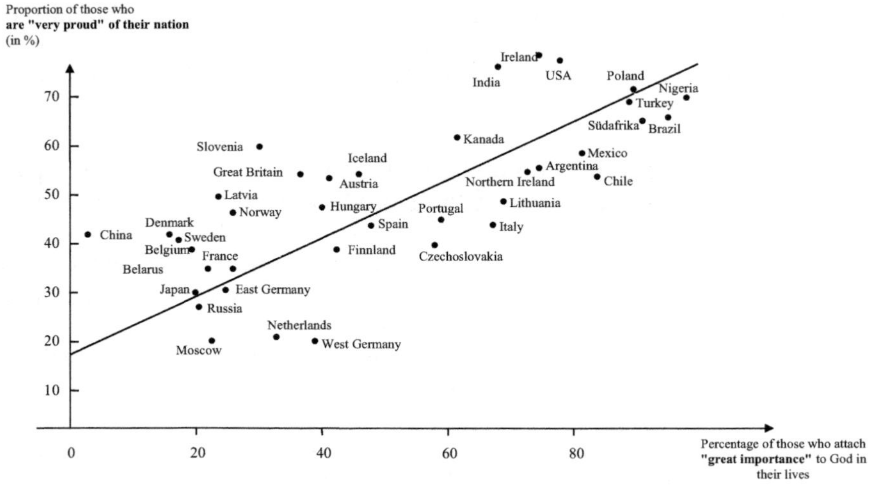

Figure 9 Religiosity and national pride.

Source: Inglehart (1998, p. 127).

Table 8 Scale for measuring fatalism

To which extent do you agree with the following statements?
Making plans only brings unhappiness because the plans are hard to fulfill.
It doesn't make much difference if people elect one or another candidate, for nothing will change.
With the way things are today, an intelligent person ought to think about the present, without worrying about what is going to happen tomorrow.
The secret of happiness is not expecting too much out of life and being content with what comes your way.

Source: Farris/Glenn (1976).

2013; Ruiu 2013). Table 8 shows a fatalism scale developed by Farris/Glenn (1976).

For Interfaith Marketing (IFM), the personality trait of fatalism is significant in many ways. One of the reasons for this is that risk perception and willingness to take risks are influenced by this individual difference. Thus, fatalists are less willing than other consumers to acquire innovative goods (cf. Tansuhaj et al. 1991). Moreover, because of their passivity, they do not tend to take on the role of advisors in their social environment (e.g., as market mavens). And because they do not strive to change a situation they perceive as unsatisfactory, fatalistic customers usually seldom complain or switch to another provider if they are dissatisfied (cf. Foxman et al. 1990).

2.9 Performance orientation

The different economic development of the Catholic and Protestant regions of Germany has led M. Weber to his well-known studies on the "spirit of capitalism." Since then, the connection between religious affiliation, work and performance ethos, and economic success has been on the agenda of research in the sociology of religion. Less than a century later, under the impression of the "Asian miracle," attention was also focused on Confucian values, which are presumably no less conducive to performance (cf. Liang 2010). But the other religions have also formulated explicit or implicit performance ethics.

2.9.1 Jewish work ethic

It is true that Jews should limit economic activity to what is necessary for survival. However, in contrast to early Christianity, which glorified poverty, Deuteronomy, the 5th book of Moses, also states (Dt 15:4), "The Lord your God will bless you abundantly in the land that the Lord your God will give you as a portion and inheritance." Despite all contradictions, this points to a success-oriented work ethic, especially since the Jewish conception of man grants each individual the "ability for responsible freedom," an essential prerequisite for entrepreneurial action.

2.9.2 Protestant work ethic

With the Reformation, Protestantism played a decisive role in "loosening the grip of the Christian medieval worldview around a considerable part of Europe" (Inglehart 1998, p. 307). As a result, from the 18th century onward, the countries and regions of Europe populated predominantly by Protestants and those populated predominantly by Catholics developed in very different economic ways. This realization had three consequences:

- First, there was an intensive discussion about possible causes of the development deficits of Catholic countries and regions.
- Second, primarily Catholic authors began to criticize "modern competitive capitalism" as a system of greed, selfishness and exploitation. After the Franco-Prussian War of 1870/71 and inspired by the resurgence of anti-Semitism at that time, it was said on both sides of the Rhine that Jews had invented modern capitalism (or capitalist rationality) and that capital accumulation, as the essence of capitalism, was immanent to the Jewish spirit or to Judaism (cf. Sombart 1911).
- Third, the thesis of the Protestant origin of the "spirit of capitalism" gained the upper hand.

Weber (1905) was the first to explicitly analyze this connection. The impetus for this was the examination paper of one of his students. He wrote that the Protestants living in Baden, Leipzig and Tübingen at that time were not only more educated but also more prosperous than their Catholic neighbors. While the latter mostly worked in small craft businesses, the management of large-scale industry was mainly in the hands of Protestants. Such observations prompted the professor, who had been interested in economic sociology all his life, to pursue a number of fundamental questions, including:

- Is there a systematic correlation between religion and economic success?
- Did Protestantism promote the spread of capitalism worldwide?

In a collection of essays entitled "Protestant Ethics and the 'Spirit' of Capitalism," the then still unknown scientist attempted to find answers to these questions. Together with the posthumously published monograph "Economy and Society," this work was to establish his scientific fame decades later.

The German sociologist and economist, who later became world-renowned, studied ascetic Protestantism in depth and demonstrated a connection between certain religious convictions and "professional ethics": the "self-evident obligation of the individual to increase his wealth." Put simply, his insight was that the economic successes of Protestant societies can be explained in general terms by their special kind of religiosity (especially Calvinism and Puritanism) and in concrete terms by their rational way of life. This manifests itself through:

- Strict self-control, thrift and an ascetic way of life (i.e., renunciation of consumption, especially luxury)
- Success at work through conscientiousness and diligence ("hard work")
- Acquisitiveness, which is not primarily intended to satisfy one's own material needs
- Awareness of living in the debt of God

One of the ways in which the Protestant work ethics differs from other religiously inspired work ethics is that work is valued for its own sake and not for its results. The Calvinist virtues made possible the capitalization of parts of the Protestant population and thus investments in industrial plants and ultimately prepared the ground for systematic industrialization. In the intellectual succession of M. Weber, other scholars were also able to demonstrate that the economic development of a society depends essentially on the religiously motivated willingness of its members to perform. For example, using a random sample of all adult Detroit residents, Mayer/Sharp (1962) demonstrated that Detroit's Jews were the most successful economically (and thus presumably more willing to perform than others) followed by Orthodox Jews, the members of the various Protestant churches, and finally Catholics. In addition, at the end of the 1980s, a ranking of the countries with the highest per capita income showed that it was predominantly Protestant countries that occupied the top positions (cf. Hoffmann/Härle 1992, p. 191).

2.9.3 *Catholic work ethic*

While Protestant ethics decidedly focuses on the personal responsibility of the individual and does not consider individual economic success as enrichment at the expense of others, from the Catholic point of view only God's grace opens the "way of salvation." Only in this way can man, who is sinful by nature, attain salvation (cf. Sood/Nasu 1995, p. 5f.). For the thesis that Catholicism has always regarded acquisitiveness with suspicion, numerous examples can be found in church history, such as the "Decree Ejicere" of canon law:

> The merchant can hardly ever please God..., therefore no Christian may engage in trade. But whoever does it is to be expelled from the church (ejicere).... He who buys or sells cannot keep himself free from perjury (legal collection "Gratian"). This conception can be traced back to the pre-Christian Greek philosophy, which, above all through Aristotle, strongly influenced Western thought. Aristotle distinguished economics, the natural art of acquisition, from chrematistics, the morally reprehensible art of enrichment, which he assigned to internal trade.
>
> ("Decretum Gratiani")

However, according to Aristotelian Roman Catholic doctrine, wealth is quite legitimate, provided it is pursued in moderation – as much as one needs for a good life.

2.9.4 *Islamic work ethic*

Ramadan costs Islamic countries around 3% of their gross national product each year (see Hasan 2017). However, it is not religion that is primarily responsible for hostility to innovation and economic stagnation, but certain personality traits that often go hand in hand with religiosity: Dogmatism, authoritarianism and an excessive sense of tradition. The exclusion of women from public life is also one of the reasons for the lower level of economic development of this region (see Figure 10).

2.9.5 *Hindu work ethic*

The fact that Hindus, like Buddhists, see life as a chain of rebirths, forming an eternal cycle, is often interpreted as an indication of surrendering to fate and a low achievement orientation. However, it is overlooked that this cycle can be broken, among other things, by a godly life and good deeds (cf. II-5.1). Karma does not mean inevitable fate but ultimately implies a message that promotes performance: everyone is responsible for his or her own fate. "A person of good deeds becomes good, a person of bad deeds becomes bad."

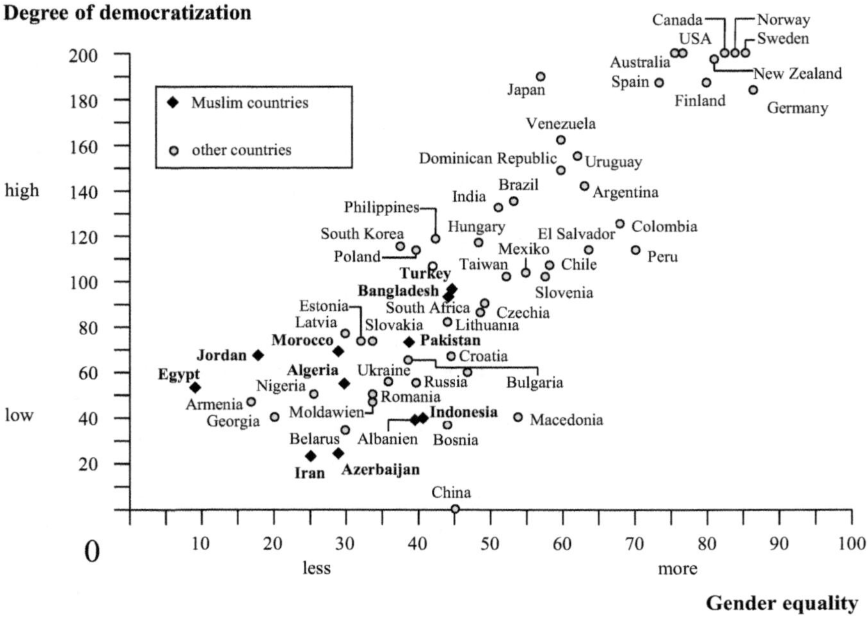

Figure 10 Sociopolitical map.

Source: Inglehart/Norris (2003, p. 68).

However, the doctrine of karma can be used to justify lack of empathy with the poor as well as lack of willingness to promote a more egalitarian society. If the current life is a consequence of the good and bad deeds done in the past life, then the starving homeless person is just as responsible for his or her fate as the rich billionaire is for his or her.

The consumer and performance-oriented side of modern Hinduism is embodied by Ganesha, the elephant-headed son of Parvati and Shiva, responsible for business and financial success and happiness. In his honor, a festival is held every year in Mumbai, India's financial center: Ganesh Chaturthi. With the participation of countless people, images (drawings, statues) of the elephant god are carried to the beach and finally sunk into the sea.

2.9.6 *Confucian work ethic*

Regarding the discussion about the causes of the "Asian miracle," it has been generally accepted that presumably not religious denomination is responsible for the strong economic growth of this region, but rather Confucian values (cf. Stiglitz 1996; Bond/Hofstede 1989; McCord 1989): hard work, special appreciation of learning, education, achievement and willingness to defer rewards and accumulate capital (see II-6.2).

The most important concern of Confucianism is to impart morality and humanity to the individual, the family and the state, and thus to ensure order. The ultimate goal is the stability of the state. Confucian values are manifested in five cardinal virtues: mutual love, righteousness, wisdom, morality and sincerity. Especially important is dutiful behavior toward others. In addition, honoring ancestors and parents is a moral duty that strengthens the bond within the family. While according to the Protestantism thesis, "hard work" provides certainty of grace, according to Confucian moral teachings the individual thereby obtains the guarantee not to bring disgrace to his or her own family, which is why in these societies performance orientation is a value in itself.

2.10 Past vs. future orientation

Willingness to save, economic success and other economically significant behaviors also depend on what the individual expects in the future. The hope for a "better future" is part of the Western worldview. Jews and Christians have placed and continue to place their hope in the Messiah or in the Second Coming of Christ. For Orthodox Christianity, however, the resurrection of Christ marks the fulfillment and not the beginning of history. For this reason, the Orthodox, who live mainly in Russia, Bulgaria or Greece, are usually said to have a weaker orientation toward the future.

The cyclical understanding of time in animistic societies is dominated by the past and the present. Polytheistic religions also lack the form of future orientation that is characteristic of Christianity. Its linear understanding of time, with the creation of the world as the zero point and the Last Judgment as the end point, has favored a quantification and economization of the scarce commodity of time: "time is money." In Western industrial societies, it was and still is reserved for the alternative movement to propagate a deceleration of consumption, (for example, cf. Husemann/Eckhardt 2019a).

3 Religion, religiosity and consumer behavior

In his influential theory of values, Rokeach (1969; 1968) described religiosity as a terminal value: the pursuit of inner harmony and redemption. Following the value typology of Vinson et al. (1977, p. 46), religiosity can be defined as a domain-specific value that directly influences concrete behavior. It is true that the values prevailing in a society do not last forever, as numerous studies have shown (cf. Inglehart 1998). But a profound change in values, such as Germany or Japan experienced after World War II, takes decades or longer. Religious affiliation and religiosity, like national culture, are therefore considered relatively stable over time and capable of influencing attitudes and behavior more or less predictably (see Delener 1990a).

However, this basic IFM thesis is very unspecific. Therefore, Mathras et al. (2016) proposed, based on the relevant literature, to understand religion as a four-dimensional construct that manifests itself in rituals, religious beliefs, values and faith communities. These four dimensions were substantiated by different subdimensions: Rituals, for example, are divided into prayers, purification rituals (e.g., confession, purifying bath in the Ganges) and time rituals (e.g., sequence of festivals and sacraments). Agarwala et al. (2019) largely adopted this structure and linked it to economically relevant consumer behaviors (see Figure 11).

The six "Consumer Outcomes" are the result of a comprehensive analysis and categorization of relevant empirical research by these scholars. Thus, this category captures:

- Materialism[10] studies on the relationship between religiosity and consumption, brand awareness, fashion awareness and attitudes toward luxury brands. This includes a study by Stillman et al. (2012). They found that spiritually oriented consumers are willing to pay less than others for products related to conspicuous consumption (e.g., smartphones).
- Intolerance[11] studies on the connection between religiosity and animosity, consumer boycotts and feelings hurt by controversial advertising. In this sense, consumers who are intolerant are those who tend to be religiously exclusivist (i.e., who regard their own religious beliefs as indisputably true and those of others as indisputably false) (cf. Trinitapoli 2007).

DOI: 10.4324/9781003506010-13

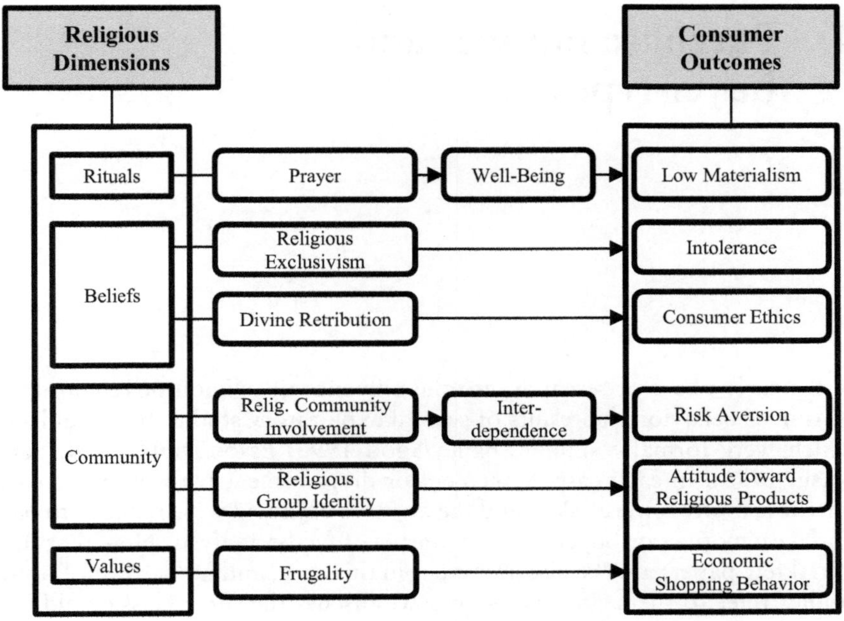

Figure 11 Structural model of research on interfaith consumer behavior.
Source: Agarwala et al. (2019, p. 35).

- Consumer ethics[12] studies on the relationship between religiosity, ethical beliefs and consumer behavior. Most people consider unethical behavior to be less reprehensible if they profit from the misconduct of others (e.g., not saying anything if the seller has miscalculated to their advantage). However, those who actively behave unethically themselves (e.g., report an exaggeratedly large amount of damage to their insurance company) can expect less leniency. This effect is somewhat more evident among the very religious than among the less religious (cf. Arli 2017).
- Risk aversion[13] studies on the connection between religiosity and acceptance of innovations, consumers' risk perception and brand- and store-switching behavior. Religious people tend to be socialized not only in a collectivist way on the basis of shared beliefs but also through participation in the rituals and events of their religious community. As consumers, they therefore do not want to deviate from the customary (cf. Agarwala et al. 2019, p. 42).
- Attitudes toward religious products[14] studies on the connection between religiosity and consumption that conforms to a particular religion (e.g., kosher products, Islamic banking) and on the use of religious symbols in brand communication. As the relevant research has shown, religious people prefer shopping venues that remain closed on Saturdays (= Jews) or Sundays (= Christians) (cf. Siguaw/Simpson 1997) and brands that are associated with religious symbols (cf. Henley et al. 2009).

4 Purchase motives and buyer types

In the early phase of research into the influence of religion or religiosity on consumer behavior, the results of several exploratory studies were published which were formally similar (Bailey/Sood 1993, Essoo/Dibb, 2004, Sood/Nasu, 1995). In each case, agreement or disagreement with pre-formulated purchase motives were asked and the answers obtained were reduced to basic purchase motives or buyer types by means of factor analysis. Note that these initial few papers are the classic studies in this area, and numerous follow-up studies refer to them. In this section, we discuss the three classic studies in this area of research.

4.1 Purchase motives across diverse religious affiliations

Bailey/Sood (1993) interviewed 349 followers of different religious affiliations in Washington, DC In addition to their religious affiliation, the respondents were asked about their religious convictions. The question "Do you believe Jesus is son of god?" was answered in the affirmative by 87% of Catholics, but, understandably, by only 9% of Buddhists. The dependent variable "purchasing behavior" was operationalized using 20 statements (semantic differentials) on product choice, place of purchase and information search (e.g., "You prefer ads that are exciting – are informative?"). A fictitious high-involvement purchase situation (i.e., purchase of a high-priced stereo system) was examined, since previous studies had shown that consumers only assess high-involvement products differently depending on their religiosity, while this does not play a role for low-involvement products.

Seven buyer types were identified by means of factor analysis in this study:

- Rational buyers are price-sensitive and prefer low-priced shopping places. They look for special offers, are satisfied with average product quality, do not draw conclusions about the quality of the products from the price and pay attention to durability, warranties, etc.
- Impulsive shoppers make their purchasing decisions spontaneously and independently of special offers, shop in the next best store and do not seek

DOI: 10.4324/9781003506010-14

advice from friends and acquaintances before making purchasing decisions, nor are they influenced by the media.
- Informed buyers also do not attach any particular importance to the advice of other people, because they obtain the necessary product information themselves. They prefer informative, subtle advertising to emotional, attention-seeking displays.
- Reluctant shoppers are extremely price-sensitive. Because they perceive shopping as a burden, they limit themselves to just a few shopping venues and settle for a limited range.
- Buyers who are willing to take risks are also interested in unadvertised, new products and are open to foreign brands.
- Skeptical shoppers generally distrust advertising, prefer to ask friends for their opinion and prefer well-known brands.
- Elitist shoppers expect above-average service and like to shop at well-stocked stores (rather than the lowest priced stores).

The two researchers then used regression analysis to examine for each religious affiliation whether and to what extent religious affiliation can be used to predict their purchasing behavior. However, the different religious affiliations were not systematically compared with each other, but each individually only with a very small sample of non-religious people (n = 37). In addition, apart from Protestants (n = 107) and Catholics (n = 90), the other religious affiliations were so few in number that the reported findings can only show a provisional trend: 28 Buddhists, 16 Hindus, 31 Jews and 40 Muslims. Leaving aside these objections, the researchers found the following:

- A disproportionately large number of the Muslims surveyed are impulsive and relatively low-information, risk-taking consumers (which may be linked to a fatalistic basic attitude).
- Hindus seem to have a propensity for rational purchasing behavior, which is consistent with the Hindu ideal of striving for simplicity, purity and self-control.
- Catholic consumers are less likely than non-denominational consumers to seek information before making a purchase decision.
- The Buddhists, Jews and Protestants interviewed in this study revealed similar consumption habits as their non-religious peers.

Delener (1989) has already observed something similar. Her study also showed Muslims to be more impulsive and Hindus more rational consumers. Furthermore, it was shown that non-religious people search for information more intensively than religious consumers. Despite various weaknesses, the work of Bailey/Sood (1993) is considered a milestone in research on Interfaith Marketing (IFM).

4.2 Purchase motives across Catholic, Hindu and Muslim consumers

Essoo/Dibb (2004) largely replicated the Bailey/Sood study. However, they restricted themselves to three religious groups (Catholic, Hindu and Muslim) and to comparing strictly religious with less religious people. Again, seven types of buyers were identified by factor analysis. The two researchers then analyzed the role played by religiosity and religious affiliation in this context.

Both variables proved to be significant moderators. However, religiosity influences behavior more strongly than religious affiliation. For example, whether a respondent is more of a demanding or more of an innovative shopper depends less on his or her religious affiliation than on the intensity of his or her religiosity. Interaction effects (e.g., systematic differences between less devout Catholics and strictly devout Hindus) could not be demonstrated.

According to this study, Catholics are more demanding, conservative customers who pay particular attention to the quality of the services offered. They also expect seriousness and credibility from advertising measures. They respond positively to sales promotions and are loyal to the store. The opinion of their social environment is also important to them.

Muslims, by comparison, are more the innovative, practical and price-conscious type. More than others, they want to be able to negotiate prices. Special offers are important to them. It also does not seem particularly risky to them to keep trying out new stores and products. This, together with their greater willingness to take risks and their lower tendency to gather a lot of information before making purchasing decisions, can be explained by the firm conviction of most Muslims that everything on earth obeys Allah's will.

Based on the insights presented here, Hindus can be described as rather passive consumers, as the antitype of the demanding and the practical. They tolerate lower product quality, poorer services and higher prices more than others. To justify this, Essoo/Dibb (2004) have pointed to the comparatively large acceptance of fatalistic beliefs in Hinduism as well as the special appreciation of serenity, self-control and detachment from evil desires.

4.3 Purchase motives across Buddhist, Shinto and Protestant consumers

Sood/Nasu (1995) wanted to know whether less religious people consume similarly or differently than strict believers. For this purpose, they interviewed Japanese (Buddhism as well as Shintoism) as well as U.S. consumers (Protestants). The participants were first asked to imagine that they wanted to buy a high-priced radio set, and then to respond to 20 statements concerning various aspects of this fictitious purchase decision: product selection (quality, brand name, etc.), choice of the place of purchase (assortment, price, etc.) and information gathering (media, friends' opinions, etc.). These 20 statements were each assigned a rating scale (e.g., "I would buy the radio that has

Table 9 Factor structure of purchasing behavior

Buyer type	*Special features*
Pragmatic	What is important is adequate quality, durability and guarantees. Pragmatic also buy new, still unknown brands.
Price-conscious	Low-priced (also foreign) products are important. Price-conscious shoppers buy selectively during clearance sales, do not feel tied to specific shopping places and do not rely on the price/quality assumption.
Self-confident	New, unknown brands that are little advertised are important. Self-confident people rely on their own informedness and decision-making ability.
Rational thinkers	Rational ad appeals are important. Rational thinkers distrust advertising statements and prefer unobtrusive advertising.
Reluctant	One-stop shopping is important. Reluctant people don't look to the media for information, and shopping is a burden to them.
Tradition-conscious	Product origin and service are important. The tradition-conscious prefer domestic products.
Purposeful	Product quality, durability and guarantees are important.

Source: Own representation based on Sood/Nasu (1995, p. 7).

the best quality… has an appropriate quality"). Through a factor analysis, the assessments obtained could be reduced to seven dimensions (cf. Table 9).

The authors used t-tests to compare the factor means as a function of religiosity and nationality. Strictly religious American participants proved to be above-average price-conscious and rational consumers. For the purchase motives of Japanese, however, their religiosity was irrelevant. The reason for this could be that Japanese society is largely secular. In addition, many Japanese are multi-confessional and feel an affinity with Shintoism, Buddhism and Confucianism, depending on which area of daily life is affected (see II-1.1).

5 Purchase decisions

The cognitive stream of marketing research assumes that consumers obtain more or less comprehensive information before making a purchase decision, whether from the company, the media or their social environment. The type and intensity of the information search are moderated by the individual decision-making style as well as by characteristics of the purchase situation and the object of purchase. For example, impulse purchases and habitual purchases are characterized by the fact that they are largely made without a specific information base.

5.1 Information search

Whether and in what way religious affiliation and religiosity influence the information search behavior of consumers is one of the rather neglected questions of Interfaith Marketing (IFM). Researchers in the buyer typology domain such as Bailey/Sood (1993) have described, among other things, the type of impulsive buyer who makes purchase decisions spontaneously and independently of information offered by the media as well as recommendations from other consumers. Another type is the informed buyer. Impulsive, rather uninformed consumers were found much more frequently among the Catholic and Muslim study participants than among the Buddhists, Jews and Protestants surveyed, as well as among the non-confessional participants. The Muslims interviewed by Essoo/Dibb (2004) also tended to obtain comparatively little information before making a purchase decision. This passivity can be explained by the firm conviction that everything on the earth obeys Allah's will.

Most often, however, scholars of Arab origin have addressed this phenomenon with a normative approach: "Good Muslims do not buy anything superfluous or useless." From an Islamic perspective, impulsive consumers have been described as self-centered hedonists, driven on the one hand by the need for variety and on the other hand as victims of their lack of structure and plan (cf. Sharma et al. 2010). This behavior contradicts Islamic values, which is why devout Muslims are less susceptible to it.

DOI: 10.4324/9781003506010-15

Delener (1989), in turn, has shown that non-religious consumers search for information more intensively than religious people. Very religious Koreans rely more heavily than less religious people on advice and recommendations from members of their church congregation (see Choi et al. 2010).

5.2 Decision-making style

A wide variety of decision-making styles are described in the literature. In addition to the brand- and quality-oriented style, the price-oriented, the risk-oriented and the value-oriented decision-making styles have attracted the interest of marketing research. In addition, there are, among others, the hedonistic leisure-oriented and the halal-conscious decision-making styles of Indonesian consumers (cf. Usman et al. 2021).

5.2.1 Brand- and quality-oriented decision-making style

Brand-conscious consumers generally prefer branded products to unbranded products. From their point of view, brands reduce the purchase risk due to their quality promise. They are also intensively advertised and therefore have a good recognition value, which creates familiarity. And buyers of prestigious brands can demonstrate their social status to others in their social environment. Brand-conscious consumers accept a corresponding price premium for this added value (cf. Table 10).

The splendor of the Catholic Church in the Baroque and Rococo periods, which contrasts with the deliberate sparseness of Protestant houses of worship, suggests an affinity between brand philosophy and Catholicism. Therefore, Catholics are likely an attractive buyer segment for brands. Essoo/Dibb (2004) have confirmed this insofar as, according to their study, Catholics

Table 10 Willingness to pay of brand-conscious German consumers

	Catholics (n = 71)	*Protestants (n = 84)*	*p*
I would prefer a brand that meets my requirements over others, even if it is more expensive.	1.30	0.78	0.03
I would pay a higher price for a brand that meets my requirements.	1.27	0.80	0.07
A brand that meets my requirements can also cost more.	1.14	0.63	0.05

Note: Mean values on a scale from –3 "strongly disagree" to +3 "strongly agree," results of a t-test.

Source: Own survey.

tend to belong to the traditional type of buyer for whom the quality of a product is important.

According to the available research, strictly religious people attach greater importance to quality in their clothing purchases, but not to prestigious brand names (cf. Islam/Chandrasekaran 2019). Rather, strong religiosity inhibits the temptation to use brand-name clothing for self-expression and to demonstrate one's own self-worth (cf. Shachar et al. 2011). Indeed, these researchers found a substitution effect between religiosity and brand purchase behavior in fulfilling consumers' self-worth needs. Specifically, highly religious consumers were less likely to purchase brand-named products because their self-worth needs were already fulfilled by their religious beliefs. Moreover, the notion of quality varies depending on religious affiliation. While for Orthodox Muslims quality means above all "halal" (cf. Mokhlis 2006b), Orthodox American Christians act like smart shoppers: they look for high quality, but at low prices (cf. Davis/Jai 2014).

5.2.2 *Price-oriented decision-making style*

The type of rational shopper identified in several studies pays more attention than others to special offers when shopping and generally makes price-sensitive decisions (i.e., they react to price changes by changing their purchasing behavior accordingly). Hindus often act rationally in this sense, followed by Buddhists, Christians and Muslims (cf. Bailey/Sood 1993) as well as religious Protestants (cf. Sood/Nasu 1995).

While for the rational type primarily a low price is a good price, the brand-conscious use a high price as a quality indicator. Admittedly, the price/quality hypothesis has often proved to be a price/quality illusion. But this does not stop many from opting for a high-priced offer when in doubt. After all, it is often very difficult and sometimes impossible to reliably assess product quality, but very easy to apply the heuristic "the higher the price, the higher the quality." Of the consumers interviewed by Mokhlis (2010), primarily Muslims agreed with the price/quality assumption (significantly more often than Buddhists), while religious Protestants tended to reject it (cf. Sood/Nasu 1995).

5.2.3 *Risk-oriented decision-making style*

Many purchasing and consumption decisions are fraught with risk. Who can be sure that the new delivery service is reliable, that the special offer will meet expectations in terms of quality or that the new smartphone is worth its price? If possible, risk-averse customers avoid behavioral changes, such as trying out a new product or changing a familiar brand or retailer (cf. Karani/Fraccastoro 2010).

Due to their generally lower self-confidence and increased sense of insecurity, religious people strive to avoid risks of all kinds in many areas of life.

Their consumer behavior is influenced by this risk aversion in many ways. Religious consumers:

- Are highly skeptical of innovative products (cf. Mansori et al. 2015)
- Avoid changing brands and retailers as much as possible (cf. Choi et al. 2013)
- Perceive the risks of consumer life particularly intensively and have less confidence in their ability to make judgments (cf. Delener 1990b)

Religious people also tend not to make impulsive purchasing decisions (cf. Mokhlis 2009a). On the one hand, this is surprising, given that their less analytical thinking style and their pronounced emotionality (cf. Zuckerman et al. 2013) would actually lead one to expect spontaneous, unplanned actions. On the other hand, however, this is countered by an above-average risk aversion, which is why religious customers apparently find the spontaneous less appealing (cf. Habib/Bekun 2021).

Singh et al. (2021) have described impulsivity as a subtype of uncontrolled buying behavior, which includes compulsive buying. However, according to their observations, only extrinsically religious individuals tend to engage in uncontrolled buying behavior. This relationship is mediated by influenceability (i.e., susceptibility to interpersonal influence) and moderated by long-term orientation.

Catholics are similar to intrinsically religious people in that they also react skeptically to innovations and, when buying consumer products, consider above all the possible negative consequences of their decisions (cf. Delener 1990b). In contrast, Jews (cf. Hirschman 1981) and Muslims (cf. Mokhlis 2009a) show a greater openness to new kinds of products.

5.2.4 Ethical-oriented decision-making style

Ethical consumption is a collective term for sustainable, environmentally conscious and prosocial consumer behavior. Consumers are not primarily concerned with increasing their personal benefit through their purchasing and consumption decisions. Rather, their attention is primarily focused on the common good. According to the General Theory of Marketing Ethics, the ethical behavior of consumers is shaped, among other things, by their religion (cf. Hunt/Vitell 1986).

At the heart of the consumer social responsibility movement is a growing awareness of and striving for justice and fairness toward other people and future generations (cf. Hoffmann/Akbar 2019, p. 195). According to the Otto Group's fifth trend study,[15] ethical consumption is increasingly accepted by parts of the population.

In the 1990s and early 2000s, when the three purchase motive studies described earlier were conducted (cf. III-4), little attention was paid to the ethical implications of consumer behavior. Consequently, they were not part

Table 11 Extract from Muncy-Vitell consumer ethics scale

Lying about a child's age in order to get a lower price. (–)
Not telling the truth when negotiating the price of a new automobile. (–)
Buying counterfeit goods instead of buying the original manufacturers brands. (–)
Purchasing something made of recycled materials even though it is more expensive. (+)
Correcting a bill that has been miscalculated in your favor. (+)

Source: Vitell/Muncy (2005).

of the variable pool from which the described buyer types were extracted by factor analysis at that time. Therefore, the ethical consumer could not be identified as a type of buyer in these studies. A few years later, however, it was on the research agenda (cf. Newholm/Shaw 2007). Ethical consumer behavior is usually operationalized with the help of the Muncy-Vitell Consumer Ethics Scale (cf. Table 11).

All major world religions ultimately propagate prosocial values (e.g., mercy or active compassion for the poor) (cf. Saroglou et al. 2005). Therefore, religious consumers should have a stronger ethical awareness than non- or low-religious consumers. For intrinsically religious consumers, Vitell et al. (2005) found this to be the case, but not for extrinsically religious people. Similar findings were reported by Vitell et al. (2006) and Arli/Tjiptono (2014). Both seem plausible, since only intrinsically religious people act out of conviction, whereas extrinsically religious people are said not to be religious at all but only want to benefit from the advantages of belonging to a religious community. In a study by Schneider et al. (2011), the relationship between religiosity and ethical behavior was more evident among Muslim consumers than among Christian consumers in Germany. In addition, recent research shows that there is a positive relationship between religiosity and consumers' purchase intentions of unethical brands due to heightened moral licensing perceptions (Cabano/Minton 2024). That is, highly religious consumers already think that they are moral and ethical individuals due to them being religious, which increases their purchase intentions of unethical brands.

A caveat, however, is that most of these studies are based on self-report and thus tend to reflect wishful thinking and the need for a positive self-image (cf. Galen 2012). It does, however, explain why ethical attitudes (e.g., willingness to adopt a modest lifestyle) mostly do not promote corresponding ethical behaviors. In this context, attitudinal/behavioral research explores the question of whether religious people are not more ethical but often more hypocritical than less religious comparative persons (cf. III-5.6).

5.2.5 Spiritually oriented decision-making style

A comparatively young field of research is devoted to the analysis of consumer spirituality (cf. Husemann/Eckhardt 2019b). This refers to the consumption of goods that promise a spiritual benefit (cf. Kale 2004). Consumption situations, which satisfy the need of many people for meaning in life, for an encounter with their inner self as well as with a higher external power, can be of a:

- Material nature (e.g., renunciation of consumption in favor of a hoped-for spiritual life after death; cf. Rauf et al. 2019)
- Physical nature (e.g., pain and the associated spiritual experiences as a result of a deprivation-filled pilgrimage; cf. Cova/Cova 2019)
- Technological nature (e.g., using online platforms such as Trip Advisor to share the experiences gained during a retreat vacation in a monastery; cf. van Laer/Izberk-Bilgin 2019)

5.3 Judgment biases

Social psychologists have identified numerous systematic perception and judgment biases. The Cognitive Bias Codex, initiated by Internet bloggers B. Benson and J. Manoogian III, as of July 2022 listed 184 such biases, ranging from the "less-is-better effect" to the "attribution error." Of particular interest to IFM is the self-serving bias. This refers to a tendency to attribute responsibility for positive events (e.g., successes) to oneself as much as possible while blaming other actors or unfavorable circumstances for negative events (e.g., failures). Psychologically, this is not simply a misperception but makes sense insofar as the daily little self-deception strengthens self-esteem (e.g., self-efficacy).

Also consumers are susceptible to self-esteem distortions. It is well known that most people tend to assume that the company is to blame in the event of product defects and other disruptions in the firm/consumer relationship (cf. Folkes/Kotsos 1986). There is evidence that religious consumers whose religion demands modesty and views pride as a sin (e.g., Christianity) are less susceptible to this bias and judge facts more accurately than others (cf. Moon 2003). Religious people in general, however, are more susceptible to this bias than non-religious people and agnostics because of their rather intuitive thinking style (cf. Pennycook et al. 2016).

The social desirability bias describes the tendency not to reveal one's actual attitudes, convictions or feelings in surveys, private conversations, etc., but to answer in the way one believes one should (e.g., because it is expected or social norms suggest this). The "social desirability effect" overlays the assessment of unethical behavior particularly clearly, for example, when a consumer survey is to determine whether one has ever committed shoplifting.

Some have described this bias as a methodological artifact, a self-fulfilling prophecy or a logical short circuit (e.g., Galen 2012). Responsible for this is the partly explicit, partly implicit equation of religiosity with morality, which religious people adopt in their self-perception. Chaves (2010) calls this "religious congruence fallacy." Others, such as Chung/Monroe (2003), have explained the social desirability bias with the particularly strong need of religious people to leave a favorable impression in social situations, as a means of self-enhancement (cf. Sedikides/Gebauer 2010). Their impression management enables religious people to bridge the gap between a mostly idealistic worldview and the often less than ideal reality and, specifically, the gap between their ethical demands on themselves (e.g., honesty) and their actual behavior (e.g., shoplifting). Leak/Fish (1989) wanted to find out whether it is really conscious impression management or rather unconscious self-deception that causes religious respondents to give more socially desirable information. Their answer is both of these factors drive the effect.

Irrespective of how the bias measurable by means of the Marlowe-Crowne Social Desirability Scale can be explained, should companies, market researchers and others apply a correction factor in their survey research to the information provided by religious people to compensate for this judgment bias? The relevant research findings do not suggest a recommendation. According to Chung/Monroe (2003), religious women give significantly more socially desirable answers than less religious women and, regardless of their religiosity, also than men. And in one survey, religious respondents exaggerated the intensity of their religious commitment (cf. Jones/Elliott 2017). However, Regnerus/Uecker (2007) report that religious respondents do not give more or less socially desirable responses than other individuals on sensitive topics. Finally, Rasmussen et al. (2018) could not confirm the widely held hypothesis that religious people systematically downplay their pornography use in surveys to protect their self-image.

5.4 Family purchase decisions

Collective purchasing decisions are most often made within the family. Delener (1994) examined the influence of religious affiliation and religiosity on role behavior using the example of Jewish and Catholic Americans. Given the specific personality profile of religious people (e.g., above-average conservatism), it was assumed that in religious families it is mostly the man who makes the important purchasing decisions, while less religious couples make their decisions together. Furthermore, Catholic families tend to have a patriarchal and often authoritarian structure (cf. Ellison/Sherkat 1993), whereas Jewish families tend to be more democratic.

So is it the case that in Catholic households it is mostly the man who decides what, when and where to buy, while Jewish couples more often decide together? The object of investigation in this field study was automobiles, since they are high-involvement products due to their price, social significance and duration of use. A total of 750 Jews and Catholics living in the northeastern United States who had purchased a new car in the past year provided information. They were asked who had the greatest influence on each phase of the purchase decision process: the man, the woman or both.

In view of the object of purchase (car), it is not surprising that in most families the man had the say and the woman only had a significant say in the choice of color. And, as expected, the very religious participants adhered more closely to traditional gender roles, while the less religious participants more often made joint decisions (e.g., the place of purchase and the model). According to this research, religious Jews adhere most strongly to traditional roles, more strongly than non-religious Jews and Catholics as a whole (except for the "female domain" of color choice). Furthermore, two interaction effects were found in this research (between religious affiliation and religiosity).

- Place of purchase: Jewish households that consider themselves to be less religious more often decide together where to buy their car. In strict Jewish households, however, it is primarily the man who makes this decision. Regardless of the intensity of their religiosity, many Catholic families also leave this decision to the "head of the family."
- Color of the vehicle: Strictly religious Catholics and non-religious Jews are somewhat more likely to jointly select the color of their future vehicle than the respective comparison group.

And what is the significance of family roles in the case of food purchases? According to the analysis by Just et al. (2007), Orthodox Jews tend to follow the will of the father and the younger children, while liberal Jews tend to follow the will of the mother and the older children.

5.5 Influence of the social environment

Very religious people consider obedience to be an important virtue. When making purchasing decisions, they therefore tend to yield to the influence of authorities even if their recommendation runs counter to their own wishes and needs. The same applies to the social environment. Because religious communities are organized like communicative networks, norm-violating purchases (e.g., of non-kosher food) usually do not go unnoticed. Hindus in particular are text-dependent in this sense. As a rule, they do not make purchasing decisions by weighing the pros and cons from their subjective point of view. Far more important to them is the advice of friends – and in a figurative sense also of saints and gods (cf. Lindridge 2005).

5.6 Purchase intention and behavior

We discuss what encourages or discourages religious consumers to purchase certain products at various points in this study. However, here we want to focus on some fundamental operationalization problems in purchasing behavior research.

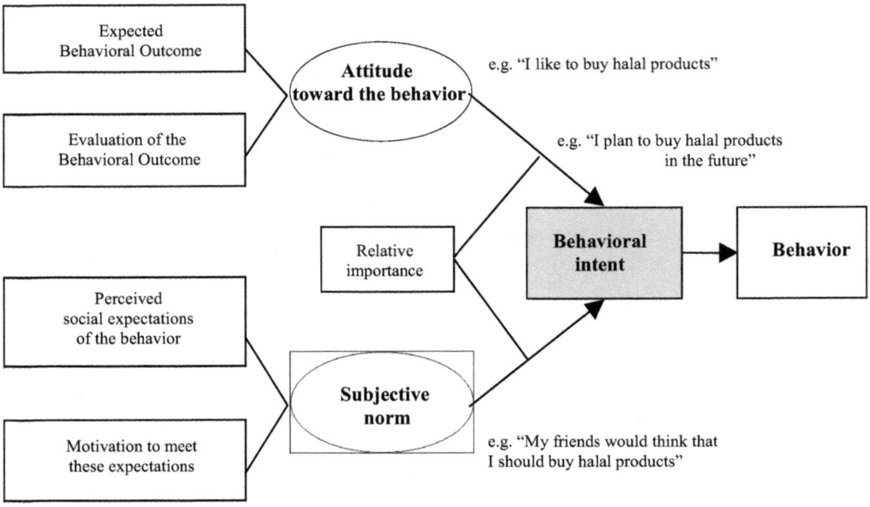

Figure 12 Intention to buy halal products according to the "Theory of Reasoned Action."

Source: Own representation based on Fishbein/Ajzen (1975) and Lada et al. (2009).

5.6.1 *Prediction of behavior*

Because it would usually be too time-consuming to survey real purchase behavior, most researchers are content to ask about purchase intention. Two constructs described by Fishbein/Ajzen (1975) in the context of the theory of planned behavior often play key roles.

- Attitude to the behavior
- Subjective norm (= expectations of the social environment regarding this behavior)

Using this measurement model, Lada et al. (2009) investigated what might induce Malaysian consumers to buy halal products. Their simplified model (cf. Figure 12) explains 66% of the variance in behavioral intention. The largest explanatory contribution is made by the subjective norm (ß = 0.814), much more than the attitudinal component (ß = 0.288). However, what their friends expect from them in this respect influences the purchase intention of the respondents also indirectly, via the path from "subjective norm" to "attitude toward behavior" (ß = 0.336). Those who believe that friends and acquaintances think it is good to buy halal products also tend to think these products are good themselves, presumably for reasons of cognitive consistency.

The theory of planned behavior is also very popular in IFM. Mukhtar/Butt (2012) have shown that, in addition to the subjective norm and the attitude toward halal products, the degree of intrapersonal religiosity is the best predictor of behavioral intention. However, since this model does not take all relevant variables into account (e.g., not habits or product knowledge), there are repeated suggestions for extensions, for example, by Rizkitysha/Hananto (2020). According to their knowledge-based research approach, the probability of purchasing a halal cleaning product depends on the perceived usefulness of this certification as well as on the knowledge about the halal label. Religious participants (mainly younger Muslims) were more convinced of its usefulness than less religious participants.

5.6.2 *Hypocrisy hypothesis*

The central problem of attitude research, however, is the attitude/behavior discrepancy. This refers to the fact that in many cases there is only a weak correlation between the expressed attitude and the observable behavior. The numerous reasons for this discrepancy include the so-called specificity problem[16] and the tendency of many people to give socially desirable responses (cf. Müller/Gelbrich 2021, p. 237 f.).

This discrepancy is usually particularly large if the purchase of socially and environmentally conscious products is the subject of the forecast model (cf. V-5.3). Whenever the demands on consumers' altruism are high (e.g., to pay a higher price than usual for environmental reasons), the probability is also high that the behavioral intention expressed in a survey will turn out to be lip service. Religious people may be increasingly susceptible to this form of hypocrisy because they have to meet particularly strict demands for a morally impeccable way of life.

So does religiosity not promote prosocial buying behavior, but rather euphemistic response behavior? As plausible as this may sound, the studies are contradictory. On the one hand, Batson et al. (1999) report that although religious people perceive themselves as prosocial and are also assessed as such by others, they are actually primarily concerned with their positive self-image and less with the needs of other people. And Ji et al. (2006) observed among evangelical Protestants with high levels of intrinsic religiosity that they internalized the "love thy neighbor commandment" on the attitudinal level, but not on the behavioral level. Various game-theoretic experiments also argue against a close link between religiosity and prosocial behavior (cf. Ahmed/Salas 2011; Tan 2006).

However, a study by Graafland (2017) does not support the hypocrisy hypothesis. It is true that only a small proportion of the Dutch Christians of different denominations surveyed stated that they had bought ethical products such as fair trade coffee, organic meat or eggs from free-range hens in the past six months. But the average attitude values were also only in the middle (i.e., neutral range of the five-point response scale (1 = not at all to 5 = completely agree)). Religious participants agreed with statements such as, "To what extent do you believe that people should buy X?" somewhat

Table 12 Attitude/behavior discrepancy in the purchase of ethical products as a function of religious denomination

	Non-religious	*Catholics*	*Orthodox Protestants*	*Other Protestants*
Setting	3.36	3.43	3.09	3.52
Price fairness	3.22	3.30	3.02	3.39
Duty	3.02	3.08	2.74	3.10
Affection	3.84	3.93	3.50	4.06
Subjective norm	2.82	3.05	2.86	3.12
Behavior	1.36	1.42	1.21	1.45

Note: Mean values, five-point rating scales, 1 = disapproval.

Source: Graafland (2017).

more than non-religious people. However, since the former bought ethical products somewhat more frequently, their attitude/behavior discrepancy in this study was somewhat smaller than that of the comparison group. According to J. Graafland, this is also more consistent with the Old Testament than the hypocrisy hypothesis. In the parable of the Good Samaritan, for example, it does not demand nice words from the believers, but active charity (i.e., the opposite of hypocrisy). Of the participating religious groups, Orthodox Protestants showed the least openness to ethical considerations in this study (cf. Table 12). This can possibly be explained by their special conception of divine grace: Out of gratitude to God, Christians are indeed called to do good. But their salvation does not depend on their good works, but on God's grace. According to J. Graafland, this doctrine can favor a division of consciousness among believers: on the one hand the economic sphere, and on the other hand the spiritual sphere.

6 Customer satisfaction and likelihood of complaint

As customer satisfaction research has shown, perceived satisfaction/dissatisfaction is not the result of an objective assessment of performance (in the sense of quality judgment), but it depends on whether a particular product or service disappoints, meets or exceeds subjective expectations. Normally, fulfilled expectations result in customers raising their level of aspiration and thus their future expectations, while disappointed expectations lower the level of aspiration and future expectations. This is not the case with Hindus, who believe in karma and presumably therefore have a weak control motivation. In addition, they have a long-term orientation. The situational adjustment of the aspiration level is characteristic for a short-term orientation, as it prevails in Western Christian culture (cf. Kopalle et al. 2010).

Under comparable conditions, religious consumers are less likely to be dissatisfied than others because they believe in the power of fate and are therefore more willing to forgive others (see Sarofim et al. 2022). If they nevertheless feel dissatisfaction, religious people comparatively seldom complain (cf. VI-4). Due to their affinity for fatalism, they tend not to assume that unpleasant things can be changed (cf. Ngai et al. 2007). Furthermore, previous work has shown that religion salience (i.e., the extent to which religious concepts are cognitively accessible) increases positive consumer responses to brand failure after recovery due to heightened forgiveness, a religious value strongly held by many major world religions (Hyodo/Bolton 2021).

DOI: 10.4324/9781003506010-16

7 Customer loyalty

Various studies show a significant correlation between religiosity and customer loyalty (e.g., Delener 1990a, p. 28). Customer loyalty is operationalized:

- Mostly as product and brand loyalty (i.e., the intention to buy a certain product or service again or on a regular basis)
- Less frequently as shopping place loyalty (i.e., as the intention to shop at a certain shopping place again or on a regular basis)

A further distinction is made between positive customer loyalty, which arises from good experiences with the product or retailer, and negative or resigned customer loyalty. The latter occurs when consumers tend to forgo a change of brand or retailer out of necessity because they fear that they will then have to accept disproportionately high switching costs (e.g., they will have to get used to unfamiliar employees, travel further distances or try out unfamiliar products). Last but not least, individual convenience and resistance to change may also play a role.

7.1 Shopping place loyalty

Religious consumers are more risk-averse and perceive purchase risks more intensively than others. Buying routines, or habits, are one way of satisfying the above-average need for security of risk-averse consumers. People who always visit the same store do not have to fear the unexpected. In most studies, however, only a weak connection between religiosity and this form of customer loyalty has been demonstrated. In the case of South Koreans, for example, who were surveyed by Choi (2010), the differences observed were statistically significant but rather minor in absolute terms. On a seven-point rating scale, the mean value of the more religious was 5.44 and that of the less religious was 5.09. Therefore, we should only speak of a slight tendency of more religious consumers to increase their loyalty to a shopping place (Choi et al. 2013).

However, mean values always run the risk of hiding interesting differences in subsamples. As Swimberghe et al. (2011) have shown, the more

DOI: 10.4324/9781003506010-17

pronounced consumers' religious convictions are, the more they evaluate the business policy of retail companies from a primarily ethical perspective. Only retailers who pass their "ethics check" can expect customer loyalty and positive word of mouth. Otherwise, for example, in the case of an unfair pricing policy, religious people will increasingly turn away and tell others about their bad experiences.

Kusumawati et al. (2020) surveyed a total of 243 Muslims in two Indonesian cities who had bought Muslim clothing at least twice in a Muslim store. This showed that religiosity has a two-fold effect. On the one hand, directly (e.g., in the form of increased repurchase and recommendation intentions), but also indirectly: religious consumers are more satisfied than average and therefore intend to shop in "their" store again and again. However, when classifying this finding, it should be noted that these were shopping venues that had been explicitly positioned as "religious." According to Suhartanto et al. (2018), religiosity also promotes the loyalty of bank customers in two ways: on the one hand, directly (ß = 0.348) and, on the other hand, indirectly, by strengthening their trust in the bank (ß = 0.691) and, consequently, the intention to demand its services in the future as well (ß = 0.393).

What influence does the consumers' religious affiliation have in this context? Theoretically, it is to be expected that Buddhists are loyal customers. This is because they do not consider change to be desirable (cf. Inglehart/Baker 2000), and their skepticism about the pursuit of material advantages also speaks against frequent change (cf. Daniels 2005). In contrast, Protestant beliefs promote the pursuit of individual success, for example, through clever switching between different providers. Catholics, however, are considered conservative consumers with a pronounced need for security. For this reason, they attach more importance to what they are used to than to the possibility of discovering more favorable opportunities for themselves through a targeted search for information. Empirically, however, Choi (2010) was unable to confirm the hypotheses derived from these considerations. The mean differences are insignificant (Protestants = 5.38; Buddhists = 5.26; Catholics = 5.21; Atheists = 5.11). Choi et al. (2013), who compared South Korean with U.S. consumers, reported similar results: no systematic influence of religious affiliation on the extent of customer loyalty. Jewish and, to a certain extent, Muslim consumers seem to be an exception. Indeed, Jews are among those who are more willing to change. This is because many of them are convinced that everyone is responsible for their own actions and can and should shape their lives according to their own ideas. In addition, they have an above-average control motivation, which is why Jews attach greater importance to being able to compare the offers of different shopping venues and then make the best choice for them (cf. Bailey/Sood 1993; Hirschman 1981). Muslims have repeatedly been observed to have a strong loyalty to an explicitly Islamic provider, such as a bank (cf. Suhartanto et al. 2018), a tour operator (cf. Abror et al. 2019b) or a clothing store (cf. Kusumawati et al. 2020). Their strong identification with their own religious group is probably responsible for this.

7.2 Brand loyalty

Brand loyalty is a two-dimensional construct with an emotional dimension (inner attachment to or commitment to a particular brand) and a behavioral dimension (repeated purchase of a particular brand) (cf. III-5.2). Emotional brand loyalty is promoted most strongly by a personal customer/brand relationship, while behavioral brand loyalty is best promoted by real incentives such as a loyalty bonus. OAhluwalia/Kaikati (2010) described lasting brand quality as the third success factor.

Various studies suggest that religious customers tend to be more loyal to brands than those who are less religious (see Choi et al. 2013; Saroglu/Dupuis 2006). The decisive reason is probably the general risk aversion of religious people and their pronounced striving to avoid uncertainty (cf. Schwartz/Huismans 1995). That is why conservative values are important to them, such as tradition, conformity and preservation of the existing social order. They are not particularly attracted to new things. Neither do they tend to:

- Engage in variety seeking (cf. Choi et al. 2013)
- Engage in novelty seeking (cf. Hirschman 1982)
- Have a strong fashion sense (cf. Islam/Chandrasekaran 2019)

Others, such as Shachar et al. (2011), argue in a more differentiated way. We discuss their findings elsewhere in the book. Xu et al. (2016) have shown that emotional brand loyalty is particularly pronounced among religious consumers.

Part IV

Strategic marketing

1 Marketing goals

More and more stakeholders (customers, employees, shareholders, the general public, etc.) expect companies to make a tangible contribution to overcoming the social and environmental challenges of our time. For this reason, brand management cannot limit itself to the classic sales or return targets but must act in a socially and ethically responsible manner and also address the concerns of society.

1.1 Corporate social responsibility

Due to the general change in values, Corporate Social Responsibility (CSR) is one of the increasingly important corporate goals: The ability and willingness to minimize the negative side effects of corporate activities, such as reducing resource consumption and pollutant emissions to a harmless minimum, ensuring compliance with human rights in all links of the supply chain, fighting corruption, etc. (cf. Carroll 1999). From an Interfaith Marketing (IFM) perspective, it is significant that religious beliefs are often used to explain and predict moral, socially responsible behavior. For example, Zaman et al. (2018) were able to show for the Islamic cultural sphere, companies that are committed to the principles of Islamic banking (see VI-2.4) are also open to CSR strategies.

1.1.1 Basic principles

Ideal precursors of the CSR movement can be found in the religious writings of the major world religions and their intellectual environment, for example, in the social encyclicals[17] of the Catholic Church or the works on "Christian realism" on the Evangelical-Protestant side (cf. Niebuhr 1953).

> For example, Catholic social teaching objects to the doctrine of classical economic theory where capital and labor are considered substitutes. It establishes priority for worker dignity and financial security, and stresses managerial responsibility for the common good. The Talmud (Jewish oral law) defines four levels of business ethical behavior,

DOI: 10.4324/9781003506010-19

> beginning at a level where an individual is just inside the basic law and reaching the highest level – the 'way of the pious'. Buddhists emphasize non-aggression, tolerance, compassion, and philanthropy.
>
> (Angelidis/Ibrahim 2004, p. 122)

Empirical CSR research mostly uses the pioneering operationalization of this construct by Carroll (1979):

- Economic responsibility: Management's ability and willingness to increase the economic welfare of society and enhance the value of the company.
- Legal responsibility: Ability and willingness to comply with legal requirements and restrictions in the process.
- Ethical responsibility: Ability and willingness to act fairly, impartially and justly in accordance with the social values of society.
- Discretionary responsibility: Ability and willingness to use discretionary powers to increase social welfare (without being forced to do so by economic, ethical or legal constraints).

It is generally assumed that there is a close connection between religion and religiosity on the one hand and CSR on the other. With regard to Islam, however, it is more difficult to make a clear statement. According to Aribi/Arun (2015), Muslim managers are clearly in favor of CSR, while Soltani et al. (2015) report the opposite. According to their respondents, Islamic values are incompatible with the CSR concept. For example, explicit CSR reporting as part of sustainability reporting contradicts the Islamic value of "Do good without talking about it" (cf. Hossain et al. 2015).

1.1.2 Empirical findings

Whether managers act in an ethically responsible manner also depends on whether the company publicly acknowledges its responsibility (cf. Singhapakdi et al. 2000). Individual commitment to moral self-improvement is also helpful. Moral self-improvement mediates the relationship between religiosity and behavioral intention. Religious individuals have an increased intention to continuously improve their moral self (e.g., "I think that it is my obligation to continue improving my moral self throughout my life."). This motivation improves their ability to recognize ethically problematic situations and their intention to behave responsibly in such situation. Religious people also increasingly agree with statements that emphasize the social responsibility of companies (e.g., "Being ethical and socially responsible is the most important thing a firm can do") and reject the opposite (e.g., "The most important concern for a firm is making a profit, even if it means bending or breaking the rules") (cf. Kurpis et al. 2008).

It is disputed whether managers are primarily responsible for the economic success of their companies and/or for their social commitment. In the early phase of this research, participants were primarily interested in the economic performance of their company, while students of economics gave priority to the assumption of ethical and discretionary responsibility (cf. Ibrahim/Angelidis 1993). Eleven years later, students of various Christian denominations surveyed by Angelidis/Ibrahim (2004) seem to have adopted the traditional viewpoint of managers: extensive incompatibility of economic and social responsibility.[18] This is surprising insofar as a contrary development could have been expected due to the growing understanding of the need for socially responsible corporate activity, especially among young people, during this period. It is true that the highly religious participants in this study placed somewhat less emphasis on assuming economic responsibility and somewhat more emphasis on assuming ethical responsibility than the less religious participants. However, the mean differences are very small (0.2 scale units on a five-point scale).

In order to find out how consumers think companies should define their corporate mission and which goals they should pursue – primarily economic or primarily ethical – Brammer et al. (2007) analyzed information from the 2003 cohort of CSR monitoring by GlobeScan Ltd. To their surprise, the data from 20 countries did not confirm the basic hypothesis of religion/CSR research: The agnostics surveyed, rather than the religious participants, were the most likely to demand that companies prioritize ethical goals. It also emerged that the different religious affiliations set different priorities. Only Buddhists and Catholics argued more strongly for a conscious ethical orientation. However, companies based in very religious countries should bear in mind that people there place particularly high demands on their CSR, irrespective of their religious affiliation (see McGuire et al. 2012).

However, it is indisputable that companies that are active in one way or another in the public sector and offer religious, social or health services are also expected to make a corresponding commitment. Most consumers concede that "normal" companies should profit financially from their business activities and take the usual marketing measures to do so. Conversely, when "social-religious" companies act in a comparable, profit-oriented manner, many consumers perceive this as inappropriate (cf. McGraw et al. 2012). In this context, critics warn of a McDonaldization of the religious, an increasing intertwining of religion and commerce (e.g., Drane 2000; Moore 1995; O'Guinn/Belk 1989).

1.2 Ethical decision-making

How managers make decisions depends not least on their image of God. For example, managers who believe in a good, forgiving God are more likely to make unethical decisions than their peers who imagine a punishing God who holds people accountable for their behavior (cf. Alshehri et al. 2021).

Intrinsically religious managers and business students are not only more sensitive to ethical issues than average but also willing to take ethical considerations into account when making decisions (cf. Singhapakdi et al. 2013). This is partly due to their self-image, which corresponds much more to the moral identity described by Hardy/Carlo (2005) than the self-image of extrinsically religious people. While extrinsically religious people find it very difficult to exercise self-control (for example, keeping the dietary laws; cf. Watterson/Giesler 2012), intrinsically religious people have repeatedly been shown to display the ability or willingness to do so[19] (cf. Vitell et al. 2009).

Mazereeuw et al. (2014) found that for Dutch managers, religious people are not generally more open to ethical issues, but intrinsically religious people are more open to the ethical aspect of CSR and extrinsically religious people are more open to the philanthropic aspect. Harjoto/Rossi (2019) have also found that Italian companies act socially responsibly on the one hand if the top management is religious, and on the other hand if the environment exerts a corresponding effect. In addition to religiosity, the proportion of female executives moderates openness to CSR.

But what does the willingness to make unethical decisions depend on? Not least on the attitude toward money and possessions (cf. VII-1.2). Managers of the Christian evangelical faith living in Malaysia, who feel motivated primarily by material incentives, were more willing to make questionable decisions than their less materialistically minded colleagues (cf. Wong 2008). In another study, 205 randomly selected managers were asked to indicate whether they would act like a fictitious video game supplier in a comparable situation (i.e., raise prices by 20–30% during the vacation season while selectively slashing supply) (cf. Singhapakdi et al. 2013). As expected, intrinsic religiosity was associated with a lower intention to behave unethically in this scenario.

Extrinsic religiosity and an above-average appreciation of money (love of money; see VII-1.2), however, promoted the intention to do so. Walker et al. (2012) had found something comparable two years earlier with a classic survey: Only intrinsically religious people used their religious beliefs to guide ethical decisions; extrinsically religious people, however, reacted primarily to the possibility of sanctions.

Finally, it is not entirely irrelevant whether CSR is also worthwhile for the companies. Will customers increasingly buy products or services from companies that act in a socially responsible manner? And are they prepared to pay a somewhat higher price for them? If one follows the insights gained by Ramasamy et al. (2010) in Hong Kong and Singapore, then customers are not only in favor of socially responsible behavior, but depending on the type and intensity of their religiosity, are also prepared to pay for it. However, the motives are different. Whereas in multi-religious Singapore, consumers were primarily driven by extrinsic values (e.g., self-respect, saving face), in Confucian-influenced Hong Kong, intrinsic values were more influential (e.g., maintaining harmony and a willingness to take responsibility).

2 Standardization vs. differentiation

In order to be able to achieve their economic goals in the best possible way, internationally active companies have to decide again and again: Should they standardize their marketing program (i.e., in extreme cases, pursue the same marketing strategies worldwide) or differentiate (i.e., adapt to different conditions) in the various markets? Since the 1960s, when more and more companies began to operate across borders, marketing scholars have been discussing whether it is advisable to design advertisements, distribution channels and, above all, products uniformly or specifically (i.e., adapted to the norms, values, needs and lifestyles of members of certain cultures, nations or religious communities) (cf. Müller/Gelbrich 2015, p. 195 ff.). For example, should luxury brands be marketed differently in a Protestant-Calvinist environment than in a Catholic environment, or is religious affiliation not a variable to be considered in this context? After the standardization thesis was initially favored, primarily due to production and cost advantages (economies of scale), proponents of the differentiation thesis increasingly gained influence in the further course of the discussion.

2.1 Contribution of marketing

"The Globalization of Markets": In this highly regarded paper, Levitt (1983) predicted that consumer needs and behaviors would converge worldwide in the long term, partly as a result of improved transnational interaction and transportation opportunities. This prediction entered the literature as the convergence thesis. A major driver of this development is the increasing spread of modern communication technologies, which enable people to communicate and act across borders relatively easily (cf. Winram 1984). In the global village created by this, companies could offer and advertise their products worldwide in a standardized manner. This in turn makes it possible to speed up the market launch of products and services, to build up a global brand image, to exploit economies of scale and to reduce price levels as a result of the possible cost reductions (cf. Douglas/Craig 1986).

Proponents of the divergence thesis consider this to be wishful thinking. There is no empirical evidence that the needs of consumers are becoming

DOI: 10.4324/9781003506010-20

more homogeneous worldwide (cf. Wind 1986). Purchasing behavior is still predominantly culturally shaped and companies are therefore forced to adapt their marketing mix to the sociocultural conditions of their target markets (cf. Diamantopoulos et al. 1995). Not only, but especially the communication policy has to take into account the various country-specific characteristics, such as the level of economic development, the respective type of media use and different legal frameworks (cf. de Mooij 2019/2003). Consequently, it is necessary to differentiate the marketing mix (i.e., to adapt it to the different conditions in the individual markets).

2.2 Contribution of religious studies

Religious scholars have developed a counterpart to the standardization/differentiation debate in marketing, which will only be briefly discussed here. Simplified, the "Theory of Sacred Canopy" states that the world religions are losing influence on the behavior of people in general and believers in particular due to increasing secularization. The most important cause is the increasing materialism of modern societies (cf. Gorski 2000).

The analogy to the divergence thesis of marketing is clear. In both cases, increasing behavioral diversity is predicted, which Berger (1967) justifies with the dwindling normative power of (world) religions. For example, Rawwas et al. (2006, p. 79) were able to show that Japanese college students who enrolled in a religious university are no more moral than students studying at a secular institution. However, this statement is based on self-reporting. For 20 behaviors (e.g., cheating on exams, using relationships for personal gain), both groups had to indicate the extent to which they considered them wrong or right. This finding supports the "Theory of Sacred Canopy" in that it could be shown that even the religious students do not behave according to the moral guidelines of their religious beliefs (i.e., standardized), but in an effort to gain an advantage (i.e., differentiated).

The opposite point of view is held by the followers of the "Theory of Rationalization." They assume that important social institutions (e.g., a religious community) still influence our attitudes and behaviors (cf. Kivisto 1998). Secularization is only a surface phenomenon and the continuation of religions is certain. In critical life situations, people still seek support and orientation in religious communities (cf. Kasper 2007). Even if everything seems to be researched and explainable, people still long for the mysterious. This presumably also explains the increased influx of new religious communities and sects of all kinds worldwide. If religious affiliation and religiosity are still relevant for the behavior of individuals, the marketing mix should also be adapted to the religion-specific characteristics of the respective target group.

2.3 Market segmentation

The easiest way of market segmentation would be to divide the world market according to the dominant religion in each country (see Table 13). This may

Table 13 Confessionally homogeneous countries

Christians	*Muslims*	*Hindus*	*Buddhists*	*Popular religions*	*Non-denominational, atheists*
2.38 billion	1.91 billion	1.16 billion	0.51 billion	0.43 billion	1.19 billion
American Samoa	Afghanistan	Bangladesh	China	Benin	Denmark
Armenia	Algeria	India	Japan	Burundi	Estonia
Barbados	Iran	Indonesia	Cambodia	Ivory Coast	France
El Salvador	Iraq	Nepal	Myanmar	Guinea-Bissau	Norway
Greece	Comoros	Pakistan	Thailand	Haiti	Sweden
Kiribati	Kuwait	Sri Lanka		Cameroon	Czech Republic
Malta	Libya	Malaysia		Sudan	Vietnam
Marshall Islands	Morocco	Mauritius		Togo	
Micronesia	Pakistan				
East Timor	Somalia				
Papua New Guinea	Sudan				
Paraguay	Tunisia				
Peru	Yemen				
Romania					
Samoa					
San Marino					
Tonga					
Venezuela					

Source: https://worldpopulationreview.com/country-rankings/religion-by-country.

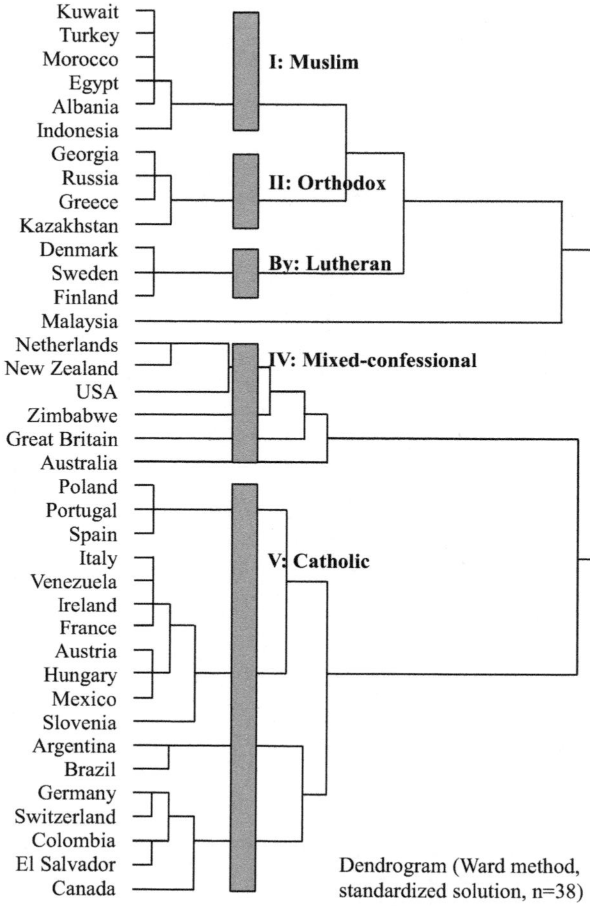

Figure 13 Confessionally homogeneous country groups as the starting point for the Differentiated Standardization strategy.

Source: Own analysis of data from the CIA World Factbook (2012).

seem to be most obvious in the marketing of halal-compliant products in the Islamic cultural sphere (cf. Rarick et al. 2012). However, this is countered by the unresolved certification problem: there is no consensus among Muslim religious scholars as to which criteria must be met for certain products or services to be considered halal (cf. Halim/Salleh 2012). Another problem is the different regulatory frameworks in the various Islamic country markets, which prevent or complicate standardized logistics processes (see Talib et al. 2015).

The majority of countries, however, are not religiously homogeneous. In most cases, religious diversity is even more pronounced than shown in

Table 14 Religious diversity in the US, in %

Protestants	*45.6*	*Buddhists*	*0.8*
Religiously unaffiliated	23.3	Muslims	0.8
Catholics	21.8	Hindus	0.5
Other faiths	1.5	Jehovah's witnesses	0.5
Jews	1.4	Orthodox Christians	0.5
Mormons	1.3	Atheists, agnostics	0.2

Source: Statista 2021, Pew Research Center, Public Religion Research Institute.

Table 14. In the course of time, numerous subgroups have split off from the religions listed here, such as Baptists, Methodists, Lutherans, Presbyterians, Episcopalians, Congregationalists, Disciples of Christ, Seventh-day Adventists, Quakers and Mennonites.

For Interfaith Marketing (IFM), it therefore makes sense to pursue the strategy of differentiated standardization instead of a standardization strategy. The main idea is to bundle country markets or consumer groups according to the similarity of their denominational structure, for example. The homogeneous clusters created in this way can then be processed in a standardized manner (either with regard to the entire marketing mix or with regard to individual instruments), while differentiation is to be made between these religious clusters. A simple way to form such homogeneous country clusters is cluster analysis, in this case based on the respective denominational structure of the population of the individual countries. As can be seen from the increase in the error rate, it might be advisable in this specific case to split the cluster of Catholic countries into the group of clearly Catholic countries (Poland, Slovenia) and the group of countries which, although also predominantly Catholic, are already more mixed denominationally (Argentina, Canada; cf. Figure 13).

3 Target groups

For reasons of cost and efficiency, companies do not usually target the market as a whole, but rather a subset that is more homogeneous than the market as a whole in terms of certain criteria that are important for the company's success. For example, a supplier of high-priced items will concentrate on the target group or target market of the affluent and a supplier of complex consumer electronics on the target group or target market of the tech-savvy. The most important target group for Interfaith Marketing (IFM) is religious consumers.

3.1 Religious consumers

Their personality profile shows religious consumers to be difficult customers in some respects. These include a tendency toward authoritarianism (cf. Weller et al. 1975), national pride or nationalism (cf. Brubaker 2012) and conservatism (cf. Jones et al. 2010). Therefore, many religious people support Buy National campaigns (cf. V-3.7). Furthermore, they are more tradition-conscious than average and unwilling to change (cf. van der Toorn et al. 2017). According to the findings of cognitive psychology research, religious people think less analytically and are less intelligent than non-religious people (cf. Razmyar/Reeve 2013). They also often endorse traditional gender roles (cf. Wilkes et al. 1986), are intolerant (cf. Gusio et al. 2003) and risk-averse (cf. Noussair et al. 2013). Thus, companies operating in a religious environment and led by religious management avoid entrepreneurial risks whenever possible (cf. Cebula/Rossi 2021). And religious consumers tend to make hoarding purchases in times of crisis (e.g., Coronavirus pandemic) (see Minton/Cabano 2021).

Due to their conservative value orientation, religious people are somewhat hostile to innovations such as online shopping (see Armfield/Holbert 2003), which is why they are not the primary target group for companies to introduce new products (see V-2.2). While non-religious or less religious Muslims adopt a technical innovation such as mobile banking mainly when it seems useful to them, it is primarily social reasons that can induce strictly religious Muslims to do so. Sun et al. (2012) explain this with the different degree of relationship orientation of these three consumer segments.

DOI: 10.4324/9781003506010-21

However, religious people also have characteristics and beliefs that favor prosocial consumer behavior (i.e., behavior that serves the community (cf. Shariff et al. 2016). For example, they are more altruistic than average (cf. Orellano et al. 2020) and optimistic (cf. Rudski 2004). Unlike atheists (cf. Gervais 2011), religious people are considered trustworthy (cf. Chuah et al. 2016). And it is comparatively easy for them to trust other people, especially if they know that their counterpart is also religious (see Tan/Vogel 2008). Furthermore, it is especially important for intrinsically religious people (cf. Vitell et al. 2005) to behave ethically:

- Consume in an environmentally conscious manner (see Raggiotto et al. 2018)
- To buy "green products" (cf. Felix/Braunsberger 2016) and fair trade products despite higher prices (cf. Salvador et al. 2014)
- To consume less (cf. Coşgel/Minkler 2004)
- To not waste food (cf. Elhoushy/Jang 2021)
- To donate to "good causes,"[20] even when it benefits members of other faith communities (see Brooks 2004)

The striving for prosociality is supported by the above-average ability of religious people to exercise self-control (cf. Minton 2018) and by their low materialistic tendencies (Balikcioglu/Kiyak 2022). In addition, all religions demand and encourage prosocial behavior in one way or another. For example, Sugden (2001, p. 9) describes fair trade as a "response of practical compassion often rooted in a Christian worldview," following the biblical command to work for social justice and care for the poor. In this context, saints and religious leaders often serve as role models for a selfless lifestyle (cf. Saroglou et al. 2005).

Religious people also cope better than average with uncertainty, as their spiritual beliefs give them a sense of security and control (see Kay et al. 2010a). Moreover, regardless of their age and religious affiliation, they are more satisfied with their lives than average, experience greater physical and mental well-being and cooperate more socially than non-religious people (cf. Habib et al. 2018; Mochon et al. 2011; Moschis/Ong 2011). This may explain why they are less prone to the following addictive behaviors than religiously unaffiliated comparison participants:

- Alcohol (see Guimarães et al. 2018; Lambert et al. 2010)
- Drugs (see van der Meer-Sanchez et al. 2008; Sanchez et al. 2011)
- Tobacco (cf. Weaver et al. 2005)
- Pornography (see Perry 2017)

They also succumb to economic temptations less frequently than others, such as being less likely to commit tax fraud (cf. Guiso et al. 2003). They are also less likely than others to try to gain an illicit advantage by buying counterfeit products (cf. Yaakop et al. 2021; Casidy et al. 2016). In addition, religious people place comparatively little value on consumption and possessions. Because of this, and due to their stronger social networks, they are more satisfied with their lives than average (cf. Balikcioglu/Kiyak 2022; Churchill et al. 2019; Wilkes et al. 1986). Since many religions portray poverty as a virtue rather than a burden,[21] the well-being of religious people depends comparatively little on their relative income position. Therefore, many more members of the lower income strata are satisfied with their lives in religion-affiliated Jamaica than in secular Norway, even though most Jamaicans are objectively much worse off materially than most Norwegians. The fact that religiosity moderates the effect of inadequate income in this way is not an isolated case but, as Berkessel et al. (2021) have shown with data from around 3 million people from up to 156 countries, it is more the rule.

Finally, religious people are socio-politically conservative, and their thinking style is not overly rational (cf. Baron 2020). If they belong to a monotheistic religion, prosociality (toward members of the in-group) is often accompanied by a tendency to prejudicial judgment (toward members of the out-group). However, this is not the case with Buddhists. They often combine prosocial attitudes with tolerance toward those who are different (cf. Clobert et al. 2015).

Religious people are above-average supporters of Corporate Social Responsibility (CSR) measures by companies. They are increasingly seen as having a duty to assume responsibility for society and to pursue social goals in addition to their original sales and earnings targets. Non-profit organizations are a special type of company that finance their business activities largely through donations. In order to increase their donations, they engage in non-profit advertising. Their success depends to a large extent on whether their target audience believes them to be socially responsible. As Hopkins et al. (2014) have shown, religiosity moderates the positive influence of the social responsibility of the organization perceived by consumers on their intention to make a donation to the organization.

The moral basis of corporate stewardship is the conviction that companies should treat the resources made available to them in a fiduciary manner. Earlier than economists (cf. Mohrman et al. 2017), religious scholars discussed this norm with regard to the human/nature relationship (cf. de Groot/van den Born 2007). That humans should deal responsibly with God's creation is part of the doctrine of nature religions and spiritual-religious currents (cf. Preston/Baimel 2021). The monotheistic religions in general and Christianity in particular, however, stand for the opposite position: "Subdue the earth…" (Genesis 1:28).

From a corporate perspective, it is problematic that the market segment of the explicitly religious is shrinking. According to a WIN Gallup survey, their share of the total population fell by an average of 9% in 37 countries between 2005 and 2012, from 77to 68%. Particularly strong secularization trends were recorded in Vietnam (–23%), France (–21%), Austria (–21%)

and Switzerland (–21%), while slight increases in the number of religious were registered in Pakistan (+6%), Macedonia (+5%) and Moldova (+5%). At the same time, other target groups, such as the environmentally conscious, are growing.

3.2 Materialist consumers

Colloquially, we understand materialists to be people whose goal and purpose in life is to accumulate possessions. Materialism can be defined as:

> the importance a consumer attaches to worldly possessions. At the highest levels of materialism, such possessions assume a central place in a person's life and are believed to provide the greatest sources of satisfaction and dissatisfaction.
>
> (Belk 1984, p. 291)

Due to their consumerism, their special appreciation of luxury goods and their above-average willingness to pay, materialists are a promising target group for profit-oriented companies (cf. Prendergast/Wong 2003). Conversely, spiritual values promote consumerism (cf. Stillman et al. 2012).

The materialistic worldview, according to which the material or tangible is the only real thing, stands in contrast to idealism. Idealism sees the real primarily in the spiritual being. For a long time it was true that materialistic values were hardly compatible with religious values (cf. Burroughs/Rindfleisch 2002).[22] More recent findings show that this is only true for intrinsic religiosity. Extrinsically religious people are quite fond of the materialistic lifestyle due to their rather functional, non-spiritual attitude toward their religion (= means to an end) (cf. Raggiotto et al. 2018). As a rule, materialists are less satisfied with their lives than others (cf. La Barbera/Gürhan 1997), because they have not learned to:

- Enjoy the "little things in life" (cf. Aronson et al. 2020)
- Maintain satisfying social relationships (cf. Banerjee/Dittmar 2008)
- Deal with stress and uncertainty in ways other than consumption (see Roberts et al. 2003)

Furthermore, it has been shown that materialistic values are one of the reasons why consumers do not pay appropriate attention to the need to protect the environment (cf. Raggiotto et al. 2018). They also promote the willingness to buy pirated goods (Furnham/Valgeirsson 2007).

Thus far, we have spoken of individualistic materialism. Awanis et al. (2017) added the concept of Collective-Oriented Materialism. According to this concept, people do not primarily strive for possessions in order to realize an individualistic consumption-oriented lifestyle. Rather, more important for collectivistic people is the symbolic function of material goods (e.g., the opportunity to signal their social status, to demonstrate belonging to a respected reference group and to take on social responsibility in a visible way).

3.3 Environmentally conscious consumers

As a rule, religions require believers to be caring. As in the case of Zakāt, one of the five pillars of Islam (cf. II-4.4), this can apply not only to people, mostly members of one's own faith community, but also to the protection of the natural environment. Theravada Buddhism, for example, teaches that all current actions have an impact on the future, including our treatment of nature (cf. Pryor 1990). Because of their image of God, an all-powerful, punishing and rewarding God, Christians and Muslims are said to feel less personally responsible for protecting the environment. They are also said to be less concerned about earthly concerns in light of their life's task of earning eternal life in God's glory or being given it by God's grace (cf. Hope/Jones 2014).

3.3.1 Anthropocentric vs. ecocentric environmental awareness

Psychological scientists distinguish between different forms of environmental awareness. Anthropocentrism sees man as the master and not the protector of nature (cf. Kortenkamp/Moore 2001, p. 262). In contrast, ecocentrism demands that nature be protected for its own sake (cf. Grettenberger 1996, p. 28f.).

The latter is similar to the concept of stewardship, which is discussed in management science (cf. Davis et al. 1997) and religious studies (cf. IV-3.4). This concept views humans as being God's stewards, who deal responsibly with God's creation, nature (cf. de Groot/van den Born 2007). Followers of alternative religions (nature religions, spiritual-religious currents, etc.) are particularly receptive to this (cf. Preston/Baimel 2021). Lynn White's thesis marks the opposite position: the monotheistic religions are partly responsible for the existing ecological problems due to their anthropocentric worldview (cf. White 1967). The biblical "Subdue the earth…" passage (Genesis 1:28), for example, has lead Christians to be less environmentally conscious than followers of other religions (cf. Shaiko 1987; Hand/van Liere 1984).

3.3.2 Religiosity, environmental awareness and environmentally conscious behavior

A positive correlation has often been observed between religiosity and environmental awareness (e.g., Guth et al. 1995) or environmentally friendly behavior (e.g., Kanagy/Willits 1993). Islam/Chandrasekaran (2016), for example, found that Indian Muslims (n = 191) are more likely to engage in environmentally conscious purchasing and consumption behavior if their religiosity is intrinsic. And according to Minton et al. (2015), both very religious Buddhists and very religious Christians consume more sustainably or environmentally consciously compared to less religious consumers. The decisive factor here is probably the close connection between religiosity and altruism as well as helpfulness, and not that between religiosity and environmental awareness (cf. Blogowska/Saroglou 2011).

The criticism of the operationalization of the central constructs of these studies was first addressed by Eckberg/Blocker (1996) by relating different forms of environmental consciousness of American Protestants to different expressions of religiosity. Religiosity was broken down on the basis of data from the General Social Survey (GSS 1993) into:

- Sectarianism (rigid, fundamentalist form of religiosity in the form of strict loyalty to authority and vehement rejection of the theory of evolution)
- General religiosity (belief in God and life after death)
- Participatory religiosity (membership in church congregation, frequent attendance at religious services, trust in local church officials)

Ten factors of environmental awareness were extracted from the data, four of which were considered in this reanalysis. Of these, 5–30% can be explained by the three forms of religiosity described. In detail, various multiple regression analyses revealed:

- Sectarianism correlates negatively with environmentally protective behavior, but positively with the conviction that nature, which was created by God, is sacred. However, protecting it in real terms is less important to this segment than achieving or preserving economic prosperity.
- General religiosity also correlates only with the appreciation of nature (= sacred), without this attitude having any consequences for real environmental behavior.
- Conversely, participatory religiosity promotes pro-environmental behavior, but not pro-environmental attitudes.

Eckberg/Blocker (1996) took these findings as an opportunity to limit the scope of Lynn White's thesis. They argue that it is not religiosity per se that prevents or hinders environmental protection, but only Christian sectarianism, which sees environmental awareness as an expression of an unfree, illiberal spirit. Recent studies even suggest that, on the contrary, religiosity can promote sustainable consumer behavior, which in turn promotes individual well-being (cf. Minton et al. 2022). Other research has also examined consumers' representations of God to reconcile when religiosity is positively or negatively associated with sustainable consumption. Specifically, previous work has shown that belief in a mystical God was positively associated with sustainable consumer spending, recycling behaviors and charitable giving to support sustainability programs (Johnson et al. 2017).

Conversely, consumers' belief in an authoritarian or benevolent God was either negatively correlated or uncorrelated with these various sustainable behaviors.

3.3.3 Religiosity, life satisfaction and environmental awareness

Is the willingness of many people to contribute to environmental protection so low because they fear a loss of quality and enjoyment of life? Probably not, and if they do, then incorrectly. Minton et al. (2018b), for example, observed that religious people across a wide range of different religions have a higher level of sustainable consumption and are subsequently more satisfied with their lives than the comparison group. Balikcioglu/Kiyak (2022), who surveyed 232 Muslims of Turkish origin, reached a similar conclusion. Together with religiosity, anti-consumption attitudes contributed to their life satisfaction, while materialistic attitudes had the opposite effect. However, since this is a structural equation analysis, it cannot be ruled out that the reverse is true: that satisfied people are more open to environmental concerns. This interpretation is supported by the results of a multilevel analysis, which Felix et al. (2018) used to evaluate the information provided by 47,130 respondents from 34 countries. They found that the positive relationship between religiosity and environmental awareness is moderated by life satisfaction. Religious people who are satisfied with their lives are inwardly closer to environmental protection than dissatisfied religious people.

Buddhism, however, favors an ambivalent attitude. For strict believers, the environment is part of the illusory, constantly changing, without real meaning. Environmental protection would mean getting caught up in the eternal cycle of becoming and passing away, instead of distancing oneself from it, as Buddha taught. However, he also spoke about responsibility, compassion and kindness. And the fact that Buddhists should not harm anyone can also be interpreted as a call to protect the environment (cf. Figh 2007).

3.3.4 Attitude/behavior gap

All studies on environmental awareness, measured as attitudes or behavioral intentions, are subject to an important caveat. Since only a few people now seriously deny the necessity and urgency of environmental protection, but at the same time many people still shy away from the sacrifices and efforts that environmentally friendly behavior would demand of them (e.g., not using packaging), the attitude/behavior discrepancy already observed in many other areas of behavior (cf. III-5.6) is particularly large in environmentally conscious consumer behavior (cf. Juvan/Dolnicar 2014).

The phenomenon of moral licensing is one of the numerous causes of this inconsistency (cf. Antonetti/Maklan 2015). This is a cognitive process in which a "good deed" (e.g., separating garbage) is used to derive the cognitive authorization ("license") to subsequently engage in less good deeds (e.g., air travel). According to this theory, only when the debit side of this mental account is burdened with more "environmental sins" than the credit side of good deeds, feelings of guilt arise, which under certain conditions increases the likelihood of a change in behavior (cf. Lasarov/Hoffmann 2020; Blanken et al. 2015).

According to a meta-analysis by Simbrunner/Schlegelmilch (2017), members of "moral societies" tend to grant themselves this license more than others. In this study, the US and Thailand, for example, were classified as moral societies, with 40.4 and 56.5% of the population, respectively, stating that religion plays an important role in their lives, and 32.7and 44.3%, respectively, stating that children should be brought up to be selfless (Data basis: WVS 2014). Central Europeans are much less likely to agree with these statements. Only 13.1% of Germans, for example, consider religion important, and only 5.9% consider selflessness an important educational goal.

3.3.5 Environmental awareness and political attitudes

Another group of consumers also tries to influence companies, markets or the economy as a whole through conscious, ethically or politically motivated purchasing decisions (cf. Micheletti 2003). Among other things, these political or politicized consumers (cf. Stolle/Micheletti 2013) differ from environmentally conscious consumers in that they are altruistically minded but tend not to be religious (cf. Wicks et al. 2017). For example, they tend not to consider the Bible to be the unchangeable word of God. Above all, however, they distrust the political system and its actors (see Copeland/Boulianne 2020).

Two types of engagement can be distinguished (cf. Lämla/Neckel 2006): Political consumerism aims at collective action (e.g., organizing buying strikes, petitions, protests), while politicized consumers see individual action as the decisive approach to a solution, such as:

- Eliminating soy products to stop rainforest deforestation
- Purchase organic goods to stop the extinction of species caused by the overuse of pesticides
- Buying second-hand goods (e.g., second-hand fashion) to stop the excessive consumption of resources by fast fashion.

Part V

Product policy

1 Types of benefits

Products primarily serve to satisfy needs and thus provide benefits to consumers. Different types of benefits can be distinguished, depending on whether they are functional or emotional benefits.

For example, a car provides the functional benefit of transportation for customers. However, for customers of a mobile communications company, the functional benefit is to be reachable at any time and any place and to be able to reach others as well.

In many cases, however (e.g., in saturated markets), the emotional benefits provided by the product often contributes more to preference formation than the functional benefits. The fact that an automobile is capable of transporting us quickly and safely from A to B seems self-evident nowadays. However, it is often more important for the purchase decision to be able to visibly express the social status and lifestyle achieved or aspired to by owning a certain car.

Cell phones are also much more than a technical means of communication. Beyond their basic use, they offer a whole bundle of additional functions such as a camera, light source, route planner or vaccination certificate. By displaying the direction of the compass on its mobile phones, LG Electronics offered Muslim customers an additional religion-specific benefit. This enabled them to determine the direction for their daily prayers ("towards Mecca") at any time.

Headgear is a good example of how much the utility and function of a product can depend on the religious affiliation of the wearer. It is true that caps, hats and headscarves also fulfill a social function in Western Christian societies, such as by demonstrating fashion consciousness and a certain group affiliation (e.g., baseball caps as a sign of a sporty, casual lifestyle). However, headgear primarily fulfills the primary function of "protection from weather." In the sphere of influence of Islam, the headscarf also serves to protect against the sun. More important, however, is its symbolic function, which can be of a religious or political nature (see Kiliçbay/Binark 2002, p. 497).

- In the most important Islamic scriptures, women are called upon to cover their hair and shoulders in order to protect themselves from the gaze of men (cf. El Guindi 1999, p. 55). In this respect, the headscarf symbolizes

DOI: 10.4324/9781003506010-23

identification with Islam and the willingness to follow its laws and rules of conduct.
- However, wearing a headscarf can also be an expression of a political stance. In this way, women document that they do not belong to the Western world, but to the Islamic world (cf. Göle 1997, p. 73).

As superficial as this brief assessment of the sociocultural function of the headscarf may be, it shows that the individual useful components of a product can be perceived and evaluated very differently depending on one's religion. For the Amish living in America,[23] for example, the shape (not body-hugging) and color (plain-covered) of their clothing are an expression of humility and a sign of their religious commitment (cf. Coşgel/Minkler 2004, p. 343).

2 Product innovation

Novel products are considered to be innovations if they offer customers a significant benefit and customers are prepared to pay a reasonable price for them. Depending on the degree of novelty and the associated benefits, one speaks of incremental (e.g., six-speed transmission) or radical innovation (e.g., self-driving car). Innovations of any kind are important for gaining competitive advantages or remaining competitive.

2.1 Innovativeness of companies

Criteria for entrepreneurial innovativeness include the number and scope or range of patents as well as the intensity of R&D activities. The latter was the subject of an analysis of corresponding data for the years 1996–2010 from 113 countries (cf. Wang/Wang 2021). The research showed that Christianity and Judaism tend to hinder R&D activity, while Buddhism[24] and atheism seem to be more conducive to it. These findings proved to be sufficiently stable against conceivable modifying influences such as form of government, income level or religious freedom. Furthermore, companies with locations in more religious societies register fewer patents (per capita) than those in less religious but otherwise comparable societies (cf. Bénabou et al. 2015b).

Especially when religiosity manifests itself as religious intolerance, it hinders the innovative activity of companies (cf. Osiri et al. 2019). Why is this the case? What is the basis for this tension between religiosity and innovation? Is it due to weaknesses in analytical thinking (see Jack et al. 2016) and a lack of creativity[25] (see Dollinger 2007)? The latter can be confirmed on the basis of a secondary statistical analysis of the Global Creativity Index. At the national level, religiosity correlates negatively with creativity (see Liu et al. 2018). Or is it the lack of ability to question the traditional, which is said of religious people in view of their conservatism? Those who want to create something new must doubt the status quo. It is true that parts of Christianity have given room to doubt under the pressure of secularization. But for a long time, orthodoxy and dogmatism were and are essential characteristics of monotheistic religions.

Another thesis is quite well-supported empirically. Innovations can have both positive (e.g., progress, novel solutions to problems) and negative

DOI: 10.4324/9781003506010-24

consequences (e.g., loss of jobs, need for change). However, due to their above-average risk aversion, religious people associate innovation primarily with negative consequences (cf. Noussair et al. 2013). From an action-theoretical point of view, innovations (e.g., solar cells) can be viewed as solutions to existing problems (e.g., climate change). This solution-oriented thinking is rather alien to religious people because of their fatalistic tendencies (cf. III-2.8). In interaction with a certain devotion to God, they form the ideological basis of the centuries-old incompatibility of religion and science (cf. Bénabou et al. 2015a). Devotion to God was also demanded by Jesus from his disciples, as it says in the Gospel of Matthew: "No sparrow falls from the eaves without the Father in heaven knowing about it. No hair gets caught in the comb when it is combed, without the Father in heaven taking care of it." Among other things, the conviction that we are all in God's hands is behind the attempt by fundamentalist religious circles to ban stem cell research or the refusal of parents to consent to life-saving medical treatment for their children (cf. Orr 2003).

This is confirmed by the following observation (see Bénabou et al. 2015a): Nowhere in the U.S. did anti-innovation statements receive as much support and pro-innovation statements as little support in their study as in the "Bible Belt" in the southeastern United States. An important question to ask is: Does the participants' religious affiliation influence the perceived link between innovation activity and company success? In order to answer this question, Recio-Román et al. (2019) used data from Eurobarometer 63.4 (2005) with the following result: Protestants are even more convinced than atheists and agnostics that innovations are a key to lasting business success. Muslims and Catholics, however, were more skeptical about innovation. They were also less likely than those of other faiths or non-believers to accept the dogma of competition policy that innovations generate overall economic growth.

2.2 Acceptance of innovations

The relevant acceptance research is highly extensive and methodologically challenging (cf. Agarwal/Prasad 1997). The technology acceptance model (cf. Davis 1989) is usually used to analyze the acceptance of technological innovations. According to this model, the decisive factors are the perceived usefulness of the innovation or the relative advantage associated with it and the ease of use. The food sector is a special case in this respect. There, innovative technologies are primarily accepted if, in addition to the perceived benefit, the perceived risk of use and the perceived naturalness are evaluated positively (cf. Siegrist 2008).

2.2.1 Influence of religiosity

Essoo/Dibb (2004) asked devout and less devout Muslims, Hindus and Catholics about their shopping behavior. Irrespective of their religious affiliation,

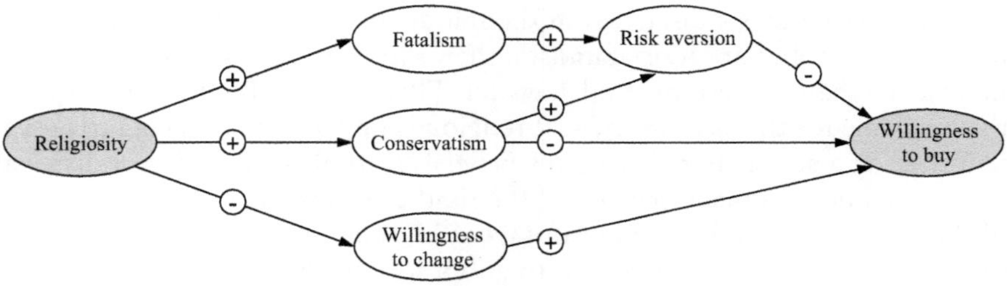

Figure 14 Religiosity and willingness to buy innovative technical products.

Source: Own representation based on Mansori et al. (2015); Ruiu (2013); Fiori et al. (2006); Tansuhaj et al. (1991).

participants who stated that they were not religious or only slightly religious proved to be comparatively trend-conscious shoppers with an above-average willingness to try new products. In contrast, very religious consumers embody the more conservative, tradition-conscious type, who shy away from risks, are skeptical of innovations of all kinds and prefer the tried and true (see Minton et al. 2022; Mansori 2012; Azam et al. 2011; Kalliny/Hausman 2007; Barton/Vaughan 1976). The more religious, the stronger the innovation resistance of South Korean Catholics and the lower their willingness to accept a digital Bible instead of the traditional book form (cf. Hong 2020). The opposite has been repeatedly reported for the Islamic cultural area. However, these researchers did not choose the adoption of innovative products as the dependent variable, but, like Baig/Baig (2013), they focused their attention on Islamic products. In contrast, broad support based on the five waves of World Values Survey (1980–2005) is provided by the study of Bénabou et al. (2015b, p. 346): "Across the fifty-two estimated specifications, greater religiosity is almost uniformly and very significantly associated to less favorable views of innovation."

The fact that religious people are less open to innovation can be explained by their personality profile: low openness to change and a tendency toward conservatism (i.e., traditionalism and conformity) (see Mansori et al. 2015). Furthermore, religiosity goes hand in hand with fatalism (cf. III-2.8) and fatalism with an increased sensitivity to risk (cf. Ruiu 2013). For this reason, and because they shy away from the associated product risk, highly religious consumers are less willing to buy new products (see Figure 14).

2.2.2 *Influence of religious affiliation*

The religious affiliation of participants also allows conclusions to be drawn about the likelihood of acceptance of new products. According to Essoo/Dibb (2004, p. 702), Catholic consumers are predominantly traditionally oriented and significantly less interested in innovative products than Jews and Muslims (see also Hirschman 1981). This is reminiscent of the anti-intellectual thesis discussed in the middle of the last century, according to which Catholics are more fatalistic than average and less determined and innovative than Protestants and Jews (cf. Ellis 1955).[26] Briefly summarized, the rationale for this is as follows: If religion is understood as a cognitive system (i.e., as a set of shared religious beliefs), Catholicism hinders individual intellectual development because of the rigid centralist-hierarchical structure of the Catholic Church. The faithful would be conditioned to internalize the canon of the Catholic Church and to adopt its worldview uncritically.

> The need or possibility for personal interpretation of events is minimized; beliefs, values, and explanations about life events are provided by the church. Behavior is ritualized, decision making is centralized in the papacy, and control of life events resides outside the individual, under the auspices of the church.
>
> (Hirschman 1983, p. 134)

Four decades later, Rigney/Hoffman (1993) confirmed the anti-intellectuality thesis, but only in relation to Jews, moderate Protestants and non-denominational Protestants. Fundamentalist Protestants proved to be the least "intellectual" group in this survey. In contrast, critics argued that this thesis may have been justified in the middle of the last century, but not in the age of secularization (cf. Lacy 2018).

According to Kahane (2012), the relatively high openness of Jews to innovation (cf. Essoo/Dibb 2004; Hirschman 1981) is related to the fact that the search for novelty and the desire to constantly improve are firmly anchored in Judaism. In this society, education is a central educational goal and Jews are therefore disproportionately motivated to search for information on their own and to educate themselves further (cf. Patai 1977). Following Midgley/Dowling (1978), these attitudes are one of the prerequisites for innovativeness: the willingness to use new products independently of the influence of others.

Muslims, together with Jews, are considered to be a type of buyer who is interested in new products and buys them frequently. Essoo/Dibb (2004) attribute this, as well as the limited interest in product information prior to a purchase decision, to the role played in Islam by the belief in the predetermination of all events. If the purchase of a new product should turn out to be a mistake, this would be Allah's will (cf. also Bailey/Sood 1993, p. 344). This probably also explains why Muslim societies as a whole do not provide a favorable environment for innovative companies, but Muslim consumers are definitely open to innovative products. Unlike Catholics, they do not find it difficult to replace a tried-and-tested product that they trust and buy regularly with an innovative product, even at a somewhat higher price. However, they usually do not understand "innovative" to mean something fundamentally new (= radical innovation), but rather an improvement of the existing (i.e., an incremental innovation) (cf. Recio-Román et al. 2019).

Hindus, however, are considered to be less innovative consumers. Possible causes are personality traits such as fatalism, hesitancy and tolerance of the status quo (see Essoo/Dibb 2004). Very religious Hindus are even said to have a tendency to flee the world, combined with the desire to renounce worldly desires.

According to a survey conducted by Mansori (2012) among the urban population of Malaysia, Buddhists are the least open to innovation, less so than Christians, Muslims and Hindus. This can be explained by Buddhism's preference for the status quo, which contrasts with the changes that usually constitute innovations (cf. Tsai et al. 2007).

2.3 Innovation Management

Usually, innovation management is divided into four phases:

- Idea generation and idea concretization
- Concept definition
- Concept evaluation and concept selection
- Market introduction

2.3.1 New product development

New product ideas can be obtained from internal sources (e.g., suggestion systems) as well as from external sources. The latter include customer and expert surveys as well as competitor observation. Various creativity techniques are used (e.g., brainstorming). Conjoint measurement analyses are often used to concretize innovative product ideas and thus make them manageable for marketing. They make it possible to determine which product features are important to potential customers and how much they would be willing to pay for them. Quality function deployment can be used to determine how customers' expectations of function and quality are to be translated into concrete design features. Ideally, various product tests are used in the next phase.

Despite the large number of tests carried out in the course of their development, the risk of failure of innovative products is high (e.g., because their benefits are not clearly recognizable or because the habits and risk aversion of potential buyers are stronger). There is also a risk of failure if suppliers and customers belong to different religious groups. In this case, companies must take into account not only the usual risks but also those arising from incompatible values and beliefs. Product innovations should not violate important religious beliefs of the target group, especially not religious affiliation-specific taboos (cf. Yun et al. 2008). A serious problem can also be the fundamental aversion to change that is said to exist among very religious people, not least with regard to innovations in the area of products and services.

Companies have various options for overcoming these barriers. For example, they can reduce unfounded fears through a targeted communication policy, or modify the product if the reservations are justified. It can also be helpful to adapt the level of innovation to the target group's willingness to change.

2.3.2 *Timing of market entry*

When introducing innovative technical products to the European market, for example, companies can be guided by the work of Recio-Román et al. (2019). They have summarized the results of their analysis of the relationship between religious affiliation and attitudes toward innovations in a diffusion curve that visualizes the probability of adoption as a function of religious affiliation (see Figure 15). Accordingly, it is advisable to start the introduction of new products in markets with a disproportionately high number of atheists, as this population group has an above-average interest in technological solutions and is generally in favor of innovations. The prospects of success are much worse in regions inhabited mainly by Catholics or Orthodox Christians. Here, it is advisable to enter the market only when the innovation is actually no longer an "innovation" at all, because it has already become established elsewhere and has achieved a high level of recognition. For these customers, "innovative" does not have a fundamentally positive connotation. They attach more importance to pragmatic solutions to problems.

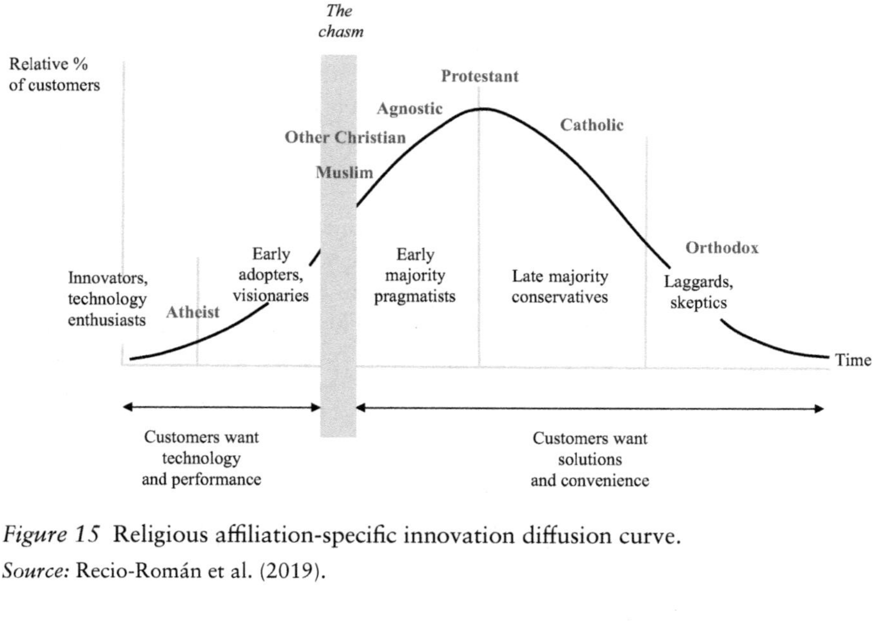

Figure 15 Religious affiliation-specific innovation diffusion curve.
Source: Recio-Román et al. (2019).

2.3.3 *Management of "problematic" innovations*

Innovation management is also required when it comes to helping morally controversial innovations achieve market success. For Interfaith Marketing (IFM), the main question is whether members of certain religious affiliations can be expected to show particularly strong resistance. It also seems conceivable that the nature and intensity of religious convictions influence the acceptance of such innovations.

The use of artificial intelligence (AI), for example, raises both great hopes (e.g., for dramatic efficiency gains) and fears (e.g., surveillance state). Although religious people are particularly trusting in many areas of life, Minton et al. (2022) expected the opposite in the case of the use of AI (e.g., in consumer electronics products). This is because religious people:

- Are relatively more resistant to change due to their personality (cf. Roccas/Elster 2013)
- View technological innovations in particular with skepticism (cf. Mansori et al. 2015)
- May be inclined to reject AI-equipped products (e.g., care robots) on principle if they interfere with human interaction (see Adnan et al. 2019)

Contrary to expectations, empirical testing of this hypothesis revealed that religiosity does not influence attitudes toward AI directly, but indirectly (mediation effect): Religious people trust AI more than non-religious ones, which is why they develop a more positive attitude (cf. Figure 16). This correlational relationship was confirmed by Minton et al. (2022) in a second study in which they did not measure religiosity but primed it. However, not only does AI appear in a more favorable light to religious people, but also companies that use this technology (e.g., in restaurants as a serving aid) and their employees.

According to further mediation analyses, the deeper reason for this unexpected result could be the fundamentally positive relationship that believers have with the intangible or the unseen.

> AI (artificial intelligence) is an unseen entity, just as faith and belief in a god or divine power are unseen entities as well. This can help to

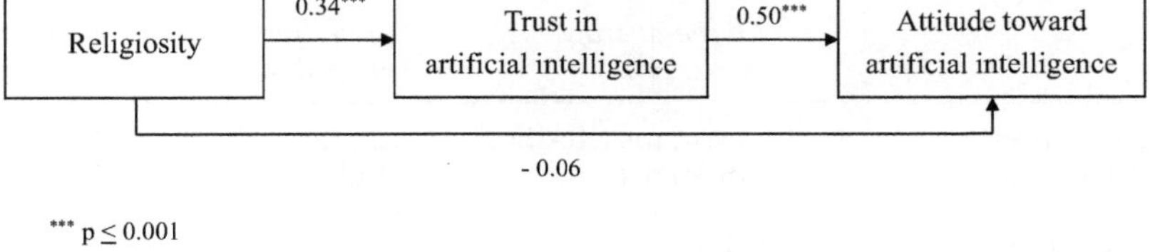

Figure 16 Attitudes of religious people toward artificial intelligence.
Source: Minton et al. (2022, p. 2060).

> explain why higher religiosity consumers are actually more trusting in AI than lower religiosity consumers, which may also translate to trust in other things that are mysterious, complex, or unable to be fully seen and understood through sight alone, such as many forms of technology like AI.
>
> (Minton et al. 2022, p. 2065)

Product innovations created with the help of genetic engineering methods are also controversial. During a public lecture held in Singapore about "genetically modified foods," Subrahmanyan/Cheng (2000) asked a total of 417 people in writing about their relevant attitudes toward and knowledge of genetic engineering. The concerns and attitudes expressed by these (33.7% Christians, 29.1% atheists, 23.2% Buddhists, 5.1% Taoists, 4.6% Hindus and 2.9% Muslims) can be summarized into four groups on the basis of a factor analysis:

- Health concerns (e.g., risky, harms environment and people)
- Ethical concerns (e.g., scientists should not play God)
- Individual benefits (e.g., better taste, higher nutrient content, lower contaminant load)
- Insufficient knowledge (e.g., level of informedness about biotechnology)

As a correlation analyses showed, people with "ethical concerns" often also have "health concerns" ($r = 0.59$) and do not expect any "individual benefit" from this method (–0.46). This explains why the mostly sweeping arguments that proponents of genetically modified foods usually put forward (e.g., better nutrition for the world's population, less pest infestation, etc.) are not convincing to those who have health concerns or fundamentally reject genetic engineering as unethical.

Furthermore, variance analysis showed that religious affiliation significantly influenced some concerns (see Table 15). The most reservations were expressed by Christians (ethical and health concerns) and Muslims (ethical

Table 15 Influence of religious affiliation on attitudes toward genetically modified foods

	Above-average expression	*Below-average expression*	*F-value*
Ethical concerns	Christians Muslims[a]	Atheists	3.60***
Health concerns	Christians	Hindus[a] Atheists	2.59**
Individual utility	Hindus[a]	Other	3.42***

[a]small sample, *** $p < 0.01$, ** $p < 0.05$.

Source: based on Subrahmanyan/Cheng (2000, p. 286).

concerns). Due to their God-centered worldview, both tend to see genetic engineering as an intervention in God's creation. In contrast, atheists and Hindus were relatively unconcerned. However, only 19 Hindus were interviewed, 12 of whom worked in areas related to biotechnology. Regardless of religious affiliation, the higher the level of education, the weaker the reservations.

3 Product design

When designing high-involvement products, the religious beliefs of the target group should be taken into account more than in the case of low-involvement products. However, this statement has to be qualified with regard to the different product and purchase risks, for example, with regard to the:

- Functional risk (e.g., "How well will the product serve its purpose?")
- Financial risk (e.g., "Is the product worth its price?")
- Social risk (e.g., "What will my friends say if I buy or use this product?")
- Psychological risk (e.g., "What kind of person am I if I buy or use this product?")

For very religious people, social risk is paramount. It is important to them above all that their decisions are accepted by their faith community.

3.1 Product quality

Perceived product quality depends first of all on product- or production-specific factors (such as the quality of the materials used or manufacturing know-how). In addition, other variables of the marketing mix play a role, such as the price/quality inference (cf. VII-3.2) or the social environment. For example, Christian symbols, if appropriately associated with the product, strengthen the product quality perceived by evangelical Christians and their purchase intentions (cf. Taylor et al. 2010). Islamic symbols placed on product packaging have a comparable effect. They also influenced very religious Muslim consumers more strongly than less religious individuals (cf. Akbari et al. 2018; Bakar et al. 2013).

Due to their increased need for security, religious people regularly articulate an above-average awareness of quality in corresponding surveys.[27] They also prefer high-quality products (see Ratnasari et al. 2020). Moreover, they perceive product risk more intensively than non-religious people (cf. Delener 1990a). It remains open whether this is a cause or a consequence of quality awareness.

DOI: 10.4324/9781003506010-25

In this context, Delener (1990a) interviewed 204 Catholics and 145 Jews who had purchased a car and a microwave oven, respectively, in the previous year. On the basis of their relevant experience since then, the respondents were asked to indicate whether the two consumer goods had the promised or usually expected characteristics. According to the respondents' self-reports, the sample was divided into strict believers and those participants who belong to one of the religious groups but do not practice their faith. First, respondents were asked to imagine that they were buying a new car or a new microwave oven but were unfamiliar with the brand. Then they had to indicate on a nine-point scale how likely they thought it was that these products would not work or would not be of the quality promised. Whether Catholics or Jews, in each case, the strict believers proved to be disproportionately skeptical: on average, 27.3% of them feared that the new car would not work (vs. 13.3% of the non-religious). Religious affiliation, however, was less significant for risk perception (Jews = 17.2%, Catholics = 20.6%). Possible interaction effects between religiosity and religious affiliation were not tested. The findings cannot be generalized either. Neither religiosity nor religious affiliation influenced the perceived functional risk of the microwave to be purchased.

Whenever a product or a certain way of using a product violates important religious beliefs, religious consumers perceive an increased social or psychological risk. This is particularly the case if consumers would violate a religion-specific taboo by purchasing or possessing it. Alcoholic beverages and revealing clothing are problematic for Muslims, pork and beef for Jews and Hindus, respectively, and contraceptives for Christians. Presumably, intrinsically religious people are mainly sensitive to psychological risk, as the match between ideal and real selves is very important to them, whereas extrinsically religious people are primarily sensitive to social risk (i.e., their reputation in the public eye) (cf. Baazeem et al. 2016).

In general, guarantees are regarded as an effective means of relieving fears such as those of increased functional risk. In Islamic culture, however, such assurances are less important, since Muslims regard the word of a fellow Muslim as guarantee enough (cf. Sanaie/Ranjbarian 1996). Kosher and halal certificates also have the effect of a quality guarantee, and not only for observant Jews and Muslims. Atheists and members of other religions perceive products labeled in this way as "pure" and "healthy" in a secular sense (cf. Lascu et al. 2016).

3.2 Denominational conformity

Allegedly, a product designer was arrested in Saudi Arabia years ago because the logo he developed for the Snow White brand in the shape of a snowflake was all too similar to the hexagonal Star of David, which is taboo in the Arab world (cf. Rothlauf 2012, p. 161). Indeed, it is indisputable that companies should observe denomination-specific specifications and restrictions, not least in the design of their products and their packaging, if they want to exploit their market opportunities with religious target groups. In the eyes of devout Muslims, companies that use "controversial packaging" (e.g., oversized or provocative) are disrespecting the purity of the community of believers and ultimately promoting immorality. Therefore, those surveyed by Almossawi (2014) (300 students in Bahrain) would also be willing to boycott such companies.

In this context, Islamic and Jewish markets play a special role due to various food laws. Indeed, numerous, sometimes very specific, regulations must be observed. For example, the strict separation of "meat" and "dairy" in Jewish cuisine or the prohibition of eating food that is harmful to health, intoxicating or illegally acquired in Islam. These requirements were formalized and institutionalized by halal[28] and kosher certificates.[29] Long a niche market confessionally compliant goods have now developed into a mega-market with a total volume of more than 2 trillion dollars. These are primarily Islam-compliant foods, but also cosmetics, drugstore items, clothing or tourist services.

Halal products are mainly consumed in Islamic countries. In surveys, however, 75% of Muslims living in the US and 84% of Muslims living in France say they always eat halal meat (see Bonne/Verbeke 2008). On the one hand, this is for many of them a confession of faith (cf. Lascu et al. 2016). On the other hand, worldly motives also play a role. One would like to:

- Protect nature (e.g., animal welfare)
- Preserve the general living conditions of future generations
- Demonstrate self-esteem and sociocultural integration

The advantages of labeling confessional goods with a halal label or certificate are clear. Believers can be sure that these products (and services) comply with the rules and regulations of their religion, which facilitates their purchasing decision. They also signal their orthodoxy to their social environment. Non-Muslim suppliers use a halal certificate like a shield against the regular anti-Western campaigns in the Islamic world (cf. Butt et al. 2017). But there are also drawbacks to consider. For example, using a sample of Indian Hindus (n = 512), Tao et al. (2022) empirically demonstrated that a halal label can trigger hostile feelings toward halal goods and ultimately toward Islam among ethnocentric and patriotic non-Muslims.

3.3 Modesty vs. grandiosity

Some consumers seek to "sacralize" consumption (cf. II-1.5). Others abstain for religious or ethical reasons. The latter is expressed in the appreciation of simplicity, frugality and naturalness (see Leary et al. 2016).

3.3.1 Luxury consumption

What distinguishes a luxury product? According to Vigneron/Johnson (2004), there are five characteristics:

- Quality (e.g., "Luxury goods are bought for their excellent quality")
- Hedonistic value (e.g., "Luxury goods bring pleasure to the owner")
- Visibility (e.g., "Luxury goods should be easily recognized by others")
- Exclusivity (e.g., "It is good to be among a very few people owning a truly luxury product")
- Expansion of the ego (e.g., "People buy luxury goods to reveal a little of who they are")

For the "nouveau riche," luxury products are attractive primarily because they allow them to demonstrate their economic success, while the "old rich" find it more important to use them to demonstrate their exclusive tastes to the world (cf. Kapferer/Valette-Florence 2019). This, however, contradicts the commandment of modesty, which the Catechism of the Catholic Church, for example, counts among the "Twelve Fruits of the Holy Spirit." Probably every religion rejects the materialistic lifestyle in one way or another, which leads to the expectation of a distance between religious consumers and luxury products. For example, previous work with American participants has shown that religiosity influences negative emotions, which then negatively influence consumers' luxury consumption intentions (Geiger-Oneto/Minton 2019). Conversely, in the case of 500 Egyptians interviewed by Kasber et al. (2022), however, this hypothesis could not be substantiated, while according to O'Cass et al. (2013), less religious young Iranians in particular are receptive to the charms of prestigious fashion.

It is possible that this contradiction is also resolved if one takes into account the type of religiosity. Unlike extrinsically religious people, intrinsically religious people favor the simple lifestyle, which speaks for a consumer-critical attitude of luxury products (cf. Wang et al. 2020; Chowdhury 2018). However, as Arli et al. (2016) found from the responses of 491 predominantly young, unmarried Muslims (Indonesians), intrinsically religious people do not expect social benefits from luxury products but are nevertheless drawn to them (e.g., "This luxury brand is the one that I would enjoy"). However, while intrinsic religiosity only encourages very brand-loyal customers to buy a particular luxury brand, extrinsically religious people are generally interested in buying luxury brands (e.g., Gilal et al. 2020; Truong et al. 2010).

Given the ambivalent role of religiosity, how can we explain the growing success of luxury goods and luxury brands (see Chandon et al. 2016)? In the Global Attitudes Survey, 62% of 38,426 respondents from 34 countries said "God is very/somewhat important in their lives" (cf. Pew Research Center 2020). Presumably, the reason is a kind of split in consciousness among religious people that Arli et al. (2020) identified among 335 Chilean students: "They love God, but they also love Gucci (i.e. luxury goods)." In addition, intrinsically religious people can soothe their guilty conscience by donating worn-out luxury products to a good cause, whereas extrinsically religious people do not feel this dilemma in the first place and therefore prefer to simply throw away outdated items. Intrinsically religious people are also relieved if the supplier credibly conveys to them that he or she has established a sustainable disposal system that makes it possible to reuse luxury products (cf. Minton/Geiger-Oneto 2020).

Apparently, religious beliefs and values are generally not a fundamental obstacle to buying luxury products. In fact, the more religious they are and the wealthier they are, the more desirable they appear to Tunisian Muslims, for example (cf. Dekhil et al. 2017a).

3.3.2 Frugal consumption

The discussion about a modest lifestyle and consumption style centers around keywords such as frugality, thriftiness or voluntary simplicity. For the first time, Essoo/Dibb (2004), in the context of comparative religion research, describe the type of frugal consumer (see III-4.2). The economic shopper pays particular attention to the price of a service, special offers and other low-cost benefits. The concept of frugal consumption goes beyond this and includes the mindful use of natural resources and living conditions (cf. Lastovicka et al. 1999). Helpful here are:

- Tendency to self-transcendence (i.e., ability to completely devote oneself to a task recognized as meaningful, such as environmental protection through self-restraint)
- Future orientation (i.e., ability or willingness to consider future consequences of current actions (cf. Chang 2021))

Religious consumers buy less than others on credit, prefer to pay cash (cf. Essoo/Dibb 2004), are frugal (cf. Renneboog/Spaenjers 2012) and rarely make impulsive purchases (cf. Habib/Bekun 2021). These indicators of a modest consumption style can also be used to describe the "frugal consumer" (cf. Shoham/Brenčič 2004). In this respect, it was to be expected that (intrinsically) religious people value a voluntarily practiced simple lifestyle (cf. Pepper et al. 2011), especially if they are older, have a higher level of education and feel spiritually comfortable (cf. Chowdhury 2018). The state of knowledge on the relationship between religious affiliation and frugality has been summarized by Agarwala et al. (2019, p. 44):

> Christianity has clear instructions regarding money and consumption. Jesus Christ spoke more about money than any other subject (Dayton 2011) and considered frugality, stewardship (being responsible for one's resources), simplicity, and contentment as valued traits. From earlier research, it is observed that devout Catholics strongly believe in

frugality and consider it to be a value that should be taught to children (Guiso et al. 2003). The studies of Protestants (Arruñada 2010), Amish and Mennonites (Dana 2009) also show that their religions propagate the values of frugality and thrift and disapprove excess consumption.

Calvinists are also considered to be particularly thrifty. According to the "doctrine of predestination" (cf. II-4.3), they regard economic success as an indication of their being chosen by God. Since diligence and asceticism are seen as precursors of success, even today thrift and renunciation of "superfluous" consumption are identity-forming for Calvinists.

3.4 Sustainability

Even more than classical marketing, Interfaith Marketing (IFM) has to take into account the fact that products and services are far more than functional and useful. They also influence the self-image and the image of the consumer (cf. Tian/Belk 2005), for example, as a moral person who buys energy-saving products. In order to better explain environment-friendly consumption, Gatersleben et al. (2019) developed a four-part typology of consumer identity based on a factor analysis.

- Spendthrifts are easily influenced, consumerist and trendy.
- The thrifty are bargain hunters, appreciate second-hand goods and tend to pay less attention to product quality.
- Moral shoppers are environmentally conscious and value fair trade products.
- Frugal people only buy things that are really needed and write one-buy lists.

Frugal and moral consumers tend to most strongly think about environmental protection when making purchasing and consumption decisions, but in different ways. Among the frugal, behaviors that can be reduced to the denominator "less-is-more" predominate: producing less waste, spending less money, etc.: Frugality as an end in itself. The moral ones live sustainably in order to do the right thing.

We speak of sustainable consumption when the livelihoods of future generations are not impaired or even destroyed by excessive consumption of raw materials, energy, clean water, etc. According to the Otto Group's fifth trend study (2020), 70% of those surveyed take ethical criteria such as product service life or material efficiency into account when making their purchasing decisions. Even if a good part of this may be wishful thinking and only a much smaller proportion actually act accordingly, the increase compared to 2009 is remarkable (= 26%). Furthermore, 63% stated that they were willing to accept additional costs for climate-neutral products.

The concept of sustainability is value-based, which suggests a close connection with religious belief systems that are also value-based. As can be seen from the sacred scriptures of the world's religions, adherents of Eastern religions support the goals of the sustainability movement primarily on the basis of an intrinsic, religiously conditioned connection with nature. This is based on the fundamental pantheistic conviction that God can be experienced in all elements of nature and is ultimately one with the cosmos. And if God is in everything, then destruction of nature ultimately turns against God. For instance, in Hinduism there is a goddess of trees (i.e., Lauma) and a goddess of rain (i.e., Prajanya) (Minton 2023; Schmidt et al. 2014). Further, Hindu sacred text also emphasizes the relationship between gods and the natural environment, such as in Bhagavata Mahapurana 2.2.41: "air, fire, water, earth, planets, all creatures, directions, trees and plants, rivers and seas – they are all organs of God's body. Remembering this, a devotee respects all species" (Minton 2023).

Conversely, Western religions teach that God created the world (nature) and charged humans with ruling it (cf. Minton et al. 2018b, p. 656 f.). For instance, in Christian and Jewish religious texts, Genesis 1:28 states: "Be fruitful and multiply, and fill the earth and subdue it; and have dominion over the fish of the sea and over the birds of the air and over every living thing that moves upon the earth" (Minton 2023). This concept of dominion can be viewed as God giving humans the right to exert control over nature. In more liberal Christian circles, however, given the current environmental crisis, the alternative stewardship approach increasingly finds approval. It assigns humans the role of faithful stewards of God's creation (cf. Eom et al. 2021a).

Overall, the study situation is contradictory. There are also repeated indications of a distanced attitude of many religious people toward the environmental movement (e.g., Pearson et al. 2018; Biel/Nilsson 2005). Presumably responsible for this is a certain inner closeness to political conservatism. For this reason, and because of their loyalty to the state and their tendency toward hierarchical thinking, they primarily see state institutions as responsible (e.g., environmental protection agencies).

In addition, there is the idea of the role that humans play in dealing with nature. As a survey of 1,101 American consumers revealed, religious people are increasingly in favor of statements such as "Mankind was created to rule over the rest of nature" (cf. Leary et al. 2016). They apparently prefer to view the "man/nature" relationship from the perspective of the biblical "subdue the earth" (Genesis 1:28 2:15; Leviticus 25:23; Psalm 24:1). Non-religious people, however, more often argue that humans are not dominators but well-meaning stewards of the earth (e.g., "Humans must live in harmony with nature in order to survive"). The respective man/nature understanding has numerous consequences for consumer behavior. Consumers who see humans as rulers are less ecologically aware, less willing to pay and less open to recycling than consumers who see humans more in the role of stewards and guardians of nature.

Eom et al. (2021a) reached a similar conclusion, but with a somewhat different study approach. First, they measured religiosity not, as usual, by self-assessment or by means of various behavioral indicators (e.g., regular attendance at religious services), but by the degree of agreement with certain beliefs, which Eom et al. (2021b) identified as "markers of religiosity."

These markers correlate strongly with religiosity: humans as stewards of God (= stewardship) vs. the idea of an all-powerful, all-controlling God (e.g., Isaiah 40:23; Romans 9:15–16; Qur'an 16:70). Second, this study did not examine the direct influence of religiosity on sustainable behavior. Rather, it examined it within the framework of a mediation model. That is, whether and how religious beliefs promote an environmental sense of guilt, and whether and how this may influence sustainable behavior. Finally, the participants' basic political orientation was included in the explanatory model, since it is known that religiosity is associated with conservative attitudes. The influence of this variable on the dependent variable (= support for environmental protection organizations) should therefore also be examined.

As can be seen from the results of the path analysis, the above beliefs favor different environment-related attitudes and behaviors. Those who see humans as God's trustees also tend to feel guilty about environmental pollution. And this feeling strengthens the willingness to support environmental concerns in real terms. In addition to this mediation effect, there is a direct "Stewardship Belief > Support" pathway (see Figure 17). However, people who are convinced that nothing happens on the earth that is not in accordance with God's will are also less inclined to feel guilt about the environmental crisis and to support institutions that want to do something about it. Feelings of guilt are also foreign to political conservatives, which is why they usually do not support environmental projects.

Willingness to participate in recycling activities depends, among other things, on the perceived or presumed effort required to do so, as well as on

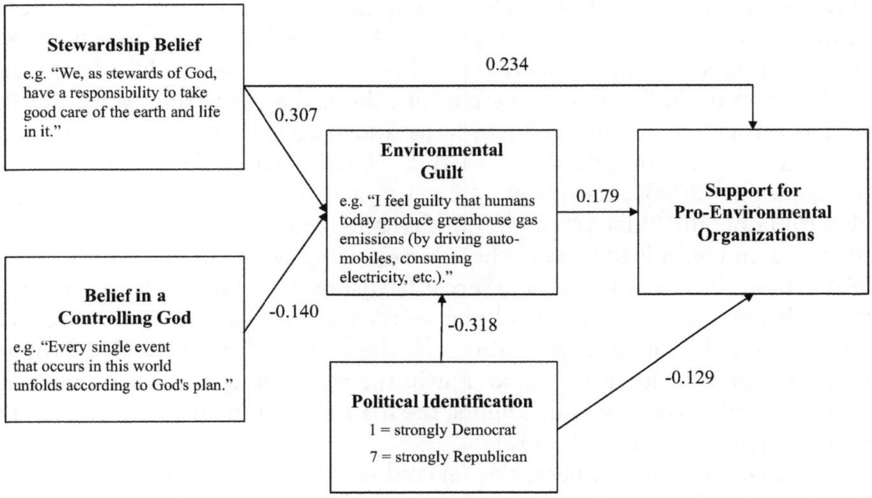

Figure 17 Influence of God/human/nature understanding on support for environmental protection organizations.

Source: Eom et al. (2021a).

the perceived or presumed efficacy. As Johnson et al. (2021) found in the case of Hindus (India) and Christians (US), the different ideas of the afterlife also play an important role. Those who believe in reincarnation, like Hindus, are more engaged in recycling, while Christian beliefs (Last Judgment, heaven, hell) reduce environmental concern. The strategy of conveying feelings of guilt to the target group in order to motivate them to increase their efforts promises success with intrinsically religious people. Extrinsically religious people seem to be immune to it, possibly because they do not perceive themselves as environmental sinners (cf. Minton/Geiger-Oneto 2020).

3.5 Color design

Colors trigger emotions and are perceived and cognitively processed much faster than graphic or even textual information. For this reason, companies use colors strategically in their corporate communications. Even more frequently, colors are used in product design to evoke certain sales-promoting associations. However, colors do not usually activate universalistic but rather symbolic associations that are partly religion- and partly culture-specific. Since different lifestyles and living conditions also give rise to different experiences and expectations, different meanings are often attributed to colors across the world (cf. Table 16).

This explains why some people associate green with liveliness, while others associate it with poison. For example, in desert regions, this color is reminiscent of fertile oases and thus embodies life. In impenetrable jungle regions, however, green stands for danger.[30] Green is also the color of Mohammed and the sacred color of Islam. That is why the national flag of Saudi Arabia bears the inscription "There is no god but Allah, and Muhammad is his messenger" in green. Jihadists wore green headbands during the Iran-Iraq war, confident that they would enter paradise immediately if they were killed. In general, green symbolizes luck, hope and success in the Islamic culture. In Syria, for example, the "green hand" signals "baraka": blessing power (cf. Schimmel 2003). Europeans, however, associate the color green above all with hope: the "first green" in the changing seasons heralds the approach of spring and with it the end of the winter season, which in prehistoric times in northern Europe was a time of great hardship. Last but not least, green is the club color of Celtic, the Catholic soccer club in Glasgow, Scotland, and blue is the color of local rival Rangers, the club of British-minded Protestants. When a "color war" broke out in the region and the green light was destroyed everywhere at traffic lights, the reason was not sporting rivalry but religious hatred (cf. Koydl 2007).

In a religious environment, the "sacred colors" are particularly effective. Besides green (Islam), blue is one of them. For Hindus, this color symbolizes the universe and the highest level of consciousness. Vishnu, one of the most important manifestations of the divine in Hinduism, is often depicted with blue skin color.

Table 16 Religion-specific color associations

	Christianity	*Islam*	*Buddhism*	*Hinduism*	*Confucianism*
Red	Blood and fire, Christ's suffering, love, saint, spirit		Happiness, power, source	Happiness, adherence, beauty	Happiness and richness, color of women (in Japan)
Blue	Calm, loyalty and tradition, Mary	Protection from ghosts, unfathomability	Dear	Color of the gods	Heaven, immortality
Green	Hope, life, resurrection, color of Catholicism (in Ireland)	Color of the prophets, sacred color of Islam, paradise	Life and death alike	Long life, mercy, femininity, life, shame (in China)	
Yellow	Not a liturgical one for worship (however, gold = divine)			Expulsion from ghosts (e.g., before a wedding), life light, truth	Masculinity, perfection (in China)
White	Enlightenment, emergence, counter part of chaos	Grief, unity, divinity	White lotus flower – mourning, sacred resurrection	Purity, peace	Grief and death
Orange	Color of Protestantism (in Ireland)		Color of the Dalai Lama		Color of change
Black	Mourning	Turmoil, misfortune, negative; but also, color of the cloth with which Ka'ba is covered			

Source: own representation based on Heller (2004).

Yellow is associated with negativity in many regions of the world: with cowardice, envy and betrayal. Jews not only had to wear a yellow identifying sign in Nazi Germany (the "Juden-Stern") but sometimes also had to wear yellow clothing under Islamic rule (cf. Schimmel 2003).

In Christian culture, white symbolizes enlightenment and purity.[31] In both Confucian and Islamic countries, however, it symbolizes death and mourning. For this reason, the advertising figure Ronald McDonald wearing white makeup did not make the desired impression on Japanese consumers. In general, the more a religion understands death as the negation of life, the darker the color of mourning, while lighter colors signal that death is more understood as a transition to another form of existence (for example, in Buddhist and Hindu societies).

The history of mourning colors, however, was not always limited to the white/black continuum. For a long time, the color red was also used for mourning, a symbolic expression of the blood that Jesus Christ shed. In Italy, until the 16th century at funerals red mourning clothes were usual and in Hungary, this lasted even into the 20th century. Purple, on the one hand a symbol of imperial power and on the other hand a liturgical color,[32] an expression of penance and fasting, was for a long time the mourning color of the European royal houses. It was not until the middle of the 19th century, after Queen Victoria of Great Britain and Ireland had made the white wedding dress acceptable, that black became established as the color of mourning.

3.6 Naming

When developing product, brand and company names, there is sometimes a lack of the necessary religious and cultural sensitivity (cf. Gürhan-Canli et al. 2018). Therefore, sometimes names are chosen or created that violate a religious taboo or social norms and damage the corporate image. The name Budweiser, for example, is inextricably linked with alcohol consumption, which is why non-alcoholic beverages should not be sold under this brand in Islamic countries. Nike was even boycotted in Saudi Arabia because in ancient Greek mythology, the "god of victory" bears that name, which is problematic in that Allah is a very jealous god and the Shahāda literally means: "There is no god but Allah." Consequently, corporate communications in Islamic countries should not refer in any way, directly or indirectly, to other gods. And Buddhists, on the basis of Ahimsā, the commandment of non-infringement, would see in a product or brand name reminiscent of an animal an insult to this living being by being degraded to an advertising figure.[33]

The art of naming is to evoke positive associations. Everything to do with luck promises particularly positive associations: lucky days, lucky names and lucky numbers. It should be noted that luck is symbolized in different ways all over the world. Just think of the eight Tibetan symbols of luck (e.g., shell, lotus flower), which are widespread in Hindu and Buddhist regions. In Korea and many other countries, however, pigs embody luck and wealth (because one could consider oneself lucky if there was a pig in one's barn), while in China this role is given to the bat. Indeed, the syllable "fu" is a homonym as it means both bat and luck.

In the Confucian region of the world, the preference for a Lucky Name is a tradition. When searching for a name that promises good luck, it is important to maintain the balance between yin and yang:

- Yang characters are composed of an odd number of strokes, while yin characters are composed of an even number.
- If a name consists of several characters, their combination is significant. The sequence Yin-Yin-Yang is more advantageous than the sequence Yin-Yang-Yin.
- Finally, it is a lucky name only if the sum of the strokes of the characters used results in a lucky number (e.g., 8, 11, 13, 15, 16, 17, 18, 25).

Technical products are preferably given alpha-numeric names. In the Western hemisphere, "7" is considered a lucky number. For this reason, the aircraft manufacturer Boeing has given its models numerical sequences such as 737. In the eastern hemisphere, other lucky numbers have to be taken into account. There, "8" symbolizes eternity, which is easy to understand if you tilt the digit: ∞.

Buddhists, in addition to lucky names and lucky numbers, also observe lucky and unlucky days. The idea is widespread there that important projects (e.g., business, building a house, getting married, traveling) can only be tackled on certain days with a chance of success. In the Middle Ages, lucky days were also determined in Central Europe with the help of the Bible, lists of saints or astrology. Even today, Tuesdays and especially Sundays are considered lucky days. In Christian societies, Friday, in particular Good Friday, is considered to be Calamity Day, the day on which Jesus Christ died on the cross. "Friday the 13th" combines both, an unlucky day and unlucky number. Phillips et al. (2001) proved that the effect attributed to unlucky symbols is not necessarily imaginary, based on the death data of Americans born in China and Japan. On the 4th day of each month, 7% more people succumbed to a heart attack than on the other days of the first week of each month. Presumably, the awareness that the ominous unlucky day has arrived is a stress factor which, like all stressors, increases the probability of a heart attack.

The idea that luck can be invoked by performing magical rituals and using symbols is widespread wherever superstitious beliefs and remnants of old folk faiths have survived, such as in many African countries. The monotheistic religions, however, teach that happiness cannot be earned or otherwise acquired but is a gift from God. Psalm 16:11 says: "You show me the way that leads to life. You give me joy, for you are with me. I cannot grasp my happiness; it never ceases." And in the Quran (Sura 9: Verse 72) it says, "But Allah's pleasure is the greatest. That is the highest happiness." Buddhists and Hindus, however, do not seek happiness, but rather inner peace.

3.7 Communication of the country of origin

As more and more products have been wholly or partially manufactured abroad in an increasingly global economy based on the division of labor, there has been a desire to know whether or how a foreign production location influences consumer preferences and purchasing behavior. Indeed, it has been shown that religious people tend to be skeptical or dismissive of imported products (cf. Haque et al. 2015b).

3.7.1 Findings of country of origin research

It is well known that the indication of CoO of a product often leads to the attribution of country stereotypes (e.g., "Made in Switzerland" = trustworthy). If the CoO suggests product characteristics such as quality, reliability or innovativeness, this is generally advantageous. There is a risk of negative consequences if country stereotypes or ethnocentric beliefs are activated by the mark of CoO, which can discourage the purchase of the product in question (e.g., "Made in China" = low quality).

Several meta-analyses confirm this to a large extent, with one limitation. CoO research consists mainly of single-cue studies, in which the product origin is the only feature addressed, or the subjects are otherwise made emphatically aware of it by the experimental design. Real consumers, however, usually do not know where a product was developed and manufactured, in whole or in part (cf. Samiee et al. 2016). In this respect, multi-cue studies, in which product origin is only one of several of the product attributes to be considered in preference formation, are more informative. The consequence of this more realistic experimental design is that the CoO effect is still detectable but noticeably smaller than under the single-cue condition (cf. Verlegh/Steenkamp 1999).

Various studies confirm that a foreign production location reduces the purchase intentions of religious consumers (e.g., Haque et al. 2015b; Tabassi et al. 2012). Due to their pronounced national pride (cf. Schmitt et al. 2008) and their tendency toward ethnocentrism and intolerance (cf. III-2.6), a strikingly large number of religious consumers attach more importance to a domestic production location than to product quality or degree of innovation.

In addition, IFM has been primarily interested in the interaction of halal certification and CoO label. According to Nasution/Rossanty (2018), CoO moderates the influence of the halal label on the purchase of imported frozen foods (i.e., a positive CoO increases and a negative CoO decreases purchase intention). Muhamad et al. (2017) offer a possible explanation. According to their surveys, religious Muslims infer the credibility of the halal logo from the CoO. However, not every CoO has the same effect. According to Rios et al. (2014), a product origin from Saudi Arabia or Kuwait promotes preference for halal products to a greater extent than a product origin from Indonesia or Malaysia. The reason is that Saudi Arabia and Kuwait are prototypes of an Islamic society (nearly 100% of the population is Muslim and Islam is the state religion). Measured against this, Indonesia and Malaysia are somewhat less clearly "Islamic." Outside the Islamic world, the United Kingdom is considered the "best address" among Muslims (see Borzooei/Asgari 2015).

3.7.2 Findings of ethnocentrism research

Ethnocentric people (see III-2.6) are proud of the symbols and values of their own ethnic or national group and reject those of others. If possible, they avoid everything foreign, including imported products (see Haque et al. 2015b; Siamagka/Balabanis 2015). Religious people are more ethnocentric than average (cf. Kusumawardani/Yolanda 2021).

For example, in the case of Tunisian consumers' attitudes toward clothing, with "Made in... France, Italy, China or Turkey," it has been shown that the CoO moderates the relationship between participants' ethnocentrism and their purchase intention (cf. Karoui/Khemakhem 2019). Specifically, in this study, products manufactured in France or Italy benefited from the respective origin label, but Chinese and Turkish products did not.

3.7.3 Findings of animosity research

Animosity research analyzes consumers' negative reactions, often in the form of reluctance to buy or boycott of products originating from certain countries (cf. Riefler/Diamantopoulos 2007). Animosity differs from ethnocentrism in that it does not reject foreign products or foreign things, but only those from a certain country. However, religious people tend toward both animosity and ethnocentrism (cf. Ahmed et al. 2013; Tabassi et al. 2012).

Kalliny et al. (2017) extended Klein et al.'s (1998) animosity model, which considers constructs such as hostility and antipathy, to include religious animosity: Intolerance and antipathy based on religious differences toward a person, nation or state. The trigger of animosity is usually a negatively critical event of a political, economic or religious nature (cf. Table 17).

Shortly after the beginning of the second intifada, Shoham et al. (2006) surveyed 135 Jewish Israelis about their attitudes toward Arab Israelis and the products and services they offer. The structural equation model developed on this basis revealed that Jews living in Israel who feel animosity toward their Muslim neighbors doubt the quality of products made by Arab Jews and are also less likely than others to intend to buy these products (see Figure 18). Dogmatic, nationalistic Jews in particular developed animosity, while internationalism weakened this feeling.

Table 17 Animosity research at a glance

Event		*Effect*
Political animosity	Massacre of the people of Nanjing in China by Japanese occupiers (1937)	Purchasing restraint: Chinese customers avoid Japanese (offered in China) products (cf. Klein et al. 1998).
	French nuclear tests in the South Pacific (ca. 1960–1996)	Boycott: Australian customers refuse to buy French products (cf. Klein/Ettenson 2005).
Economic animosity	Asian crisis (1997–1998)	Preference: Imported products (e.g., from Thailand) are preferred to products from the US (cf. Ang et al. 2004).
	Unfair trade practices of Japanese companies	Reluctance to buy: Americans avoid Japanese products (cf. Klein/Ettenson 1999).
Religious Animosity	Second Intifada in Israel (2000–2005)	Reluctance to buy: Jewish customers avoid Arab products (cf. Shoham et al. 2006).
	Publication of Mohammed-cartoons in Denmark (2005)	Boycott of Danish products in Islamic countries (cf. Jensen 2008).

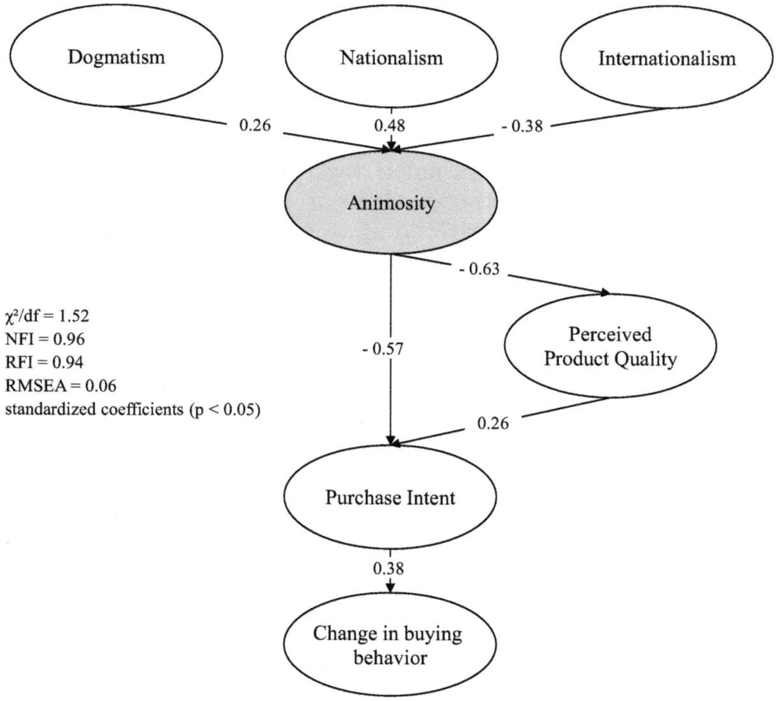

Figure 18 Animosity of Israeli consumers toward Arab products.

Source: Adapted from Shoham et al. (2006, pp. 97, 102).

In addition, against the background of the Israeli-Palestinian conflict, Farah/Newman (2010) were able to demonstrate on the basis of a random sample of 500 Lebanese consumers that Muslims are more open to boycott measures than Christians. However, it is not religious affiliation that seems to be responsible for this but rather normative beliefs of varying intensity. More Muslims than Christians perceived a strong social pressure to participate in a boycott.

In the case of the anti-Koran film by the Dutch political activist G. Wilders (cf. Al-Hyari et al. 2012), this was exacerbated by the fact that in the opinion of religious Muslims, caricatures also violate Islam's commandment of imageless worship of God, which is often misinterpreted as a ban on images. While in the Greek Orthodox Church, for example, painting an icon is equivalent to a cultic act, the pictorial representation of saints is problematic in Islam but not forbidden. Thus, in moderate Islamic countries or communities, there are countless iconic representations of the prophet holding the Koran in his hands. Regarding the use of images, Islamic doctrine distinguishes five gradations, from "commanded" to "strictly forbidden" (cf. Almir 2004). Incidentally, the prohibition of images, which was enacted with the aim of preventing a superficial veneration of images that drifted into the pagan or superstitious, is not peculiar to Islam. It also played an important role in Europe in the course of the Reformation. While the Lutherans developed a comparatively pragmatic attitude towards it in the course of time, the Reformed Church, under the influence of Calvin and Zwingli, took a fundamentalist position, which became known as "iconoclasm."

3.7.4 *Synopsis of findings*

The structural model developed by Ahmed et al. (2013) provides an illustrative summary of this research (see Figure 23). It is based on data from 410 middle-aged Malaysian respondents of both genders and different religious affiliations (46.4% Muslim; 30.3% Buddhist/Taoist; 11.7% Christian; 6.7% Hindu; 4.2% non-religious). All had been repeat customers of American fast food. Based on their experiences, they were asked to rate their quality level (e.g., "Products made by US fast-food restaurants are generally very well suited to needs of Malaysian consumers") and to provide information about their consumption behavior (e.g., "I bought from US fast-food restaurants even though cheaper foreign fast-food restaurants were available"). In detail, this research found:

- Religious consumers are often ethnocentric (e.g., "Malaysian consumers should always buy Malaysian made products instead of imports").
- Their hostile attitude toward the US (animosity) can be traced primarily to ethnocentric convictions and only secondarily to religious convictions (e.g., "I will never forgive the US for occupying and killing the civilians in other countries").

- While ethnocentrism influences consumer behavior only indirectly (through an upstream devaluation of perceived product quality), animosity has a weaker but direct effect.

This is in contrast to the findings of Shoham et al. (2006) and Kalliny et al. (2017), according to which animosity also manifests itself in a devaluation of product quality. Possibly, however, this inconsistency can be explained by fundamental differences in the evaluation of consumer products vs. services. In any case, in the case of Kang/Yang (2019), the socio-political animosity of Taiwanese respondents reduced their intention to watch Japanese TV shows, but not their assessment of the artistic quality.

Furthermore, according to recent animosity research, only consumer products are suitable as projection surfaces for consumers' hostile feelings, and not intermediate products or raw materials. For example, the negative reporting by the Chinese media on the stationing of a missile defense system in South Korea only affected the sales prospects of South Korean end products on the Chinese market (see Kim/Kim 2020).

However, the real economic consequences of a product's perceived negative origin are far too rarely examined. According to Saeed/Azmi (2016), American and British companies suffered sales losses of up to 40% in the Islamic markets during the Iraq war (2003). Until now, individual, mostly prominent companies have been targeted (e.g., Coca-Cola representing the US). In view of the Palestinian conflict, very religious Tunisian Muslims in particular heeded the call to boycott the soft drink manufacturer. In this case, the relationship between religiosity and intention to boycott was moderated by the intensity of brand loyalty: religious people did not join the buyers' strike if they felt an inner connection to the Coca-Cola brand (cf. Dekhil et al. 2017b).

4 Branding

Like certain marks of origin (e.g., Made in the US), a strong brand name also signals quality and reliability. What these characteristics have in common is a close relationship to certain values, above all trust. Consumers use brands as a visible expression of their social identity (cf. Escalas/Bettman 2005). Brands are preferred which correspond to the consumer's own values, be they more materialistic (cf. Rindfleisch et al. 2009) or religious-spiritual in nature (cf. Al-Hajla et al. 2019). In this context, Interfaith Marketing (IFM) is interested in questions such as:

- Religions as brands that can be marketed with the classic instruments of brand management (e.g., Alserhan 2010b).
- Religions as value systems that can be marketed using brands (e.g., Taylor et al. 2010).
- Religion and brands as substitutes, both of which can be self-valorizing for consumers (e.g., Shachar et al. 2011).
- Secular brands that consciously communicate religious values (e.g., Halstead et al. 2009).

4.1 Brand types

In addition to individual, family and umbrella brands, classic brand types or brand strategies also include regional, national, international and global brands. Special brand concepts such as spiritual or Islamic brands are of particular interest for IFM.

Spiritual brands are brands that are recommended by (local) spiritual leaders. Naturally, they are mainly bought by religious consumers. Apparently, the purchase or use of such brands helps consumers to reassure themselves of their social identity and to communicate this to others (cf. Sardana et al. 2021).

The brand concept of an "Islamic brand" is defined in three ways (cf. Alserhan 2010; Williams/Sharma 2005):

- "Sharia-compliant" brand identity that appeals primarily to devout Muslims.

DOI: 10.4324/9781003506010-26

- Origin from an Islamic country, whereby "halal" does not always have to be the exclusive guideline for entrepreneurial action (for example, Emirates Airlines serves alcoholic beverages to its passengers).
- Targeting of Muslim customers by suppliers originating from a non-Islamic country. In fact, the halal brands of Nestlé, L'Oréal and Unilever dominate a large part of the markets for Islamic food, cosmetics and health products.

The opposite type is embodied by global or, from a strict Islamic perspective, infidel brands such as McDonald's or Coca-Cola. Such brands can be considered infidel brands insofar as they allegedly tempt Muslim consumers to immoral behavior and can thereby betray the ideals of Islamic societies (cf. Izberk-Bilgin 2012). This, based on the real or perceived crises of a globalized world, is linked to the accusation that market-based societies prevent social justice and promote immoral behavior. In order to restore the golden age of Islam, a "consumer jihad" would ultimately be needed.

The numerous halal and kosher certificates are also a religion-specific form of branding. The strictest approach is taken by the courts of ultra-Orthodox Jews, while the most liberal is taken by the communal rabbinates. Moderate are also the K and OU certificates popular in the US (cf. Heiman et al. 2019). Especially among strict believers, these trigger a number of positive effects. On the one hand, quality advantages are attributed to the goods branded in this way, and on the other hand, respondents express an increased willingness to buy. However, only the well-known brands benefit from this (cf. Kamins/Marks 1991).

In general, religious affiliation and/or intensity of religiosity moderate the responses of religious consumers to the various forms of religious branding. They increase its impact if the actions taken are in line with the religious convictions of the target group and weaken it if there is a serious disagreement (cf. Liu/Minton 2018, p. 306). Thus, it does not diminish the brand loyalty of very religious consumers if religious brands are involved in a moral controversy with religious reference. Rather, they tend to forgive "their brand" in such cases (cf. Chowdhury et al. 2022).

4.2 Brands as a substitute for religion

Since the 1970s, affluent industrial societies have been the scene of a complex interplay between the secularization of public life and the sacralization of private consumption (see II-1.5). The Apple community is exemplary for the phenomenon of the "religion-substitute brand" (cf. Sarkar/Sarkar 2017) as well as for the phenomenon of the "brand evangelical." Measured by their comparatively small share of the overall PC market, Apple users are far inferior to Microsoft users in terms of numbers. But they identify more strongly with "their" brand and are also extremely loyal (see Belk/Tumbat 2005).

4.2.1 *Brand religiosity and brand evangelism*

Brands and religions are connected in many ways. Some scholars describe their relationship as substitutive, as mutually interchangeable. Especially for materialistic, non-religious consumers, the brand world can literally replace the religious world (cf. Sarkar/Sarkar 2017). Others emphasize more strongly what unites them. Accordingly, consumers can use both – brands and religion – to strengthen their self-worth (cf. Shachar et al. 2011). Still others emphasize the possibility of positioning religions as brands and using established branding techniques to disseminate the respective faith content as effectively as possible (cf. Usunier/Stolz 2016; Taylor et al. 2010). And Wang et al. (2018) speak of brand religiosity, by which they mean the final stage of an increasingly intensive relationship between brand and consumer. This relationship begins with the appreciation of a brand and leads to brand religiosity via romantic brand love and brand veneration.

Finally, brand cult is characterized by an extremely strong brand loyalty, a religiously formed consumer fanaticism. The followers of this cult, the brand evangelists, not only stand up for "their" brand like brand advocates, but they also fight competing brands by talking badly about them (see Chung et al. 2018). To identify brand evangelicals, Wang et al. (2019) developed a brand sacredness scale. Their nomological network includes brand love, emotional brand attachment and brand loyalty.

4.2.2 *Brand communities*

The sacralization of the brand world can be well described by the success stories of Apple, Harley-Davidson, Mercedes-Benz, Nintendo and Rolex. Kilian (2009) introduced the prolog to his critical declaration of love for the myth of the brand with the complaint of a Coke customer who wrote to Atlanta in 1985, on the occasion of the launch of New Coke: "In my life there were only two quantities of lasting value: God and Coca-Cola. You have taken one away from me." The author shows the reader the numerous overlaps between the sacred and profane spheres: "God promised us eternal life, brands eternal youth" (p. 15).

He paid tribute to the Harley-Davidson phenomenon with the words of an evangelical pastor: "Harley is ... a myth ... companion for the Lonesome Cowboy. But the myth also includes a community, that is, a congregation that lives the cult" (Kilian 2009, p. 41). Of particular importance for its members is the willingness to wear a visible sign of belonging to the community of believers (or brand owners). And what would be more binding than a sign burned into the skin in the form of a tattoo? When asked "What brand, if any, would you be willing to have tattooed on your arm?", 18.7% of respondents named Harley-Davidson, but "only" 7.7% named Coca-Cola, 6.6% Google, 5.6% Rolex, 2.6% Adidas and 1.5% Nintendo (cf. Lindstrom 2005).

Whereas in the last century it was primarily churches and other religious communities that offered people an inner home and an opportunity to identify, today other social groups are increasingly taking over this function. In a hedonistic, consumer-oriented environment, strong brands can be the focal point for such a "community." As is the case for religious communities, unique, emotionally charged symbols and rituals are also identity-stimulating for brand communities (cf. Schouten/McAlexander 1995).

Pogačnik/Črnič (2014) have analyzed the Apple community according to the four criteria that, according to E. Durkheim, constitute a religion: a community, religious beliefs, sacredness and rites (cf. Pickering 1994). "The products act as religious fetishes to Apple devotees, and Apple stores function as temples. Followers perform public pilgrimages to store openings and Apple conferences, and private rituals of product unboxing."

Because of their strong need to belong, religious people are on average receptive to the appeal of communities. The feelings they derive from this act as a halo effect, which makes them see the products or brands that are part of this community in a particularly positive light (cf. Minton/Liu 2021).

4.3 Brand trust

Trust, which arises from perceived competence, reliability, goodwill and integrity, is an important prerequisite for a favorable course of transactions of all kinds (cf. Singh/Sirdeshmukh 2000). Brand trust, which can be traced back to quality guarantee and high brand awareness, reduces various purchase risks (e.g., quality risk, social risk), which facilitates purchase decisions. Pebri/Bakti (2022) report that brand trust, as well as religiosity, has a positive influence on the decision for Mudharabah financing among Islamic business customers (see VI-2.4.2). In addition, more than members of other religious affiliations, Catholics prefer well-known, heavily advertised brands (see Bailey/Sood 1993, p. 343), which is often associated with the grandeur of the Catholic Church.

In general, religious people trust more than non-religious or less religious people (cf. Minton 2019; Iftikhar et al. 2017). This can be explained, firstly, by the close correspondence between the causes of trust and the mostly positive worldview of religious people (see IX-2.1.1). The connection is particularly close among those consumers for whom brands are an important part of their self-concept (cf. Liu/Minton 2018). Secondly, religious people generally tend to trust other people more (cf. Tan/Vogel 2008).

How then can we explain that Shachar et al. (2011) found religious consumers to have lower brand trust? Possibly this is due to the different operationalization. For this study, brand trust was not defined, as is usually the case, as "shared beliefs" or as "perceived probability that a branded product possesses the promised characteristics" (i.e., as a cognitive-emotional phenomenon preceding the purchase decision). Instead of brand trust, Shachar et al. (2011) speak of brand reliance, referring to the likelihood that a consumer will prefer a branded product over a functionally equivalent but unbranded product. To explain their findings, the researchers refer to the human need for affiliation, which religious people can satisfy through their church community, while the non-religious or less religious seek and find fulfillment through brands: Possession of prestigious branded products as an alternative to the spiritual search for meaning. However, this speculative thesis primarily describes only the motives of high-income consumers. Lower income consumers could not afford the luxury of such a search for meaning and would essentially have to prefer the cheapest product.

4.4 Brand awareness and purchase intention

There is much to suggest that religious people are more brand-conscious than average. From their point of view, brands are supposed to simplify purchasing decisions and help avoid risks thanks to the brand-specific quality guarantee. However, they should also fulfill important social functions, such as communicating the personality of the brand owner (e.g., uniqueness) and his or her social identity and conveying enthusiasm (e.g., joy of living, magical brand worlds). According to Essoo/Dibb (2004, p. 703), however, moderately religious people in particular attach great importance to brands. Obviously, there is no simple, linear relationship between religiosity and brand awareness. This is also suggested by the findings of Shachar et al. (2011) and Mokhlis (2006b), which we have already discussed previously (see V-4.4).

The latter differentiated religiosity in two ways: in terms of content (intra- vs. interpersonal religiosity) and according to intensity (weakly, moderately and strictly religious). As their analysis revealed, moderately interpersonal religious participants pay significantly more attention to branded products than weakly and strictly interpersonal religious participants. This also tends to be the case for intrapersonal religious people, albeit at a low, statistically insignificant level.

According to Rindfleisch et al. (2005), the relatively low brand awareness of very religious people can be explained by their special understanding of religiosity: as a search for and attainment of transcendent experiences. In contrast, material things like branded products embody the profane, an obstacle in the search for salvation.

Agarwala et al. (2021) conducted three experiments to investigate how religious signs influence Hindus' brand evaluation and purchase intention. Specifically, the communicative effect of religious icons was compared with the effect of religious symbols on the acceptance of secular products. The participants, predominantly male, were shown print advertisements for soap. These differed only in the motif of a picture hung in the background of a family situation:

- Experiment group "Icon": The picture shows Ganesha, the most popular deity in Hinduism.

- Experiment group "Symbol": The picture shows Om, the sacred sign of the Hindus.
- Control group: The image shows an abstract motif.

The key findings of this study were that both types of religious signs strengthen brand evaluation and purchase intention, but religious icons more strongly than religious symbols. Moreover, it was found that very religious Hindus react more positively to this type of advertising than less religious people.

4.5 Brand loyalty

Some consumers regularly buy a certain brand and report positively about it: personally, to friends and acquaintances, or anonymously in online forums. If this happens out of inner conviction and not more or less forced by external circumstances (e.g., a limited selection, price reduction or other material advantages), then we speak of brand loyalty. Suppliers benefit from this in many ways. In addition to the aforementioned willingness to spread word of mouth (even to the point of assuming the role of brand ambassador) and reduced price sensitivity, the positive effects of brand loyalty include increased cross-selling potential.

Related concepts are brand loyalty and brand retention. The concept of brand loyalty accentuates the emotional relationship to a brand. In extreme cases, this is referred to as brand love. In this case, a particular brand is an important part of the consumer's self-concept. Brand loyalty links the emotional level with the behavioral level (cf. Grace et al. 2020).

Brands like Coca-Cola have so much brand strength that even a fatwa cannot harm them. A fatwa is a legal opinion in which a Muslim jurist comments on how Muslims should deal with certain life problems that are not regulated in the Koran or the Sunna. Are Muslims allowed to get Botox injections, watch gossip TV shows or participate in a lottery? While fatwas ensured that Malaysian students enrolled in an Islamic university smoked less and listened less often to popular Western music, they were not forbidden to drink soda (cf. Muhamad/Mizerski 2013).

So far, comparative religion research has examined this topic area only sporadically. Among the exceptions is Djupe (2000). Based on a remark by Stark/Glock (1968, p. 1) on the relationship between religion and loyalty ("the heart of religion is commitment"), he has shown by means of a secondary statistical evaluation of data from the General Social Survey 1993 that religious people are more willing than others in many areas of life to commit themselves and to stand up for a cause. They are more willing to stand up for their faith community, for political issues or even for brands that are important to them. This was contradicted by Davis/Jai (2014) as they found that strictly devout American Christians are not only quality-conscious but also price-conscious when buying clothing, which results in a relatively low level of brand loyalty. Regarding the connection between religious affiliation and brand loyalty, reference can be made to Rindfleisch et al. (2005). According to these researchers, Muslims are less open than members of other religious groups to a close, possibly emotional relationship with a brand (i.e., to something that could be interpreted as brand loyalty). Possibly, according to Mathras et al. (2016), Muslims have learned to understand consumption primarily as a way of satisfying primary needs (utilitarian vs. hedonistic lifestyle) due to the strict consumption and behavioral imperatives of Islam.

Chowdhury et al. (2022) found that suppliers of religious brands that are involved in sociocultural controversies (e.g., dealing with minorities) can count on the loyalty of their religious customers. The decisive factor for their motivation is whether they are extrinsically or intrinsically religious: While intrinsically religious people do so because of their great willingness to forgive others, extrinsically religious people act primarily because of reactance. They perceive criticism of "their brand" as a restriction of their freedom of expression and as an attack on their membership of this brand community. They defend themselves against both.

According to Gilal et al. (2020), brand loyalty moderates the relationship between the type of religiosity (extrinsic/intrinsic) and the intention to buy luxury brands. According to this, intrinsic religiosity only strengthens the intention of brand-loyal customers to buy a luxury brand, while extrinsic religiosity has a similar effect on customers with low brand loyalty.

5 Product types

Products can be classified in various ways, including whether they offer primarily a material benefit (e.g., food), an immaterial benefit (e.g., ethical products) or a spiritual benefit (e.g., sacralized products).

5.1 Convenience products

Goods such as frozen foods or baking mixes offer an important additional benefit: They make life easier. On this basis, McWilliams et al. (2016) investigated the extent to which religious affiliation and religiosity influence whether consumers prefer foods that take relatively little time to prepare. The theoretical background to their considerations is the Theory of Social Custom, according to which people take into account the consequences of their decisions for their social environment, for example, for their family or their religious community (cf. Akerlof 1997).

In terms of the acceptance of convenience products, this means that Orthodox Judaism and Orthodox Islam require believers to observe strict rules of conduct when preparing food and to follow the respective dietary laws. Christianity has similar, though less strict, rules. The ultimate certainty that one is following the purity law can only be provided by traditional dishes prepared within the family circle. Only then can you be sure that you are eating kosher or halal food. Also, elaborate cooking procedures and high-quality ingredients testify to respect for the family and guests. Consequently, it can be assumed that strictly observant Jews and Muslims tend to reject convenience products. To empirically test this hypothesis, McWilliams et al. (2016) asked 388 Jews, Muslims and Christians living in Israel whether they prefer fresh or frozen poultry, and in one piece or cut up. Indeed, those who buy poultry parts (e.g., breast) save time in preparation but have to pay more. Frozen poultry, however, allows for flexible preparation and is cheaper but less tasty.

The results of the study confirmed their hypothesis. They found that neither for Jews nor Muslims is convenience an argument for buying frozen food. However, while predominantly conservative Jews prefer fresh meat (= quality consciousness) and poultry parts (= time saving), religious as well

DOI: 10.4324/9781003506010-27

as non-religious Muslims prefer fresh poultry, but as a whole (= quality consciousness and traditionalism). The fact that, in contrast, ultraorthodox Jews prefer frozen poultry parts (= cost and time advantage) may have less to do with their religious convictions than with the lifestyle of their religious community as they generally have many children and limited income. Many ultraorthodox Jewish men do not work and instead devote their lives to their religion. The preferences of Christians could not be examined in this research due to the limited sample size.

5.2 Religious vs. sacralized products

The relationship between religion and consumption is complex. The loss of significance suffered by institutional churches in industrial societies (on secularization, see II-1.5) is countered by the undiminished need of many people for faith and the sacred (see Belk 2013). The latter manifests itself in a variety of ways, such as consumption as a substitute of religion, but also in the increased demand for religious products: "Products and services that contain religious associations" (Agarwala et al. 2019, p. 42). These associations can take different forms:

- Normative religious associations refer to what believers may eat and when and how they should dress or consume. Believers, for whose religion orthopraxy ("right action") is central, prefer offers that trigger such associations. Muslims, for example, prefer halal food (cf. Jamal/Sharifuddin 2015), halal pregnancy clothing (cf. Krisjanous et al. 2021) or Islam-compliant (e.g., interest-free) banking services (cf. Albashir et al. 2018).
- Symbolic religious associations are usually triggered by the use of religious signs (images, figures, words, melodies, etc.) in marketing communications (cf. IX-6.2).

There is ample empirical evidence that religious consumers respond more positively than average to religious products, such as halal products (cf. Khan et al. 2019; Nurhayati/Hendar 2019) or sharia-compliant financial services (cf. Abou-Youssef et al. 2015). This can be explained in a number of ways, such as in terms of social identity. By buying religious products, religious people assure themselves of belonging to the social group of believers and demonstrate their religious affiliation to others (cf. Tajfel 1974). As Rizkitysha/Hananto (2020) have found, the perceived usefulness of the halal label continues to play a role in the purchase of household cleaners, for example. This primarily improves the attitude of religious people toward halal products and ultimately their purchase intention of such products.

But how do consumers who are not religious or belong to a different religious group react? For them, the halal logo is usually not an incentive to buy (cf. Kawata et al. 2018). On the contrary, if, as in the case of Indian Hindus, their own religious group's relationship with Islam is conflictual, many of them feel animosity toward overtly "Islamic" products (cf. V-3.7). And, as Tao et al. (2022) found, the animosity felt by their 512 Indian participants mediates the negative influence of ethnocentrism, willingness to boycott and religiosity on the intention to buy halal products. A few years earlier, Schlegelmilch et al. (2016) found similar findings. In their study, religiosity promoted animosity and this promoted aversion to halal products. Wilkins et al. (2019) explored the question of what determines how European non-Muslims assess the quality of halal food and how this product assessment affects their purchase intention. Of the British, Canadians and Spaniards interviewed, primarily those who are ethnocentric (cf. V-3.7) and identify strongly with their nation (national identity) tended to devalue halal products and not to buy them. In contrast, cosmopolitan participants and those who identify strongly with their religious group (religious identity) expressed a stronger positive attitude.[34]

More and more people of other faiths are also convinced that halal products are healthier, cleaner and have a higher overall value than non-certified products. Knowledge about the halal system emerged as the second most important reason for purchase in an online survey of Indonesian non-Muslims (see Purwanto et al. 2020).

Do non-Muslims feel cognitive dissonance when they subsequently learn that halal food was served to them in a restaurant without their knowledge? As the researchers found, the effect is rather weak. On the seven-point rating scale used, the country averages of Spain and Canada are only just above the category "2 = disagree." Only among the British surveyed by Wilkins et al. (2019a) does the deception seem to have triggered somewhat more dissonance. They rated the statement, "I feel frustrated by the lack of information about halal food served in restaurants" with a mean of 3.63 (i.e., between "rather disagree" and "neither nor"). The intention to continue eating halal food[35] in the future is also in the undecided range. However, it is noticeably lower among the British participants than among the Canadians and Spaniards. Overall, this speaks for a weak but nevertheless detectable "cognitive dissonance > repurchase intention" effect in this subsample. In addition, in this study, participants with a pronounced religious identity (i.e., those who identify strongly with their own religious affiliation) experienced above-average dissonance. The same applies to participants who were very interested in the welfare of animals. The reason for this could be negative reports about slaughtering practices in halal farms.

5.3 Socially and environmentally conscious products

Important manifestations of ethical products are fair trade products and environmentally friendly or sustainable products (i.e., "green products") (cf. Mazar/Zhong 2010). In all these cases, social or moral values are more important than consumers' price and quality preferences. But since they are obviously morally "good" (for the protection of the environment, disadvantaged population groups, etc.), corresponding surveys usually reflect more the social desirability of this product category than the actual willingness to pay or purchase intention of potential customers (cf. Saracevic et al. 2022).

5.3.1 *Motives of consumers*

Socially acceptable products are particularly popular with consumers who are older, female, well-educated, financially well-off and religious (cf. Vitell 2009; de Pelsmacker et al. 2005). However, especially among religious people, it often remains a matter of wanting, which is discussed in the literature as the hypocrisy hypothesis (cf. Ji et al. 2006). This alludes to a systematic attitude/behavior discrepancy in this case (cf. III-5.6). If we restrict ourselves to the behavioral level, then the relevant research speaks relatively clearly for the fact that religious people buy fair trade coffee, organic meat or eggs from free-range chickens much less often than assumed. Graafland (2017) has demonstrated this for Dutch Christians and Doran/Natale (2011) for religious consumers of different religious affiliations.[36] In Section VII-4.3, we discuss in more detail the willingness to pay for socially and environmentally conscious products.

In view of various crises in recent years, the way we eat has triggered numerous controversies (environmental, climate, obesity crises). It is true that movements such as "vegan" or "dietary" seem at first glance to primarily serve individual well-being motives. However, on closer inspection, one also recognizes how these relate to socially responsible consumer behavior, some of which are indirect (reduced-sugar diets) and some of which are direct (e.g., vegan diets). According to Minton et al. (2019), very religious consumers prefer dietary foods, where this relationship is mediated by the moral idea of purity (mediation effect). In contrast, less religious consumers favor sustainably produced foods. They primarily follow the insight that our environment is threatened and needs our care.

5.3.2 *Motives and possible actions of companies*

And what about the firm side? For what reasons do companies engage in fair trade? Cater et al. (2017) have identified three types of fair trade entrepreneurs, albeit on a narrow empirical basis (35 in-depth interviews):

- Ethics First: Their primary drive is human rights and the pursuit of social justice.
- Faith First: They follow their faith/religious beliefs.
- Business First: The prospect of being able to combine business and doing good with fair trade appeals to them.

Since previous willingness-to-pay research (see VII-4) primarily consists of studies that describe the characteristics of potential customers that promote or inhibit their willingness to pay, Wei et al. (2018) wanted to know what firms of socially and environmentally conscious products can do to increase their customers' willingness to pay. Can participation be such a lever, for example, by manufacturers implementing customer-specific design suggestions? Yes, at least according to the responses obtained from 334 predominantly younger Americans, most of whom had higher educational qualifications. In this study, participation[37] ensured that the low willingness to pay of participants with low environmental awareness[38] for an environmentally friendly T-shirt was significantly increased.

In this context, Berger (2019) tested the signaling hypothesis experimentally. In fact, the participants (Swiss students) were willing to pay significantly more than usual for various everyday products (e.g., soap, lemonade) if their social environment found out about them. Firms that want to profit from this effect should design their green products in such a way that they are easily recognizable as "green" and send out appropriate signals to friends, acquaintances, etc. The basic message that the "consumer was willing to pay a considerably higher price" can be provided with a status appeal or a social appeal. Both provide social benefits, but in different ways:

- Status: "Buyer can afford it" (e.g., Tesla buyer).
- Social compatibility: "Buyer accepts disadvantages for the sake of a good cause" (e.g., inconvenience due to not using plastic bags in a grocery store).

5.4 Taboo products

Some behaviors pose an existential threat to societies. In such cases, commandments or rules are not enough. Rather, taboos are necessary, as they are rarely explicit, but particularly strict forms of prohibitions. Whoever disregards a taboo must reckon with (social) exclusion from the community. Perhaps the best-known taboo is the incest taboo, which is supposed to protect societies from the spread of hereditary diseases. Generally known are religious taboos that refer to the consumption of meat: Pork for Jews as well as Muslims, beef for Hindus and, much less strictly, meat of mammals on Holy Friday for Christians.

Like the Catholic Church, Islam also rejects contraceptives, but not tolerant Hinduism (cf. Iyer 2002, p. 713). Nevertheless, Hindus and Muslims living in India use contraceptives with roughly equal frequency (cf. Pinter et al. 2016). This can be explained by the fact that it may be annoying or unpleasant to follow religiously motivated commandments, norms, taboos, etc., which concern, for example, holidays, food or clothing (i.e., rather peripheral areas of life). However, if this could lead to negative-critical life events such as the birth of an unwanted child, which would change the entire further course of one's life in an undesirable way, then many religious people also find ways to reconcile everyday reality with their religious convictions.

Iyer (2002, p. 720) determined which factors influence contraceptive use in a survey of 173 women living in India. A logistic regression analysis identified the educational level of the spouse for both subsamples (57% Hindus, 43% Muslims). Also true for both religious groups was that relatively few women (37% of Hindus and 23% of Muslims) discuss this with their husband. The advice of female family members is much more important. However, the fact that a woman is less likely to use contraception the more female family members live in the household is probably the result of a spurious correlation. Religious women are more likely to live in an extended family than more or less secular women, which is why the degree of religiosity is likely to be the decisive variable here and not the number of women in a household.

In general, religious people perceive the social risks associated with the purchase or use of religiously questionable products more intensively than average consumers. However, to the extent that they believe they have moral potency and are convinced of their own judgment in ethically controversial matters, the perceived risk does not reduce their purchase intention (cf. Mortimer et al. 2020).

5.5 Counterfeit products

Product and brand piracy is an increasingly global phenomenon that causes enormous economic damage and fuels distrust between market participants. Traditional piracy, which involves imitating real products, is increasingly fading into the background, and digital piracy is dominating the scene for two reasons. First, it is easier to copy software of any kind compared to hardware. Second, existing property rights are hardly enforceable due to the global reach of online offerings (cf. Miric/Jeppesen 2020).

Casidy et al. (2016) surveyed 400 younger Indonesians on their use of pirated digital products. According to their findings, religious people are less likely than others to intend to buy and share pirated goods and to recommend this to others (see Table 34). Kasber et al. (2022) report similar findings. This is probably due to the fact that very religious people regard the purchase of illegal copies as a sin (see also Souiden et al. 2018). Moreover, they are more concerned than less religious people to behave in accordance with their social environment and God's teachings. This in turn has to do with the close social networking of religious people and the great importance of obedience for monotheistic religions (cf. Ellison/Sherkat 1993). Deviating from this view, others assign the key role to fear of punishment.

Do attitudes toward the purchase or use of pirated goods change over the course of a lifetime? Only 26% of the 706 young Canadian Baptists (14–18 years old) surveyed by Fawcett et al. (2013) were able or willing to see something wrong with copying music videos without permission. With increasing age, however, the concerns grew, presumably as a result of the then deeper involvement with religious scriptures.

And what about religious affiliation? Does a decidedly Christian upbringing make people more resistant to the temptation to buy illegal goods at a discount? Rather not, according to Lewer et al. (2008), who asked American students about their attitudes toward product piracy. None of the following statements were judged significantly differently by students who were enrolled at a Christian university than by students at state universities:

- "It is morally wrong to copy CDs or DVDs for friends."
- "It is morally wrong to download unauthorized music, movies, or TV shows from the Internet."
- "The record and movie industries should prosecute those who have downloaded songs illegally from the Internet."

Part VI

Service policy

1 Forms and characteristics of services

Services can be marketed on the one hand as an independent offer (e.g., haircut by a hairdresser) and on the other hand as an accompanying product. Product-accompanying services are divided into those that are close to the product (e.g., use of samples) and those that are far away from the product (e.g., childcare while shopping). Services differ from products in three ways (cf. Grönroos 2001). Services:

- Are not physically tangible
- Can neither be transported nor stored. Production and consumption often coincide in time (e.g., bus ride)
- Are created in direct interaction with the customer and often in the customer's presence (e.g., measurement)

What is remarkable about this from a marketing point of view is that the direct involvement of the customer in the production process transforms what appears to be a purely economic transaction into an interpersonal encounter. And this often has a decisive influence on the quality of the service. For example, it is more difficult to serve an unfriendly, impatient and disproportionately demanding hotel guest in a satisfactory manner than a well-meaning, well-balanced customer. Disruptions also frequently occur when service providers and customers belong to different value communities (e.g., different religious affiliations, national cultures or subcultures).

The influence of the country's culture on the service process has already been extensively researched (see Müller/Gelbrich 2015). Accordingly, service providers find favorable conditions in feminine societies (as caring is an identity-forming value there, which underpins traditional services such as childcare or nursing) and in societies that tolerate uncertainty (since the service process is fraught with uncertainties compared to the manufacturing of material products, which can mostly be standardized and controlled down to the last detail).

Divergent religious values give rise to different perceptions and expectations. For example, the more customers are convinced that everything on the earth depends on non-earthly powers, the less likely that they will be to

DOI: 10.4324/9781003506010-29

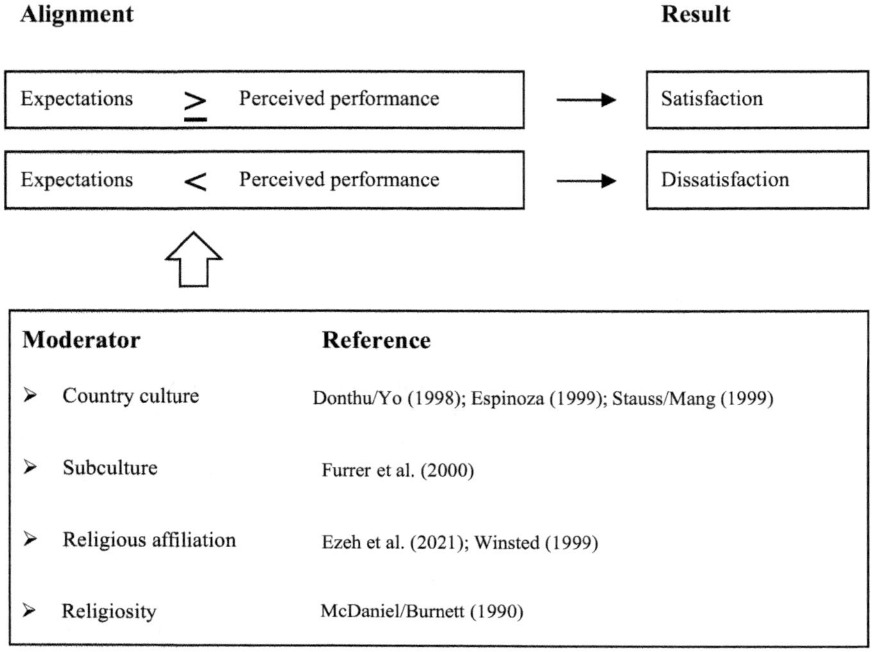

Figure 19 Structure of value-based satisfaction research in the service sector.

respond by complaining or spreading negative word of mouth if they are dissatisfied with a service. For Interfaith Marketing (IFM), this is significant as customer satisfaction can usually be explained less by the absolute quality level of a service offered than by the ratio of expected to received performance (cf. Oliver 1997, p. 13). Customers are more satisfied the more a service meets or exceeds their expectations (see VI-3.2 and Figure 19).

2 Service businesses

Religious similarity and, even more so, religious diversity across different countries promote international trade in services. Religious similarity does so because it creates mutual trust, and religious diversity because it fosters the sociocultural openness that is beneficial to cross-border exchanges of all kinds. This also explains why the dominance of one religion in an economic area inhibits cross-border trade, while religious tolerance strengthens it (see Lee/Park 2016).

2.1 Evening entertainment

Hirschman (1983) asked 330 New Yorkers of different religious groups in writing what criteria they used to decide on a particular service (e.g., price). According to this study, when Catholics and Protestants want to go out on a Saturday night, their expectations are largely similar. However, given their tendency to be thrifty, it is particularly important for Protestants to spend little money on entertainment but still have a good time. Jews, however, place a conspicuously high value on going out with others, preferably in a larger group. More than Christians, they make their decision dependent on the weather and make sure to spend Saturday evening at their favorite place. The importance Jews attach to socializing can also be seen in their actual going-out behavior. More often than Christians, they meet in bars, have fun in nightclubs, go to the ballet or visit friends. Unlike Catholics (= 3%) and Protestants (= 13%), they also consider sex to be a typical Saturday evening activity (= 53%). Catholics, however, spend the evening at home more often than others, enjoying a good meal.

2.2 Tourism

Religion is a significant pull factor in the tourism industry. One need only think of the demand for travel services triggered by pilgrimages, for example, to Jerusalem or Rome (see Collins-Kreiner 2010; Timothy/Olsen 2006). As can be seen from the fuel consumption and capacity utilization of buses, trains and airplanes, the demand for transport services increases considerably on the occasion of major religious festivals and holidays. Before the

DOI: 10.4324/9781003506010-30

pandemic, almost 2 million Muslims took part in the Hajj, the great pilgrimage to Mecca. As these pilgrimages usually involve long distances, average expenditure per pilgrimage is estimated at €5,000 (for visa, flight and accommodation). This adds up to a market potential of over $10 billion.

When choosing their destinations, religious tourists also pay attention to climate, sights, purchasing power and other classic selling points of the travel industry. In addition, the religious similarity/dissimilarity between the country of origin and the destination country also plays an important role for them. Numerous studies support that shared religious identity is a good predictor of tourist flows and is subconsciously used by many travelers as a heuristic for their decisions (cf. Vietze 2012). Even though they did not consider pilgrimages in their analysis, according to Fourie et al. (2016), 52% of travel volume can be attributed to the "religion" factor. Religious similarity is primarily responsible for this. However, religious diversity (i.e., if there are known religious minorities living in a destination) also plays a significant role (cf. Fourie et al. 2015). Regardless of the religious fit, countries where Christianity, Buddhism or Hinduism are the majority religions that attract the most tourists. Conversely, Islam tends to deter travelers of other faiths.

Among the topics that are increasingly attracting the interest of comparative religion research, besides the factors that influence the satisfaction of religious tourists (cf. Preko et al. 2020), is their environmental awareness. It should be noted that there is a special connection between "religious tourism" and "sustainable travel." On the one hand, there is this connection because of the personality of religious people (caring, modesty, etc.). And on the other hand, it recalls the centuries-old tradition of pilgrimages, which have always been carried out in an environmentally friendly manner (cf. Romanelli et al. 2021). Religiosity also proves to be a key moderator in this context. Research has shown that among Chinese hotel guests, intrinsically religious people are particularly concerned about the state of the environment and are interested in a simple, nature-oriented vacation (cf. Wang et al. 2020). Among Buddhist Chinese people, however, extrinsic religiosity increases the positive attitude toward "green tourism" and the intention to stay in an environmentally friendly hotel slightly more than among Taoist and Muslim participants (cf. Wang/Zhang 2020).

2.3 Transportation services

Those who have to decide between a cab, their own car and the bus can use various selection criteria to do so. In the 1980s, when environmental awareness was not yet on the agenda, Jews, Catholics and Protestants alike focused primarily on costs and convenience (easy access). They attached somewhat less importance to speed and security at that time (cf. Hirschman 1983). Two factors had a religious affiliation-specific effect.

- Far more often than Catholics and Protestants, Jews made their decision dependent on the weather, as they disproportionately fear becoming ill as a result of external influences. This seems to be a generalized fear that radiates to other areas of consumption. More than half of the Jews, but only a quarter of the Catholics and Protestants, considered the risk of allergies when buying a pet.

- Protestants as well as Jews are considered to be distinctly time-oriented. Jews are known for their impatience, and Protestants pay more attention to productivity and efficiency. Accordingly, significantly more Protestants (= 47.4%) and Jews (= 45.0%) than Catholics (= 15.6%) preferred cabs as a means of transportation (at that time, in the New York City survey area, cabs were the fastest mode of transportation).

2.4 Financial services

So far, Interfaith Marketing has mainly focused on Islamic banking: the specifics and effects of Islam-compliant financial services.

2.4.1 Basic principles

One important way of reducing search and control costs in transactions of all kinds is to trust the other party. This strategy is particularly suitable for the purchase of so-called credence goods. Laypersons cannot check their properties (credence qualities) even after purchase or can do so only at a disproportionately high cost. A classic example of a credence good is the investment of money. When signing a contract, investors cannot know whether the equity fund will actually achieve the optimal return, whether the management costs for investment funds are justified or whether the "value corrections" of the term life insurance are appropriate. If you trust your provider, you don't have to worry about any of this, but you take a different kind of risk: Whose interests will the agent represent? Will he or she justify the trust placed in him or her, or abuse it?

This leads to the question of whom to trust. First of all, people, institutions, etc. with whom one has had good experiences in the past will most likely be trusted by consumers. However, this cannot be assessed in a first-time interaction. Then we tend to trust those who are similar to us because they have similar beliefs and values as we do (e.g., because they belong to the same religious community). As Tan/Vogel (2008) found with a game-theoretic experiment, religious actors actually enjoy more trust and also trust others more than non- or low-religious actors: for example, Indonesian bank customers of an Islamic bank. As a result, trust strengthens the intention to continue using the services of this bank in the future. In addition to this mediation effect, Suhartanto et al. (2018) have described a direct influence of religiosity on customer loyalty.

Is it therefore advisable to position financial innovations as "religious" (such as an Islamic credit card) in order to increase their acceptance in a religious environment (see Johan/Putit 2016)? As plausible as this assumption may sound, to the best of our knowledge, there is no reliable empirical evidence to date.

(see also Demirguc-Kunt et al. 2014)

2.4.2 *Islamic-compliant financial services*

All major world religions are more or less critical of financial transactions. However, no religion has had such a lasting influence on this economic sector as Islam. Islamic banking is the term used when all banking transactions are conducted in accordance with the religious rules of Islam.

Its bases are the "pillars of Islam," the five basic obligations that all Muslims should fulfill: Creed (Shahada), prayer (Salat), compulsory social contributions (Zakat), fasting in Ramadan (Saum) and, if possible, pilgrimage to Mecca (Hajj). Together, they are intended to ensure equality and solidarity among Muslims. Zakat is an expression of the responsibility that the wealthy bear for the poor. According to the commandment of charity, Muslims are supposed to help their neighbors in need without demanding a tribute (i.e., interest) in return.[39] At a time when the economy was based on exchange and commodities, and loans for investments to expand business activities and increase the productivity of companies were unknown, the prohibition of usury and interest arose.[40] That is, Muslims should not take advantage of the neediness of others, and moneylenders should not charge interest for emergency loans (riba).

Ultimately, this ensured that purely financial transactions were generally considered impure. Real economic objects should always be exchanged or transferred (see Hassan/Lewis 2009). But even then, certain transactions and investments are not Sharia-compliant. For example, Muslims are forbidden to invest in or trade in the production of alcohol or the processing of pork. Nor should they profit from prostitution and pornography. The Accounting and Auditing Organization for Islamic Financial Institutions represents 155 members from 40 countries. Its standards are binding in Bahrain, Dubai, Jordan, Lebanon, Qatar, Sudan and Syria and are a recommendation in other Islamic countries.

However, Islamic companies also need funds to be able to invest. And professional investors as well as private savers want to be able to invest money profitably. Therefore, various methods have been created that make this possible in an Islam-compliant manner (cf. El-Gamal 2006).

A first approach is of a purely semantic nature and is exhausted by referring to interest not as interest but as a profit markup. It is also possible to charge a fee for loans instead of interest. And since the authoritative Sura 30:39 is ambiguous and is interpreted partly as "any kind of interest" and partly as "usury interest," one can speak thirdly of a prohibition of usury instead of a prohibition of interest altogether.

More economically relevant is the profit-sharing model: profit and loss sharing instead of interest. This principle corresponds to the Islamic sense of justice: If investors share in possible profits of an investment, they should also share in possible losses.

- In Murabaha, a form of short-term financing, the bank first acquires the asset to be financed itself. It then sells it to the borrower for a corresponding price premium.[41]
- The common feature of the Mudaraba and Musharaka financing instruments is that, within the framework of a joint venture, the business partners divide profit or loss according to the capital they have contributed. Unlike Mudaraba, Musharaka is used for longer term financing. The investors have voting rights, can appoint representatives of their company to the joint venture's board of directors and can influence business policy.
- Sharia-compliant financing instruments continue to include sukuk (i.e., interest-free bonds whose buyers use them to acquire a stake and receive a premium for the associated risk).
- Ijara is a lending transaction comparable to leasing. A party that lets an asset to a contractual partner for a certain period of time receives a lease in return.

However, the Koran not only prohibits (usurious) interest or investments in drugs, alcohol, weapons, pornography and gambling but ultimately also insurance. Because neither insurers nor their customers know when they take out a policy whether a claim will ever be made, insurance is similar to a forbidden game of chance from an Islamic perspective. Takaful offers a way out: a cooperative insurance model in which customers pay into a fund that then invests the collected capital in a Sharia-compliant manner. The surpluses generated are used to settle any claims. The insurance company receives fees for the transactions it has to carry out.

2.4.3 Findings from comparative religion and financial services research

Little is known about the attitudes of the general population toward the interest rate ban in Islamic banking and of bank customers in particular. However, it is known that Muslim customers of religious banks do not react differently to unfavorable interest rate changes than Muslim customers of conventional banks (see Aysan et al. 2018). Accordingly, the interest rate is also an important decision criterion for them. In contrast, the influence of religiosity on the attitude toward and use of Islamic banking and on customer loyalty has been studied relatively frequently.

- Souiden/Rani (2015) observed in a Tunisian convenience sample that it is above all the ideological dimension of religiosity that allows a prediction: Believers with a pronounced fear of God's judgment as well as particularly strict believers (= believe in Islamic Law) showed above-average positive attitudes in this study. In contrast, the behavioral dimension of religiosity (i.e., the extent to which specific commandments are followed and rites are practiced) had no systematic influence on attitudes toward Islamic banking.

- The literature contains contradictory statements on the relationship between religiosity and intention to use. Some researchers have not been able to find any significant correlation (cf. Hanudin et al. 2011). Others describe a mediation effect in that religious people develop positive attitudes toward Islamic banking, which in turn promote the intention to use it (cf. Bananuka et al. 2019).
- Religiosity also plays an important role in the intention of customers of an Islamic bank to remain loyal to it. However, Suhartanto et al. (2018) found no direct effect of religiosity > customer loyalty. Rather, this relationship is mediated by trust. Religious Muslim customers trust their Islamic bank, and because they trust it, they also intend to use its services on a permanent basis (religiosity > trust > customer loyalty).

Does the technology acceptance model (cf. Davis 1989; Davis et al. 1989) predict the intention of Islamic bank customers to use an innovative Islamic credit card in the future? According to Jamshidi/Hussin (2016), the classic constructs of the original model (perceived usefulness of the technological innovation, perceived ease of use and attitude toward the technology) are indeed meaningful in this case as well. However, two additional constructs, religiosity and trust, significantly increase the explanatory power of the model to 57.1% of behavioral intention.

Is there a Ramadan effect in the financial markets? According to Gavriilidis et al. (2016), the answer is yes. This is because the usually positive mood during the month of fasting promotes optimism among market participants. This in turn means that, in contrast to many other consumer sectors, stock markets in Muslim countries are buoyant during Ramadan, which drives up prices (see Białkowski et al. 2012).

Other studies are devoted to the question of whether there is a connection between religiosity and the results of the business activities of financial service providers. In most cases, it is not the individual religiosity of the management or employees that is meant, but the location of the company's headquarters (i.e., whether it is located in a religious region or not). In fact, in this sense, "religious banks" were less affected by the 2007–2009 financial crisis than others (see Adhikari/Agrawal 2016; Kanagaretnam et al. 2015). This can be explained by a conservative approach to business and a preference for risk-averse strategies. This is reflected, among other things, in a lower-than-average volatility of return on assets and a lower insolvency risk (see Cantrell/Yust 2018). Furthermore, such banks can expect more encouragement than comparable institutions in a more secular environment if they offer new investment opportunities (cf. Hilary/Hui 2009).

2.5 Health services

Especially when a service affects sensitive areas of life (e.g., health), the type of relationship between service providers and consumers plays a decisive role. Based on this consideration, Nix/Gibson (1989) first examined whether the religious orientation of a hospital is important to patients. The answer was very different depending on the questioning technique used. Yes, if supported questions were used, and no if unsupported questions were used. Similar results were obtained a little later when Andeleeb (1993) wanted to know whether patients would be treated in a religious hospital that corresponded to their own religious beliefs. However, he tested how this fit affects the perceived service quality. For this purpose, 130 residents of a city in the northeastern United States were interviewed in writing. All respondents or their family members had already had experiences as patients with both types of facilities (religiously oriented vs. secularly oriented hospitals). Specifically, it was found that when patients were asked:

- Directly after the importance of individual selection criteria for a hospital, the religious affiliation of the facility is rated as secondary, regardless of whether the participants had their last illness treated in a hospital of their religious affiliation or in a neutral hospital.
- Which hospital comes to mind first, then the religious hospital enjoys the highest degree of familiarity among people who belong to the same religious affiliation. In contrast, atheists and members of other religious affiliations disproportionately often named a non-religious hospital ($p < 0.001$).
- When asked which hospital they would choose in the event of a family emergency (future preference) and where they or one of their family members had last been treated (past preference), the importance of religious orientation was confirmed once again: religious people had chosen or would choose a religious hospital, while people of other religions or non-believers preferred a neutral institution.
- According to medical competence and service quality, patients belonging to the same religious affiliation rated the religious hospital significantly better than patients of other faiths or of no faith. In contrast, the assessment of the services provided by the state hospital was not systematically influenced by religious affiliation.

The effect described is stable (i.e., it can be traced back to fundamental beliefs and not to environmental variables, such as the distance between home and hospital). If the latter is taken into account as a control variable, it becomes clear that non-religious people are more likely to consider a religious hospital if it is much easier to reach than a comparable state hospital. In the case of strong commitment, however, "When controlling for respondents with the same religious background as the hospital, however, the results indicated that closeness to home was not significantly related to recall, preference, or choice" (Andeleeb 1993, p. 47).

To summarize, in isolation, religious fit is less important for patient satisfaction. Patients primarily want a hospital in which they are well treated and well cared for. However, if there are several comparable hospitals to choose from, religious orientation is the deciding factor for patients with a religious affiliation. They then prefer the hospital of their own faith. This fit benefits above all the perceived quality of service.

3 Perceived service quality

Like the quality of products, consumers can only very rarely assess the quality of services objectively. Therefore, research usually uses subjective measures, in this case perceived service quality.

3.1 Measuring service quality

Attempts to capture perceived service quality using a one-dimensional scale are rather rare. Among the exceptions are Saptasari/Aji (2020), who operationalized service quality by means of general statements such as "Islamic banks have consistent quality." The central finding of this survey of 575 younger Indonesians is that religious Muslims attest to a higher level of service quality in an Islamic bank than non-religious people. This, as well as the above-mentioned finding that religious hospital patients are more satisfied than average with "their" hospital, can be explained with the help of findings from social psychological attractiveness research: People feel attracted to people (and organizations) with similar interests, abilities and attitudes (cf. Aronson/Worchel 1966). Irrespective of this, the fact that very religious patients are generally more satisfied with the services they receive than less religious patients is also likely to play a role (see Shuv-Ami/Shalom 2017; Benjamins 2006).

Mostly multidimensional measurement instruments are used to measure service quality, most notably SERVQUAL, consisting of five subscales (cf. Parasuraman et al. 1988):

- Amenity of the material environment (tangibility)
- Reliability
- Responsiveness
- Performance competence (assurance)
- Empathy

Gayatri/Chew (2013) have developed an "Islamic service quality scale" that primarily takes into account Islamic values such as sincerity, modesty, humanity and trustworthiness as well as Muslim rules of conduct

DOI: 10.4324/9781003506010-31

and rituals. However, neither empirical basis (n = 36) nor methodology (= qualitative interviews) correspond to the usual procedure of a scale development. Another, an exclusively conceptual proposal, conceives service quality as a three-dimensional construct, with the subdimensions of environment, outcome and interaction quality. In addition to general requirements such as the equipment of the service provider, waiting time or food quality, this measurement method also takes into account special features of the Islamic cultural environment such as halal quality (cf. Sumaedi/Yarmen 2015).

3.2 Influence of expectations on perceived service quality

According to the influential confirmation/disconfirmation model of satisfaction (cf. Oliver 1977), customers have expectations before they buy or use a service. If the service received or perceived meets or exceeds the expected service (confirmation), then the service quality is judged positively. Accordingly, unfulfilled expectations (disconfirmation) lead to a negative quality assessment (see Figure 20).

Essoo/Dibb (2004) have described moderately religious people as the more demanding type of buyer who places comparatively high demands on product and service quality (cf. III-4.2). In comparison, very religious people are regarded as indulgent customers (cf. Wiebe/Fleck 1980), submissive and trusting (cf. Kahoe 1974). However, this does not mean that quality is completely unimportant to them and that they are generally undemanding. Rather, religious people are more tolerant and complain less frequently, for example, about product and service deficiencies. However, they attach greater importance to the quality of relationships, especially

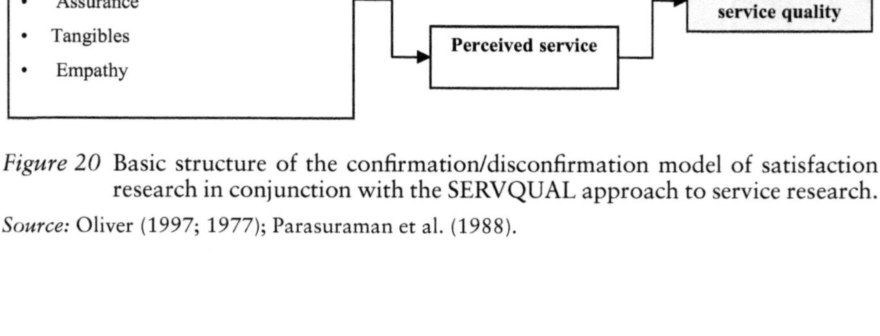

Figure 20 Basic structure of the confirmation/disconfirmation model of satisfaction research in conjunction with the SERVQUAL approach to service research.

Source: Oliver (1997; 1977); Parasuraman et al. (1988).

friendly sales personnel. Religious affiliation is also significant in this context:

- Religious Hindus regard their present life as a stage of an infinite cycle. Therefore, they have lower expectations of their existence than others (cf. Hermann 1991).
- The general tolerance attributed to Buddhists speaks for an above-average tolerance of errors in services (cf. Bailey/Sood 1993, p. 331).

As members of a strictly hierarchically structured religious community, Catholics are used to following strict rules, at least more so than members of other faiths. Essoo/Dibb (2004, p. 704) suggest that devout Catholics expect the same from others and not least from service providers, which indicates an above-average level of aspiration. What this faith community has in common with Hindus and Buddhists are high standards for the quality of their personal relationship with service providers.

3.3 Influence of perceived service quality on customer satisfaction

According to Abror et al. (2019a), there is a strong positive correlation between the service quality perceived by 335 Indonesian bank customers and their customer satisfaction. This effect is somewhat weaker for religious customers (slightly negative moderation). Presumably, the fact that the Muslim respondents are customers of an Islamic bank acts as a buffer, ensuring that their satisfaction is somewhat less dependent on the quality of the service they receive than is the case for non-religious or less religious individuals. The positive relationship between perceived quality and customer loyalty is mediated by perceived customer satisfaction. Finally, good service quality strengthens customer commitment, by which the researchers mean emotional attachment to the brand or the bank.[42]

4 Managing service failures

For successful relationship management, companies need information about what customers perceive as service failures, why and how they complain and what compensation they expect or feel is appropriate. Since forgiveness plays an important role in many religions, it is of particular interest to Interfaith Marketing (IFM) under which conditions customers are willing or able to deal with service failures leniently.

4.1 Customer reactions to service failures

Customers usually react to service failures with dissatisfaction. This is because the actual service does not correspond to the expected service. In addition, the following reactions can be observed:

- Cognitive reactions: Customers find an explanation for the unpleasant occurrence, place it in their belief system (e.g., "Nobody is perfect") and ultimately forget the occurrence.
- Emotional reactions: Customers get annoyed, frustrated or angry.
- Behavioral reactions: Disgruntled customers complain to their service provider or record their dissatisfaction in a customer survey, tell other consumers about their bad experiences and advise against this provider (negative word of mouth). Their "toughest" sanction options are to switch providers and call for a boycott.

Conversely, generous customers avoid any form of negative reaction: they forgive the unreliable service provider.

4.1.1 Dissatisfaction

Whether service failures lead to a noticeable decline in customer satisfaction depends on a number of moderators. Some of these, such as the severity of the failures, are more universally valid: the more serious the failures, the greater the dissatisfaction. The effect of other moderators, however, is subject to cultural or religious influences. These include, on the one

DOI: 10.4324/9781003506010-32

hand, customer characteristics such as their preferred attribution style and country-specific sociocultural norms. On the other hand, contextual factors such as the presence of religious symbols in the service environment also play a role.

Service failures regularly raise the question of who is responsible: one of the acting persons (the service provider or oneself) or the circumstances of the critical incident (i.e., the "situation")? The answer depends to a large extent on the customers' attribution style.

- Protestant beliefs favor the personal or dispositional attribution. According to the focus on the individual, which is typical for this religious group, either the provider is seen as responsible (= view of the customer) or the customer (= view of the provider). The attribution style fixated on the acting individuals is called fundamental attribution error (cf. Li et al. 2012). It leads to higher levels of customer dissatisfaction.
- Chinese, Koreans, Japanese and other Confucian Buddhist-influenced people of East Asia share a value system according to which all those involved in an event are subject to a common fate (cf. Norenzayan/Lee 2010). Therefore, they are less inclined to hold manufacturers, sellers or other persons responsible for service failures. Their attention is primarily focused on external circumstances, in which ultimately no one is at fault. These can be excessive time pressure, unfavorable working conditions and much more (= situational attribution). This thesis has been empirically confirmed by Yau (1988), among others. In his study, Confucian Chinese customers expressed less dissatisfaction after a service failure than Christian customers due to their situational attribution style. As Americans, they preferred the dispositional attribution style.

Furthermore, the degree of dissatisfaction after a service failure is influenced by sociocultural norms such as "saving face" and "faith in fate." The norm of "saving face" is a consequence of the need for social acceptance and respect that is paramount in Confucian societies (cf. Hwang et al. 2003). "Face" is understood to mean the honor or reputation of a person and the social position derived from it (cf. Ho 1977). The Confucian imperative is, "What you do not wish for yourself, do not do to others. Then there will be no wrath against you - neither in the state nor in your family." A story, which we do not know if it is true or just well invented, illustrates this.

> Allegedly, a foreign guest in a Japanese tea house asked for sugar with his green tea. When the waitress kindly informed him that green tea is drunk unsweetened in Japan, the guest was not satisfied and finally asked to speak to the manager. When the manager replied that there was no sugar in the tea house, the foreigner changed his

order. Instead of green tea, he ordered a cup of coffee, which was immediately served to him - with sugar. The solution to the riddle: the staff and the manager not only felt compelled to prevent their guest from losing face because he was drinking green tea with sugar in public, but they also had to save their own face, which would have been seriously threatened if they had allowed their guest to embarrass himself.

The norm "belief in fate," however, is particularly relevant in societies, whose members, mostly for religious reasons, have a tendency to fatalism and are not very convinced of their self-efficacy. There, people explain negative events such as a service failure often as a misfortune or as a consequence of the action of a mysterious anonymous power: fate.

What is the impact of these two cultural norms? Chan et al. (2009; 2007) first measured the extent to which the participants (students from Hong Kong and the U.S., respectively) internalized the norms of "saving face"[43] and "believing in fate."[44] In addition, the type of service failure and the social setting of the event were varied in a scenario experiment. The service failure could be either social (= the employee taking the order does not smile) or non-social (= the requested menu item is sold out). The social setting was described as a private event (= without witnesses) or a public event (= other diners observed the scene). The results showed:

- The more the participants internalized the norm of saving face, the stronger dissatisfaction the service failure triggered, especially if it was a social in nature.
- Belief in fate: The more the participants believed in the power of fate, the less dissatisfied they were (under the condition "non-social without witnesses"). If, however, other guests observed the incident, the saving face norm was activated.

Customer characteristics and contextual factors can weaken or intensify dissatisfaction after a service failure. In this sense, religious symbols that are placed in the service environment on the occasion of religious festivals (e.g., Christmas trees, stars or angels during Christmas time) are "double-edged." In a series of experiments, Newton et al. (2018) demonstrated that such symbols are not only decorative but also capable of appeasing religious customers affected by a service failure. However, the effect reversed when others were affected by the service failure and they belonged to a vulnerable social group (e.g., elderly retirees vs. business people). Then, Christmas decorations increased observers' dissatisfaction, and they were also more likely to switch providers and to warn other customers about the issue. Presumably, religious symbols activate not only the norm that one should forgive others in case of conflict but also the norm that disadvantaged people are in need of protection.

4.1.2 Complaints

How often and where or how do customers complain when a company does not meet their expectations?

- Directly to the company, in a personal conversation, by telephone or in writing a message (= voice response)
- Through negative word of mouth (WoM) in the private environment (= private response)
- By publicly expressing their dissatisfaction, for example, on social media (= third-party response)

Confucian-Buddhist socialized customers are much less likely to complain than Christian and Islamic socialized customers. In the event of a conflict, Chinese, Japanese, Koreans, etc. do not usually regard the provider as an adversary, but as a partner with whom they would prefer not to have a dispute (cf. Au et al. 2014; Jahandideh et al. 2014; Ngai et al. 2007). On the one hand, this restraint is the result of a pronounced need for harmony. On the other hand, the cultural standard of "saving face" also plays an essential role here. After all, not only would the person who caused the damage lose face and thus his or her social standing but also the complainant would as well. In addition, there is the striving for long-term social relationships and the shyness to show emotions in public. Asians also do not a priori consider self-confidence and assertiveness to be desirable traits, which is why they are less likely than Europeans or North Americans to strive for self-esteem enhancement through a successful complaint. If "Confucians" do complain, they do so in a face-saving manner. They then prefer to report the critical event only to their immediate social environment or change the provider from the outset. In contrast, American customers, who are characterized by Christian individualism, often vent their anger publicly by complaining to the company or its employees (see Liu/McClure 2001).

4.1.3 Negative word of mouth

Most consumers trust recommendations from friends and acquaintances more than advertising messages from companies. Marketing then speaks of WoM: informal or non-professional advice that people give to others in certain areas of life (e.g., consumption). Thanks to the networking of large sections of society, it has become very easy to evaluate all conceivable facts and to disseminate one's own opinion. In the course of this development, electronic WoM (eWOM) has become a frequently used and efficient marketing tool.

However, the mostly anonymous eWoM does not enjoy the same level of trust as personal recommendations in face-to-face communication. Since anonymous positive reviews are increasingly suspected of being fake reviews, primarily critical comments and reviews influence consumers' decisions (see Ahluwalia 2002). This is also the reason why on the Internet negative WoM predominates, while positive reviews dominate in the case of personal advice among acquaintances (cf. Hornik et al. 2015). Overall, according to Review Trackers 2018, consumers are 21% more likely to criticize (vs. positively rate) providers, products, services, etc. And 94% of respondents would avoid a provider who is the subject of negative comments.

Religiosity and religious affiliation also play a significant role in this context. As they react more sensitively than others to a violation of the fairness norm (cf. Henrich et al. 2010), religious people engage in more negative WoM behavior if they are convinced that a service provider has not treated them fairly (cf. Casidy et al. 2021). Furthermore, Confucian-Buddhist socialized customers (= Chinese) tend to engage in private responses (i.e., they prefer to talk about a negative experience in their private environment). Christian-Protestant customers (= Americans), however, tend toward voice responses and usually complain directly to the provider (Chan/Wan 2008).

4.1.4 *Switching service providers*

Customers switch service providers, products or brands for a variety of reasons: mainly due to dissatisfaction with the quality of the current offering or in view of more favorable competitive offers (e.g., price advantage, better accessibility, friendlier employees). But curiosity and a need for variety are also important triggers of declining customer loyalty (see Kocas/Bohlmann 2008). For the previous provider, changers cause a loss of sales and, if the customer talks badly about the company damages its reputation. For the new provider, however, they are often particularly valuable customers as they usually have above-average customer satisfaction, customer loyalty, willingness to pay and increased cross-selling potential (cf. Ganesh et al. 2000).

How does religiosity influence the willingness to switch? It is well known that religious people are risk-averse and value security and predictability more than others, which is why they should prefer products and businesses that are familiar to them. Numerous studies confirm this: Religious customers are mostly loyal customers (e.g., Muslim customers of an Islamic bank (see Wahyoedi et al. 2021)). More than ten years earlier, Choi (2010) used the example of Korean consumers to show that very religious people are less willing to switch than the less and non-religious, irrespective of religious affiliation (Buddhism, Catholicism and Protestantism).

For loyalty management, this means that service providers should pay particular attention to consumers who are not very religious and those who are. Customer loyalty programs (for a service provider's own customers) and attempts to poach outside customers (e.g., switching bonus) promise more success with less religious consumers than with very religious consumers.

4.1.5 Forgiveness

The Old Testament "eye for an eye, tooth for a tooth" is often misinterpreted as a call for or justification of revenge. In fact, however, it is a guide to how victims of crime are to be justly compensated. Analysis of religious scripture shows that all major world religions promote forgiveness as an important virtue (cf. Hyodo/Bolton 2021, p. 809; McCullough et al. 2005):

- "If a person forgives and makes reconciliation, his reward is due from Allah." – Qur'an 42:40 (Islam)
- "Forgiveness subdues (all) in this world; what is there that forgiveness cannot achieve?" – Mahabharata, Udyoga Parva Section XXXIII (Hinduism).
- "And forgive us our trespasses, as we forgive those who trespass against us." – Matthew 6:12–14 (Christianity)

Are religious people therefore more willing than average to forgive others in cases of conflict (cf. Escher 2013)? At any rate, this corresponds to their self-image (cf. Barnes/Brown 2010). However, this can only be partially proven empirically:

- Harrison-Walker (2019) and Mullet et al. (2003), among others, report on increased compliance and conciliation. Among other things, the relatively low tendency of religious people to act out their anger in conflict situations is responsible for this (cf. McCullough/Worthington 1999).
- Others recognize a systematic discrepancy between the official doctrine of the religion to which the respondents belong and their willingness to actually forgive others (cf. Tsang et al. 2005).

It is undisputed, however, that religiosity is better able to explain the willingness to forgive than religious affiliation (cf. Fox/Thomas 2008). This is especially surprising in the case of Christianity. That is because the forgiveness of sins is essential for the Christian faith. Thus we encounter the, "And forgive us our debts, as we have forgiven those of our debtors" (Matthew 6:12), in a slightly modified form in the Lord's Prayer. Catholics also confess, "I believe in the Holy Spirit, the holy Catholic Church, communion of saints, forgiveness of sins, resurrection of the dead and eternal life. Amen."[45]

However, the experimental design has not accounted for important mediators and moderators, such as:

- Severity of the service failure: It is easier to forgive minor failures.
- Fairness norm: If religious people gain the impression that a service provider is acting unfairly, their willingness to forgive this provider diminishes (cf. Casidy et al. 2021).
- Belief in fate: Belief in fate mediates the relationship between religiosity and forgiveness. Religiosity corresponded with belief in fate in the study

by Sarofim et al. (2022). This in turn promoted the willingness to forgive the provider of a defective service, which ultimately increased satisfaction. In addition, this study was able to rule out the possibility that interpersonal justice moderates the mediation model (religiosity → belief in fate → forgiveness → emotional well-being).
- Visibility of religiosity: Service failures are more easily forgiven if the provider is perceived as religious. In the case described by Cowart et al. (2014), the critical event was a service interruption during a religious holiday. As expected, religious customers reacted relatively leniently to this, but surprisingly agnostics and non-religious people did as well.

Hyodo/Bolton (2021) examined how salience or cognitive-emotional availability of religious values influences willingness to forgive in the face of a service failure. Salience was primed in this study using sentence-construction tasks. Specifically, this meant that the experimental group had to insert terms such as "divine, heaven, or religion" into the sentence to be re-constructed (scrambled sentence) and the control group had to insert neutral terms. Furthermore, as described by the researchers, corporate reparation measures can also be understood as an admission of guilt and a request for forgiveness, just as Catholics can obtain forgiveness when they confess their sins during a confession.[46] Based on this, they tested the following research hypothesis:

- Consumers for whom religion is made salient will be especially likely to forgive a service failure when it is accompanied by strong recovery efforts.
- An apology from the service provider provides a stronger trigger of religion-driven forgiveness than does monetary compensation (Hyodo/Bolton 2021).

These hypotheses could be supported by a series of eight experiments. It remains to be explained why an apology moderates the willingness to forgive more strongly than monetary compensation. After all, monetary compensation is generally considered to be the most effective instrument of complaint handling (cf. Gelbrich/Roschk 2011). Hyodo/Bolton (2021, p. 810) cited two reasons for the superiority of an apology in the present case:

- Forgiveness requires empathy, which is better expressed with an apology than with material compensation (cf. Ohtsubo/Watanabe 2009).
- In a materialistic context, monetary compensation signals that the perpetrator of the harm is serious about making amends. However, given the ambivalent relationship of most religions to money and possessions, compensation in a religious context loses this special quality (cf. Watson et al. 2004).

So can companies achieve more with a free apology than with paid compensation if they embed themselves and their activities in a religious context? On the surface, yes. However, if complainants suspect or recognize that they are being manipulated in this way, there is a risk of a boomerang effect. Then the company's attempt to influence them achieves the opposite of what it actually intended (cf. Hyodo/Bolton 2021, p. 821). Forgiveness is a multidimensional construct: on the one hand, it is a psychological event (= emotional forgiveness), and on the other it is a social event primarily intended to enable the persons affected to interact constructively in the future (= forgiving behavior). According to Tsarenko/Tojib (2012), religious people practice both forms of forgiveness, not only in interpersonal relationships but also in their role as consumers.

Contrary to expectations and in contrast to religiosity, spirituality does not strengthen consumers' willingness to forgive, which in retrospect can be explained in two ways:

- First, spirituality is egocentric in that it is inwardly focused and primarily serves personal growth. Forgiveness, however, aims at stabilizing interpersonal relationships.
- Second, however, the decisive reason may be the youth of the student participants, an age when individual spiritual development is still at its very beginning.

However, if consumers get the impression that the service failure is particularly serious, this reduces their willingness to forgive the service provider emotionally. Emotional intelligence moderates this relationship. Emotionally intelligent customers are therefore less influenced by the severity of the service failure. They have the ability to regulate their emotions and are apparently not at the mercy of their negative feelings toward the service provider but are able to put aside their anger or rage in search of a modus vivendi: an acceptable and ultimately beneficial form of continuation of the interaction for all parties involved. Customers who consider the service failure to be serious and have no intention of forgiving the service provider tend to break off the relationship (intention to change). Companies whose customers are not prepared to forgive emotionally or to behave in a forgiving manner must reckon with negative WoM.

4.2 Complaint management by companies

Ideally, companies avoid service errors. However, due to the special features of services (e.g., limited standardization, integration of the customer into the service process), this is an ideal to be strived for continuously but never to be fully achieved. More realistic are strategies and measures that increase customer resilience. Among other things, this inoculation strategy can cause them to react less sensitively to service failures. Customers who have been warned in advance about possible defects experience them as less serious than customers who have not received a warning (see Mikolon et al. 2015).

Furthermore, good human relations between employees and customers have proven to be an effective buffer (cf. Worsfold et al. 2007). Last but not least, religious symbols (e.g., a cross displayed at the place of service) have a calming effect, and not only on religious customers (cf. Mikolon et al. 2015).

As a rule, however, service failures occur and are then complained about by customers in at least one third of cases. In this case, service providers have three main options for dealing with them constructively: They can:

- Explain to the complainants how the failure could have occurred
- Apologize to them
- Offer compensation to those affected

4.2.1 *Explanation*

Obviously, the first step is often to try to explain to the complainant how the service failure could have occurred. After all, it is one of the universal needs of people to look for causes for unusual events. But are such explanations also important to customers affected by a service failure?

In contrast to comparative cultural research, comparative religion research has not yet addressed this issue. Mattila/Patterson (2004), for example, empirically demonstrated that customers of different nationalities valued this form of complaint handling equally. Whether Americans, Malaysian or Thai nationals, they all found it relieving to understand why the service failure occurred. For Malaysians and Thais, moreover, the explanation paradoxically led them to feel particularly well compensated (Distributive Justice) and treated (Interactional Justice). The team of authors explained this effect with the culturally typical striving for harmony.

4.2.2 *Apology*

Although it is undisputed how effective apologies can be, most customers who experience a service failure wait in vain for them. The reasons are different attributions of responsibility, unwillingness to apologize for the mistakes of other employees, inability or unwillingness to show feelings and lack of empathy. More than elsewhere, Confucian customers resent it if the company does not apologize for the mistake. This is because in their countries of origin, apologies play a key role in avoiding conflict (cf. Barnes 2007), not least in the judiciary and the administration of justice (cf. Lee 2005). There, apologies are an expression of fair interpersonal interactions and indispensable for preserving or restoring face (cf. Wong 2004).

4.2.3 *Compensation*

The most effective instrument of service recovery management is compensation, usually in the form of a replacement offer, a voucher, a discount or, in extreme cases, a refund of the purchase price (see Gelbrich/Roschk 2011). Individualists such as Americans or Australians attach even more importance to material compensation of the damage caused to them than do complainants who come from collectivist countries, such as China (cf. Hui/Au 2001). This can be explained by the pronounced goal orientation of Christian individualistically socialized people. In their view, complaints should lead to a concrete result and, if possible, to material reparation. Like all forms of compensation, material compensation increases the perception of justice of individualists, while for collectivists the transaction climate is more important.

Mattila/Patterson (2004) reached a similar conclusion. They were able to show experimentally that the material compensation of a service failure appeases American customers more than Thai or Malaysian customers. Different expectations regarding the type and intensity of reparation could be ruled out as a possible explanation. Rather, different self-concepts are likely to be the decisive factor. Whereas Americans strive for individual benefit maximization on the basis of their independent self-construal, the interdependent self-construal predominates in Asia. It focuses on mutual social obligations. This has cultural-religious reasons. People who grew up in the Chinese tradition believe in "Pao": Whether someone is blessed or cursed depends on his good and bad deeds; an intervention by others cannot change this (cf. Chiu 1991). Thais, however, are influenced by Buddhism and believe that sacrifices and good deeds benefit people in their next life (cf. Mattila/Patterson 2004).

4.3 Customer reactions to complaint management

Whether the redress measures that companies take have the desired effect depends first of all on the expectations that customers have in this regard and whether they perceive these measures as fair (cf. Abd Rashid et al. 2022). This ultimately results in emotional reactions (e.g., anger), cognitive reactions (extent of complaint satisfaction) and behavioral reactions (likelihood of repurchase, WoM).

4.3.1 Expectations

What do customers expect from the company responsible for a service failure? Based on the insights gained in semi-structured in-depth interviews, Ringberg et al. (2007) described three "expectation types":

- Relationship-oriented people hope for an improvement in the relationship with the service provider. They react very emotionally, ultimately want to be comforted and are willing to forgive the provider and tolerate weaknesses. With these customers, a credible apology promises success.
- Opponents are suspicious, react angrily and are sometimes distant, sometimes aggressive. It is more important to them to publicly reproach the

service provider than to forgive it. The chances of success of complaint management are relatively low. Still, a combination of apology and compensation may work.

- Utilitarians rationally weigh the advantages and disadvantages of the various options for action. They react pragmatically and expect a significant compensation for the damage suffered.

It can be assumed that religious norms and beliefs also influence complainants' expectations of corporate complaint management. However, comparative religion research has not yet analyzed this connection. However, it seems indisputable that national culture plays a role (cf. Ringberg et al. 2007). Customers from individualistic societies (e.g., Australia, US) expect that the employees of the company responsible for the service failure have a sufficiently large scope for decision-making for reparation measures. Customers from collectivist societies (e.g., Panama, Venezuela) attach particular importance to a credible explanation of how the service failure could have occurred. In masculine societies (e.g., Japan, Austria), a convincing explanation is equally important. In addition, customers there expect appropriate external circumstances (e.g., respectable appearance of employees and business premises). This is also important in long-term-oriented societies (see Kanousi 2005).

Whether complainants are satisfied with the company's response depends not only on their expectations, however, but above all on how they experience the complaint management process (in terms of the length of time they have to wait, the way they are dealt with and the outcome of complaint handling). Is the amount of compensation offered experienced as fair or unfair (cf. Grönroos 1988)? What is perceived as:

- Interactional justice, when the way the company treats their complaint seems fair and humane to the complainants.
- Procedural justice if the entire process of complaint handling appears transparent and comprehensible to them.
- Distributive justice, if the compensation offered by the company is, from the complainant's point of view, in reasonable proportion to the damage suffered.

4.3.2 *Complaint satisfaction*

According to Matikiti et al. (2018), all three forms of perceived justice promote complaint satisfaction. La/Choi (2019) and Jha/Balaji (2015), for example, argue similarly. On the one hand, this seems theoretically plausible, but on the other hand, it was also to be expected due to the high intercorrelation between these constructs. In the study by Abd Rashid et al. (2022), for example, the correlation coefficients varied between 0.526 and 0.681 (with a sample size of 338 Muslim participants). Surprisingly, no influence of religiosity on the correlation between "type of complaint handling" and "complaint satisfaction" could be found in this study.

Hyodo/Bolton (2021), however, formulated a different assessment with regard to the consequences of distributive justice. According to their analyses, customers are more satisfied with a material reparation of service deficiencies if their religious beliefs have been updated through priming and have thus become conscious to them. Companies can support this effect by being obviously penitent.[47] The "ashes on my head" strategy triggers the willingness of religious customers to forgive the "sinner."

After successful service recovery, complainants are sometimes even more satisfied than customers who had no reason to complain (cf. de Matos et al. 2007). This complaint paradox can be explained by the fact that a successful complaint strengthens the complainant's self-esteem. However, this effect only occurs if the service failure is not serious and the service provider's efforts to make amends are considerable (cf. McCollough 2009).

To our knowledge, there are no specific studies on the role of religious affiliation and religiosity in the development of the complaint paradox. However, we can assume that religious people are particularly susceptible to this phenomenon. This is because the complaint paradox is based on the satisfaction customers feel when they have prevailed against an apparently overpowering service provider. This is particularly important to people with a pronounced control orientation. They are fundamentally convinced that they can achieve something through their actions. Religions that offer believers the prospect of being rewarded for a virtuous life after death promote this form of self-control (cf. Vitell et al. 2009, p. 605). Monotheistic religions also provide believers with a large number of concrete rules of conduct (cf. Carter et al. 2012a; Geyer/Baumeister 2005). Therefore, it seems plausible to assume that religious people are control-oriented and tend to self-regulate (cf. Carver/Scheier 2012; McCullough/Willoughby 2009). If this is true, religious people would likely feel particularly good if their complaint was successful. This proposition awaits empirical investigation.

Part VII

Pricing policy

1 Attitudes toward money and possessions

"Thou shalt not covet thy neighbor's goods and chattels." These and other warnings or prohibitions are found in the scriptures of all world religions. However, even they cannot overlook the fact that money and possessions are important motivators of human behavior.

1.1 Statements of the religious scriptures

In Hinduism, prosperity is considered a favor of the gods (cf. Lindrige 2005). Manu Smriti (ch. 3, verse 40) states that material prosperity is a component of a good life but subordinate to spiritual prosperity (ch. 3, verse 66). Hindus should provide for hard times and save (ch. 7, verse 213) as well as honor the gods and the deceased with diverse offerings (ch. 4, verse 226).

One of the basic principles of Buddhism is change. Everything is subject to the cycle of birth, death and rebirth (samsara). As a consequence of this worldview, material possessions are considered subordinate to mental possessions. Desires and striving for material wealth are considered to cause suffering (cf. Choi 2010, p. 159).

In Confucianism, the cult of ancestors and family obliges the individual to care for his or her ancestors, the children and for himself or herself. The thriftiness that is particularly pronounced in these societies is not primarily based on economic rationality but on social considerations: the obligation to provide for the (extended) family.

Islam forbids trying to get something for which one has not worked hard (Maisir). Following this logic, it is also not correct to raise the price without increasing the quality or quantity of the supply accordingly (cf. Saeed et al. 2001, p. 138). Wealth is a gift from God and should not be sought through unfair practices. This includes all measures by which prices are artificially inflated. However, price increases are permissible when there is a natural scarcity.

1.2 Findings of empirical research

Most commonly, attitudes toward money and possessions are operationalized as "Love of Money" (LoM). Some researchers also use individual

DOI: 10.4324/9781003506010-34

items from the World Values Survey (WVS) or the European Values Study for this purpose.

1.2.1 Love of money

Money plays a key role in the life of modern societies (e.g., as a neutral unit of account for the efficient exchange of a wide variety of services or as an emotionally conditioned driving force of social life (motivator, measure of success, symbol of freedom and power, etc.)). The attitude toward money was operationalized as a three- or four-dimensional construct LoM with items such as:

- "Money is a symbol of my success" (success).
- "I am highly motivated by money" (motivator).
- "I want to be rich" (rich).
- "Money is an important factor in the lives of all of us" (importance).

Are people with this LoM attitude, for example, more satisfied with their lives than people for whom money and possessions are less important? Not according to Hoetoro (2020), who surveyed 99 younger, educated Muslims. On the contrary, they found that LoM had a negative, albeit non-significant, influence on participants' life satisfaction (ß = –0.127). The satisfaction of employees with their remuneration also suffers from this attitude (cf. Tang/Chiu 2003). Moreover, it is empirically well established that LoM promotes the acceptance or probability of unethical behavior, such as tax avoidance or the willingness to steal intellectual property (cf. Walker et al. 2012; Vitell et al. 2007; 2006).

1.2.2 Materialistic lifestyle

Should people place less emphasis on money and material possessions in the future? The answer to this question depends, among other things, on the religious affiliation of the respondents. As an analysis of WVS data (fourth wave) revealed, more than 60% of Protestants and almost three quarters of Jews, but only a good third of the Russian Orthodox respondents, favor a less materialistic lifestyle (see Figure 21).

Using a combination of field and laboratory experiments, Kurt et al. (2018) demonstrated a relationship between frugality and the intensity of religious beliefs (see also Price et al. 2015). In the U.S., a religiously diverse country, religious customers spent significantly less in grocery stores than less religious comparison consumers. Apart from the general tendency toward a modest lifestyle already mentioned, two special features of religious consumers are responsible for this: They are relatively less susceptible to impulse buying and spend less time shopping. This is also supported by the fact that

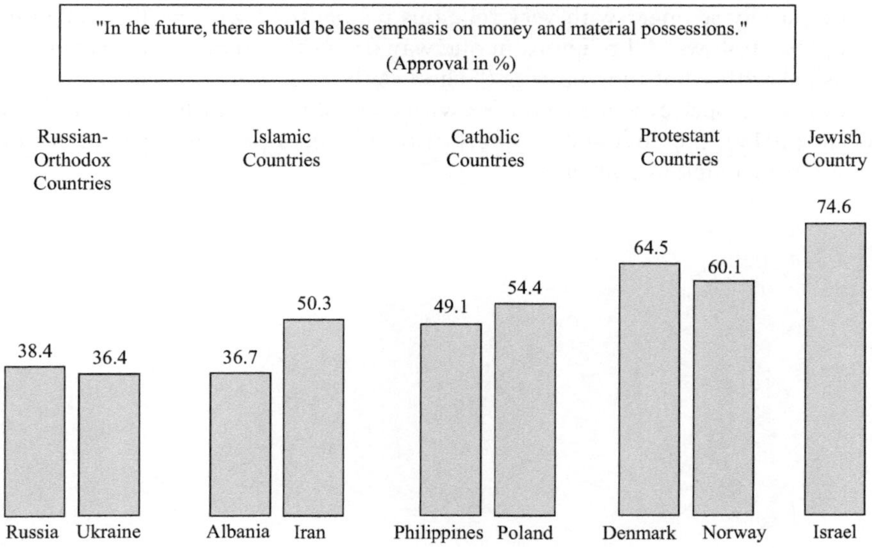

Figure 21 Materialism in selected countries.
Source: EVS-Group, WVS-Association (1999–2004).

they do not tend to go into debt to finance their consumption or make greater efforts to pay off existing debts. Moraru (2012) found similar findings when comparing young Muslims with young Christians (predominantly Evangelical Lutherans).

1.3 Endowment effect

It is well known that the subjective value of an object often does not correspond to its objective, monetary value. Enthusiasts of classic cars, for example, sometimes pay sums of money even for extremely battered older cars that others just shake their heads over. Within this field of research, the endowment effect describes the systematic divergence between the price expectations of buyers and sellers. Those who own a good regularly perceive it to be worth more than those who do not own it (cf. Knetsch/Sinden 1984). This phenomenon is explained:

- Economically as generalized loss aversion (cf. Kahneman et al. 1991).
- Psychologically as consequence of the integration of possession into the extended ego of the owner (cf. Morewedge 2009).

Qin et al. (2017) have empirically investigated the connection between religiosity and the endowment effect. They explain the fact that this phenomenon is essentially stronger with very religious people than with weakly religious people as follows: All religions in one way or another require believers to be satisfied with what they possess ("Thou shalt not covet thy neighbor's…"). This gives a special value to one's own possessions. According to Shtudiner et al. (2019), the endowment effect also influences pricing behavior in the market for religious souvenirs.

2 Price fairness

Given that buyers and sellers no longer exchange goods for goods, but goods for means of payment, the question arises as to what is "right and cheap." The concept of price fairness, however, does not primarily focus on "cheap" (which is primarily captured by the construct of price satisfaction) but on "fair." Does the consumer perceive the provider's pricing behavior as fair – fair in terms of both the procedure and the outcome of pricing?

2.1 Fair price

The discussion about the just price is one of the classics of the sociology of religion. In the Middle Ages, this construct was initially intended to protect the seller. In principle, freedom of contract applied in the application of Roman law. However, if the buyer had bargained the seller "more than half below the fair price," the seller could either withdraw from the contract or claim damages. Later, the construct of the just price was also applied to protect the buyer, although less decisively than to protect the seller.

But what do people living today think of the way in which prices are now formed? How fair does it seem to them? Starting from these questions, de Noble et al. (2007) investigated whether there is a noteworthy relationship between religiosity and attitudes toward price formation. As their survey of American business students revealed, intrinsic religiosity correlates with rather skeptical attitudes toward the fairness of price setting by the market.

According to a survey of restaurant visitors in Bangladesh (cf. Ahmed et al. 2023), perceived price fairness promotes customer satisfaction to a comparable extent ($ß = 0.376$) as does perceived service quality ($ß = 0.326$). More important for companies, however, are the effects on customer loyalty. Customer loyalty benefits significantly more from fair pricing ($ß = 0.202$) than from service quality ($ß = 0.326$) ($p = 0.051$). The extremely plausible thesis that religious customers are particularly sensitive to fairness and unfairness has been neglected by comparative religion research. Sayuti/Amin (2019) are among the exceptions. According to their analyses, perceived price fairness promotes the demand of Muslim bank customers for financial products of an Islamic bank in Malaysia.

DOI: 10.4324/9781003506010-35

2.2 Fairness signaling

Due to the systematic asymmetry of information between suppliers and customers, customers are usually unable to reliably judge whether a price is fair. In this case, the only option is to infer fairness from the supplier's behavior or other signals. Suppliers can express their price fairness by means of price guarantees, for example: The promise that customers may withdraw from the purchase or have the difference paid out if they can prove that a competitor's price is cheaper.

Another increasingly popular means of signaling price fairness and trustworthiness are seals or certificates (e.g., sustainability seals) (cf. Hamilton/Zilberman 2006). In order to prevent opportunistic suppliers from taking advantage of the special situation in the market for "pure goods" to demand disproportionately high prices, halal and kosher seals of approval have been established which are awarded by neutral institutions (third-party certification; cf. Starobin/Weinthal 2010). These markets are special because religious regulations have to be observed in the production and distribution of pure foods and other goods, which cause additional costs. Added to this is the disadvantage of production for the rather small market of strictly religious consumers (costs of small scale).

3 Price consciousness

Gabor/Granger (1961) introduced this construct into the scientific literature. By price consciousness, they are referring to "the extent to which housewives are conscious of the price of an article at the time of its purchase." However, since this "pre-feminist" definition proved to be too general for empirical research, price consciousness is mostly split into price interest, price orientation and price sensitivity in the more recent literature.

3.1 One-dimensional operationalization

The construct in its previous form found its way into some comparative religion studies. Hirschman (1983), for example, described not only Protestants but above all Catholics as price-conscious. Mokhlis (2006a) found Muslims to have the strongest price consciousness ($\bar{x} = 3.74$) and Hindus the weakest ($\bar{x} = 3.45$).[48] For the Christian study participants, on the five-point Likert scale, they had a mean of 3.65, while the Buddhist study participants had a mean of 3.64. Based on these minor mean differences, the conclusion can only be that there are no significant differences in the price consciousness[49] of above-average educated Malaysian consumers of different religious affiliations. Here, too, the degree of religiosity makes a somewhat larger explanatory contribution (cf. Mokhlis 2009b): Very religious people are somewhat more price-conscious than moderately and weakly religious people ($\bar{x} = 3.94$ vs. 3.66 vs. 3.34).[50]

Sood/Nasu (1995) have studied very religious and moderately religious people in Japan (Buddhists and Shintos) and in the US (predominantly Protestants). The participants were first asked to imagine that they were buying a high-priced radio and then to evaluate 20 statements concerning various aspects of this fictitious purchase decision:

- Product selection (quality, brand name, etc.)
- Shopping place preference (assortment, price, etc.)
- Information gathering (media, friends' opinions, etc.)

Whereas religious beliefs did not significantly influence the purchase motives of Japanese consumers, Sood/Nasu (1995) were able to identify two effects

DOI: 10.4324/9781003506010-36

among American consumers. Compared with less religious consumers, very religious Protestants are the more rational and price-conscious consumers who specifically look for advantageous offers during sales and in low-price stores. They also doubt that higher prices guarantee good quality. One possible explanation is that the Protestant work ethics goes hand in hand with a preference for rational consumption.

Our own empirical study in Germany supports this finding. Very religious, predominantly Protestant young Germans were somewhat more price-conscious than less religious young Germans.

Usman et al. (2022) wanted to know how the price consciousness of Indonesian consumers affects their intention to buy halal-certified food. The results are generally negative; however, the effect is moderated by the intensity of the participants' religiosity. Thus, very religious price-conscious consumers tend to be less reluctant to buy halal products than moderately or weakly religious consumers with comparable levels of price consciousness.

In summary, very religious consumers are somewhat more price-conscious than those who are less religious. This may be due to the personality profile of religious people. They are considered disciplined and responsible, including in financial matters (cf. Wiebe/Fleck 1980). This is also supported by the pronounced willingness of religious households to save (see Renneboog/Spaenjers 2012).

3.2 Multidimensional operationalization

In the early phase of Interfaith Marketing (IFM), several researchers identified dimensions of buyer behavior using factor analysis. Some of these are also referred to as buyer types (cf. III-4). Important criteria for the formation of buyer types are the respondents' interest in price and their price orientation.

3.2.1 Price interest

Price interest is understood as the need of consumers to obtain price information before making a purchase decision. As the work of Bailey/Sood (1993, p. 342) shows, the "rational buyer" very consciously pays attention to the general price level of a store, always buys at the lowest possible price and therefore primarily purchases products on discount. The "informed buyer" actively seeks price information, and "practical buyers" value price negotiations, special price promotions and the opportunity to buy on credit.

According to this study, Catholics are among the less informed shoppers. Due to their tendency to be thrifty, they do pay attention to which special offers are available in which stores at which times. When it comes to more complex purchasing decisions, however, they are primarily guided by the views that prevail in their social reference groups. This is partly because social relationships and the opinions of other people are important to them, and partly because it is less important for them to form their own opinions. In addition, Muslims also pay attention to special offers and other price advantages when making purchasing decisions. However, their need to obtain intensive information before making a purchase decision is also rather low. In their case, this can be explained by a relatively fatalistic worldview and external locus of control. Accordingly, events are less dependent on the individual than on a higher power. Hindus are also said to have a below-average price interest. This is probably due to the relatively large distance of this religious community from the world of consumption.

The type of economic shopper identified and described by Essoo/Dibb (2004) is disproportionately common among religious people, especially Hindus and, to a certain extent, Muslims. Economically minded consumers pay close attention to the price of goods and systematically try to take advantage of special offers. Impulsive purchasing decisions are alien to them.

An indirect indicator of price interest is the importance of price bargaining in a society. While haggling is of relatively little importance in the Christian cultural sphere, it fulfills an important social function in all relationship-oriented collectivist societies. This applies, for example, to all Arab countries, where buyer and seller enter into a personal relationship during a price negotiation, on which the business relationship is then built.

3.2.2 Price orientation

This construct captures the importance attached to the price of a product in purchasing and consumption decisions. Special attention is paid to price-oriented quality assessment. Since buyers are often unable to adequately assess the quality of an offered service or can do so only with great effort, many infer quality from price. This is because the price/quality heuristic offers consumers the invaluable advantage that price information is easily accessible and can be judged supposedly objectively.

This thesis has not yet been explicitly investigated by comparative religion research. Based on the study by Mokhlis (2006b), one can only assume that very religious people assume a close connection between price and quality, provided that the consumers are high in intrapersonal religiosity. This is because they attach great importance to the quality of an offer and less to its price.

The "economic shopper" (cf. Essoo/Dibb 2004; Sood/Nasu 1995) is found with above-average frequency among religious consumers. When making purchasing decisions, they pay attention first and foremost to price. It is important for them to systematically take advantage of special offers, for example, by planning their purchases accordingly. As such, they do not tend to make impulsive purchasing decisions.

So far, only Davis/Jai (2014) have investigated the influence of religiosity on price orientation. In their online survey, religious American students (n = 333) identified themselves as above-average price-conscious buyers of clothing. They agreed with the following statements to a significantly greater extent than their less religious peers:

- "I buy as much as possible at sale prices."
- "The lower price products are usually my choice."
- "I look carefully to find the best value for the money."

3.2.3 Price sensitivity

The concept of price sensitivity is similar to that of price elasticity. Both indicate the extent to which consumers react to a price change and compare prices before making a purchase decision. Price sensitivity is moderated by various factors. Not surprisingly, low-income consumers are more price-sensitive than high-income consumers.

To the best of our knowledge, comparative religion research has largely ignored this topic. We have found only one conceptual contribution, which is largely inadequate (see Abd Aziz et al. 2015). In addition, Islam/Chandrasekaran (2016) also indicate that very religious people are somewhat more price-sensitive than others. And for non-profit organizations, previous research has shown that donors are less price-sensitive if the appeal for donations has a religious background (cf. Gruber 2004).

Indirectly, a positive relationship between Confucianism and price sensitivity can be inferred from the study done by Lee et al. (2020). Admittedly, these researchers investigated the influence of acceptance of power distance[51] on price sensitivity. But in China, Korea, Vietnam and other countries where the teachings of Confucius have permanently shaped sociocultural life, acceptance of power distance is among the cultural standards. Therefore, the assumption Confucianism > Price Sensitivity seems plausible, especially since it can also be theoretically justified. Consumers who accept more power distance due to their Confucianism are less price-sensitive, because their "need for closure" motivates them to complete an action as quickly as possible. When making a purchase decision, the search for the most advantageous price would be hindering.

4 Willingness to pay

Willingness to pay is the fundamental intention of consumers to pay at least or at most a certain amount for a product or service. In the behavioral models of marketing research, willingness to pay is often used as the outcome variable of study. And companies want to know whether their target market not only accepts a product innovation or product modification[52] at the introductory level but is also willing to pay an appropriate price for it. Various moderators must be taken into account in the corresponding analyses:

- Socioeconomic variables (e.g., disposable income)
- Psychographic variables (e.g., frugality, lifestyle)
- Product type (e.g., socially responsible products)
- Marketing measures (e.g., branding)

Furthermore, the type of business activity plays a role. Even if the profit motive is generally accepted, companies that position themselves as being oriented toward the common good or are associated in one way or another with "religion" or "health" must expect that many consumers will not appreciate it if they use the usual marketing strategies (e.g., optimizing the price appearance[53] in order to be able to charge the highest possible price (cf. McGraw et al. 2012)).

4.1 Influence of product origin

Their personality profile (e.g., conservative, ethnocentric) predisposes religious people to reject imported products and prefer local, preferably regional, products (see V-3.7). The region of origin effect is moderated, among other things, by the age and educational level of consumers. Thus, the preference for regional products increases with age (cf. Pícha/Skořepa 2018).

But does this preference also increase the willingness to pay for regional products? Yes, to a certain extent, as our own empirical study shows. A total of 100 young people from Germany (50 not very religious and 50 very religious) were surveyed. According to their self-assessment, very

DOI: 10.4324/9781003506010-37

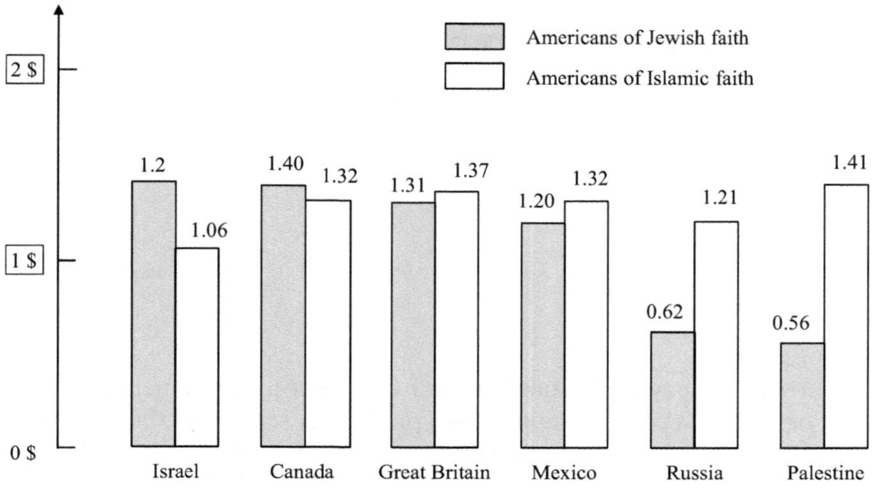

Figure 22 Willingness to pay as a function of religious affiliation.
Source: Own representation based on Byrne et al. (2021, p. 27).

religious consumers would pay an average of 14.3% more for a product from the region, while moderately religious people considered a surcharge of only 6.3% acceptable. Heiman/Just (2021) observed something similar. On average, the 442 Israelis they surveyed self-reported that they would be willing to pay up to 15% more for locally produced fruits and vegetables than for produce from other countries. The more religious the participants were, the greater their expressed willingness to pay.

Last but not least, the price consumers would pay may also depend on their religious affiliation. Byrne et al. (2021) asked the American participants in their online survey what they would pay for a kilo of qualitatively equivalent grapes from six foreign growing regions if American grapes cost $2.00. The averaged data reveal a clear country-of-origin effect which can be broken down into region of origin and country of origin. The averaged data (see Figure 22) reveal a clear Country of Origin effect, which can be divided into a:

- Home bias:[54] The participants would be willing to pay considerably more for domestic grapes than for foreign products, despite their qualitative equivalence.
- Animosity effect (cf. V-3.7): Willingness to pay is particularly low for grapes originating from enemy countries. For Americans of the Jewish faith, these are "Palestinian grapes" and for Americans of the Islamic faith these are "Jewish grapes." "Russian grapes" play a special role. Given the traditional rivalry between Russia and the U.S., the overall sample (n = 10,049) would want to pay the least for them. Muslim-Americans are

excluded from this because they perceive Russia as an ally in the Palestinian conflict.

The region-of-origin and country-of-origin effects are probably caused by the religious people's sense of community and, in connection with this, by their desire to support companies based in the region and their employees through their purchasing behavior. In fact, in the study by Byrne et al. (2021), in addition to the economic patriotism mentioned here, general patriotism, nationalism and xenophobia correlated negatively with willingness to pay, all of which are typical characteristics of very religious people in particular. They thus lack what is indispensable for the purchase of imported goods: cultural openness.

4.2 Influence of brands

The central role that branding plays for companies and thus also for marketing has already been discussed in more detail in the context of product policy (see V-4). In the following, we will discuss basic forms of branding: secular and religious branding.

4.2.1 Secular brands

The willingness of consumers to pay more for a branded product than for comparable competing products is a measure of brand strength (see V-4). Quality- and status-conscious consumers in particular are generally prepared to do this. This is more common among Catholics. As a survey of 154 German consumers showed, Catholics are more receptive than Protestants to the promise of quality and prestige of branded goods and are also prepared to pay a price premium for them (see Table 18).

However, this does not apply to spiritually oriented consumers. They are not prepared to pay the usual extra price for conspicuously consumed products (e.g., smart phones) (see Stillman et al. 2012).

Table 18 Willingness to pay more depending on religious affiliation

Willingness to pay more	*Catholics*	*Protestants*	*P*
I would prefer a brand that meets my requirements over others, even if it is more expensive.	1.30	0.78	0.03
I would pay a higher price for a brand that meets my requirements.	1.27	0.80	0.07
A brand that meets my requirements can also cost more.	1.14	0.63	0.05

Note: Mean values on a scale from –3 "strongly disagree" to +3 "strongly agree," results of a t-test (n = 154).

Source: Own survey (2007).

4.2.2 *Religious brands*

The various halal and kosher certificates can be seen as a religious form of labeling. Indeed, they are referred to as "faith labels." In principle, most Muslims accept a higher price for certified products, especially for halal food. According to Verbeke et al. (2013), Belgian Muslims would be willing to pay up to 13% more for certified meat in an Islamic butcher shop than in a supermarket. A positive attitude toward halal labels and a decidedly religious self-image are conducive to this effect (cf. Iranmanesh et al. 2019).

Muslims who are aware that it is not enough if only the product is halal (e.g., "Halal logistics is important to prevent contamination during transportation") would, by their own admission, also pay an appropriate price for halal logistics and increasingly demand appropriately certified services (cf. Fathi et al. 2016). In the case of halal transportation services, religiosity moderates the relationship between relevant knowledge and willingness to pay. According to self-reports, religious Muslims who are well-acquainted with the goals and background of halal certification would pay significantly more for appropriately marked transport services than less religious and rather ignorant peers (cf. Ngah et al. 2021).

Others have investigated whether and in what way the knowledge that a provider belongs to the same religious community as oneself influences willingness to pay. According to Siala (2013), there is a positive but non-significant correlation ($r = 0.131$ and 0.164, respectively) between the religiosity of consumers or their religious centrism[55] and their willingness to pay a price premium for car insurance.

4.3 Influence of social and environmental certificates

Probably all religions and religious communities demand fairness and caring from believers (e.g., toward disadvantaged population groups or nature (cf. Williams/Zinkin 2010; Saroglou et al. 2005)). Consequently, religious people should be more willing to pay a fair price for environmentally friendly or socially acceptable services. Surveys generally confirm this, provided that only the attitude toward this issue or the behavioral intention is measured. At the behavioral level (i.e., actual price acceptance), however, this correlation cannot be proven in many cases. This can be explained on the one hand by the fact that in surveys, people do not always state what they actually think or do, but what they consider desirable. And it is possible that this bias has a particular influence on religious consumers' self-reports in studies because responsible behavior promises more social recognition than self-interested behavior, especially for religious people. However, it may also be that religiosity does not favor prosocial behavior in general, but only under certain conditions (cf. Preston et al. 2010) (e.g., in a context that activates religious beliefs (cf. VII-4.3.2)).

4.3.1 *Individual purchasing behavior*

Trudel/Cote (2009) asked their American respondents how much they would pay for a pound of premium coffee. Among other things, they also received information about the production conditions. Under the condition "normal production," the respondents named a mean price per pound of $8.31, while they wanted to pay $9.81 for fairly produced coffee and only $5.89 for unfairly produced coffee. According to the current state of knowledge, companies can promote consumers' willingness to accept an appropriate price premium for fair trade products in three ways:

- Reputation: People who are convinced that the supplier always acts ethically and takes the well-being of society into account consider a much higher price premium acceptable than skeptical individuals (cf. Trudel/Cote 2009).
- Knowledge: Those who are aware of the goals of the fair trade movement develop an above-average positive attitude toward it and accept higher prices (cf. de Pelsmacker/Janssens 2007).
- Customer values: People who care about protecting the environment also accept a higher price level (cf. Doran 2009).

But how do religious consumers react in such a case? Is fair trade a "Christian mission" (cf. Sugden 2001)? Is it a way to follow divine commandments (justice, care, etc.) even as a consumer, to assure oneself of one's own religious identity and to demonstrate it to others (cf. Reinstein/Song 2012)? On the basis of our own findings, this question can be answered in the affirmative, even though we did not ask specifically about fair trade coffee, but about fair trade products in general (see Figure 23). The price premium accepted by the religious participants (+24.7%) is significantly higher than the +11% calculated by Trudel/Cote (2009) for the general population.

Overall, however, the findings of the relevant research vary widely depending on how religious beliefs have been operationalized (e.g., Hwang 2018;

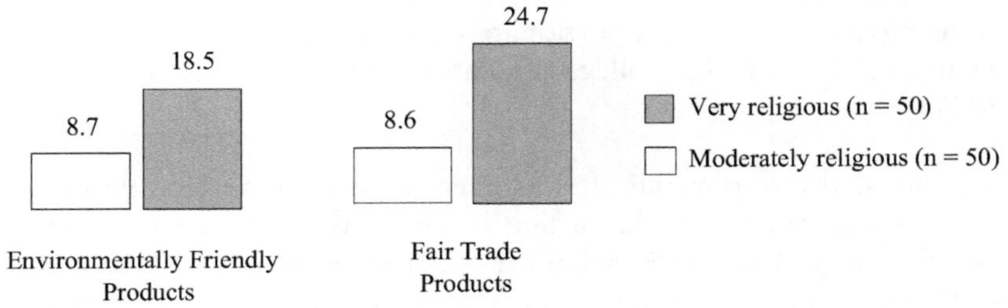

Figure 23 Percentage willingness to pay more as a function of product benefit.

Source: Own survey (2011).

Doran/Natale 2011; Dietz et al. 1998). In addition, the effect sizes found are small in many cases (e.g., Pepper et al. 2011). Also, these studies are usually based on participants' self-assessments. Due to the widespread tendency to give socially desirable responses, the frequency or level of prosocial behavior is usually systematically overestimated (cf. Andorfer/Liebe 2012).

The connection between religious affiliation and willingness to buy fair trade products despite a higher price level is also less clear-cut than many may expect. For example, the fair trade movement is rooted in the religiously motivated Christian charity movement. But in a survey by Doran/Natale (2011), Catholics and Protestants reported lower purchase intentions than non-religious or atheist respondents. Buddhists and Hindus were the most open-minded.

Suppliers who want to know how best to persuade customers to pay a higher price for fair trade products can take four recommendations from the relevant research:

- Moral appeals ("It is right to...") increase willingness to pay for fair trade products more than justice appeals ("It is fair to..."),[56] and this is independent of consumers' religious affiliation and religiosity (cf. Minton et al. 2018b).
- Increasing knowledge about fair trade is another key. According to Kapusuz/Kimzan (2016), among younger, predominantly male Turkish Muslims, this can increase trust in the fair trade sector and ultimately the willingness to pay a higher price for fair trade products (mediation effect).
- Another possibility is to communicate how fair trade provides more justice, at least in the economic sphere (e.g., through fair wages). With this message, companies can satisfy many consumers' needs for the world to be a just place and thus increase the willingness to pay an appropriate price for fair trade products. This thesis is based on the theory of a just world (cf. White et al. 2012).
- Finally, it is advisable to strengthen customers' perceived self-efficacy by communicating that they make a tangible contribution to the big picture with their individual purchasing decisions. It is possible that religious consumers are particularly receptive to this message. For example, religious Egyptians are disproportionately convinced of their self-efficacy, as a survey of 702 Muslim college students revealed (cf. Abdel-Khalek/Lester 2017).[57]

It is also socially responsible if consumers base their purchasing decisions on environmental criteria. According to an analysis of relevant data from the South Korean General Social Survey (2014), religious South Koreans are more willing than non-religious comparative people to pay higher prices for "green products" and even to accept a reduction in their standard of living in return. The same applies to Protestant and Catholic South Koreans, in relation to Buddhist consumers. Hwang (2018) attributes this to the fact that

Buddhism, in contrast to Christian teachings, is a very self-referential religion without a deeper connection to communal goals.

In addition to religious beliefs, brand trust also influences the attitude toward green products and the willingness to buy them. In particular, the intrinsically religious among 300 Pakistani Muslim students expressed an increased willingness to buy when "green" was associated with a trustworthy brand (cf. Iftikhar et al. 2017).

4.3.2 *Organizational buying behavior*

As a result of five case studies, Bezençon/Blili (2009) reported that traditional distributors do increase the sales potential of fair trade products. However, by listing them (i.e., including them in their product range), these actors primarily pursue their own strategic goals (e.g., product differentiation, access to market niches, positioning as a responsible company). However, they contribute little to the dissemination of the ideas and ideals of the fair trade movement. Competently informing the mass of consumers about this and convincing them of these goals is still the task of the fair trade movement.

Salvador et al. (2014) were the first to investigate the factors that determine whether professional buyers from intermediaries accept the higher price level of fair trade products. The starting point of their considerations is the realization that people also have different social roles or identities in their working lives. These can be profane (e.g., "dutiful employee," "soccer fan") or religious (e.g., "practicing Catholic"). It is true that behavior at the workplace is primarily guided by mundane role expectations (e.g., "dutiful employee" > "only calls in sick when actually ill"). However, to the extent that religious cues are present in the work environment (e.g., religious symbols, colleagues who are visibly religious), religious role expectations gain influence. The more this happens, the more likely people are to behave according to the role expectations of their religion. The same applies to decisions such as the purchase of fair trade products.

> All these arguments and findings suggest that when religion is highly salient in a decision making context, religious commitment will positively predict an individual's support for fair trade products.
>
> (Salvador et al. 2014, p. 359)

The researchers manipulated the context by giving the two randomly selected test groups different information about a fictitious restaurant at which the research participants were to buy coffee. While the "low contextual salience" group received general information with a focus on competence and professionalism (e.g., the company slogan "Professional Cuisine"), the information intended for the "high contextual salience" group had obvious religious references (e.g., the company slogan "Prayerful Cuisine"). As Figure 24 shows,

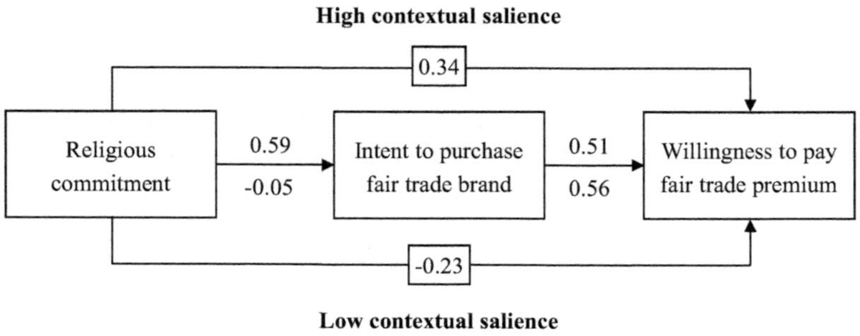

Figure 24 Willingness to pay for fair trade coffee as a function of the presence of religion.

Source: Salvador et al. (2014, p. 366).

the religious commitment of the fictitious purchasing managers increased their intention to buy fair trade coffee instead of conventional coffee only if the experimenter had addressed religion through the instructions. The willingness to accept a price premium for such products also depends on the visibility of religion.

4.4 Influence of religious holidays

In the run-up to important religious holidays, it is not only spending on food, gifts and clothing that increases but also the willingness of the faithful to pay increases. On the one hand, this is due to anticipation (e.g., of Aid al-Fitr, the festival at the end of Ramadan ("breaking of the fast"), or of Christmas). On the other hand, there is also increasing social pressure not to be stingy on such days. Retailers take advantage of this and increase the price of food during this period, although this is not permitted.

> Prices for food traditionally needed for Ramadan dishes are rising two or threefold. In August of this year, the Moroccan High Planning Commission (HCP) calculated a 5.1% increase in the cost of living index and a 9.1% increase in food prices compared to 2007.
>
> (Hackensberger 2008)

However, not all price increases can be explained socioculturally but are sometimes the result of behavioral changes. For example, the sharp increase in sugar consumption during Ramadan is accompanied by a significant increase in sugar prices on the commodity markets (cf. Hossain et al. 2018), which indirectly also suggests a corresponding increase in consumers' willingness to pay.

During Ramadan, the month of contemplation, Muslims should spend as much time as possible with their families. A Ramadan effect can then be observed in many markets. Contrary to what might seem plausible, people do not consume less intensively than usual but on the contrary intensify their consumption behaviors. For example, the "Santa Claus rally" can be explained on the one hand by the positive, rather carefree mood of many people during these weeks and on the other hand by herd behavior (i.e., the orientation toward the behavior of other people) (see Gavriilidis et al. 2016).

Part VIII

Distribution policy

1 Fundamentals

The subject of distribution policy is operational decisions and measures that are intended to help make the route from products and services to the customer as efficient and effective as possible. Internationally active companies in the manufacturing industry as well as service companies are faced with four simple questions:

- Where? Which country markets do we want to sell?
- How? With which market entry and market development strategies?
- When? In what chronological order?
- Who? Which customers do we want to attract?

Retailers have to deal with the following considerations, among others:

- Storage and distribution of the object (products and, to a certain extent, services) in order to ensure its availability in terms of time and space
- Product range design tailored to needs of the target market(s)
- Procurement, preparation and evaluation of supply-specific information as well as information about customers and competitors
- Advice to customers
- Financial transactions (establishment and operation of payment systems) and credit functions
- Sales support services (delivery service, assembly, maintenance/repair, exchange)

DOI: 10.4324/9781003506010-39

2 Market entry barriers

Before a company becomes involved in a foreign market, it will analyze the economic (e.g., purchasing power, competitive situation), legal (e.g., import regulations, patent protection) and sociocultural environmental conditions. For example, it is important to know whether corruption and protection are outlawed, tolerated or even encouraged in a society, whether people deal with each other in a trusting manner or whether mistrust prevails.

2.1 Mistrust

Trust is the subjective certainty that other persons, companies, organizations, etc. will behave as expected and in accordance with common values. Trust is essential for all kinds of cooperation (e.g., between companies (cf. La Porta et al. 1997)). In market economies, customers can usually trust that suppliers will always supply them, despite differing moral convictions. However, as an exception, in the US Christian fundamentalist service providers sometimes deny market access to members of the LGBTQ community (cf. Cabano/Minton 2023; Minton et al. 2017).

In trust-based societies, all participants benefit from the fact that cost-intensive and time-consuming control measures are not necessary (e.g., theft protection, attendance checks). Conversely, distrusting societies tend to make arrangements or agreements that are disadvantageous for all participants (e.g., because they require a disproportionate amount of control).

As Daniels/von der Ruhr (2010) have deduced from corresponding data from the General Social Survey, fundamentalist Protestants and Catholics trust other people less than people who do not belong to any religious group. In contrast, liberal Protestants seem more likely to trust their peers, with the strength of the effect correlating with the frequency of attendance at religious services. Conservative Protestants, on the other hand, tend to be distrustful regardless of the intensity of their religious practice. For Ghana, for example, members of world religions trust other people and state institutions more than Ghanaians who are affiliated with traditional or African religions or are non-denominational (cf. Addai et al. 2013).

DOI: 10.4324/9781003506010-40

Furthermore, according to the World Values Survey (WVS), religious people agree less often with the statement, "Most people can be trusted" than non-religious people. On closer inspection, however, it becomes clear that this applies primarily to the Western industrialized countries and the Northeast Asian countries (exceptions: Argentina and Russia). In the countries of Central and South America, in North Africa, Southeast Asia and Southeast Europe/Middle East, distrust prevails, regardless of the extent of religiosity ("Religion is important in life").

However, people do not only distrust people of other faiths. Other causes can be a conflict-ridden past in the countries of origin or large genetic differences, as dissimilarity increases distrust. Low relative trust between citizens of different countries has highly detrimental economic consequences, such as restricted exchange of goods between the countries and less direct investment (see Guiso et al. 2009).

2.2 Corruption

In markets that are more susceptible to corruption than average, transaction costs are significantly higher than elsewhere. Among other things, this is because bribes have to be paid as well as excessive fees for permits. Furthermore, there are time delays (e.g., due to overlong processing procedures). But this is not the only reason why foreign investors find it difficult to gain a foothold in such markets. In addition, corruption creates intransparency and uncertainty, which makes decision-making and forward-looking corporate management more difficult.

2.2.1 Religion and corruption

Actually, one would think that the keyword corruption has no place in a book for Interfaith Marketing (IFM). After all, all religions oblige believers to behave morally and clearly reject corruption (cf. Ahmed 2018; Schirrmacher 2005):

> You shall not bend justice, you shall not look at the person, and you shall not take a bribe. For the bribe blinds the eyes of the wise and perverts the cause of the righteous.
>
> (Deut. 16:19)

> By Allah, you have certainly known that we did not come to cause corruption in the land, and we have not been thieves.
>
> (Quran 12:73)

Nevertheless, numerous studies on the religion/corruption thesis can be found in the sociology of religion and economic literature. For example, according to the analyses of Kilkon/Seong-Gin (2014), North et al. (2013) and Paldam

(2001), followers of hierarchically organized religions (Catholics, Orthodox Christians and Muslims) are particularly susceptible to bribery. These religions, according to an ex post explanation, promote respect for social hierarchies as well as for authority and foster distrust. The former increases the willingness to "do good" to the decision-makers responsible at the numerous levels of the hierarchy: to bribe them. And faith in authority does not allow a self-confident civil society to emerge that resolutely fights corruption.

Treisman (2000) has shown that the greater the proportion of Protestants in the population, the less susceptible societies are to corruption (also Arvate et al. 2009). Moreover, property rights can be better enforced there (see Stulz/Williamson 2003). Furthermore, companies in predominantly Protestant countries are less likely to try to gain an advantage through lobbying (see Faccio 2006). These findings are explained by the fact that Protestant Christianity is an egalitarian-individualistic religion with a flat organizational structure. The Calvinist doctrine, according to which the fate of every human being is predetermined by God and does not depend on his or her deeds during his or her lifetime, also plays an important role. In a figurative sense, this means that the success of a company is also predetermined, and management should not try to help it along through corruption.

At first glance, this is confirmed by the ranking of the Corruption Perception Index compiled by Transparency International. Indeed, predominantly Protestant nations (e.g., New Zealand, Denmark) are at the top of the list (100 = "very clean"), while Catholic (e.g., Venezuela) and Muslim countries (e.g., Somaila) are at the bottom (0 = "highly corrupt").

However, the religion/corruption thesis ignores the explanatory power of economic and cultural variables. In addition, it is not sufficiently theoretically grounded and empirically validated. Ex post explanations mentioned at the beginning are "explanations after the fact" and consequently epistemologically unconvincing. Ko/Moon (2014) reviewed the most important explanatory attempts using data from the fourth wave of WVS (87,988 individuals from 64 countries) but found insufficient empirical evidence for various theses. Neither could susceptibility to corruption be explained by belief in authority (e.g., Catholicism) nor by the priority of family obligations over moral considerations (e.g., Confucianism).

Empirical evidence tends to support an alternative explanation. That is, it is not a specific religion that drives corruption, but the intensity of religiosity (see Gokcekus/Ekici 2020; Borlea et al. 2019). On the one hand, religious people are particularly trusting and, on the other, they are convinced that sins or misconduct such as corruption will be sanctioned by a higher authority or in a later life.

2.2.2 *Sociocultural environment and religion*

Transparency International's ranking of corruption-prone countries can also be interpreted differently. Only economically prosperous industrialized countries were rated as comparatively free of corruption, while poor countries devastated by wars and weak governments were at the bottom of the scale. Does the corruption climate of a country thus depend less on the dominant religion there than on the economic situation and the reliability of government action? This is supported by the fact that in the forecasting models of La Porta et al. (1997) and Treisman (2000), the influence of the independent variable religion (e.g., "proportion of Protestants in a society") on the dependent variable ("perceived corruption in a society") is noticeably reduced when economic variables such as the respective gross domestic product are included in the analysis: the wealthier, the less susceptible to corruption.

A separate analysis belonging to the comparative culture approach confirms and expands this view (cf. Müller/Gelbrich 2015, p. 763). Accordingly, wealthy societies that tend to be culturally individualistic, tolerant of uncertainty and reject power distance are less corrupt than average, all of which applies to Protestant societies, but not to Catholic nor Islamic societies. While this study is based on the Hofstede cultural dimensions, the structural equation model presented in Figure 25 was calculated using the corresponding values of the GLOBE culture dimensions.[58] It also shows that collectivist societies, which primarily include not only Islamic countries, but also non-European Catholic countries such as Mexico, generate a lower-than-average gross domestic product and are more prone to corruption than average. Uncertainty-tolerant societies, on the other hand, combine a lower intensity of corruption with above-average prosperity. Note that although

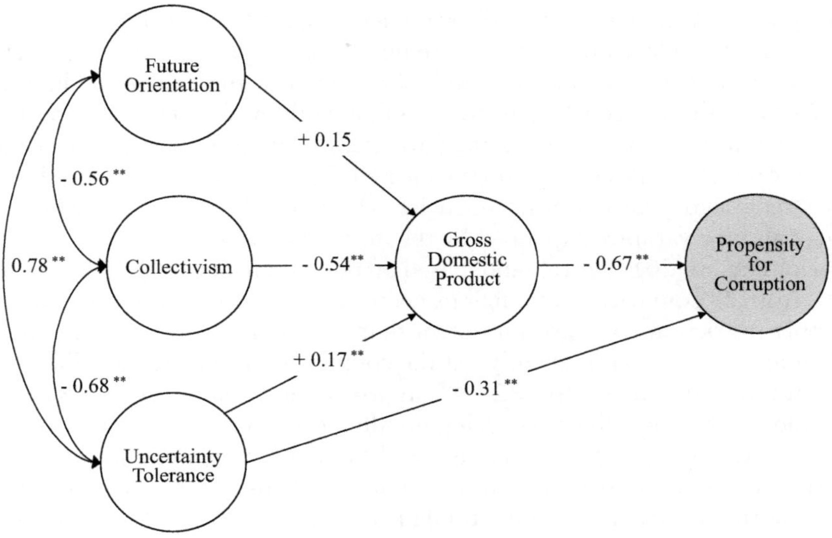

Figure 25 Structural equation model of willingness to engage in corruption.

Source: Own analysis.

the Hofstede framework has been widely criticized as being empiricist and not sufficiently theoretically grounded (see Gelbrich et al. 2021, p. 99 for details), we refer to work based on the Hofstede culture dimensions because Hofstede's measurement approach is still frequently used, it consistently provides good explanations despite the weaknesses mentioned above, and no more suitable measurement approach is available to date.

2.3 Protectionism

Protectionism often takes the form of trade barriers that states erect to give their companies an advantage by making it more difficult or impossible for foreign competitors to enter the market. Several scholars have investigated whether there is a systematic connection between religion, religiosity and protectionism. This is because many religions prioritize care and compassion over the right of the strongest. Free trade is incompatible with this in that unrestricted competition leads to employees of less efficient companies losing their jobs.

Lam (2006b) examined the influence of religiosity on attitudes toward protectionism using two statements:

- "Goods made in other countries can be imported and sold here if people want to buy them." (Free Trade)
- "There should be stricter limits on selling foreign goods here, to protect the jobs of people in this country." (Protectionism)

Religiosity was measured with the statement "Apart from weddings, funerals and baptisms: How often do you attend a church service?" The data from 32,719 respondents from 35 countries obtained in the course of the third WVS wave allowed conclusions to be drawn, with the results being a positive correlation: the more religious the participants, the more protectionist they were. And the wealthier and more educated they are, the more their religiosity strengthens protectionist tendencies. However, the effects described are weak and the variance explained by the model as a whole is low.

Domínguez (2013) also found, based on the statements of 42,154 respondents from 28 countries, that religious people across various countries support import restrictions to a greater extent than comparative people who attend religious services less frequently. At the country level, the greatest difference was found between Swedes (= 28.9% approval) and Arab Israelis (= 81.9%).

And what is the influence of religious affiliation? According to Guiso et al. (2003), American Catholics, Baptists and Methodists are more likely to support trade restrictions than non-denominational Americans. Since many of these faiths are strict, sometimes fundamentalist, the thesis of "binding social capital" is discussed in the relevant literature. According to this theory, these faith communities function like social networks that create strong internal solidarity, while at the same time rejecting or even showing hostility toward outsiders (cf. Braun 2011). In contrast, moderate or liberal faith communities resemble bridging networks. They perceive industrialization and globalization not as a fundamental challenge. As a result, they do not react with hostility toward those of a different faith (cf. Putnam 2003, p. 23).

Daniels/von der Ruhr (2005, p. 470) reported similar findings. According to their secondary statistical analyses of data from the 1996 International Social Survey Program, Catholics and fundamentalist Protestants are more in favor of import restrictions than followers of other faiths. The external validity of these findings and the socioeconomic openness of (non-fundamentalist) Protestants are supported by the above-average import rates of countries with a predominantly Protestant denomination, while Catholic and especially Islamic countries are relatively closed and consequently have lower import rates (see Mehanna 2003).

2.4 Religious distance

Constructs such as cultural, psychological or social distance are subjective measures of dissimilarity that play an important role in intercultural marketing. The more dissimilar a foreign market is to the domestic market, the more difficult it is to obtain and process information and to make decisions, and the greater the various risks (see Kraus et al. 2016). This can be explained, among other things, with the similarity/attraction effect described by social psychologists: people are attracted to what or who is/are similar to them.

While cultural distance has been and continues to be the subject of numerous studies, such as regarding the preferred market entry strategy (cf. Tihanyi et al. 2005), religious distance and other distance measures have received less attention thus far (cf. Berry et al. 2010). Exceptions include Guiso et al. (2009) and Dow/Karunaratna (2006). According to their work, religious similarity promotes bilateral commodity exchange by strengthening mutual trust, which ultimately strengthens trade relations (mediation effect). Hergueux (2011) has elaborated on this statement. According to his gravity model, developed on the basis of the OECD database of global bilateral stocks of direct investment, he explains:

- Religious similarity disproportionately increases reciprocal direct investment by less developed countries with weak, low-performing institutions (more precisely, by companies headquartered in these countries).
- Religious diversity disproportionately increases reciprocal direct investment by developed countries with strong, efficient institutions (or, more precisely, by companies headquartered in these countries).

Presumably, in developing countries, the mutual trust that grows out of religious similarity counterbalances the distrust caused by weak institutions there. In addition, in order to comprehensively explain the market entry decisions of small and medium-sized enterprises (SMEs), Martín Martín/

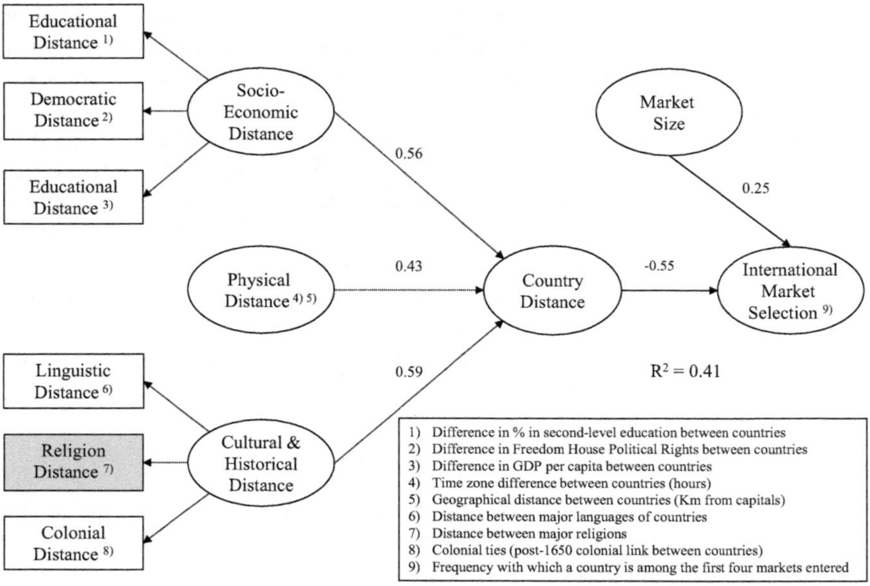

Figure 26 Influence of different distance measures on market entry.

Source: Martín Martín/Drogendijk (2014).

Drogendijk (2014), based on the work of Dow/Karunaratna (2006), have developed a multidimensional distance measure that integrates the distance measures that have so far mostly been considered in isolation. Accordingly, the management of Spanish SMEs prefers foreign markets that have a low distance to their home market. This "country distance" is influenced by all three subdimensions, above all by the "cultural and historical distance," which is made up of linguistic distance, religious distance and shared colonial past (see Figure 26).

3 Negotiations

Is there a connection between ethical convictions and negotiation style? Do religious managers negotiate differently (e.g., more fairly or more willing to compromise) than non-religious managers? The insights available so far suggest that shared religious convictions and common membership in a particular religious community create trust, improve the flow of information, standardize the evaluation of information and facilitate communication overall. This benefits both the success of negotiations and the success of joint ventures (see VIII-4.3).

Li/Sai (2020) are a case in point. Using data from the Thomson Financial Security Data Corporation, they have shown that the smaller the religious distance between the investor's home market and the location of the investment and the lower the religious diversity in the target country, the more likely it is that negotiations on the acquisition of a foreign investment will be concluded successfully. Linguistic distance and diversity have a comparable effect. The performance capability of the institutions in the target country moderates these relationships. If courts, public administrations, etc. operate reliably, then similarities in language and religion contribute less to the success of business transactions than in countries with weak institutions. There, the trust that arises from similarity acts as a social cement that holds society together and compensates for the inefficiency of state or public institutions.

Richardson/Rammal (2018) conducted 27 in-depth interviews with Muslim managers to find out how Islam influences their negotiation skills. They summarized their insights as follows:

- First, Muslims are unfamiliar with the idea that negotiations, like the professional sphere as a whole, should be viewed in isolation from the ethical principles of their faith. Muslims are obliged to inform their negotiating partners comprehensively, not least about the limits and risks of their own offer. For Mohammed had said that on the Day of Judgment, the place of the honest merchant would be at the side of the martyrs. Applying this to the real case of the sale of real estate, which had been the scene of two murders, this means that although a German court ruled that the seller

DOI: 10.4324/9781003506010-41

was not obligated to inform the buyer, the seller should have done so according to Muslim legal and, above all, moral understanding.

- Second, the interviewees had the impression that belonging to the same faith community would make it easier for the negotiators to establish a harmonious social relationship with each other, which would promote negotiation success in the long run. Also, their religious affiliation would make it easier for them to use emotional appeals and, for example, to remind people of their religious-spiritual affiliation instead of trying to convince the counterpart of the advantageousness of the draft agreement through rational arguments.
- Third, many study participants succumbed to the intergroup bias: the tendency to perceive and evaluate members of a social group to which one belongs (e.g., a religious community) more positively (e.g., more likeable, more competent) than persons who belong to another, possibly even competing social group (cf. Johnson et al. 2012). This observation goes back to social identity theory. In order to increase their self-worth and to define their social identity, people systematically prefer members of their own group to members of another group (cf. Tajfel 1974).

Yadav et al. (2016) wanted to know whether spiritual intelligence makes students and managers negotiate in a more socially compatible way (e.g., more fairly). The negotiation style was not observed in real life but was derived from self-assessments using the Self-Reported Inappropriate Negotiation Strategies Scale (SINS Scale). Spiritual intelligence was measured with the "Integrated Spiritual Intelligence Scale (ISIS)." The results revealed that spiritually intelligent participants reject ethically inappropriate negotiation strategies such as false promises or deliberate misinterpretation of information more clearly than less spiritual individuals.

4 Market entry strategies

4.1 Overview

Companies use a wide variety of market entry strategies to enter foreign markets (e.g., export, franchising, direct investment). These strategies differ, among other things, in whether they tie up many resources (e.g., setting up a new foreign company) or few (e.g., contract manufacturing) and are therefore more or less risky. As a rule, foreign commitments are accompanied by increased uncertainty and additional risks (e.g., exchange rate risk, non-transparent import and profit transfer regulations). For this reason, many companies favor markets that are culturally similar to their home market, especially at the beginning of their internationalization, when management still has little experience abroad (cf. Shenkar 2001; Beugelsdijk et al. 2018; Kogut/Singh 1988). Which market entry strategy is preferred in a particular case also depends on the psychological distance (e.g., differences in mentality) (e.g., Ellis 2008).

Since their religious background has a significant influence on the values and behaviors of business partners, religious distance could play an important role as well. Indeed, Muslim managers systematically prefer foreign markets with a Muslim-majority population (see Richardson 2014). Surprisingly, however, little research has been done on the influence of religiosity and religious affiliation on this decision (cf. Richardson/Ariffin 2019). This is also noteworthy in that, according to numerous studies, religious people tend to be risk averse, which can lead to overly defensive market entry decisions given the numerous risks of foreign engagements (e.g., Mortimer et al. 2020; Miller/Hoffmann 1995).

4.2 Foreign direct investment

Direct investments or foreign investments include not only the establishment or expansion of production, sales and service facilities abroad, but also the acquisition of companies or majority/minority stakes in foreign companies. In the case of portfolio investments, only capital is transferred, while in the case of direct investments, both capital and know-how are transferred.

DOI: 10.4324/9781003506010-42

Table 19 Religious freedom ranking in 2019

Chile	0.83	Great Britain	0.69	Greece	0.50
Taiwan	0.81	Italy	0.68	Brazil	0.49
Australia	0.81	Israel	0.63	Indonesia	0.32
New Zealand	0.79	Spain	0.62	Russia	0.29
US	0.71	Belgium	0.60	Afghanistan	0.27
Netherlands	0.71	Germany	0.59	Morocco	0.24
Norway	0.70	Denmark	0.59	Iran	0.21
Luxembourg	0.69	Poland	0.55	Saudi Arabia	0.07
Switzerland	0.69	Austria	0.55	China	0.00
Canada	0.69	France	0.55	North Korea	0.00

Note: 1 = complete freedom of religion, 0 = complete lack of freedom.

Source: https://govdata360.worldbank.org/indicators/hd6a18526?country=BRA&indicator=41930&viz=line_chart&years=1975,2019; 02/06/2022

4.2.1 *Establishment and expansion of facilities for production, sales, and services abroad*

Dolansky/Alon (2008) used the Toyo Keizai Foreign Investment Database (1986–2001) to investigate whether and how religious freedom (see Table 19) and religious diversity in the target countries influence direct investment by Japanese companies. According to their findings, Japanese companies prefer to invest in economically strong countries and in countries where religious diversity is guaranteed. It is obvious that economically prosperous locations are preferred. Companies have better sales prospects there than in poorer regions. The variable "gross national income" clearly makes the largest explanatory contribution in the regression model. The attractiveness of locations where several religions are practiced on an equal footing can be justified in two ways. Religious diversity:

- Strengthens economic growth (see Barro/McCleary 2003)
- Promotes tolerance, presumably not only toward other religions, but also toward the foreign investors

Indeed, religious freedom also goes hand in hand with economic prosperity (see Alon/Chase 2005) and should therefore be an incentive for direct investment. Conversely, countries with a state religion develop less well, which is why they are less attractive markets.

Furthermore, the social environment in which direct investments are to be made is important to consider. Attitudinal data obtained by Jamal/Milner (2022) showed that in a Muslim country such as Tunisia, the acceptance of a foreign investor dwindles noticeably if the population fears that the investor might prevent future employees and other social groups from practicing religious rites (e.g., prayers, Ramadan, clothing).

Religious fundamentalism that manifests itself in terrorist acts plausibly deters foreign investors. The relevant literature tends to confirm this thesis; however, the empirical evidence is less strong than might be expected (cf. Khalil/Surendran 2006). American investors avoid locations where the legal system combines customary law with religious law and prefer locations where civil law applies (cf. Globerman/Shapiro 2003).

4.2.2 Mergers and acquisitions

Beginning in the 1980s, several developments fundamentally changed the market: liberalization of the financial markets, shortening of product and market life cycles, growing competitive intensity and increased return expectations of investors. As a result, more and more companies sought to achieve a company size that was presumably necessary to achieve certain strategic goals by merging with other companies (mergers) or buying companies (acquisitions).

Specifically, the M&A strategy aims to "leverage" synergies and exploit economies of scale[59] as well as economies of scope. The latter can include cost advantages due to a broader product range, which enables better capacity utilization in the case of products for which there are seasonal differences in demand. In the case of acquisitions, a distinction is made between friendly and hostile takeovers. An "unfriendly or hostile takeover" is when the necessary shares in a company are acquired without the consent or against the resistance of the top management team of the acquired company.

Mergers put everyone involved in a state of great uncertainty, partly because the previous corporate identity is lost and serious consequences are possible for each individual. Dwindling job security and career prospects jeopardize employees' trust in company management (cf. Drori et al. 2013). This is one of the reasons why more than half of all mergers are considered to have failed when measured against classic success criteria such as an increase in return on equity or stock market value and accelerated market access (cf. Schoenberg 2006). Many takeovers also do not go as planned. In such cases, post-merger integration, the merging of previously independent companies into a single entity with a common corporate culture and identity, is supposed to provide a remedy (cf. Shrivastava 1986). In the case of a hostile takeover, the management of cultural differences is particularly imperative, but also particularly difficult, given that the fierce resistance of some employees is likely.

While the importance of country and corporate cultural diversity for M&A success has received considerable attention in the literature, to our knowledge, only two studies on the consequences of religious diversity for this market entry strategy are available to date: Dow et al. (2016) and Kwok et al. (2020). The latter started from the following consideration: if the employees of the business units to be integrated belong to the same religious group, this will lead to shared values and increased credibility. Particularly in early integration phases, when there is still a great deal of information asymmetry, the participants will likely use this heuristic often. In a field experiment with

Malaysian managers, the researchers found supportive evidence. Specifically, they found that employees of the acquired company trust the management of the foreign investor more quickly if they both belong to the same religious group. Higher religiosity levels strengthen this effect as well.

In the case of M&A abroad, the question regularly arises as to what share an investor will acquire. This also depends on the religious-cultural-linguistic distance between the countries involved. However, according to Dow et al. (2016), distance research suffers from a blind spot. It is a mistake, they argue, to consider only the relevant distance measures between the investor's country of origin and the location of the foreign investment. Religious, cultural or linguistic diversity within the acquirer's country of origin is no less influential. Depending on how large or small this is, it moderates the effects of linguistic and religious distance on the foreign investor's ownership share.

As Dow et al. (2016) found in data from the Thomson Financial Security Data Corporation (SDC), the level of participation depends, among other things, on religious diversity in the investor's home country. Two opposing effects can be distinguished:

- The more faith communities are active in the location of the investment, the lower the percentage of participation of the foreign acquirer. Presumably, in this case, diversity within the target country is perceived as another source of behavioral uncertainty and information asymmetry, and thus as an additional risk.
- Religious diversity in the investor's home country enhances the cognitive complexity and cultural sensitivity of management (i.e., ultimately their ability to deal competently with the challenges of foreign locations).

4.3 Joint ventures

4.3.1 Basic principles

When two or more companies establish a new, legally independent company and manage it jointly, it is referred to as a joint venture. Such cooperative forms of market entry enable the partner companies to pool the necessary resources and share the costs (e.g., for marketing, product development and sales). Both companies can also benefit from the know-how of the other company. One of the particular difficulties that joint ventures have to overcome is the different, usually interest-driven understanding of how to distribute effort and revenue fairly. This is all the more true the greater the cultural distance between the participants.

Joint ventures involve the cooperation of partners that is contractually regulated in detail. For this purpose, a new business unit is established that is organizationally independent of the partner companies and has clearly defined responsibilities. In a non-equity alliance, the parties cooperate but remain legally independent (e.g., licensing).

Transaction cost theory assumes that joint ventures are susceptible to opportunistic decisions. For the sake of their own advantage, they do not adhere to agreements, break promises and withhold information. As a countermeasure, the parties can establish binding rules, sanction violations or only give the partner company access to so-called specific technologies (i.e., technologies that are worthless outside the alliance).

One argument against the introduction of such control measures is the cost of agreeing and monitoring rules and regulations. In addition, controls generate mistrust and provoke countermeasures. In comparison, religions are a mostly efficient and free way to control opportunistic behavioral tendencies. Their moral standards help to shape the working relationship in a more just and fair way.

4.3.2 Influence of religious affiliation and religiosity

Religious people are suitable cooperation partners because they trust other people and state institutions and are convinced of the fairness of the market more than others (cf. Guiso et al. 2003). But do managers who are Christian really act less opportunistically than those who are not religious? And does this behavioral disposition influence the preferred market entry strategy? Starting from these questions, Li (2008) used data from SDC to study 22,156 cross-border engagements in 48 industries over nine years worldwide. Countries with a population of more than 50% Christians were classified as Christian, and countries with more than 50% atheists were classified as atheist.

If it is true that atheists behave opportunistically more often than religious people, then joint ventures, at least one in which one of the partners is an atheist, would be more likely to choose the legal form of a joint venture. This is because it would then be legally required to protect knowledge and know-how on a contractual basis. As the logistic regression analysis showed, business partners from religiously different or non-religious countries are indeed more likely to choose a joint venture. This is because their contracts protect them from opportunistic behavior. On the other hand, less legally binding market entry strategies such as the strategic alliance are more likely to be pursued if both companies come from Christian countries and, therefore, presumably share central values and trust each other more.

5 Distribution channels

Modern media enables a more efficient exchange of goods, such as in the form of e-commerce. In this context, Interfaith Marketing (IFM) is particularly interested in whether the above-average risk aversion and relationship orientation of religious consumers are an obstacle to acceptance of online shopping or whether their greater trust in other people is an advantage. Another research focus is on shopping place preference and the acceptance of sales channels that conform to religion.

5.1 Importance of the characteristics of shopping places

Customers evaluate shopping places on the basis of certain criteria (e.g., depth and breadth of the assortment, product quality, price level, competence and friendliness of the sales staff, accessibility). In order to find out whether consumers express different preferences depending on their religious affiliation and religiosity, McDaniel/Burnett (1990) conducted a written survey with 550 American consumers of different religions. The researchers measured participants' cognitive and behavioral religiosity. They then presented the participants with a list of 30 "Retail Store Evaluative Criteria" to be rated on a seven-point importance scale. Twenty-two of these criteria loaded sufficiently high on one of the extracted factors (factor loadings ≥ 0.67). These seven factors (e.g., shopping efficiency, product assortment, sales personnel friendliness) can be understood as meta-criteria by which consumers judge department stores. According to the two researchers, these results are transferable to other distribution channels, as a study by Hansen/Deutscher (1978) showed. They noted "that consumer evaluations of the importance of these particular attributes were similar for both grocery stores and department stores" (McDaniel/Burnett 1990, p. 104).

In order to rule out the possibility that sociodemographic characteristics are confounded with the independent variable (religiosity), the authors controlled for the possible influence of age, income and level of education. In all analyses, these variables made a smaller explanatory contribution than religiosity. The most important results of this study are:

- Regardless of which religious affiliation they belong to and whether they are cognitively religious or religious in their behavior, religious department

DOI: 10.4324/9781003506010-43

store customers place more value on being served in a friendly manner compared to less religious customers.
- Customers with a high degree of cognitive religiosity also attach greater importance to the convenience and efficiency of shopping and to product quality compared to customers with a low degree of cognitive religiosity.
- Religious affiliation proved to be largely irrelevant. Whether Jews, Catholics or Protestants, their responses differed only insignificantly from one another (cf. McDaniel/Burnett 1990, p. 109 ff.).

5.2 Brick-and-mortar distribution channels

In view of the fascinating triumph of online retailing (see VIII-5.3), it is easy to forget that the vast majority of retail sales are still made locally in brick-and-mortar retail stores.

5.2.1 Traditional shopping places

As a result of the division of labor and the decline of self-sufficiency, markets, bazaars and other informal market events developed worldwide. In the course of industrialization, these were then pushed into the background by the forms of distribution with which we are familiar, in some regions (western industrialized nations) more so than others regions (developing countries). This development did not leave the prosperous but very structurally conservative Gulf states unscathed: "The presence of hypermarkets has attracted customers away from traditional souqs" (Belwal/Belwal 2017 on the situation of trade in Oman).

In some places, sales fairs developed in a different way. They were usually organized in connection with an already existing church festival, preferably in honor of the local patron saint. From modest beginnings, economically very important fairs such as the Hanover Fair or the Frankfurt Fair emerged, especially in Germany.[60]

For success in personal selling, external appearance, credibility, professional competence and the persuasiveness of individual employees are critical. The spectrum of applications of personal selling ranges from door-to-door sales, to the service counter in the supermarket, to the sale of turnkey industrial plants. The influencing strategies that salespeople use can be divided into two categories:

- Soft selling (informing, convincing, promising success)
- Hard selling (persuading or influencing, often by limiting the time or quantity of the offer)

In hard selling, the salesperson deliberately builds up pressure (e.g., through language or supposed time pressure). People differ in their ability to be influenced. Moderately religious people are considered to be more flexible than average and are therefore easier to influence than very religious or non-religious people (cf. Bock/Warren 1972).

In Confucian countries, it is also important in sales situations to not seek short-term advantages, but rather a long-term harmonious relationship (cf. Zhou et al. 2017). Chinese business partners, for example, attach great importance to solidarity, responsiveness, empathy and trust (cf. Yau et al. 2000).

In Saudi Arabia and other strictly Islamic countries, it is generally problematic if the customer and the seller are of different genders (see Tuncalp/Erdem 1998). Door-to-door sales, for example, can lead to an unwanted encounter between men and women. In this region, clothing stores must ensure that female customers can try on clothes without offending common decency, such as having special sales hours, online shopping, and women-only shopping centers (e.g., Al-Jazeera Women's Shopping and Recreational Center in Riyadh). Last but not least, in business meetings and sales pitches, prayer times should be observed (cf. Sanaie/Ranjbarian 1996).

5.2.2 Local shopping places

Among the first to scientifically address the influence of religion and religiosity on preferences for particular shopping venues were Yavas/Tuncalp (1984). According to their observations, religious Saudis at that time preferred to shop in a traditional neighborhood store because they feared that meat, poultry and other food would not be prepared in a halal-compliant manner in a modern supermarket. Also, with their large assortment of packaged goods, it is often questionable whether all ingredients comply with the dietary laws.

Years later, this assessment still held true. Hino (2010, p. 68), who surveyed Jordanians and Arabs living in Israel on this topic, summarized his insights as follows: "Muslim consumers attach high importance to religious values and hence are more likely to shop for most of their food needs in traditional outlets, thus decreasing the proportion of product lines they purchase at supermarket formats."

In one of our surveys, young German religious people also gave smaller stores near their homes a more positive rating than their less religious peers (see Figure 27). During the Covid pandemic, religious customers in particular appreciated small neighborhood stores even more. This effect is mediated by the social norm "caring for one's neighbor" (cf. Minton/Cabano 2022). As this study has further shown, local retailers can take advantage of this by thematizing religion and neighborhood in their advertising measures, thereby priming the caring motive.

Mokhlis (2009a) asked participants how often they had made purchases in various modern retail outlets in the past 12 months. The five-point Likert scale used for this purpose ranges from "never" (= 1) to "very often" (= 5). It is noteworthy that he operationalized preference by a behavioral measure (= actual purchase frequency) rather than qualitatively, as a preference

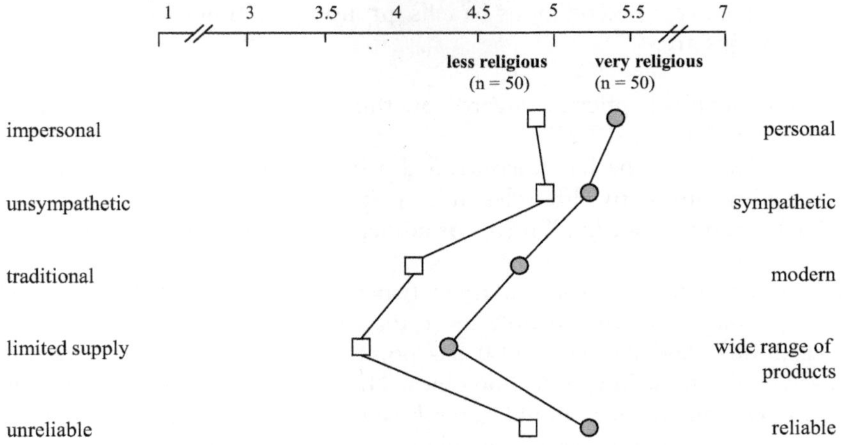

Figure 27 Image profile of smaller neighborhood stores.
Source: Own survey.

(e.g., "Where do you prefer to shop?"). Participants were residents of Kuala Lumpur (Malaysia) of different religious affiliations. The main result that can be reported is that shopping place preference depends primarily on the type of retail operation and less on customers' religious affiliation. Whether Buddhists, Christians, Hindus or Muslims, at that time, all shopped most frequently in department stores and least frequently in specialty stores. This held true except for Hindus, who visited shopping malls even slightly less frequently than specialty stores.

5.3 Electronic distribution channels: online shopping

Global online sales have more than quintupled in the past ten years (2021 = \$4.9 trillion; Statista). This corresponds to around 20% of total retail sales. Since online shoppers can only assess the quality of the products on offer themselves after completing the purchase, trust is the decisive factor.

5.3.1 Influence of religiosity

Regardless of their religious affiliation, religious people use Internet services less frequently than non-religious or less religious people (see Lissitsa/Kol 2016). On the other hand, data from the Baylor Religion Survey (2017) shows that intensive Internet users are less likely than others to pray, read scriptures or participate in religious services. They also consider religion to be less important (cf. McClures 2020). And unlike intensive television users, intensive Internet users endorse atheistic attitudes. Davidson/Farquhar

(2014) have explained religious Israelis' pronounced "internet anxiety." The causes of this are:

- Fundamental skepticism toward new things, resistance to innovation and risk aversion (cf. V-2.2).
- Fear that everyone has uncontrolled access to undesirable content (e.g., sexuality, alternative lifestyles) (cf. Lissitsa/Madar 2018).
- Lack of confidence in all forms of modern communications technology

However, according to a secondary statistical analysis of the WVS-2005, religious people trust other people more than non-religious people (cf. Guiso et al. 2006). And Barnes (2009) has pointed out that religiosity promotes goodwill and trust in new technologies. Therefore, a disproportionate number of religious people should actually shop on the Internet. But the sales figures tell a different story as religious consumers contribute less than non-religious consumers to the online boom. However, it is important to note that even strictly religious Jews now shop online (cf. Hong 2020), including male ultra-Orthodox Jews (see Lissitsa/Cohen 2018). However, religious people still react skeptically to innovations such as mobile shopping (see Lissita/Kol 2021). One reason could be that online shopping has long had an image problem with this consumer segment.

Research on the acceptance of innovative technologies has shown that along with quality guarantee, service quality and usability (cf. Tarhini et al. 2018), trust is crucial for the intention to shop online (cf. Ingham et al. 2015). In relationship-oriented societies (e.g., Buddhist, Confucian and Muslim societies), trust depends primarily on belonging to the same social group (e.g., religious group) and less on concrete actions.

E-commerce has to contend with a number of specific problems due to the psychological and real distance between supplier and buyer. These range from abuse[61] of the right to return or exchange goods to clearly criminal acts, with which platforms such as eBay in particular have to contend. Vacation homes are rented out that don't even exist. And a stolen identity can be used to make purchases free of charge. Others obtain the account data of customers through fraudulent websites. According to Sharma et al. (2022), religious (extrinsic and intrinsic) people are less likely to engage in such fraudulent online shopping. Based on the theory of planned behavior (cf. III-5.6), perceived behavioral control (= conviction not to get caught) and social norms (= conviction that such behavior is common) were found to exacerbate the problem.

The findings of Sohaib/Kang (2014) suggest that a distinction should be made between two forms of trust. Cognitive trust arises from the reliability of the transaction partner (e.g., "Promises made by this website are likely to be reliable"), and emotional trust comes from the impressions users have during the transaction visit to the website. In the present case, religiosity explains relatively well the cognitive trust of Pakistani customers and generally the emotional trust of Australian customers.

Trust is destroyed when users get the impression that the provider uses unfair practices (e.g., "This website/store takes advantage of less experienced consumers to make them purchase"). The more religious online shoppers are, the more sensitively they react to such unethical business practices and devalue the provider. Agag/El-Masry (2016), who interviewed mainly younger male Egyptians, explain this with the discrepancy between the idealistic worldview of very religious Muslims and obviously self-serving business behaviors.

5.3.2 Influence of religious affiliation

The influence of religious affiliation on trust is less clear than the influence of religiosity. While Protestants and, to a lesser extent, Catholics seem to be more trusting, Hindus tend toward (slight) distrust. No clear tendency was found among Buddhists, Jews and Muslims (see Guiso et al. 2006).

Does whether the provider is recognizably a member of the same or a different religious community as the customers affect customers' trust in the online store? To this end, Siala et al. (2004) have examined a total of 91 Christians, Muslims and followers of other faiths or atheists. Specifically, they wanted to know to what extent the participants trusted online booksellers and what role the religious identity of the bookstore's website played in this. The study participants were shown real websites of Christian, Islamic or neutral online booksellers. As expected, sites whose operators belong to one's own religious group appeared significantly more trustworthy than sites with

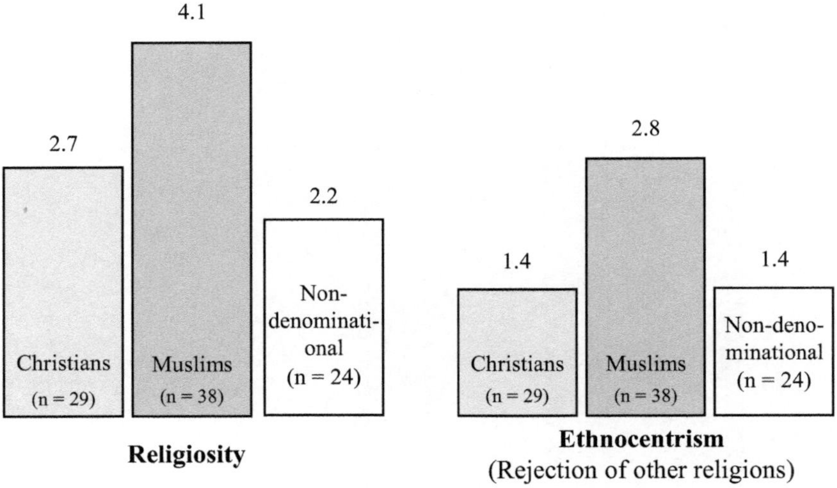

Figure 28 Religiosity and ethnocentrism as a function of religious affiliation.
Source: Based on Siala et al. (2004, p. 15).

a provider who was of a different or no religious affiliation. However, while Muslims only trusted Islamic providers, the Christians surveyed were more religiously tolerant. By their own admission, they also trust providers who do not belong to any religion or who belong to a different religion. This is probably due to the fact that the Muslim participants were not only more religious than average, but also significantly more ethnocentric (see III-2.6) and thus more negatively disposed toward other religious groups (see Figure 28).

Azam et al. (2013) report similar findings. In their study, too, the common religious affiliation (Islam) of the online merchant and customer proved to be advantageous. Participants said they trusted an "Islamic website" more than a neutral site.

6 Store management

What distinguishes successful retailers? The success of discount retailers such as ALDI points first of all to the factor of pricing. Furthermore, brick-and-mortar retail stores should be easy to reach in terms of both distance and store opening hours. Even more than others, religious consumers also pay attention to a high-quality range of products and friendly sales staff. Last but not least, the location of the business plays an important role.

6.1 Location

While customers attach particular importance in this context to the easy accessibility of shopping venues, retailers are mainly interested in the purchasing power of the consumers living in a particular location, as well as the intensity of competition there. Remarkably, a disproportionately large share of religious households in the area is seen as a location disadvantage, except by explicitly religious retailers. This is because religious people tend to be frugal and lead modest lifestyles, partly out of conviction and partly due to their below-average income. As Kurt et al. (2018) calculated from Economic Census (2012) data, the US retail stores in counties with an above-average number of religious residents actually generate significantly lower sales than those in less religious counties. From the explanatory model, we can deduce that an increase of 20% in religious residents means an average drop in sales of 3.4%. This is due, among other things, to the fact that religious consumers spend less time in the store and plan their purchases better than others. The latter is reflected in a slightly lower number of unplanned purchases (–2.7%).

6.2 Reputation

Consumers prefer retailers with a good public reputation. This is all the more important for retailers because reputation reinforces the positive effects of good accessibility, value for money and attractive product ranges (see Arnold et al. 1996). The social reputation of shopping venues is particularly important to religious consumers (cf. Mokhlis 2008). On the one hand, this is because they are risk averse and fear that a bad reputation could rub off

DOI: 10.4324/9781003506010-44

on them. And secondly, they want to lead a godly life and observe religious norms and values. As a survey of Malaysian participants also revealed, the value that participants attach to the reputation of a place of purchase depends on their religious affiliation (cf. Mokhlis 2006a). Whether Buddhists, Christians, Hindus or Muslims, the good reputation of retail stores was even more important than their pricing or product range.

Can retailers pro-actively promote their reputation (e.g., by volunteering themselves and their employees for environmental projects or by getting involved in their community)? As West et al. (2016) found out from a survey of 216 visitors to a trade fair in Canada, such actions primarily offer the opportunity to convince less religious consumers of the company's good intentions. No comparable effect was observed among very religious consumers. While for the more secularly oriented consumers, there is a direct connection between concrete actions and trustworthiness, very religious consumers are convinced that this also or primarily depends on God's will and cannot be influenced by humans.

6.3 Assortment policy

There are several reasons for retailers to consider the religious affiliation and religiosity of their customers when composing their assortment:

- Religious holidays, such as Christmas or the breaking of the fast after Ramadan
- Religious affiliation-specific dietary laws or regulations (e.g., halal, kosher)
- Moral concepts (products with sexual connotations, addictive potential, revealing clothing)
- Pilgrimages and proximity to important sacred buildings

In most cases, the question is: which additional products should be included in the range, especially for the religious holiday (e.g., Christmas tree decorations) or in larger quantities (e.g., toys in the run-up to Easter)? And which ones should not be included? However, there are also cases of buying restraint due to religious festivals and customs. During Lent, for example, and especially during Holy Week, less food is sold in Christian neighborhoods. The same interplay of weakening and intensifying consumption can be observed in Islamic regions during the fasting month of Ramadan and on the occasion of Eid al-Fitr, the subsequent breaking of the fast (cf. Touzani/Hirschman 2008). Suppliers of food, for example, are accustomed to taking account of such fluctuations in demand by adjusting their procurement and stock-keeping policies.

Assortment policy is also influenced by the practice of giving gifts to friends and family members on the occasion of religious holidays. Since social considerations (e.g., generosity) usually take precedence over economic rationality in gift-giving (cf. Lemmergaard/Muhr 2011), the price sensitivity of gift-givers is comparatively low and their willingness to pay is above average.

Apparently, there is a connection between religiosity and the importance of branded products for assortment design (cf. V-4). In the US districts with an above-average number of church congregations and an above-average number of churchgoers, a disproportionately large number of retailers can be found that underweight branded products in their assortment and primarily offer private labels and unbranded goods. This emphasis is supported by the results of a microeconomic experiment. In this experiment, very religious, especially wealthy participants, gave preference to unbranded products more often than less religious people (cf. Shachar et al. 2011). Retailers who want to promote the sales of their own brands should therefore subtly remind their customers of religion (e.g., by playing religious music as background music in the store).

6.4 Store opening hours

All religions know days of rest, days on which believers are not supposed to work (Sabbath, Sundays, holidays, etc.). Much stricter than the Christian commandment of Sunday rest, the Sabbath obliges religious Jews to temporarily refrain from worldly activities. In strongly religious regions, most stores then remain closed. As a rule, the preceding days are the preferred shopping days, such as Saturdays in Christian and Fridays in Jewish communities.

Although Islam "only" recognizes Friday prayers, but not an explicit day of rest, merchants in Saudi Arabia often offer longer opening hours on Thursdays and Fridays in the afternoon and evening hours. And during Ramadan, not only eating but also buying behavior shifts to the time after sunset.

In the course of secularization, however, the formerly predominantly restrictive store closing laws have been liberalized in many places, even to the point of introducing being open on Sundays. Even in very religious America, the requirement of Sunday rest has become less binding in recent decades. A telephone survey of 338 American consumers, three quarters of whom were women, revealed that very religious consumers are less likely to visit stores on Sundays than their less religious counterparts. But they also shop comparatively frequently on Sundays (= 11 times per year). And the percentage of these purchases compared to the expenditures they make during the week is 17.0%, which is above the expected value.[62] Still smaller are the differences between members of different religious groups (both on the attitudinal and on the behavioral level). Overall, the findings presented by Siguaw/Simpson (1997) suggest that very religious consumers did not want shopping hours to be extended at that time. In their opinion, only stores that are absolutely necessary (e.g., gas stations, hotels) should be open on Sundays.

This assessment has changed little in the following two decades. As Swimberghe et al. (2014) observed, consumers with a higher level of intrapersonal religious commitment in particular rate the Sunday rest of companies positively. As a result, the perceived corporate image and the intention to remain loyal to the retailer improve.

6.5 Accessibility

The attractiveness of a shopping location also depends on its accessibility. However, this is not an objectively definable variable, but rather depends on the procurement effort that consumers are willing to take on themselves. More than others, religious people prefer to shop in their immediate neighborhood (cf. Siguaw/Simpson 1997, p. 27). The reasons for this, however, are primarily traditionalism and a sense of home, and rarely convenience. The narrower radius of action of religious people opens up opportunities for profiling, especially for neighborhood stores. This is because they are a relatively loyal, less mobile clientele. Consumers' religious affiliation does not influence their attitude toward the accessibility of a shopping location.

6.6 Sacralization

The overriding goal of the technique of sacralization is to create an ideational added value for the profane. For example, the goal of sacralization is to make businesses, products or lifestyles the object of spiritual debate with the religious and the question of the meaning of life (cf. II-1.5; V-5.2). In order to turn customers into members of a (faith) community, companies make use of a number of cultural techniques (cf. Dion/Borraz 2015):

- Exaggeration of places (e.g., the parental garage where S. Jobs and S. Wozniak allegedly constructed the first Apple computer)
- Creation of myths (e.g., J. Rockefeller's extreme thrift and godliness as the driving force behind corporate success)
- Development of rituals (i.e., rigid rules in dealing with sacred places or objects) (e.g., fashion shows in which the sacred objects are only presented by models who outwardly conform to very specific, exaggerated specifications, such as through their catwalk)
- Scarcity of access to "sacred" spaces (e.g., the offices or private rooms of the mythically enraptured founding personality)
- Iconography (i.e., symbolic charging of images and other optical stimuli) (e.g., a certain gray as the corporate color of Dior: the Dior gray)

7 Shopping place preference

Where consumers shop (i.e., which shopping venues they visit to meet their needs) depends on numerous influencing factors, such as the available mix of shopping venues. The fit between the functional (e.g., good accessibility) and social needs of customers (e.g., friendly employees) and the service portfolio of retail companies also plays a role. In addition, there are different religious-driven shopping orientations. For very religious consumers, the religious identity of the supplier can also be an important decision criterion.

7.1 Customer expectations

Following Sheth (1983), shopping preference depends on the one hand on supply-side factors. These include market conditions (e.g., retail structure) and company conditions (e.g., service quality). On the other hand, consumers also have an influence, such as through product-related factors (e.g., brand loyalty or product use) or personal factors (e.g., values and norms).

7.1.1 Classic criteria of shopping place preference

McDaniel/Burnett (1990) were among the first to address this issue from a comparative religion perspective. The starting point of their study was a literature analysis. In a next step, they asked their 550 US respondents to rate a department store on the basis of 30 evaluation criteria (on a seven-point rating scale). Their responses were then combined into seven superordinate criteria (factors) using a factor analysis. According to the participants' self-assessment, product quality, friendliness of the sales staff and efficient shopping had the greatest influence on their choice of department store, while the credit facilities offered by a store and its equipment had the least influence.

The next step was to examine what the expressed expectations depended on. The researchers examined the type and intensity of the participants' religiosity (intrinsic/extrinsic) and/or their religious affiliation (= 48% Protestants,

DOI: 10.4324/9781003506010-45

28% Catholics, 15% non-denominational and 7% Jews). The results of this study revealed:

- The expectations of the followers of the different faiths are largely similar.
- Consumers with particularly strong religious convictions (intrinsic religiosity) place slightly more value on the efficiency and convenience of shopping than others, as well as on friendly sales staff and high product quality.
- The degree of extrinsic religiosity is significant in this context in only one respect: those who rarely attend religious services place somewhat less value on the convenience of shopping than do consumers with an average level of attendance at religious services.

Khraim et al. (2011) asked 800 Jordanian consumers for their views and motives. They were asked to rate 19 store attributes on a five-point scale (1 = not at all influential; 5 = very influential). Most important to the participants was a "reasonably priced offer" ($\bar{x}$ = 4.53) and least important was "proximity to the workplace" ($\bar{x}$ = 3.55) and a "range of local products" ($\bar{x}$ = 3.66). However, it is particularly noteworthy that the criteria "the owner is an acquaintance" is hardly weighted more heavily than the criteria "relatives work in this business" ($\bar{x}$ = 3.31). This is because, given the strong relationship orientation of Jordanian society and the great importance that family ties have there, higher agreement values are expected. Once again, religious beliefs proved to be an important moderator. Very religious people rated all shopping place characteristics as "more influential" than moderately religious and especially as nonreligious people, with an average mean difference of 0.6 scale units between the very religious and the nonreligious.

Taylor/Minton (2021) investigated whether retail companies can influence shopping preferences through the nature of their communication policy (active vs. passive). In this study, individual Christmas gift cards were regarded as "active" and general Christmas advertising as "passive." The results of this study revealed that gift cards have a better effect on extrinsically as well as intrinsically religious people, although in different ways:

- It fills extrinsically religious consumers with pride to be thought of personally in this way.
- Among intrinsically religious consumers, gift cards elicit lower levels of guilt than general Christmas advertising.

7.1.2 *Social criteria of shopping place preference*

In the recent past, many consumers began to expect more from a shopping place than "just" high-quality products at low prices. Now, many also attach importance to a good reputation and social commitment on the part of the retailer. This was confirmed empirically by Mokhlis (2009a). Regardless of

Table 20 Importance of shopping place characteristics

	Muslim (n = 103)	*Buddhist (n = 57)*	*Hindu (n = 34)*	*Christian (n = 32)*
Reputation	4.34	4.10	4.17	4.17
Value for money	4.09	3.56	3.91	3.78
Sales promotion actions	3.43	3.25	3.19	3.20
Attractiveness	2.98	3.15	3.29	3.06

Legend: Scale: 1 = not important, 5 = very important.

Source: Mokhlis (2009a, p. 72).

religious affiliation, the most important factor for the Malaysian participants was the good reputation of the retailer, ahead of its value for money (see Table 20).

In this context, a study in which Dinh et al. (2022) interviewed 388 Vietnamese Catholics about the background of their loyalty to shopping places is also of interest. Unlike extrinsically religious people, intrinsically religious Vietnamese people tend to evaluate the market presence of retail companies from an ethical point of view (e.g., fairness in dealing with others). If their judgment is positive, they intend to continue shopping at the store. In the case of extrinsically religious customers, this relationship is mediated by their life satisfaction. Extrinsically religious people who are satisfied with their lives tend to be loyal to retailers.

How important is the corporate social responsibility (CSR) commitment of retail companies for consumers' decisions on where to buy food, clothing, shoes, electronics and household goods? Friske et al. (2021) investigated this question. They found that intrinsically religious people are influenced by CSR (cf. IV-1.1), but under two limiting conditions:

- First, it is a mediated relationship, which means that perceived CSR commitment only indirectly influences purchasing site preference (via attitudes toward CSR).
- Second, only corporate misconduct proved to be significant. Perceived corporate social irresponsibility reduced the likelihood that intrinsically religious people would shop in the store. If, on the other hand, their presumed high expectations of the moral integrity of retail companies are met or even exceeded, this is not reflected in their purchasing behavior.

7.1.3 *Relevance of scientific findings*

The effects described by Mokhlis (2009a) and Wilkes et al. (1986), among others, are substantial theoretically, but not very meaningful in terms of practice. For example, the largest mean difference found by McDaniel/Burnett (1990) in absolute terms is only 0.32 units on a seven-point importance scale (both for friendliness of sales personnel and for product quality).

As such, the observed effects are weak. However, they fit in well with what we know about religious people in general. For example, they attach great importance to personal relationships and are well connected socially (e.g., in their church community). Accordingly, it is particularly important to them to be served by friendly and supportive staff. Furthermore, there are numerous findings that speak for an above-average risk aversion of religious people (see III-5.2). They are less likely than others to make impulsive purchasing decisions (see Mokhlis 2009a). And because of their increased need for security, the quality of the product range is even more important to them than to less religious consumers.

However, since this effect is observed for all 19 individual criteria, the question arises as to whether this really captures differences in importance or rather different response styles.

7.2 Shopping frequency

Where consumers shop most often seems to depend relatively little on their religious affiliation. At least, this is how the results of a study conducted by Mokhlis (2009a) in Kuala Lumpur (Malaysia) can be summarized. When asked where they had shopped in the past 12 months and how often (1 = never, 5 = very often), all religious group subsamples named the department store first, with Hindus being relatively the most frequent ($\bar{x} = 3.56$) and Christians somewhat less frequent ($\bar{x} = 3.19$). Mail order played the smallest role (Muslims: $\bar{x} = 2.15$; Buddhists: $\bar{x} = 1.86$). The only significant difference in mean values, although not too large, relates to shopping in the specialist department of a larger type of business (or specialist department store). There, Hindus ($\bar{x} = 2.79$) shop somewhat more frequently than Buddhists ($\bar{x} = 2.11$). There are no differences in frequency of shopping in a hypermarket or shopping center (Muslims = 2.92, Hindus as well as Christians = 2.56) and in a specialty store (Hindus = 2.76, Muslims = 2.39).

7.3 Products conforming to religion

But what about shopping places that offer religiously certified products exclusively or to a significant extent? Do they profit significantly from this by attracting a disproportionately large number of religious consumers? And do Muslims appreciate it if a store does not offer alcoholic beverages?

While the influence of appropriate product labeling on purchase intention and brand loyalty has already been studied more frequently (see V-5.2), only a few have analyzed the effects on the choice of shopping place. Among the exceptions are Jamal/Sharifuddin (2015). They explain the positive influence of halal products on the loyalty of shoppers. The halal label acts as a quality guarantee, which creates trust and thus unifies shopping.

It is known to be extremely important to many Muslims that "their" place of purchase does not offer alcoholic beverages. If they did, this would even be a reason for devout Turkish customers to boycott the store (cf. Uysal/Okumuş 2019). However, the exceptionally high approval rating determined by Khraim et al. (2011) ($\bar{x} = 4.52$ on a five-point response scale) raises questions. This is because it is not based on a representative sample, but on the information provided by mainly younger, well-educated Jordanians with an upper income and a mostly urban, secular lifestyle. Therefore, a more tolerant attitude toward alcohol would have been expected. It is therefore possible that the strict rejection of alcoholic beverages is more the result of a response tendency than an expression of actual convictions. This is supported by the fact that Muslim respondents answer socially desirable questions much more frequently than Jewish respondents, for example (see Baron-Epel et al. 2010).

However, retailers can behave in a religion-compliant manner not only in the composition of their assortment, but also, for example, in setting their opening times. They seem to be able to score points with very religious consumers. Faithful Catholics and Protestants, for example, prefer stores that remain closed on Sundays (cf. Siguaw/Simpson 1997). This has not changed two decades later, as the stronger their intrapersonal commitment, the more Christians in the southern US value companies that respect the commandment of Sunday rest. This strengthens the corporate image and ultimately the loyalty to the retailer (cf. Swimberghe et al. 2014).

In addition to a Sharia-compliant product range and a trustworthy pricing policy, the special features that make up an Islamic store include gender segregation (cf. Abu Bakar/Hussin 2013). Does this mean that shopping places in Islamic societies that require women and men to shop separately have an advantage? In the eyes of Muslim consumers from northern Nigeria, no. By their own account, they feel comfortable shopping with members of the opposite sex in the same supermarket. They also found no fault with the price strategies of the suppliers, the shopping atmosphere and the product selection, but they did find fault with the advertising messages, which seemed deceptive or dishonest to them (cf. Yusuf/Madichie 2012).

7.4 Religious identity and ethical positioning of the provider

Members of religious minorities in particular tend to trust primarily, and sometimes exclusively, providers who belong to the same religious community as they do and to buy from them (e.g., Bonne/Verbeke 2008). This preference is referred to as religious centrism. As Siala (2013) has shown using the example of the purchase of car insurance, the common religious identity of providers and consumers (Muslims of different ethnic backgrounds) strengthens their customer loyalty, which ultimately results in an increased willingness to pay and to provide positive word of mouth (WoM) for the provider (see Figure 29).

This finding is in line with Belk's (1988) view that the preference of many customers for a place to shop depends to a large extent on the identification potential of the company. Since religious beliefs and values are essential for

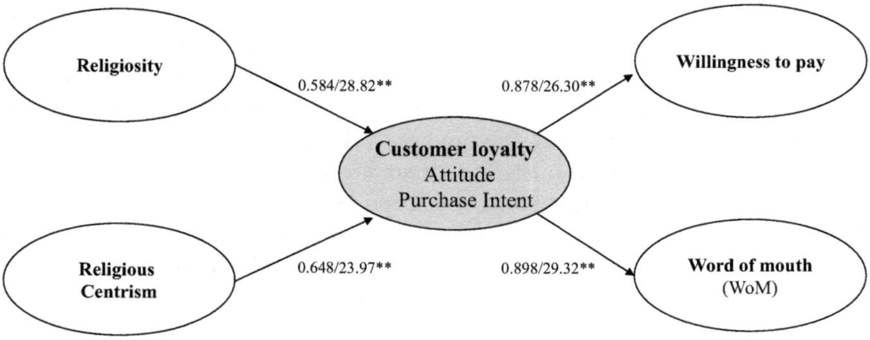

Figure 29 Influence of religiosity and religious centrism on customer behavior: Results of a path analysis.

Source: Own representation based on Siala (2013, p. 585).

the identity and self-concept of religious people, they prefer to shop in stores whose product range (e.g., organic, local production), personnel policy (e.g., no low-wage jobs), etc. correspond to their values (cf. Swimberghe et al. 2009). In the US, the growing segment of Christian "Faith Driven Consumers" is estimated at 46 million with a total purchasing power of over 1.75 trillion dollars. For the opportunity to shop in stores that visibly stand for the same religious values as themselves, they also accept higher prices (cf. Davis 2016).

What would customers think of a retailer who publicly advocated same-sex marriage? First, Swimberghe et al. (2009) gave this scenario to 425 American consumers. They found that to the extent that this commitment does not correspond to the religious identity and moral convictions of the consumers, their intention to switch increases and their willingness to engage in word-of-mouth advertising (i.e., to tell other consumers positive things about this retailer) decreases.

Part IX

Communication policy

1 Communication goals

Marketing usually distinguishes between economic (e.g., increasing sales) and non-economic communication goals (e.g., increasing awareness). Due to the imputability problem, however, the fulfillment of economic goals is usually not sufficiently verifiable. This is because none of the marketing instruments works exclusively on its own, but only in combination. In addition, there are often many environmental influences. No matter how successful and convincing the advertising campaign for a particular product may be, it will not be able to stimulate sales to the extent hoped for if:

- The price is set too high.
- The product quality is poor.
- An economic slump has decisively worsened the consumer climate.

Therefore, academic research and marketing departments mostly focus on the extra-economic goals, such as awareness, attitude and purchase intention. In order to achieve this, the attention of the target market must be gained. In addition, the central advertising message must be conveyed and communicated in a credible and likeable manner.

1.1 Convey central advertising message

According to a secondary statistical analysis of the World Values Survey 2005, religious people trust other people more than non-religious people (see Guiso et al. 2006). This may be the reason why they are less critical and defensive of advertising messages. But religious affiliation also influences how advertising messages are received. While Protestants and, with some reservations, Catholics seem to be more trusting, Hindus tend to be (slightly) distrustful. No clear tendency was found among Buddhists, Jews and Muslims.

As members of relatively competitive societies, Christians and Jews are especially receptive to advertising messages that communicate the unique selling proposition. What benefit does a product offer the consumer? For this reason, the advertising message in these countries often focuses on the product advantage offered by the advertised product (e.g., long shelf life).

DOI: 10.4324/9781003506010-47

Buddhism, Islam and Confucianism, on the other hand, are particularly widespread in relationship-oriented societies. There, it is more important to increase the quality of the relationship (e.g., through trust-building messages, such as 24/7 customer service). A high level of awareness also contributes to this. After all, the known (i.e., the familiar), is usually more trustworthy than the unknown. In these markets, advertising is therefore primarily intended to make a product known, to anchor it in the memory of those being advertised to and to build up a communicative relationship with the customer. Campaigns that are intended to influence too superficially run the risk of appearing obtrusive and exaggerated and of triggering reactance.[63]

1.2 Attract the attention of the target market

Advertising messages have to stand out from the vast amount of information available, which is characteristic of information societies. In most cases, advertisers have little time to attract the viewer's attention with a social media campaign or a traditional newspaper ad. For example, ordinary ads in general-interest magazines are viewed for an average of only 1.5–2.5 seconds (cf. Kroeber-Riel et al. 2019, pp. 60 ff.. 304 ff., 542). In order to nevertheless be able to capture the attention of the target market, companies use various ad appeals. Whether this should include religious advertising appeals is debatable and seems to depend on the context (cf. IX-6.2.5). From an Islamic perspective, advertisers should refrain from anything that violates the principle of fairness in business transactions, including exaggerated and misleading advertising messages and designs (cf. Behravan/Masoudi 2012).

1.2.1 Religious symbols

Symbols are frequently used in advertising. They are very attention-grabbing and, when used appropriately, can give the advertising message a positive emotional charge. Symbols can be of many kinds, even the environment in which a product or service is embedded. If a TV commercial shows a beer bottle against the backdrop of a forest, nature is supposed to symbolize "purity": the purity of the beer. If an off-road vehicle drives through the steppe in a TV commercial, then this type of ad symbolizes "freedom," which viewers can (supposedly) attain as soon as they are in possession of the advertised vehicle.

Since hardly any system of ideas is as symbolic as a religion, it makes sense for Interfaith Marketing (IFM) to use religious symbols in advertising. Sacred images, figures and texts are still deeply rooted in society's collective consciousness despite increasing secularization. As such, this can draw the viewer's attention to the advertising message more quickly than other symbols (cf. Taylor et al. 2010). Furthermore, it is assumed that companies that specifically use religious symbols in their marketing communications are perceived as particularly credible and trustworthy.

As Halstead et al. (2009) found out through in-depth interviews with managers of smaller Christian service providers, they mostly use religious symbols in their advertising to signal their Christian convictions to consumers. On the one hand, they want to target the religious market segment (see Zehra/Minton 2020). On the other hand, religious symbols should also be understood as an implicit promise to the market as a whole to be a particularly trustworthy and efficient service provider (see Taylor/Halstead 2014). It is true that explicit promises, such as a quality guarantee, usually have a stronger effect (cf. Wirtz et al. 2000). But implicit promises are less obvious, less easy to see through, and less enforceable or criticizable.

Can companies expect more success if they advertise with religious symbols and themes instead of secular ones? Ideally, the former would activate the religious values of those being advertised to, which would promote acceptance of the advertising message. But the research findings on this thus far are contradictory. On the one hand, Muralidharan/La Ferle (2018) and van Esch et al. (2014) found that "religious ads" are more appealing to very religious people than to less religious consumers. And in a study by Taylor et al. (2010), Christian symbols (cross) significantly improved the acceptance of ads by evangelical Christians. This effect was moderated by the religiosity of the participants, as the more religious they were, the more positive the responses. Certain characteristics of the advertising company (e.g., trustworthiness, professionalism) acted as mediators. On the other hand, the attitude toward the brand and the purchase intention of very religious Christians deteriorated when a cross was shown in an advertisement for pet insurance and the participants were not interested in animals (cf. Dodson/Hyatt 2000).

The obvious explanation that religious symbols do not work for low-involvement products was indirectly empirically refuted by Agarwala et al. (2021) using the example of advertising for a commonplace product (soap). In their study, Hindu symbols (lantern) improved brand evaluation and strengthened purchase intention. As Henley et al. (2009) found out, religious symbols work better if they have a content-related connection to the advertised product (beer) or the advertised service (family counseling). And it is obviously also important what motives the consumers ascribe to the company. According to Zehra/Minton (2020), only some of the participants consider such a design to be a religious statement. Others see it as an easy-to-see-through marketing strategy. Furthermore, it became clear that religious symbols only improve the attitude of Muslims toward the company, but not of Christians. One explanation is offered by the moderator open-mindedness: only those who are fundamentally skeptical of new ideas and think dogmatically are not bothered by religious advertising symbols (see Minton 2020). Religious people in general (see IV-3.1) and Muslims in particular meet this condition (see Albaghli/Carlucci 2021). Other influencing factors are the type and strength of the religious convictions of those being advertised to and their product involvement. In the study by Dotson/Hyatt (2000) mentioned above, advertisements on which the Christian symbol of the cross was clearly visible were only successful with religiously dogmatic participants who were interested in the advertised product (pet insurance) (= involvement). The comparison group (dogmatic, low involvement) reacted less positively. The advertising message did not improve their attitude toward the brand, nor did it increase their purchase intention.

Muslims and members of other religious groups generally react positively to religious symbols, including in advertising (see Butt et al. 2018). However, their use is not without risk. As a rule, religious symbols are only unreservedly recommendable if the target consumers are very religious. For less religious consumers, there is a risk of a backlash effect. According to Taylor et al. (2017), in their study, the Christian fish symbol inserted in an advertisement fueled skepticism toward the provider, and the perceived quality of the service offering deteriorated. Similar findings were reported by Nickerson et al. (2023), where they showed that advertisements for a cell phone with Islamic symbols (lantern, crescent moon) and an Islamic greeting ("Ramadan Kareem") did not promote either the attitude or the purchase intention of Muslim consumers compared to a neutral ad. Even the very religious participants in this study did not react positively to the Islamic symbols to the extent expected. However, they did worsen the purchase intention of Christians and non-religious people. Under certain conditions, religious symbols may do more harm than good, even among very religious consumers. According to Dotson/Hyatt (2000), this is the case when believers feel that their religion is being misused to help something trivial, such as a product, succeed (cf. IX-6.5).

1.2.2 Controversial topics and designs

Companies can also attract attention by provoking and, for example, offending deep-seated social, societal or religious feelings. This advertising strategy has been called shock advertising (c.f. Hubbard 1993). Examples of shock advertising include oil-smeared ducks, naked buttocks stamped "HIV-positive" and a blood-stained shirt of a soldier with a bullet hole.

But how does shock advertising work? It is undoubtedly often effective at attracting the attention of the target consumers (cf. Myers et al. 2020). However, it usually has a negative effect on the downstream phases of information processing. Apart from legal risks, controversial advertising is usually associated with a serious danger known as the vampire effect in which particularly eye-catching design elements attract all the attention and ultimately distract attention from the actual advertising message, provided that the design does not relate to the content of the advertising message. Advertising with sexual cues is regularly exposed to this danger (cf. IX-6.2).

However, as acceptance research has shown, shock advertising is not rejected in principle. Many non-profit organizations use such advertising with certain limits, like no religious taboos or important social norms being violated in the process. Otherwise, however, "in the opinion of the respondents, the end justifies the means in this case" (cf. Parry 2013).

1.3 Be credible

Attention is usually a necessary, but not sufficient condition for successful communication. Although hardly anyone would dispute this, it happens time and again that the success in attracting attention is achieved at the expense of the credibility of the advertising message or the company (e.g., through exaggerated promises or the violation of religious taboos) (cf. Greenough 2021). The credibility strategy promises greater success, especially in the marketing of high-involvement products. As Sarofim/Cabano (2018) recently demonstrated with a sequential mediation analysis, this is particularly true if the target market consists largely of religious consumers. This is because all religions have high standards for the truthfulness of communication. However, advertisers can benefit from the fact that (moderately) religious people a priori rate the truthfulness of advertising messages higher than non-religious or less religious people. Presumably because of their above-average positive view of the world and of humanity, they usually assume more than others that the advertised product will actually offer them the promised benefit. The credibility they accord to advertising increases the purchase intention of the advertised product for religious consumers.

However, this positive attitude does not relieve companies of the task of paying greater attention to the credibility of their advertising in terms of form and content. According to the source-attractiveness theory, the similarity of the communicator to the target consumers, as well as his or her familiarity and likable appearance, are important antecedents to perceived credibility of the communicator (cf. McGuire 1985). The source credibility theory (cf. Hovland et al. 1953) describes the credibility of the communicator as a three-dimensional construct: competence, attractiveness, and trustworthiness.

Various studies suggest that trustworthiness is the primary factor of perceived credibility (see Wang/Scheinbaum 2017). Furthermore, the religiosity of the celebrity endorser has proven to be an important moderator (see Silalahi et al. 2021). The trustworthiness and attractiveness of a celebrity endorser disproportionately increases the purchase intention of the consumers, provided that the target group perceives the endorser as religious.

2 Target groups of communication

The most important target group or target market for IFM is religious consumers, since they have many things in common (values, beliefs, behaviors) regardless of their religious affiliation. Of course, it is also possible to target consumers of a particular religious group. However, since homogeneous societies are the exception and a diversity of religious groups is the rule, it is often very difficult for IFM to target just one particular religious group. Moreover, there is a risk of undesirable side effects among members of other faiths.

2.1 Religious consumers

We have already described the personality profile of religious people in detail (cf. IV-3.1). On the one hand, these are characteristics such as conservatism and unwillingness to change, which indicate a low receptiveness to innovative products and services. On the other hand, religious people have prosocial characteristics. Their altruism, modesty and willingness to place trust in others predestine religious people as a target market for prosocial corporate strategies.

2.1.1 Trust

Religious people not only trust our economic system more than non-religious people, but they also do not fundamentally doubt that charitable organizations fulfill their purpose and actually act in a charitable manner, which is why they are increasingly willing to support them through donations (cf. Hopkins et al. 2014). And they trust various advertising measures more than average (cf. Minton 2019; 2015). Since trust is an important prerequisite for advertising success, religious consumers are a receptive target market for any form of commercial communication. However, the exception to this is political advertising, where religious people distrust such messages more than non-religious people (cf. Nelson et al. 2021).

Why is that so? Why do religious people, regardless of their religious affiliation, usually trust other people? One decisive reason is the conviction that our world is in principle a just place (cf. Bègue 2002). This is explained, on

DOI: 10.4324/9781003506010-48

the one hand, by corresponding convictions and values that presumably all religions teach. On the other hand, the above-average frequency of interaction among religious people is likely to play a role. In order for their numerous social encounters, such as with other members of the community, to be positive, it is necessary to believe in the good in people and to trust others. In addition, all religions demand respectful interpersonal interaction from believers, with trust being considered an important manifestation of respect (cf. Berggren/Bjørnskov 2011). In this context, trust in God, which primarily intrinsically religious people have, serves not only as a model for dealing with other people (= interpersonal trust), but also with the marketplace.

According to Li et al. (2008), the common basis of general trust, which includes interpersonal trust and "economic" trust (including brand trust, trust in business partners, etc.), is a positive image of humanity derived from trust in God. This manifests itself, among other things, as the conviction that people are in principle well-meaning and competent. However, this is not blind trust. Rather, religions also impart values and convictions to believers that help them to recognize undesirable developments, such as morally inappropriate attempts to influence people through advertising and other forms of manipulative communication.

2.1.2 Risk acceptance

Buyers take risks: will the product fulfill its purpose (= functional risk)? What will my friends say about it (= social risk)? Is the purchased product worth its price (= financial risk)? It is well known that risk perception is highly subjective. In Christian societies, for example, it is mainly the functional risk that counts, whereas in relationship-oriented Confucian societies, it is mainly the social risk that is important. There, "saving face" is one of the decisive cultural standards (cf. Bao et al. 2003).

Materialistic buying behavior can represent a high social risk for religious people, since, for example, conspicuous consumption of luxury goods is hardly compatible with religious values such as modesty (cf. IV-3.2; V-3.3). Therefore, this group of consumers appreciates ads that do not highlight the material symbolic value of the advertised product but convey advertising messages that support them in consuming without feelings of guilt (c.f. Veer/Shanker 2011). Specifically, they prefer advertising messages that:

- Demonstrate the affiliation of the buyer or user of the advertised good to a socially recognized reference group (e.g., sustainable, fair and ecological fashion).
- Communicate to the social environment that the owner or user is individually fulfilling his or her social responsibility (e.g., by buying a Tesla).

Companies can counter the increased risk sensitivity of religious consumers (see Figure 30) with risk-reducing strategies. This is particularly advisable if

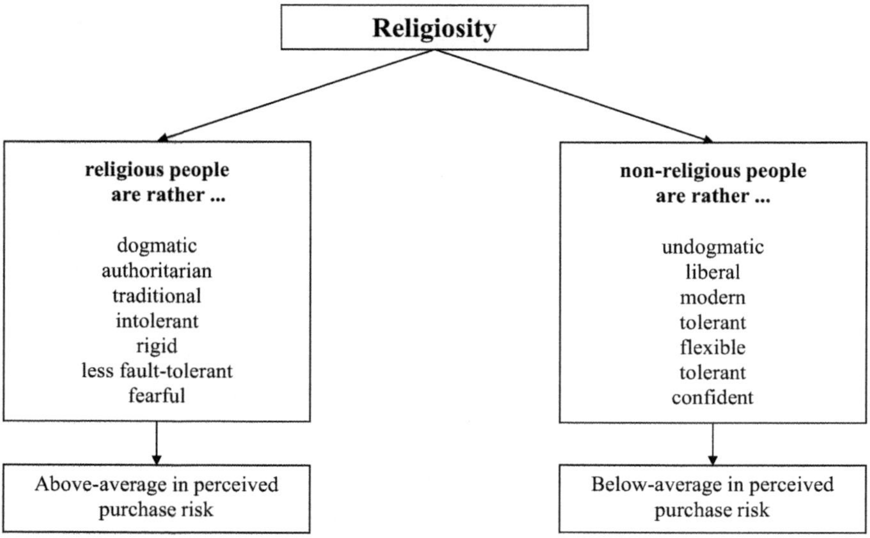

Figure 30 Personality and risk perception.
Source: Delener (1990a, p. 29).

the target market consists of devout Catholics. Promising strategies are, for example:

- Information from independent external institutions (e.g., official seals of approval, reliable test ratings)
- Advice from credible personalities (cf. IV-6.1)
- Generous guarantees (e.g., money-back guarantee, extension of product warranty)

2.2 Religiously diverse societies

Most societies are religiously diverse. Therefore, advertisers should always consider how advertising messages that meet the needs and beliefs of a particular religious group will affect members of another religious community. Intrinsically religious people in particular are likely to reject messages designed for other religious groups. Aji/Dharmmesta (2019) studied how Indonesian Catholics react to "Islamic TV commercials." Their finding was that intrinsically religious people increasingly doubt the credibility of foreign cultural advertising messages. Since their religious convictions are firmly established, competing religious convictions trigger greater cognitive dissonance in them than in extrinsically religious people, whose relationship to their faith is primarily superficial and purpose-oriented (see II-1.2). Doubting the credibility of what is seen or heard is a good way to avoid or reduce cognitive dissonance.

3 Time and subject of communication

Particular sensitivity is required in the context of important religious holidays and festivals. Buddhists associate the spring festival with the beginning of a new life. Especially during the first 15 days, companies there should refrain from advertising "controversial products" such as underwear (see I-6.3). In Malaysia, advertising for underwear and contraceptives in the mass media is prohibited. The only exceptions are media whose target market is predominantly non-Muslims. Advertising for feminine hygiene products is generally not permitted until after 10 p.m. (see Fam et al. 2004).

According to tradition, the angel Gabriel delivered the revelation to Mohammed in the ninth month of the Islamic calendar (cf. Braswell 1996). Since then, the holy month of Ramadan has been the fourth of the five pillars of Islam. Muslims are then supposed to fast from sunrise to sunset and reflect on the original Islamic values. TV stations take advantage of the fact that during this time, Muslims spend a lot of time with their families. In Egypt, for example, the prospect of a large audience leads to the production of TV series and shows especially for Ramadan and with a considerable increase in advertising during this period (cf. Ansari et al. 2017), especially for high-calorie foods (cf. Alyousif et al. 2020). However, from a purely economic point of view, the pricing policy of broadcasters often negates this gain in reach. This is because disproportionately higher fees are charged during Ramadan, which is why the price per thousand contacts actually deteriorates during this month.

As a content analysis of the commercials revealed, advertising during the holy month is also different from that during the rest of the year. The advertising style is traditional and garish, while provocative things are undesirable. Since Muslims are supposed to remain pure during Ramadan, it is advisable for suppliers of controversial products to take a break from advertising during these weeks. Products with sexual connotations (e.g., underwear) should be advertised in more "discreet" media (e.g., Internet, direct mailings, special magazines) at most. Just as the Christmas season is in Christian societies, in Islamic societies, Ramadan creates a favorable environment for campaigns for public services as well.

DOI: 10.4324/9781003506010-49

4 Media usage

Target markets can also be described and distinguished on the basis of their media usage behavior. Since the 1980s, research has focused primarily on the media preferences and types of media use of members of the various Christian denominations (print media, electronic media, Internet). Current research has also focused on social media and examines, among other things, the attitudes and online behavior of Muslim (cf. Mostafa 2019) and Jewish users (cf. Lev-On/Lissitsa 2018).

4.1 Motives for media usage

According to gratification theory, people prefer media offerings from which they expect certain rewards. If religious people, especially Catholics, read newspapers more often than others, it is presumably to minimize the probability of making wrong decisions (e.g., a wrong purchase) (cf. Severin/Tankard 2001). Jews, on the other hand, are likely to be motivated by curiosity, given their openness to innovation.

However, research in the sociology of religion prefers the secularization theory. According to this theory, after the Enlightenment, the primacy of rationality, scientific thinking and technical progress led to the loss of importance of the religious worldview and the decline of spirituality and mysticism (cf. Swatos/Olson 2000). Not only from a conservative point of view, the messengers of secularization are "the media," above all the electronic media and even more so social media. Both are an instrument and a mirror of the secular world and in constant conflict with traditional religious values. For this reason, it is to be expected that religious people tend to avoid their predominantly entertainment-oriented offerings, and orthodox people and fundamentalists avoid them as much as possible. To them, superficial media enjoyment seems more or less sinful, which is why they do not want (or are not allowed) to expose themselves to content that is incompatible with their worldview. In fact, religious people are generally not guided by the escape motive (i.e., the quest to escape the impositions and challenges of everyday life by spending a lot of time in the illusory world of the media) (cf. Charlton et al. 2013).

DOI: 10.4324/9781003506010-50

When the very religious or ultra-Orthodox use social media, they do so for very different reasons, as a survey of Israeli Jews revealed. While the secular participants in this study primarily cited social needs as a motive for using the service (maintaining contact with like-minded people), ultra-Orthodox participants stated that they were primarily pursuing professional goals (establishing and maintaining business relationships). Although they are less open to different opinions overall, this group of people comes into contact with people of other faiths much more frequently (cf. Lev-On/Lissitsa 2018). This opens up the possibility for IFM to reach this otherwise rather skeptical target market via professional online networks.

4.2 Credibility of and trust in the media

One of the key questions of communications policy is which media are more or less trusted by which target markets? From the beginnings of religion media research (cf. Buddenbaum/Stout 1996), it is known that in the eyes of Catholics and Protestants, newspapers are the most trustworthy sources of information (cf. Westley/Severin 1964). Mormons, however, consider them to be untrustworthy, immoral and politically one-sided (i.e., too liberal) (cf. Golan/Baker 2012). However, this may have less to do with their reporting than with the fact that strict believers in Mormonism reject the modern media as a whole.

Not only these studies, but the entire sociological research on the credibility of media seems contradictory and unconvincing. Even if the described, partly positive, and partly negative correlations are significant, with correlations in the range of ±0.10 to 0.20, they contribute only little to explain the overall variance (e.g.. Golan/Day 2010).

4.3 Intensity of media usage

Catholics read newspapers more frequently than average (cf. Jelen 1996), more frequently than people who never go to church (cf. Sobal/Jackson-Beeck 1981), and more frequently than Protestants (e.g., Penrose et al. 1974). Jews are likewise avid newspaper readers, more so than nonreligious people and adherents of other faiths (cf. Rigney/Hoffman 1993).

Religious people also prefer print media (cf. Croucher/Harris 2012), especially those published by their faith community (cf. Davie 2008). As a telephone survey by Finnegan/Viswanath (1988) showed, Americans who are members of a church read local magazines more often than their peers who do not belong to a church community (67% vs. 33%). The explanation was that those who are involved in their church and connected to its congregation are interested in local news. The survey also showed that parishioners read daily newspapers significantly more often (70% vs. 30%) and watch cable TV more often than those who do not belong to a church (72% vs. 28%). Overall, religious people seem to have a greater need for information than others.

However, they watch television relatively little (see Armfield 2003). In addition to others, Tankard/Harris (1980) have analyzed the differences that distinguish people who do not watch television from those who watch it a lot. Accordingly, the latter are more often dissatisfied with their life as a whole and their family life in particular. On the other hand, many "socially committed" and religious people belong to the group of non-viewers. However, there was one unsurprising exception as people who consider themselves religiously conservative watch religious TV programs more often than people with a liberal worldview (cf. Roberts 1983). With regard to the use of the Internet, it is known, among other things, that religious people:

- Approach this media in a rather distanced way (cf. Croucher/Harris 2012)
- Use social media primarily to maintain their social relationships with like-minded people and less often to inform or entertain themselves (cf. Almenayes 2014)
- Are less likely to develop an Internet addiction (cf. Meerkerk et al. 2006)

However, the negative correlation between religiosity and the intensity of Internet use seems to be only weak (see Armfield/Holbert 2003; Bedell 2000). According to Nyland/Near (2007), religious people do not spend significantly less time on online platforms than non-religious people, and young religious Muslims living in Istanbul now even use Instagram more actively than non-religious people (cf. Kurtulus et al. 2018). Presumably, the decisive difference is not the intensity but the objective of use.

This was already indicated by a classification of Internet users by Mathwick (2002). Using data from the "10th WWW User Survey" of the Georgia Institute of Technologies, Graphics, Visualization and Usability Centers, she analyzed the profile of American online users. Four groups could be distinguished by cluster analysis:

- Active Surfers (Transactional Community Members)
- Socializers
- Observers (Lurkers)
- Contact Seekers (Personel Connnectors)

As can be seen from the surfing behavior of the different user types, the socially religious prefer to use the Internet to exchange views with members of their faith community. They attach great importance to personal contact and interaction with others, while impersonal expressions of opinion (via feedback forms, e-mail or chat forums) are less important to them (see Figure 31).

This typology is confirmed by Nyland/Near (2007), whose study found that religious people primarily use the Internet to maintain existing contacts with family members and friends. The fact that religious women also use the Internet more frequently to find out about social events or to get to know

Surfing behavior	Active (n = 290)	Sociable (n = 85)	Observer (n = 270)	Contact finder (n = 171)
Contact with online providers				
- E-mail and chat forums	●	○	○	○
- Feedback on products	●	○	○	○
Member of ...				
- Leisure groups	○	●	○	○
- Political groups	○	●	○	○
- Religious organizations	○	●	○	○
-Charities	○	●	○	○
Social Relationships				
- Contact with family	○	●	○	●
- Contact with colleagues	○	○	○	●

Note: ● above-average mean value

Figure 31 Typology of American online users.
Source: Mathwick (2002, p. 48).

new music is explained by the role they play in their church community. They are the ones who organize charitable events, for which they use the Internet (e.g., to publicize these events).

Finally, on the connection between religious affiliation and attitude toward the Internet, reference should be made to Kluver/Cheong (2007), who interviewed selected spiritual leaders of the religious groups active in Singapore on this topic. Whether Buddhists, Protestants, Taoists, Hindus, Catholics or Muslims, on the one hand, they all perceive the Internet as a valuable means of disseminating and searching for information about religions (e.g., prayer instructions, songs, information about the congregation). On the other hand, they also know that it facilitates access to content that they consider immoral and illegal (e.g., pornography). In addition, false information about the individual religious communities is often disseminated there. The concern that unorthodox content is shared in Internet forums and on social media is also widespread among Muslim users (cf. Campbell/Evolvi 2019).

McClure (2020) indirectly confirmed what has been described thus far. He chose a different approach and did not examine media use as a function of religious affiliation or religiosity, but rather the extent of religious practice as a function of media use. As his evaluation of data from the Baylor Religion Survey revealed, frequent Internet users rarely pray, rarely participate in religious services, etc. However, this does not apply to frequent TV users. They practice their religion just as intensively as infrequent TV users. The conclusion of this study was that most religious people have made their peace with television, but not with the Internet. However, a gender effect should be noted here. While male religious people spend hardly any less time on the

Internet than other men, religious women spend significantly less time there than less religious comparison people. This is presumably due to the greater willingness of women to respect the rules of their religion (in this case, the commandment to stay away from the vain aspects of the world (cf. Charlton et al. 2013).

What does the different usage behavior of religious consumers mean for providers who market products and services on the Internet or via social media? It would undoubtedly be a mistake to limit oneself to the company website and not also post one's own content on relevant forums and social media channels. A sporting goods manufacturer, for example, could advertise on relevant sports forums. Since "social Internet users," who include a disproportionately large number of religious people, frequently communicate with others on the Internet, word of mouth and online experience reports from reference consumers are also important strategy components. Through these methods, religious Internet users, who are generally relationship-oriented, can be better convinced of the advantages of a product or service than through the usual advertising communications. Ultra-Orthodox people, who use social media primarily to maintain business contacts, can be approached relatively well via career platforms, provided that the product or service corresponds to this medium (e.g., financial investment, laptop).

5 Personal communication

Especially before buying high-involvement products, many people ask friends and acquaintances for advice. As research has shown, hardly anything convinces consumers as much as recommendations from friends and acquaintances (cf. Casidy et al. 2021). According to the 2015 Nielsen study "Global Trust in Advertising," 92% of respondents trust them more than commercial advertising. In contrast to professional advisors and testimonials, people attribute altruistic motives to "friends and acquaintances". As a rule, they do not benefit financially when others follow their recommendations (see Berger 2014).

Wherever close social ties in the family and other living communities are the norm, advice from the closer social environment is understood as a form of social support. Religious people in particular, who prefer to communicate within their faith community, prefer to rely on personal references rather than anonymous information from the mass media, especially in the Islamic cultural area (cf. Yousaf/Malik 2013; Sanaie/Ranjbarian 1996). Also when searching for product information, religious Koreans primarily heed advice from their religious community, while they view external sources (sales staff, media) with more skepticism than less religious people do (cf. Choi et al. 2010; Shin et al. 2010; Saroglou et al. 2005). Presumably, shared religious beliefs act as a form of external control (cf. Kay et al. 2010a), protecting advice-seekers from opportunistic behavior by advisors (i.e., from abusing their informational advantage).

Another question is whether the willingness to report positive or negative word of mouth depends on the strength of consumers' religious beliefs or their religious affiliation. According to Siala (2013), religious Muslim consumers would be more likely to tell others positive information about a car insurer that provides Islam-compliant insurance policies. However, the relationship is weak ($r = 0.159$). In contrast, religious consumers' increased willingness to advise others against a provider they are disappointed with (negative word of mouth) is clearly demonstrable. Casidy et al. (2021) explain this by the fact that religious people are highly sensitive when they have the impression that they have not been treated fairly by a provider. This makes it difficult for

DOI: 10.4324/9781003506010-51

them to be forgiving and forgive a service failure. They process their anger by reporting the negative experience to their friends and acquaintances or to the general public on the Internet via electronic word of mouth.

Wisker/McKie (2021) argue similarly. In their study, religious people also reacted more strongly to perceived anger with increased negative word of mouth. The trigger was misinformation as the meat offered was not halal (i.e., the animal had not been slaughtered in accordance with Sharia law). This and other studies (e.g., Wisker 2020) suggest that religious people are very susceptible to fake news campaigns.

In communication networks, religious people not only assume the role of information seekers more often than average, but also that of information providers or opinion leaders (cf. Wilkes et al. 1986). For this reason, companies should look after their religious customers particularly intensively. They are regarded as credible multipliers and are particularly good at convincing other members of their faith network of the benefits of a product or service.

6 Advertising

Advertising (i.e., paid messages disseminated via the media (e.g., TV, print media, social media)) is still the most important communication tool. In the process, even experienced multinational companies repeatedly make astonishing mistakes, such as when Coca-Cola advertised on posters in Russia in the fall of 2007 with motifs characteristic of the Russian Orthodox Church (i.e., onion domes). However, it was not considered that the majority of Russians generally reject advertising with religious symbols. In addition, some of the posters were hung upside down, showing an upside-down church. In the end, the advertising campaign had to be stopped due to massive protests.

6.1 Attitudes toward advertising

A positive attitude toward advertising in general and toward a specific advertising measure in particular is one of the preconditions for positive advertising effects (MacKenzie et al. 1986; Gelb/Pickett 1983). Religious people have an ambivalent attitude toward this. On the one hand, they are generally more trusting than suspicious of their fellow human beings, which is also reflected in a more positive attitude toward advertising messages (cf. Minton 2015). On the other hand, all religions are said to have a more or less advertising-critical attitude. For example, commercial TV advertising in many Islamic states was for a long time only possible to a very limited extent and was even banned in Saudi Arabia until 1986. At that time, advertisers could only use alternative advertising media (e.g., magazines, billboards). Although even in the particularly conservative countries of the Arab world, there is largely freedom of advertising today, Sharia law has not lost its influence (see Rice/Al-Mossawi 2002). However, in some countries (e.g., Saudi Arabia), its requirements are observed more strictly than in others (e.g., Malaysia).

In an exploratory study (n = 43), Al-Makaty et al. (1996) surveyed male Muslims' (in Saudi Arabia) attitudes toward TV advertising. They were able to identify three types of attitudes:

- Modern advocates largely accept TV ads but object to Muslim women appearing in commercials.

DOI: 10.4324/9781003506010-52

- Tolerant traditionalists fear that advertising threatens Islamic values, but nevertheless consider further state intervention unnecessary.
- Conservative opponents reject TV advertising on principle.

Current research paints a somewhat more nuanced picture. According to Niazi et al. (2019), even devout Muslims do not fundamentally reject commercial advertising, but only advertising as seen in the Western media. Islamic advertising, on the other hand, was appreciated by the study participants (210 male and female students from Peshawar, Pakistan). Islamic advertising is in accordance with the relevant religious regulations of the Quran and:

- Refrains from sexual motives, strongly emotional, especially fear-inducing appeals as well as untrustworthy testimonials
- Respects the special dignity of families and the elderly and places faith above knowledge (i.e., prioritizing religious beliefs over scientific knowledge)

However, this form of advertising promises little success with people who are different or not believers. Malaysian consumers who do not profess Islam, for example, associate Islamic advertising mainly with derogatory terms: unattractive, boring, and not suitable for attracting attention (see Shafiq 2020). And according to a study by Aji/Dharmmesta (2019), intrinsically religious Christians even reject Islamic television advertising in principle and doubt its credibility.

6.2 Design of advertisements

There are various ways and means of influencing the target market's attitude to advertising and thus its chances of success, such as the use of religious symbols (cf. Naseri/Tamam 2012). More important, however, are the conformity of the advertising message and design with the values of the target group, the use of testimonials with identification potential as models or role models, and the credibility of the advertising message. Different types of advertising appeals can be distinguished: rational vs. emotional, religious vs. spiritual and moral vs. justice appeals.

6.2.1 Value conformity

Advertising is usually seen as a "mirror of society" (Gilly 1988), which is why the advertising message and design forms are usually adapted to the values of the target market. Since in countries such as Turkey, Malaysia or the US, the majority of society leads a religiously influenced life, the respective religious convictions are in the foreground there (cf. Fam et al. 2004). The striving for value conformity affects, among other things, the portrayal of gender roles in advertising. In the Koran, depending on the interpretation and translation, there are relatively strict guidelines on the clothing of women. Accordingly, advertisements in Arab media show significantly more women in long robes (83%) than in American ads (29%). Also, women in Arab media are only seen as good testimonials for "typically female products" such as cosmetics, food or cleaning products (cf. Al-Olayan/Karande 2000). Muslims are required to cover their hair. Therefore advertising messages for shampoo (e.g., "incomparably full, shiny hair") should not be illustrated with images of women with loose hair.

Nike was heavily criticized when the sporting goods manufacturer published advertisements in Arab media in 2017 that showed women acting in public spaces (e.g., playing various sports). This was unrealistic and did not reflect the traditional role of women in the Arab world (see Keshkar et al. 2019; Aswad 2017). Since women have not been allowed to participate in sports there, manufacturers of bicycles have only been able to advertise with female models if they stand next to the bicycle veiled or push the bicycle, but not ride the bicycle. For internationally active companies, this restrictive practice means that they cannot standardize their advertising worldwide but must differentiate regionally and adapt to the strict conditions of the Islamic region.

In the Islamic world, all products that are considered impure may not be advertised. These include in particular pork and alcoholic beverages. Impure services (e.g., betting, interest transactions) are also taboo. Furthermore, everything that is reminiscent of other religions should be avoided. In the case of the cross, there is also the fact that it not only symbolizes the Christian faith but also evokes associations with the crusaders in this region, who have a very bad reputation in the Arab world. Even fantasy figures, like those in children's books, can be problematic. In 2006, the Turkish TV station TRT had to take programs with Winnie-the-Pooh off the air at the behest of the government, because of the character's friend, the timid piglet (pig = unclean).

Products and services fulfill different functions. These can be "value-expressive" or "social-adjustive" (cf. Wilcox et al. 2009). Consumers with value-expressive attitudes prefer products and services that enable them to demonstrate to their social environment which values are important to them. Like many other areas of life, they place their consumption in the service of their need for self-expression (e.g., stylish, exquisite taste). Others express primarily socially conformist attitudes. They, too, ultimately want to attract attention through their consumption style, but for a different reason. They are concerned with the recognition of their peer group. As Pace (2014) has shown, extrinsically religious Americans (n = 375) respond almost equally well to socially adjusted and value-expressive ads for wristwatches (purchase intention: $\bar{x}$ = 3.24 vs. 3.37 on a four-point scale). Intrinsically religious consumers, on the other hand, are significantly more motivated to make a purchase with the socially adjusted ad ($\bar{x}$ = 3.17 vs. 2.60). As expected, this is because intrinsically religious people are not so concerned with outward appearances. It is more important to them to be in harmony with their religious values. Since it promises equal success with both target groups, advertisers should prefer the value-expressive advertisement.

Value conformity is also the reason why intrinsically religious people feel attracted to a social media campaign for the sustainable disposal of luxury products (positive attitude toward the brand, purchase intention), whereas extrinsically religious people do not. For the former, it is important to live in accordance with their religious values. Responsible action (e.g., sustainable disposal) corresponds to the social identity of religious people (cf. Minton/ Geiger-Oneto 2020).

6.2.2 Use of testimonials

In addition to or instead of presenters who introduce the advertised product, guide the viewer through the advertising video, etc., testimonials are often used in advertising. These human models have, allegedly or actually, gathered their own experience with the advertised product and can ideally give a credible account of it. Testimonials are also used so frequently to spread advertising messages because hardly anything is as attention-grabbing as images and representations of people, especially the eye area of the face. A distinction can be made between four types of testimonials:

- Experts who, as specialists, report positive things about the advertised product, such as "As a dentist, I recommend this toothpaste to my family" (success factor: competence).
- Celebrities, also known as celebrity endorsers, are well-known public figures (e.g., Michael Jordan) whose prominence is transferred to the advertised product (e.g., Hanes) by the advertisement. In some cases, celebrities act as advocates who directly support the advertised product, while in others they are indirectly associated with it (success factors: likeability and familiarity).
- Normal consumers ("people like you and me") who report on their positive experiences with the advertised product (success factor: identification).
- Influencers, who play a central role in social media marketing. These are people with a high reach on social media who share content from their lives with their many followers and also promote products. Influencers often combine all three success factors because, like fitness influencer Kayla Itsines, they are considered experts in a particular field (fitness and health), are very well known with the target market due to their high reach (almost 16 million followers), and at the same time come across as "normal" and approachable people (success factor: identification).

Advertising research has shown that it is worthwhile for companies to use testimonials, especially with religious customers in mind. For these customers, it is very important to act in accordance with the values of their faith community. And because they also believe in authority (cf. III-2.2), religious people are easily convinced by prominent advocates, especially if the advertised product conforms to their religion. Due to the pronounced orthopraxy of Islam (cf. El-Menouar 2014), Muslims are more susceptible than others to be influenced by such recommendations and advice. This was most recently confirmed by a study of 300 Muslim millennials from Malaysia. The celebrity advertising shown to them disproportionately strengthened the attitudes of very religious study participants toward advertising, their attitudes toward the advertised brand and their purchase intention (cf. Azizan et al. 2022).

Based on the results of a survey of Muslim consumers from Sudan by Mansour/Diab (2016), however, it should be borne in mind that it is problematic if the advertising models are "celebrities" (i.e., prominent representatives of entertainment and consumer society). Then religious Muslims distrust this type of advertising more than others. And because of their negative image of women, they react with skepticism to female testimonials in particular, unless they act within their traditional familial role.

Apart from this, testimonials are successful if they are perceived as credible. Since similarity has a trust-building effect, people consider others who belong to the same religious community as them to be more credible than people who do not believe or who believe differently. This is especially true for religious people who belong to a religious minority in their social environment. In the case of testimonials, the trustworthiness attributed to members of one's own religious group leads to more positive attitudes toward the brand advertised by them.

6.2.3 *Credible advertising messages and stylistic devices*

Ultimately, advertising messages are nothing more than a promise of benefits that the advertiser makes to potential customers. Like adherents of other religions, Muslims in particular should not promise anything that they cannot deliver. This applies not only to private life or dealings with business partners, but also to the design of advertising messages. Even more so than elsewhere, advertising messages in Arab media should be formulated simply and unambiguously, as they should be particularly credible. This moral claim is in contrast to the prevailing view in Western culture, according to which advertising should not be measured against reality. For it is generally known and accepted that advertising is part of the artificial media reality.

6.2.4 *Rational vs. emotional ad appeals*

The art of saying a lot with just a few words is highly valued in Islamic culture. It is one of the high-context cultures in which the indirect, implicit style of communication dominates. What is said there is not always what is meant, which is why the recipient of a message often has to infer its actual message from the context of the communication (cf. Kim et al. 1998). An important contextual factor is facial expressions. For example, the sentence "You've made an effort" says something fundamentally different, depending on whether it is said with a serious or an ironic, smiling facial expression.

However, it is not only the words used to convey a message that are important, but also the number of words used. In Arab print media, advertisements convey less product information than in American magazines: 88% of the advertisements evaluated by Al-Olayan/Karande (2000) contained at least two pieces of information (vs. 63% in the Arab comparison sample). As indicated previously, this may be due to cultural factors, but it may also be a consequence of the adaptation of ad design to different levels of literacy (cf. Al-Deen 1991).

Emotions also play an important role in advertising. There are numerous strategies to specifically arouse them, predominantly with fear appeals, humorous messages or sexual stimuli (cf. Hornik et al. 2017). In addition, it is easily overlooked that other advertising messages also trigger emotions as a side effect. For example, Taylor/Minton (2021) found, using the example of a fictitious retailer's Christmas advertising, that Christmas greetings in the guise of an individualized gift card filled extrinsically religious consumers with pride (compared to a standardized Christmas greeting card), while reducing intrinsically religious consumers' feelings of guilt. Both the pride of the extrinsically religious people, who were primarily interested in their self-image, and the lower feelings of guilt of the intrinsically religious people,[64] strengthened their attitude toward and emotional attachment to the retailer as well as their purchase intention.

In France, advertising is more often emotional than in the US (cf. Biswas et al. 1992). There, and especially in the sphere of influence of Islam and Buddhism, advertisers focus on information and rational ad appeals. In doing so, they address the practical or functional benefits that the advertised product offers to the target consumers (cf. Hornik/Miniero 2011).

Cabano/Minton (2023) investigated whether it depends on the degree of religiosity how consumers react to rational and emotional ad appeals. In view of their rather analytical cognitive style aimed at rational problem solving (cf. Zuckerman et al. 2020), it was to be expected that less religious people would react more positively to the rational than to the emotional ad appeal. Cabano/Minton (2023) were able to find support with this prediction through four online surveys (MTurk). However, the effect size of the observed significant mean differences is relatively small (e.g., "Attitude toward the advertised product": rational: $\bar{x} = 5.42$ vs. emotional: $\bar{x} = 4.82$; "Purchase intention": rational: $\bar{x} = 5.93$ vs. emotional: $\bar{x} = 5.30$). Seven-point rating scales were used in each case. Religious participants' responses to both types of advertisements, as expected (cf. Wollschleger 2017), are not significantly different, but under both conditions, they form a much more positive "attitude toward the advertised product" than their less religious counterparts (rational: $\bar{x} = 6.09$

vs. emotional: $\bar{x} = 6.15$). This speaks for a more open-minded basic attitude of religious people, which is reflected to a smaller degree in "purchase intention" (rational: $\bar{x} = 5.55$ vs. emotional: $\bar{x} = 5.78$).

> The results suggest that marketers should use rational rather than emotional appeals in their marketing communications to low religiosity consumers (identifiable through such means as demographic data for geographic regions or self-identified classifications on social media). Marketers can also prime low religiosity in their messages (e.g. using words such as "evolution") and, when doing so, should couple that prime with a rational (vs. emotional) appeal.
>
> (Cabano/Minton 2023)

In the programs of religious American TV stations, not only are devotional objects (e.g., crucifixes, religious books) advertised, but often so are medical products and life insurance. In most cases, this is done by means of fear appeals (cf. Gray et al. 2017). Presumably, accidents, illnesses, death and other risks of life are so frequently addressed because these advertisements are mainly aimed at fundamentalist Christians, and fears and moral pressure are characteristic of this religious trend. Fear of death, which according to terror management theory is the main driving force of human behavior (cf. Becker 1973), is omnipresent in fundamentalist thinking (cf. Altmeyer/Hunsberger 1997).

As widespread as the use of fear appeals is, they are also controversial. Under certain circumstances, there is even a risk of the vampire effect (see I-1.2). This happens when, due to strong emotionalization, the viewers do not even perceive the actual advertising message, because the visual or acoustic elements of the ad capture all their attention. Fear appeals are most effective when they do not primarily generate fear but convey to the viewers that they can use the product advertised (e.g., strong toothbrushes) to avert the danger invoked in the advertisement (e.g., bleeding gums). Fear appeals fail, however, with people who are very convinced of their self-efficacy. They assume that they can cope with the problem without buying the advertised product (cf. Farías 2020). Fear appeals can further be "defused" by a positive image of God, as Wu/Cutright (2018) have shown through a series of seven experiments. Those who have a loving, supportive God in mind will feel less fear and respond to it with avoidance behavior than people with a negative image of God (punishing God).

Caution is also advised when trying to advertise humorously. It is true that it can be very effective in attracting the attention of those being advertised to (cf. Cline 2003). But, used incorrectly, the vampire effect threatens here as well. The relevant literature contains a wide variety of suggestions for describing and classifying different humor styles, including affiliative, self-enhancing, self-defeating and aggressive humor. As members of a collectivistic society focused on social relations, Arab Muslims prefer the affiliative style, while American Christians, due to their individualistic, achievement and success-oriented socialization, tend to prefer the self-enhancing as well as the self-defeating style. This is because the subject of "American humor" is mostly the individual (cf. Kalliny et al. 2006).

Important stylistic devices of advertising are exaggeration, surprises and aggression. They are all incompatible with central religious values. Thus, modesty, which all religions demand from believers (cf. Taylor/Raymond 2000), is not compatible with the exaggerated style, and the value of caring (cf. Beck 2006) is not compatible with aggressive elements. The constructive handling of surprises, in turn, presupposes cognitive and emotional abilities which many religious people do not have.

> It appears that, from a psychological, and especially from a personality psychology perspective, religion associates negatively with personality traits, cognitive structures and social consequences typical to humor: incongruity, ambiguity, possibility of nonsense, low dogmatism and low authoritarianism, playfulness, spontaneity, attraction to novelty and risk, lack of truthfulness and finality, affective and moral disengagement, loss of control and order as implied by emotionality, and finally transgression, especially transgression of prohibitions related to aggression/dominance and sexuality.
>
> (Saroglou 2002, p. 205)

Apart from that, however, there are relevant differences between religions. While the Western Christian religions have always been said to have a negative view of secular humor[65] (cf. Joeckel 2008), the relationship of the Eastern religions and Zen Buddhism in particular to humor is considered to be rather relaxed (cf. Morreall 2008). But even in its sphere of influence, humor in advertising can be problematic, albeit for other reasons. An American manufacturer of eyeglasses had to recognize this when he advertised in Thailand with an animated film in which animals wear eyeglasses. What was meant to be funny, the vast majority of the population found blasphemous. This is because Buddhists worship animals as incarnations of divine beings. Wordplay, on the other hand, can be problematic on the Arabian Peninsula and in other Islamic countries. This is because, as the language of the Koran and of prayer, Arabic is an important part of the cultural identity of language-conscious Arabs (cf. Barakat 1993).

Whether in traditional print media (cf. LaTour/Henthorne 1994) or in social networks, such as sponsored Facebook pages (cf. Kadić-Maglajlić et al. 2017), sexual advertising appeals are as popular as they are controversial. Admittedly, they are usually very attention-grabbing. However, women in particular react negatively to them at the attitudinal and behavioral level (purchase intention) (cf. Wirtz et al. 2018). In Islamic countries and many other world religions, nudity in general and sexuality in particular are among the taboo topics (cf. Alam et al. 2019; Sarpal et al. 2018; Rice/Al-Mossawi

2002). Even more than members of other religious affiliations, Muslims reject sexual advertising appeals (cf. Farah/El Samad 2014). As de Run et al. (2010) have shown among younger Malaysians, even this generation has internalized Islamic sexual morality to such an extent that very and less religious Muslims are equally critical of such ad appeals. Among members of other religious groups, it is primarily the very or intrinsically religious who reject sex appeals (cf. Vitell et al. 2006). This results in negative attitudes toward the advertised brand and the advertising company. The purchase intention of religious consumers also dwindles (cf. Putrevu/Swimberghe 2013).

6.2.5 Religious ad appeals

Religious symbols and themes are used for advertising in a variety of ways, such as by printing a Bible verse on shopping bags as the retailer Forever 21 does. In many cases, number symbolism, which has numerous religious references, is also used for communicative purposes (see V-3.6; Table 13). In many societies, for example, the number seven is part of the creation story or the founding myth. For example, the Egyptians believed in the creation of the world by the Goddess Neith with seven words, and Rome was built on seven hills. According to the Judeo-Christian creation story, God created the world in seven days. For Muslims, the seventh heaven is the place of the final transfiguration. In addition, there are the seven wonders of the world, seven pillars of wisdom, seven deadly sins, seven virtues, seven sacraments and, in the Revelation of John, the book with seven seals. The reason for the special appreciation of this number may be due to the fact that Babylonian astronomers discovered the seven planets of the earth 4,000 years ago (Mercury, Venus, Mars, Jupiter, Saturn, Sun and Moon).

Numerous animals also have symbolic value. Sacred animals populate the myths and legends of people worldwide. Indians, for example, worship not only cows, but also elephants (as incarnation of Ganesha, god of luck), tigers (mount of goddess Durga) and the king cobra. The fox has great significance in Shintoism as it relates to Inar (god of rice and fertility). And the goat, which plays a major role in Egyptian as well as Greek mythology, is one of the 12 signs of the Chinese zodiac for Chinese people.

As a rule, however, these animals are not worshipped for their own sake, but as embodiments of gods or god-like beings. In Buddhist countries, it would be a mistake to advertise with animals for another reason. While Christianity suggests a hierarchy of living beings, at the top of which is the human being, this superiority or subordination is foreign to the Buddhist belief in reincarnation. Rather, the animal is seen as the brother of man. In other cultures, the problem is not whether, but how animal symbols can be advertised. When the Carlsberg brewery advertised its elephant beer in sub-Saharan Africa, the people responsible were probably not aware that two elephants symbolize bad luck there. Therefore, a third elephant had to be added to the advertising material.

Since religious consumers respond well to religious symbols in advertising, the increasing secularization of Western industrial societies in particular raises the question of whether other symbols can have a similar effect. The background for an experiment in which La Ferle et al. (2022) tested the effectiveness of spiritual symbols in comparison with religious symbols is the following religion sociological trend: although more and more people in countries such as Germany or the US are turning away from the institution of the church, they define themselves as spiritual, searching for meaning in their lives, but without believing in a specific God. For this purpose, 98 American consumers were shown a digital advertising campaign for an online seminar with a religious ("connect with your religious self") or a spiritual appeal ("connect with your spiritual self"). The Christian participants rated both campaigns positively but would only use the religious appeal as an opportunity to search for more information about the advertised service. In contrast, the non-religious participants responded better to the spiritual appeal (more positive attitude and a stronger intention to search for information about the seminar). Consequently, advertisers could take into account the increasing secularization of numerous industrial societies by increasingly addressing the spiritual needs of their target markets in their marketing communications.

6.2.6 *Moral vs. justice ad appeals*

Moral and justice ad appeals are similar in that both call on recipients of the message to do the right thing. What is different, however, is the theoretical reasoning. While the moral argument (right vs. wrong) is more self-centered (e.g., "I don't buy counterfeit branded goods because I don't want to participate in intellectual theft"), the justice argument (fair vs. unfair) aims at balancing social relations (e.g., "I buy fair trade products so that the workers involved in their production can be adequately compensated").

Moral appeals are more open to interpretation, since there are often different views of what is right and what is wrong, depending on religious socialization, for example. In comparison, there is greater consensus on what is fair and what is unfair. Religious people often take an idealistic position from a philosophical point of view, according to which there are absolute moral standards. Non-religious people, on the other hand, usually take the relativistic position, according to which moral standards have to be adapted to the respective decision situation (cf. Barnett et al. 1996).

Minton et al. (2018b) had 197 American adults rate commercials for three common fair trade products (ice cream, hoodies, tea) to empirically test whether these considerations could be used to derive advice for formulating advertising messages. The justice appeal was operationalized by the following advertising slogan: "You should buy our ice cream/sweatshirt/tea because it is fair" and the moral appeal by the slogan "You should buy our ice cream/sweatshirt/tea because it is right". As expected, the researchers found that advertising appeals that portrayed the purchase of fair trade products as a question of morality ("right") worked better for members of monotheistic religions and appeals to a sense of justice ("fair") worked better for non-religious participants.

6.3 Special forms of advertising

Various forms of advertising are particularly sensitive to IFM because they are in tension with important religious norms and values.

6.3.1 Advertising for controversial products

In Western European countries, it is customary to advertise with strong stimuli. Even breaking taboos is permissible according to Supreme Court rulings. Indeed, provocative advertising campaigns may be an effective means of attracting the attention of those being advertised to in societies flooded with stimuli. In most other regions of the world, however, they violate important social norms. Buddhists, for example, place great value on respectful interaction with one another. Therefore, lying, talking about others and frivolous topics are not allowed. Strong emotions such as anger are not expressed loudly. And sexuality is a taboo subject.

In Islamic societies, too, resistance to the commercialization of nudity, sexuality and intimacy is strong (cf. Sugiarto/De Barnier 2019). Secularized Christian societies may be more liberal. But even here, religious people find sexually charged social media campaigns offensive and react to them with rejection (Kadić-Maglajlić et al. 2017).

Since the study by Michell/Al-Mossawi (1995), what will hardly surprise anyone has been empirically supported. Controversial advertising is conceivably unsuitable for convincing or influencing religious people. As the researchers found, very religious Christians and Muslims reject controversial advertising motifs, and conservative Muslims remember them worse than liberal Muslims. Comparable findings were reported by Farah/El Samad (2014) and de Run et al. (2010). In addition, there have been other similar findings, such as:

- Religious people are less responsive to advertising for alcoholic beverages (cf. Thomsen/Rekve 2003).
- Since ancestors are revered in the Confucian cultural area, the subject of burial is taboo there as an expression of respect for elders (cf. Waller/Fam 2000). While it is accepted in Christian countries that funeral companies advertise their services in the daily newspapers, Confucian, Taoist or Buddhist people would see this as a bad omen for the whole day.

In a still noteworthy study, Fam et al. (2004) investigated the extent to which members of different religious groups perceive advertising for controversial products as offensive (e.g., products with addictive properties). For this purpose, they surveyed Buddhists (Taiwan and China), Muslims (Malaysia and Turkey) and Christians (Great Britain and New Zealand). A total of 1,393 students from six countries indicated the extent to which they found various advertising measures provocative or offensive. Factor-analytically, the 17 advertising objects examined could be grouped into four groups of different offensiveness:

- Products with sexual reference (e.g., condoms, underwear)
- Social or political groups (e.g., parties, religious groups)
- Addiction-producing products (alcohol, cigarettes)
- Health and care products (e.g., drugs for sexually transmitted diseases).

Measured by the group mean values, the participants' reactions on the five-point response scale (1 = not at all objectionable; 5 = extremely objectionable) were rather moderate overall. Strict Buddhists particularly disliked advertisements for addiction-producing products ($\overline{x}$ = 3.37), followed by advertisements for political groups ($\overline{x}$ = 3.20), while they found advertisements for products with sexual connotations ($\overline{x}$ = 2.38) and for health products ($\overline{x}$ = 2.15) rather less problematic.

Because of the moral strictness of Islam, it was expected that Muslims would be most offended by all issues. But their reactions were more moderate than expected. In absolute terms, they were still most disturbed by advertising for weapons, funerals and religious communities ($\overline{x}$ = 3.73), while only a few rejected advertisements for medical and social issues (e.g., avoiding STDs) ($\overline{x}$ = 2.42). Responsible for this "tendency toward the middle" are:

- In Turkey and Malaysia, a relatively moderate Islam was practiced at the time of the study.
- Students were surveyed who are generally more liberal than the general population and prefer the cosmopolitan lifestyle.
- Strictly speaking, the survey did not ask about attitudes to "advertising for controversial" products, but to "advertising for very controversial" products. Instead of the usual designation of the poles of the rating scale (1 = strongly disagree; 5 = strongly agree), they used more extreme designations (1 = not at all offensive; 5 = extremely offensive). As comparative cultural marketing research shows, the worldwide tendency of respondents to use extreme answers (not at all, extremely) has a particular influence on the response behavior of members of collectivist societies (including Malaysia and Turkey).

The Christian participants surveyed especially rejected advertising for weapons, political parties and other socio-political topics ($\overline{x}$= 3.34) as well as advertising for addictive products ($\overline{x}$ = 2.82), while products with sexual connotations ($\bar{x}$ = 2.17) as well as health-related topics such as avoiding STDs ($\bar{x}$ = 2.01) irritated them less.

Wang et al. (2018) largely confirmed the findings of the Fam et al. study. These researchers found that Muslims were also the most likely of their respondents (1,402 university students from 11 countries in North America, Europe, Asia, and Australia) to feel offended by controversial advertisements. Accordingly, they felt that the relevant requirements of government regulators were not strict enough to protect them from inappropriate advertising. Christians and Hindus, on the other hand, rated the existing level of protection as adequate, given their more liberal attitude toward this issue, while Buddhists/Taoists and non-believers surveyed felt that the current regulations were too strict.

Almost at the same time, Tariq/Khan (2017) surveyed Indian students on this topic. Of a total of 17 product areas, female underwear, condoms and alcohol were rated as the most controversial, although with different weighting depending on the religious affiliation of the participants. Hindu participants were most bothered by advertising for female underwear, while Muslims were most bothered by alcohol advertising.

With the results of their qualitative research approach (focus groups and content analysis of diaries), Wilson/Ayad (2021) wanted to draw a more nuanced picture of Muslims' attitudes toward advertising. The respondents were Egyptian Muslim millennials whom they interviewed after the Arab Spring and whom they described as socially mobile, educated and digitally connected. According to their own statements, this social class is primarily disturbed by advertising whose messages, themes or executions offend their intelligence. They also reject the escapism of the advertising world in view of the precarious living conditions in their country. Moreover, their parents and their wider social environment have a greater influence on them than religion.

6.3.2 Comparative advertising

This form of advertising directly compares a product or service with that offered by a competitor in order to highlight the advantages of the company's own product or service. While this advertising strategy is widely accepted in the USA and other competitive countries, less competitive societies such as Germany tend to regulate its use (for example, with the law against unfair competition). Elsewhere, religious rules argue against it. For example, a hadith (i.e., a saying of Muhammad passed down and documented in the Sahih Al-Bukharyy) states: "A Muslim is one from whose tongue and hand Muslims are safe." Against this, a Muslim who disparages or criticizes another Muslim for the sake of its own advantage would be in violation.

According to the Muslim view, comparative advertising is a form of manipulative advertising and is therefore immoral. From a comparative cultural perspective, Islamic societies are collectivist societies that place great value on caring for others and social well-being. Advertising that criticizes or even belittles others violates these values. Therefore, adjectives such as "better" (than the competitor) and comparable should not be used. In general, reference to competitors is much less common there than in the USA, for example (see Al-Olayan/Karande 2000). In Confucian societies, comparative advertising is rejected primarily because there is a great danger that a competitor will lose face (see Lin 1993).

6.3.3 *Sponsorship*

Alongside sales promotion, public relations, guerrilla marketing and many others, modern sponsorship is one of the below-the-line measures of communication policy. "Below the line" because in the broad and constantly swelling stream of general social media communication, they operate below the media-critical radar of those being advertised to and are often not recognized as advertising (see Gelbrich/Müller 2023). In return for the provision of financial, in-kind or other services to the sponsor (= individuals, groups or institutions), the sponsor (= advertising company) receives the right to use the goodwill of the sponsor for communication purposes within the framework of a contractual agreement (i.e., the sponsor's name recognition and image) (cf. Cornwell 2014).

Whether sponsorship is successful or not depends on various factors, including sympathy, customer proximity and image. In the case of cross-border sponsorship commitments, the prevailing attitudes and valid legal provisions on charitable acts and the binding nature of contracts in the countries concerned must be taken into account. Ultimately, however, the socio-cultural fit between sponsor and sponsor recipient is decisive, to which values arising from a common religious orientation also contribute.

Nevertheless, research has so far only touched on this topic in passing. In essence, it is limited to relatively banal considerations, such as which taboos should be observed in sponsoring. Casinos and other gambling providers, for example, cannot act as sponsors wherever gambling is prohibited, especially in the sphere of influence of Islam (cf. McKelvey 2004). For a long time, this also seemed to apply to the producers and marketers of alcoholic beverages (cf. Dun 2014). Qatar, however, has given priority to business interests, at least for the 2022 World Cup. In any case, the sponsors of this major sporting event include not only the well-known main sponsors (Adidas, Coca-Cola, Kia, McDonalds, Visa, Qatar Airways) but also the beer producer Budweiser.

6.3.4 *Price advertising*

Sanaie/Ranjbarian (1996) have derived from the Islamic prohibition of usury that companies should not aggressively advertise for loans. This can be applied to aggressive price advertising, not least because it is considered impolite in Arab countries (cf. Lin 1993). As in other relationship-oriented societies, the reputation of a company or the goodwill of a brand is more important than the financial value of a product. According to Al-Olayan/Karande (2000), who analyzed the content of advertisements, the majority of advertisers respect this expectation. While only 8% of the advertisements in family and women's magazines distributed in the Middle East and North Africa at the time contained price appeals, while the figure was 20% in comparable US media.

6.4 Advertising effectiveness

Advertising research distinguishes between economic and non-economic effects. To our knowledge, only Oh et al. (2020) have so far compared the economic effects of advertising measures on the basis of company data from 1992 to 2014. First, they showed that American companies with Protestant or Catholic CEOs invest more than average in advertising. Secondly, the volume of the advertising budget mediates the influence of the CEO's religious affiliation on the company's value (measured as shareholder value).

The most important criteria for the non-economic impact of advertising include awareness, attitude (toward the advertisement, the brand or the company) and purchase intention. According to a survey of Muslim consumers, religious symbols in advertising for car financing promote the development of positive attitudes toward this advertising and the advertised brand (cf. Butt et al. 2018).

For a comprehensive analysis of the effectiveness of the communication policy measures taken, research often uses the elaboration likelihood model. It explains under what conditions people process advertising stimuli, with what probability (likelihood) and with what intensity (elaboration) (cf. Petty/Cacioppo 1986). A distinction must be made between a high-involvement and a low-involvement situation.

If the addressees of an advertisement are highly involved (i.e., interested in the advertising message or the advertised product), then they are very likely to take the "central path of information processing" and cognitively process the arguments of the advertisement intensively. On the other hand, those who are less involved are hardly interested in information and arguments. They prefer to process advertising messages peripherally and superficially and respond primarily to key stimuli (e.g., the emotional quality of the background music or a seal of approval displayed). Religious symbols, such as the Christian cross, the Muslim hijab or the Jewish Star of David, can also be key stimuli (cf. Naseri/Tamam 2012).

In order to be able to test the Elaboration Likelihood model, Dotson/Hyatt (2000) surveyed 341 American students of the Christian faith. As expected, participants who were strongly involved tended to process information centrally. As such, these participants who read strong arguments subsequently expressed a more positive attitude toward the advertisement and the brand than the less involved comparison group. According to theory, the contrast group with weak levels of involvement should be more receptive to peripheral stimuli. However, this could not be supported empirically. Rather, as the moderation analysis showed, the effect in this case depends on how religious the participants are. Among less involved very religious participants, a religious symbol in the ad did not trigger more attention or a more positive attitude toward the ad than among less religious people. On the contrary, they even expressed a more negative attitude toward the brand. The boomerang effect can presumably be explained by the fact that very religious participants who are not very involved (i.e., not interested in the advertising object) feel uncomfortable when religious symbols are used or, from their point of view, misused to achieve profane goals such as selling a product or service. Apart from that, however, the results of the study support the elaboration likelihood model in one central point, as highly involved consumers can best be convinced by strong arguments.

Notes

1 Using time series (1960–2010), Burke et al. (2015) calculated the optimal mean temperature for economic performance of 165 countries.
2 On the "curse of resource wealth," also called the "Dutch disease," see Torvik (2001) or Gelbrich/Müller (2011, p. 1233 f.).
3 A Buddhist economic ethics was explicitly formulated only after World War II, and even then not as a closed system of thought, like the Catholic Social Teaching, but as a mosaic of "culturally differentiated answers to economic questions" (Brodbeck 2022).
4 When Pope Paul VI issued a decree in 1966 relaxing the ban on eating meat on Fridays that had been in effect until then, demand for fish in the United States declined significantly, causing the US fishing industry to suffer threatening losses in sales (see Bell 1968).
5 The priming method offers the advantage that it is possible to "manipulate" individual religiosity in an experimental research approach. In contrast to the prevailing practice of quasi-experimental field research, which uses a naturally occurring variation of the independent variables, this type of controlled research allows causal statements.
6 Orthodox Jews value time-saving products (e.g. frozen chicken giblets) significantly less than do strict Jews.
7 "The most consistent relationship found was between religious commitment and the importance placed by the consumer on sales personnel friendliness/assistance" (McDaniel/Burnett 1990, p. 101).
8 Clayton/Gladden (1974) essentially confirmed this by surveying two larger samples of American students at a liberal university in Florida. In both cases, one dimension (Ideological Commitment) accounted for most of the variance (78% and 83%, respectively) in a factor analysis.
9 Coefficient of determination r^2.
10 Importance of owning material goods.
11 Inability or unwillingness to accept views or behaviors that are fundamentally different from one's own.
12 Moral principles and standards of behavior regarding the "right" way to handle products and services.
13 Preference for the decision alternative with the lowest possible loss probability.
14 Products associated with religious beliefs.
15 www.ottogroup.com/de/newsroom/meldungen/Trendstudie-2020-Ethischer-Konsum (11/23/2021).
16 In many studies, attitudes are asked in very general terms (e.g. "Do you think we should do more to protect the environment?"), but behavior is asked in very concrete or specific terms (e.g. "How often do you use a bicycle?"). However, one can be environmentally conscious and rarely or never ride a bicycle (e.g. for

health reasons or because there are no bike lanes available). And you can be an enthusiastic cyclist and think nothing of environmental protection.

17 "World Circular Letters of the Popes dealing with fundamental questions of the order of the social spheres of life" (www.kas.de/de/web/geschichte-der-cdu/sozialenzykliken).

18 Although this was not asked directly, it can be seen from the fact that the economic dimension of CSR correlates negatively with the legal, ethical and discretionary dimensions (cf. Angelidis/Ibrahim 2004, p. 123).

19 In the scale developed by Tangney et al. (2004), self-control is operationalized by items such as, "I am good at resisting temptation."

20 "Brooks found that on average, American religious individuals gave $1,568 more in charitable donations than non-religious persons" (Salvador et al. 2014, p.357).

21 Islam teaches that poor people will enter paradise 500 years earlier than the rich, and the New Testament says, "It is easier for a camel to go through the eye of a needle than for a rich man to enter the kingdom of God."

22 "Materialism and religiosity are generally considered antithetical, as the major, underlying motives of materialism (such as self-promotion) tend to contrast religious values like spirituality or humility" (Raggiotto et al. 2018, p. 620).

23 Artistic creativity, which expresses itself in poems, paintings, sculptures, etc., is excluded from this. Religiosity seems to be conducive to this (cf. Day 2005).

24 The "proportion of Protestants and Catholics in a country" correlates positively with national creativity and the "proportion of Muslims" negatively correlates with national creativity. As a result, the ranking of the Global Creativity Index is headed by Anglo-Saxon (e.g. Australia) and Scandinavian countries (e.g. Denmark) (cf. www.edutopia.org).

25 Recio-Román et al. (2019, p. 611) clarified this finding in their groundbreaking study, albeit limited to Europe: "For Catholics, innovations did not imply the creation of new products but the improvement of existing ones. Should an innovation be introduced in the market, which substitutes an existing product that the Catholics already trust, they would maintain their fidelity with the old product, and they would not pay any more for the new one." According to a recent meta-analysis, there is a "negative intelligence – religiosity relation" (Zuckerman et al. 2020).

26 The "belief in the predetermination of events" attributed to Muslims is more characterized by the confidence of being in God's protecting hand, while the fatalism meant here is more rooted in a pessimistic worldview.

27 According to Mokhlis (2006b), the respondent's religious affiliation has only a slight influence on quality awareness (mean values: Muslims = 3.90; Christians = 3.81; Hindus = 3.75; Buddhists = 3.71).

28 Halal (Arabic) means permitted or permissible and Haram means forbidden (in each case according to the Sharia). Makruh is the gray area between halal and haram: frowned upon, unwanted, but not explicitly forbidden. As a precaution, Muslims should also avoid anything that is makruh.

29 Kosher (Hebrew) means suitable or pure.

30 But this is not why we speak of poison green, but because in the Middle Ages green paint was made by adding highly toxic arsenic (which, in the form of green wallpaper, is said to have hastened Napoleon's death).

31 Initially, Christians also used white as a mourning color. In its place, black was used hesitantly from the 6th century and completely from the 14th century, as an expression of the spiritual darkness of the soul.

32 An informative outline of the history and function of liturgical colors can be found at https://de.wikipedia.org/wiki/Liturgische_Farben.

33 In the case of "Lurchi", for example, an advertising figure of the shoe manufacturer Salamander, it could be a human being reborn in the shape of a salamander.
34 The fact that, according to Wilkins et al. (2019b), non-Muslims are more positive about halal products the more they identify with their own religion contradicts not only their research hypothesis but also, to some extent, the findings of Tao et al. (2022) and Schlegelmilch et al. (2016). Now, religiosity and religious identity are similar but not identical constructs. Therefore, the counter-intuitive finding of Wilkins et al. (2019b) can possibly be justified speculatively as follows: Let us imagine, in addition to religious identity in the narrower sense, a broader religious identity that includes all those who, in contrast to atheists, "believe in something at all." Then it could be that the cross-denominational community of believers still views religious products with benevolence even if they are associated with a religion other than their own.
35 "I will likely consume halal-produced meat in restaurants in the future."
36 In this study, Buddhists were still relatively the most open-minded about buying fair trade products. This could be due to Buddhist values such as caring for humanity (caring for humankind).
37 e.g. "This online retailer offered me many options to customize the t-shirt to my needs and taste."
38 e.g. "Environmental problems are not affecting my life personally."
39 However, the motives of zakat donors are only altruistic to a limited extent. Many see it primarily as a means of protecting themselves against "the realm of evil spirits" (cf. Kashif et al. 2018). Donations are preferably made individually rather than to a charity. The reasons are a lack of trust in charities and their limited relevant product offerings.
40 "And whatever you lend in riba, that it may increase with the good of men, it does not increase before Allah" (Sura 30: 39). "Ye believers! Fear Allah! And henceforth leave off taking interest" (Sura 2: 278).
41 Mudaraba dates back to the caravan era, when wealthy merchants provided capital to caravan leaders. While profits were shared, the financiers had to bear losses alone. Today, however, mudaraba contracts stipulate that all participants share equally in profits and losses.
42 However, the operationalization of this construct contradicts its verbal definition. None of the three items addresses the emotional level: "I intend to stay on as a customer of this bank"; "I want to help other customers with their questions"; and "I want to help the bank to improve its service."
43 Concern for Face: e.g. "I care about praise and criticism from others."
44 Belief in Fate: e.g. "Many things in life are predetermined."
45 Excerpt from the Apostles' Creed.
46 Judaism (teshuvah) and Islam (tawba) know something similar (cf. Rye et al. 2000).
47 Ultimately, these two studies are not comparable because Abd Rashid et al. (2022) operationalized religiosity in a traditional way (agreeing or disagreeing with given statements), whereas Hyodo/Bolton (2021) primed religiosity (see I-4).
48 Essoo/Dibb (2004) likewise reported that devout Hindus make conspicuously little effort to obtain price information.
49 The operationalization consisted of three statements: "I prefer to buy things on sale"; "I usually watch the advertisements for announcement of sales"; and "I can save a lot of money by shopping around for bargains."
50 These statements refer to interpersonal religiosity. Differentiation according to intrapersonal religiosity resulted in largely equal mean values.

51 The cultural dimension "acceptance of power distance" described by Hofstede (2001) expresses the extent to which hierarchical differences exist in a society and the extent to which this is accepted, especially by lower social classes.
52 Product modification is subsumed under product variation and product differentiation. Product differentiation is when a company launches different variants of a product on the market in order to be able to address different target markets according to their needs (e.g. chocolate with 30, 50 or 70% cocoa content). In the case of product variation, parts of an existing product are changed (e.g. the linen content in the trouser fabric is increased in order to improve the wearing comfort in view of climate change) and, therefore, offered only in the improved version.
53 Measures aimed at influencing the subjective price perception of consumers and making a price appear relatively favorable. For example, a tie for $79 offered together with a high-priced suit ($599) appears cheaper than in combination with a low-priced suit ($199).
54 Originally overweighting domestic equities in the portfolio; has been generalized to systematically favor domestic products.
55 "Religious centrism (or religio-centrism) is defined as the extent to which a consumer is inclined to buy exclusively from within their own religious group" (Siala 2013, p. 580).
56 Moral appeal: "You should purchase our ice cream because it is the right thing to do." Justice appeal: "You should purchase our ice cream because it is the fair thing to do."
57 Adeyemo/Adeleye (2008) reported differently. They found no correlation between religiosity and perceived self-efficacy (among 291 adolescent, predominantly Christian students in Nigeria).
58 On the similarities and differences between the Hofstede and GLOBE culture dimensions, see Müller/Gelbrich (2021, pp. 71 ff. and 102 ff.).
59 e.g. Bundle purchasing volumes to generate cost advantages.
60 Five of the world's ten most important trade fairs are held in Germany. In 2019, the German trade fair industry recorded more than 10 million visitors.
61 Many seem to feel that it is their right to order the product they want in several sizes, colors or configurations, knowing that they will only keep one product at most and return the others.
62 If the total purchases were evenly distributed throughout the week, each day would account for 1/7 of 100% = 14.3%.
63 If a subjectively important freedom is restricted (e.g. freedom of opinion or decision), many people feel reactance, a restriction of freedom. They then strive to regain this freedom by consolidating their previous opinion, developing a negative attitude toward the influencer (e.g. advertiser) (boomerang effect) or even trying to harm the advertising company (by boycotting purchases, negative purchase recommendations, etc.).
64 For intrinsically religious people, classic Christmas advertising triggers stronger feelings of guilt because it reminds them of the commercialization of Christmas more than a personalized gift card (which is not compatible with the religious beliefs of intrinsically religious people).
65 Religious humor is supposed to directly support people in coping with the problems of daily life, while secular humor is at best attributed as an indirect relief function.

Bibliography

Abbasi, A.S.; Akhter, W.; Umar, S. (2011): Ethical Issues in Advertising in Pakistan. An Islamic Perspective, *World Applied Sciences Journal*, 13(3): 444–452.

Abd Aziz, E.Z.; Jusoh, M.S.; Amlus, M.H. (2015): The Moderating Effect of Product Quality on Religiosity, Price Sensitivity, Personnel Responsiveness and Purchase Intention, *Australian Journal of Basic and Applied Sciences*, 9(13): 218–224.

Abd Rashid, M.H.; Hamzah, M.I.; Mansor, A.A.; Mat Ali, S.A. (2022): Coping with Service Failure and Recovery in Restaurant. Does Being Religious Matter? *Journal of Foodservice Business Research*, 25(4): 396–413.

Abdel-Khalek, A.M.; Lester, D. (2017): The Association between Religiosity, Generalized Self-efficacy, Mental Health, and Happiness in Arab College Students, *Personality and Individual Differences*, 109: 12–16.

Abdel-Samad, H. (2019): *Integration. A Protocol of Failure*, Munich: Droemer.

Abou-Youssef, M.M.H.; Kortam, W.; Abou-Aish, E.; El-Bassiouny, N. (2015): Effects of Religiosity on Customer Attitudes toward Islamic Banking in Egypt, *International Journal of Bank Marketing*, 33(6): 786–807.

Abror, A.; Patrisia, D.; Engriani, Y.; Evanita, S.; Yasri, Y.; Dastgir, S. (2019a): Service Quality, Religiosity, Customer Satisfaction, Customer Engagement and Islamic Bank's Customer Loyalty, *Journal of Islamic Marketing*, 11(1): 1691–1705.

Abror, A.; Wardi, Y.; Trinanda, O.; Patrisia, D. (2019b): The Impact of Halal Tourism, Customer Engagement on Satisfaction. Moderating Effect of Religiosity, *Asia Pacific Journal of Tourism Research*, 24(7): 633–643.

Abu Bakar, A.R.; Hussin, S.R. (2013): What Constitutes an Islamic Retailer, *International Journal of Sales, Retailing and Marketing*, 2(1): 4–84.

Addai, I.; Opoku-Agyeman, C.; Ghartey, H.T. (2013): An Exploratory Study of Religion and Trust in Ghana, *Social Indicators Research*, 110(3): 993–1012.

Adeyemo, D.A.; Adeleye, A.T. (2008): Emotional Intelligence, Religiosity and Self-efficacy as Predictors of Psychological Well-Being among Secondary School Adolescents in Ogbomoso, Nigeria, *Europe's Journal of Psychology*, 4(1): 22–31.

Adhikari, B.K.; Agrawal, A. (2016): Does Local Religiosity Matter for Bank Risk-Taking? *Journal of Corporate Finance*, 38: 272–293.

Adnan, A.A.Z.; Yunus, N.K.Y.; Ghouri, A.M. (2019): Does Religiosity Matter in the Era of Industrial Revolution 4.0? *Asian Academy of Management Journal*, 24(2): 67–77.

Adorno, T.W.; Frenkel-Brunswik, E.; Levinson, D.J.; Sanford, R.N. (1950): *The Authoritarian Personality*, New York: Harper & Row.

Agag, G.M.; El-Masry, A.A. (2016): Cultural and Religiosity Drivers and Satisfaction Outcomes of Consumer Perceived Deception in Online Shopping, *Internet Research*, 26(4): 942–962.

Agarwal, R.; Prasad, J. (1997): The Role of Innovation Characteristics and Perceived Voluntariness in the Acceptance of Information Technologies, *Decision Sciences*, 28(3): 557–582.

Agarwala, R.; Mishra, P.; Singh, R. (2019): Religiosity and Consumer Behavior. A Summarizing Review, *Journal of Management, Spirituality & Religion*, 16(1): 32–54.

Agarwala, R.; Mishra, P.; Singh, R. (2021): Evaluating the Impact of Religious Icons and Symbols on Consumer's Brand Evaluation. Context of Hindu Religion, *Journal of Advertising*, 50(4): 372–390.

Ahlheim, H. (2012): *Deutsche, kauft nicht bei Juden! Antisemitism and political boycott in Germany 1924 to 1935*, Göttingen: Wallstein.

Ahluwalia, R. (2002): How Prevalent Is the Negativity Effect in Consumer Environment? *Journal of Consumer Research*, 29(9): 270–279.

Ahmed, A.M.; Salas, O. (2011): Implicit Influences of Christian Religious Representations on Dictator and Prisoner's Dilemma Game Decisions, *Journal of Socio-Economics*, 40(3): 242–246.

Ahmed, F.B.J. (2018): Corruption According to the Main Sources of Islam, *Intellectual Discourse*, 26(1): 91–110.

Ahmed, S.; Al Asheq, A.; Ahmed, E.; Chowdhury, U.Y.; Sufi, T.; Mostofa, M.G. (2023): The Intricate Relationships of Consumers' Loyalty and Their Perceptions of Service Quality, Price and Satisfaction in Restaurant Service, *The TQM Journal*, 35(2): 519–539.

Ahmed, Z.; Anang, R.; Othman, N.; Sambasivan, M. (2013): To Purchase or Not to Purchase US Products. Role of Religiosity, Animosity, and Ethnocentrism among Malaysian Consumers, *Journal of Services Marketing*, 27(7): 551–563.

Aji, H.M.; Dharmmesta, B.S. (2019): Subjective Norm vs Dogmatism. Christian Consumer Attitude towards Islamic TV Advertising, *Journal of Islamic Marketing*, 10(3): 961–980.

Akbari, M.; Gholizadeh, M.H.; Zomorrodi, M. (2018): Islamic Symbols in Food Packaging and Purchase Intention of Muslim Consumers, *Journal of Islamic Marketing*, 9(1): 117–131.

Akerlof, G.A. (1997): Social Distance and Social Decisions, *Econometrica. Journal of the Econometric Society*, 65(5): 1005–1027.

Alam, M.M.; Aliyu, A.; Shahriar, S.M. (2019): Presenting Women as Sexual Objects in Marketing Communications. Perspective of Morality, Ethics and Religion, *Journal of Islamic Marketing*, 10(3): 911–927.

Albaghli, B.; Carlucci, L. (2021): The Link between Muslim Religiosity and Negative Attitudes toward the West. An Arab Study, *International Journal for the Psychology of* Religion, 31(4): 235–248.

Albashir, W.A.; Zainuddin, Y.; Panigrahi, S.K. (2018): The Acceptance of Islamic Banking Products in Libya, *International Journal of Economics and Financial Issues*, 8(3): 105–111.

Albertini, F.Y. (2022): Jewish Business Ethics, in: Aßländer, M.S. (Ed.), *Handbuch Wirtschaftsethik*, 2nd ed., Heidelberg: J.B. Metzler

Al-Deen, H.S.N. (1991): Literacy and Information Content of Magazine Advertising. USA versus Saudi Arabia, *International Journal of Advertising*, 10(3): 251–257.

Al-Hajla, A.H.; Nguyen, B.; Melewar, T.C.; Jayawardhena, C.; Ghazali, E.; Mutum, D.S. (2019): Understanding New Religion-Compliant Product Adoption (NRCPA) in Islamic Markets, *Journal of Global Marketing*, 32(4): 288–302.

Al-Hyari, K.; Alnsour, M.; Al-Weshah, G.; Haffar, M. (2012): Religious Beliefs and Consumer Behavior. From Loyalty to Boycotts, *Journal of Islamic Marketing*, 3(2): 155–174.

Allison, L.; Wang, C.; Kaminsky, J. (2021): Religiosity, Neutrality, Fairness, Skepticism, and Societal Tranquility. A Data Science Analysis of the World Values Survey, *PloS one*, 16(1): e0245231 (12/16/2022).

Al-Makaty, S.S.; Van Tubergen, G.N.; Whitlow, S.S.; Boyd, D.A. (1996): Attitudes Towards Advertising in Islam, *Journal of Advertising Research*, 36(3): 16–26.

Almenayes, J.J. (2014): Religiosity and the Perceived Consequences of Social Media Usage in a Muslim Country, *Journal of Arts and Humanities*, 3(5): 108–117.

Almir, I. (2004): *Das Bilderverbot im Islam*, Marburg: Tectum.

Almossawi, M.M. (2014): Impact of Religion on the Effectiveness of the Promotional Aspect of Product Packages in Muslim Countries, *Asia Pacific Journal of Marketing and Logistics*, 55(5): 1440–1468.

Al-Olayan, F.S.; Karande, K. (2000): A Content Analysis of Magazine Advertisements from the United States and the Arab World, *Journal of Advertising*, 29(3): 69–82.

Alon, I.; Chase, G. (2005): Religious Freedom and Economic Prosperity, *Cato Journal*, 25(2): 399–406.

Alserhan, B.A. (2010a): On Islamic Branding. Brands as Good Deeds, *Journal of Islamic Marketing*, 1(2): 101–106.

Alserhan, B.A. (2010b): Islamic Branding. A Conceptualization of Related Terms, *Journal of Brand Management*, 18(1): 34–49.

Alshehri, F.; Fotaki, M.; Kauser, S. (2021): The Effects of Spirituality and Religiosity on the Ethical Judgment in Organizations, *Journal of Business Ethics*, 174(3): 567–593.

Alston, J.P. (1975): Three Measures of Current Levels of Religiosity, *Journal for the Scientific Study of Religion*, 14(2): 165–168.

Altemeyer, B.; Hunsberger, B. (1992): Authoritarianism, Religious Fundamentalism, Quest, and Prejudice, *International Journal for the Psychology of* Religion, 2(2): 113–133.

Altemeyer, B.; Hunsberger, B. (1997): *Amazing Conversions. Why Some Turn to Faith & Others Abandon Religion*, Amherst/NY: Prometheus Books.

Alyousif, Z.; Alkhunain, N.; Dahl, W.J.; Mathews, A.E. (2020): A Content Analysis of Food Advertising in Arab Gulf Countries During Ramadan, *Health Promotion International*, 35(6): 1267–1272.

Andeleeb, S.S. (1993): Religious Affiliations and Consumer Behavior. An Examination of Hospitals, *Marketing Health Services*, 13(4): 42–49.

Andorfer, V.A.; Liebe, U. (2012): Research on Fair Trade Consumption. A Review, *Journal of Business Ethics*, 106(4): 415–435.

Ang, S.H.; Jung, K.; Kau, A.K.; Leong, S.M.; Pornpitakpan, C.; Tan, S.J. (2004): Animosity toward Economic Giants, *Journal of Consumer Marketing*, 21(3): 190–207.

Angelidis, J.; Ibrahim, N.A. (2004): An Exploratory Study of the Impact of Degree of Religiousness upon an Individual's Corporate Social Responsiveness Orientation, *Journal of Business Ethics*, 51(2): 119–128.

Ansari, J.; Khalid, F.; Jalees, T.; Ramish, M.S. (2017): Consumer's Attitude towards Ramadan Advertising, *South Asian Journal of Management*, 11(1): 14–31.

Antonetti, P.; Maklan, S. (2015): How Categorization Shapes the Attitude-Behavior Gap in Responsible Consumption, *International Journal of Market Research*, 57(1): 51–72.

Appadurai, A. (1988): How to Make a National Cuisine, *Comparative Studies in Society and History*, 30(1): 3–24.

Aribi, Z.A.; Arun, T. (2015): Corporate Social Responsibility and Islamic Financial Institutions (IFIs). Management Perceptions from IFIs in Bahrain, *Journal of Business Ethics*, 129(4): 785–794.

Arkoun, M. (1982). *Humanisme Arabe Au Iv/Xe Siecle*. Vrin.

Arli, D. (2017): Does Ethics Need Religion? Evaluating the Importance of Religiosity in Consumer Ethics, *Marketing Intelligence & Planning*, 35(2): 205–221.

Arli, D.; Cherrier, H.; Tjiptono, F. (2016): God Blesses Those Who Wear Prada. Exploring the Impact of Religiousness on Attitudes toward Luxury among the Youth of Indonesia, *Marketing Intelligence & Planning*, 34(1): 61–79.

Arli, D.; Gil, L.D.A.; van Esch, P. (2020): The Effect of Religiosity on Luxury Goods. The Case of Chilean Youths, *International Journal of Consumer Studies*, 44(3): 181–190.

Arli, D.; Nguyen, T.M.; Nham, P.T. (2021a). Are Atheist Consumers Less Ethical? Investigating the Role of Religiosity and Atheism on Consumer Ethics, *Journal of Consumer Marketing*, 38(5), 525–539.

Arli, D.; Septianto, F.; Chowdhury, R.M. (2021b): Religious but Not Ethical. The Effects of Extrinsic Religiosity, Ethnocentrism and Self-righteousness on Consumers' Ethical Judgments, *Journal of Business Ethics*, 171(2): 295–316.

Arli, D.; Tjiptono, F. (2014): The End of Religion? Examining the Role of Religiousness, Materialism, and Long-term Orientation on Consumer Ethics in Indonesia, *Journal of Business Ethics*, 123(3): 385–400.

Arli, D.; Tjiptono, F. (2017): God and Green. Investigating the Impact of Religiousness on Green Marketing, *International Journal of Nonprofit and Voluntary* Sector *Marketing*, 22(3): 1–11.

Armfield, G.G. (2003): Structural Equation Model of Religiosities Effect on Mass Media Use and Civic Participation, *Paper Presented at the 2003 Annual Meeting of the Association of Educators in Journalism and Mass Communications*, Miami/FL.

Armfield, G.G.; Holbert, R.L. (2003): The Relationship between Religiosity and Internet Use, *Journal of Media and Religion*, 2(3): 129–144.

Arnold, S.J.; Handelman, J.; Tigert, D.J. (1996): Organizational Legitimacy and Retail Store Patronage, *Journal of Business Research*, 35(3): 229–239.

Arnoldi, J. (2001): Niklas Luhmann. An Introduction, *Theory, Culture & Society*, 18(1): 1–13.

Aronson, E.; Wilson, T.; Sommers, S.R. (2020): *Social Psychology*, 10th ed., Harlow: Pearson.

Aronson, E.; Worchel, P. (1966): Similarity versus Liking as Determinants of Interpersonal Attractiveness, *Psychonomic Science*, 5(4): 157–158.

Arruñada, B. (2010): Protestants and Catholics. Similar Work Ethic, Different Social Ethic, *The Economic Journal*, 120(547): 890–918.

Arvate, P.R.; Curi, A.Z.; Rocha, F.; Miessi, S.F. (2009): Corruption and the Size of Government. Causality Tests for OECD and Latin American Countries, *Applied Economics Letters*, 17(10): 1013–1017.

Assheuer, T. (2021): What Comes after Faith, *Die Zeit*, 76(48): 68–69.

Aswad C. (2017): Women in Sports Ad Strikes Nerve in Arab World, www.reuters.com/article/us-arab-women-nike/women-in-sports-ad-strikes-nerve-in-arab-world-idUSKBN1620I7, 23/02/2017.

Au, N.; Buhalis, D.; Law, R. (2014): Online Complaining Behavior in Mainland China Hotels. The Perception of Chinese and Non-Chinese Customers, *International Journal of Hospitality & Tourism Administration*, 15(3): 248–274.

Awanis, S.; Schlegelmilch, B.B.; Cui, C.C. (2017): Asia's Materialists. Reconciling Collectivism and Materialism, *Journal of International Business Studies*, 48(8): 964–991.

Ayoub, M.M. (2013): *Islam. Faith and History*, New York: Simon & Schuster.

Aysan, A.F.; Disli, M.; Duygun, M.; Ozturk, H. (2018): Religiosity versus Rationality. Depositor Behavior in Islamic and Conventional Banks, *Journal of Comparative Economics*, 46(1): 1–19.

Azam, A.; Qiang, F.; Abbas, S.A.; Abdullah, M.I. (2013): Structural Equation Modeling (SEM) Based Trust Analysis of Muslim Consumers in the Collective Religion Affiliation Model in E-commerce, *Journal of Islamic Marketing*, 4(2): 134–149.

Azam, A.; Qiang, F.; Abdullah, M.I.; Abbas, S.A. (2011): Impact of 5-D of Religiosity on Diffusion Rate of Innovation, *International Journal of Business and Social Science*, 2(17): 177–185.

Baazeem, T.; Mortimer, G.; Neale, L. (2016): Conceptualizing the Relationship between Shopper Religiosity, Perceived Risk and the Role of Moral Potency, *Journal of Consumer Studies*, 15(1): 440–448.

Baig, A.K.; Baig, U.K. (2013): The Effects of Religiosity on New Product Adoption, *International Journal of Research in Business and Social Science*, 2(2): 28–37.

Bailey, J.M.; Sood, J. (1993): The Effects of Religious Affiliation on Consumer Behavior. A Preliminary Investigation, *Journal of Managerial Issues*, 5(3): 328–351.

Bakar, A.; Lee, R.; Rungie, C. (2013): The Effects of Religious Symbols in Product Packaging on Muslim Consumer Responses, *Australasian Marketing Journal*, 21(3): 198–204.

Balabanis, G.; Diamantopoulos, A.; Mueller, R.D.; Melewar, T.C. (2001): The Impact of Nationalism, Patriotism, and Internationalism on Consumer Ethnocentric Tendencies, *Journal of International Business Studies*, 32(1): 157–175.

Baldauf, A.; Cravens, D.W.; Wagner, U. (2000): Examining Determinants of Export Performance in Small Open Economies, *Journal of World Business*, 35(1): 61–79.

Balderjahn, I. (2013): *Sustainable Management and Consumer Behavior*, Konstanz: UVK.

Balikcioglu, B.; Kiyak, F.M. (2022): The Trio of Religiosity, Materialism, and Anti-Consumption in Explaining Life Satisfaction, in: Cherrier, H.; Lee, S.W. (Eds.), *Anti-Consumption*, 162–181, London: Routledge.

Bananuka, J.; Kasera, M.; Najjemba, G.M.; Musimenta, D.; Ssekiziyivu, B.; Kimuli, S.N.L. (2019): Attitude: Mediator of Subjective Norm, Religiosity and Intention to Adopt Islamic Banking, *Journal of Islamic Marketing*, 10(2): 166–186.

Banerjee, R.; Dittmar, H. (2008): Individual Differences in Children's Materialism. The Role of Peer Relations, *Personality and Social Psychology Bulletin*, 34(1): 17–31.

Bao, Y.; Zhou, K.Z.; Su, C. (2003): Face Consciousness and Risk Aversion. Do They Affect Consumer Decision-making? *Psychology & Marketing*, 20(8): 733–755.

Barakat, H. (1993): *The Arab World. Society, Culture, and State*, Berkeley/CA: University of California Press.

Barnes, B.E. (2007): *Culture, Conflict, and Mediation in the Asian Pacific*, Lanham/MD: Rowman & Littlefield.

Barnes, C.D.; Brown, R.P. (2010): A Value-Congruent Bias in the Forgiveness Forecasts of Religious People, *Psychology of Religion and Spirituality*, 2(1): 17–29.

Barnes, S.J. (2009): Strength of Religious Faith, Trusting Beliefs and Their Role in Technology Acceptance, *International Journal of Innovation and Learning*, 6(1): 110–126.

Barnett, T.; Bass, K.; Brown, G. (1996): Religiosity, Ethical Ideology, and Intentions to Report a Peer's Wrong-Doing, *Journal of Business Ethics*, 15(11): 1161–1174.

Baron, J. (2020): Religion, Cognitive Style, and Rational Thinking, *Current Opinion in Behavioral Sciences*, 34 (August): 64–68.

Baron-Epel, O.; Kaplan, G.; Weinstein, R.; Green, M.S. (2010): Extreme and Acquiescence Bias in a Bi-ethnic Population, *European Journal of Public Health*, 20(5): 543–548.

Barrett, D.B. (Ed.) (1982): *World Christian Encyclopaedia*, New York: Oxford University Press.

Barro, R.J.; McCleary, R.M. (2003): Religion and Economic Growth across Countries, *American Sociological Review*, 68(5): 760–781.

Barton, K.; Vaughan, G.M. (1976): Church Membership and Personality. A Longitudinal Study, *Social Behavior and Personality*, 4(1): 11–16.

Batson, C.D.; Schoenrade, P.; Ventis, W.L. (1993): *Religion and the Individual. A Social-Psychological Perspective*, New York: Oxford University Press.

Batson, C.D.; Stocks, E.L. (2005): Religion and Prejudice, in: Dovidio, J.F.; Glick, P.; Rudman, L.A. (Eds.), *On the Nature of Prejudice*, 413–427, Malden/MA: Blackwell.

Batson, C.D.; Thompson, E.R.; Seuferling, G.; Whitney, H.; Strongman, J.A. (1999): Moral Hypocrisy. Appearing Moral to Oneself without Being So, *Journal of Personality and Social Psychology*, 77(3): 525–537.

Baucal, A.; Zittoun, T. (2013): Religion as Dialogical Resource. A Socio-Cultural Approach, *Integrative Psychological and Behavioral Science*, 47(2): 207–219.

Baumann, C.; Winzar, H. (2017): Confucianism and Work Ethic, in: Oh, I.; Park, G.-S. (Eds.), *The Political Economy of Business Ethics in East Asia*, 33–60, Cambridge: Elsevier.

Bechert, I. (2021): Of Pride and Prejudice. A Cross-National Exploration of Atheists' National Pride, *Religions*, 12(8): 648–672.

Beck, R. (2006): Defensive versus Existential Religion, *Journal of Psychology and Theology*, 34(2): 142–152.

Becker, E. (1973): *The Denial of Death*, New York: Free Press.

Becker, J. (2019): *Marketing Conception*, 11th ed., Munich: Vahlen.

Bedell, K. (2000): Dispatches from the Electronic Frontier. Explorations of Mainline Protestant Use of the Internet, in: Hadden, J.K.; Cowan, D.E. (Eds.), *Religion on the Internet*, 183–204, Amsterdam: JAI/Elsevier.

Bègue, L. (2002): Beliefs in Justice and Faith in People. Just World, Religiosity and Interpersonal Trust, *Personality and Individual Differences*, 32(3): 375–382.

Behravan, N.; Masoudi, R. (2012): A Review Study of Developing an Advertising Strategy for Westerner's Companies among Middle East Countries. The Islamic Perspective, *Information Management and Business Review*, 4(3): 107–113.

Belk, R.W. (1984): Three Scales to Measure Constructs Related to Materialism. Reliability, Validity, and Relationships to Measures of Happiness, in: Kinnear, T. (Ed.), *Advances in Consumer Research*, Vol. 11, 291–297, Provo/UT: Association for Consumer Research.

Belk, R.W. (1988): Possessions and the Extended Self, *Journal of Consumer Research*, 15(2): 139–168.

Belk, R.W. (2013): The Sacred in Consumer Culture, in: Rinallo, D.; Scott, L.; MacClaran, P. (Eds.), *Consumption and Spirituality*, 69–80, New York: Routledge.

Belk, R.W.; Ger, G.; Askegaard, S. (2003): The Fire of Desire. A Multisited Inquiry into Consumer Passion, *Journal of Consumer Research*, 30(3): 326–351.

Belk, R.W.; Tumbat, G. (2005): The Cult of Macintosh, *Consumption Markets and Culture*, 8(3): 205–217.

Belk, R.W.; Wallendorf, M.; Sherry Jr, J.F. (1989): The Sacred and the Profane in Consumer Behavior, *Journal of Consumer Research*, 16(1): 1–38.

Bell, F.W. (1968): The Pope and the Price of Fish, *American Economic Review*, 58(5): 1346–1350.

Belwal, R.; Belwal, S. (2017): Factors Affecting Store Image and the Choice of Hypermarkets in Oman, *International Journal of Retail & Distribution Management*, 45(6): 587–607.

Bénabou, R.; Ticchi, D.; Vindigni, A. (2015b): Forbidden Fruits. The Political Economy of Science, Religion and Growth, *Working Paper 21105*, Cambridge/MA: National Bureau of Economic Research.

Bénabou, R.; Ticchi, D.; Vindigni, A. (2015a): Religion and Innovation, *American Economic Review*, 105(5): 346–351.

Benjamins, M.R. (2006): Does Religion Influence Patient Satisfaction? *American Journal of Health Behavior*, 30(1): 85–91.

Berger, P. L. (1967). A sociological view of the secularization of theology. *Journal for the Scientific Study of Religion*, 6(1), 3–16.

Berger, J. (2014): Word of Mouth and Interpersonal Communication. A Review and Directions for Future Research, *Journal of Consumer Psychology*, 24(4): 586–607.

Berger, J. (2019): Signaling Can Increase Consumers' Willingness to Pay for Green Products. Theoretical Model and Experimental Evidence, *Journal of Consumer Behavior*, 18(3): 233–246.

Berger, P.L. (1986): *The Capitalist Revolution*, New York: Basic Books.

Berggren, N.; Bjørnskov, C. (2011): Is the Importance of Religion in Daily Life Related to Social Trust? Cross-Country and Cross-State Comparisons, *Journal of Economic Behavior & Organization*, 80(3): 459–480.

Berkessel, J.B.; Gebauer, J.E.; Joshanloo, M.; Bleidorn, W.; Rentfrow, P.J.; Potter, J.; Gosling, S.D. (2021): National Religiosity Eases the Psychological Burden of Poverty, *Proceedings of the National Academy of Sciences*, 118(39): 1–6.

Berry, H.; Guillén, M.; Zhou, A. (2010): An Institutional Approach to Cross-National Distance, *Journal of International Business Studies*, 41(9): 1460–1480.

Beugelsdijk, S.; Kostova, T.; Kunst, V.E.; Spadafora, E.; van Essen, M. (2018): Cultural Distance and FIFM Internationalization. A Meta-Analytical Review and Theoretical Implications, *Journal of Management*, 44(1): 89–130.

Bezençon, V.; Blili, S. (2009): Fair Trade Managerial Practices. Strategy, Organization and Engagement, *Journal of Business Ethics*, 90(1): 95–113.

Białkowski, J.; Etebari, A.; Wisniewski, T.P. (2012): Fast Profits. Investor Sentiment and Stock Returns during Ramadan, *Journal of Banking & Finance*, 36(3): 835–845.

Biel, A.; Nilsson, A. (2005): Religious Values and Environmental Concern. Harmony and Detachment, *Social Science Quarterly*, V6(1): 178–191.

Binark, M.; Kılıçbay, B. (2002): Consumer Culture, Islam and the Politics of Lifestyle, *European Journal of Communication*, 17(4): 495–511.

Biswas, A.; Olsen, J.E.; Carlet, V. (1992): A Comparison of Print Advertisements from the United States and France, *Journal of Advertising*, 21(4): 73–81.
Blackburn, S. (1996): *The Oxford Dictionary of Philosophy*, Oxford: Oxford University Press.
Blanchard, C.M. (2008): The Islamic Traditions of Wahhabism and Salafiyya, in: Malbouisson, C.D. (Ed.), *Focus on Islamic Issues*, 21–30, New York: Nova Science. https://sgp.fas.org/crs/misc/RS21695.pdf/ (13.08.2024)
Blanken, I.; van de Ven, N.; Zeelenberg, M. (2015): A Meta-Analytic Review of Moral Licensing, *Personality and Social Psychology Bulletin*, 41(4): 540–558.
Blogowska, J.; Saroglou, V. (2011): Religious Fundamentalism and Limited Prosociality as a Function of the Target, *Journal for the Scientific Study of Religion*, 50(1): 44–60.
Bock, D.C.; Warren, N.C. (1972): Religious Belief as a Factor in Obedience to Destructive Commands, *Review of Religions Research*, 13(3): 185–191.
Bond, M.H.; Hofstede, G. (1989): The Cash Value of Confucian Values, *Human Systems Management*, 8(3): 195–200.
Bonne, K.; Verbeke, W. (2008): Muslim Consumer Trust in Halal Meat Status and Control in Belgium, *Meat Science*, 79(1): 113–123.
Borlea, S.N.; Achim, M.V.; Rus, A.I.D. (2019): Behavioral Determinants of Corruption. A Cross-Country Survey, Studia Universitatis Vasile Goldiş Arad, *Seria Ştiinţe Economice*, 29(1): 21–39.
Borzooei, M.; Asgari, M. (2015): Country-of-Origin Effect on Consumer Purchase Intention of Halal Brands, *American Journal of Marketing Research*, 1(1): 1–10.
Brammer, S.; Williams, G.; Zinkin, J. (2007): Religion and Attitudes to Corporate Social Responsibility in a Large Cross-Country Sample, *Journal of Business Ethics*, 71(3): 229–243.
Braswell, G.W. (1996): *Islam. Its Prophet, Peoples, Politics, and Power*, Nashville/TN: Broadman & Holman Publishers.
Braun S. (2011): Associative Lifeworld, Bonding Social capital and Migrant Clubs in Sport and Society, in: Braun, S.; Nobis, T. (Eds.), *Migration, Integration and Sport*, Wiesbaden: Verlag für Sozialwis-senschaften.
Brodbeck, K.-H. (2022): *Buddhist Business Ethics*, in: Aßländer, M.S. (Ed.), *Handbuch Wirtschaftsethik*, 2nd ed., 669–672, Berlin: Metzler.
Brooks, A.C. (2004): Faith, Secularism, and Charity, *Faith & Economics*, 43(Spring): 1–8.
Brown, B.A. (1996): Authoritarianism in the New States of Central Asia, *Report of BIOst 46/1996*, Cologne: Bun-desinstitut für Ostwissenschaftliche und Internationale Studien.
Brown, C.; Zsolnai, L. (2018): Buddhist Economics. An Overview, *Society and Economy*, 40(4): 497–513.
Brown-Iannuzzi, J.L.; McKee, S.; Gervais, W.M. (2018): Atheist Horns and Religious Halos: Mental Representations of Atheists and Theists. *Journal of Experimental Psychology: General*, 147(2), 292–297.
Brox, T., Williams-Oerberg, E.; Rowe, M.M. (Eds.) (2020): *Buddhism and Business: Merit, Material Wealth, and Morality in the Global Market Economy, Honolulu*: University of Hawaii Press.
Brubaker, R. (2012): Religion and Nationalism. Four Approaches, *Nations and Nationalism*, 18(1): 2–20.
Buddenbaum, J.M.; Stout, D.A. (1996): Religion and Mass Media Use. A Review of the Mass Communication and Sociology Literature, in: Stout, D.A.; Buddenbaum,

J.M. (Eds.), *Religion and Mass Media. Audiences and Adaptations*, 12–34, Thousand Oaks/CA: Sage.
Burke, M.; Hsiang, S.M.; Miguel, E. (2015): Global Non-linear Effect of Temperature on Economic Production, *Nature*, 527(7577): 235–239.
Burris, C.T.; Navara, G.S. (2002): Morality Play or Playing Morality? Intrinsic Religious Orientation and Socially Desirable Responding, *Self and Identity*, 1(1): 67–76.
Burroughs, J.E.; Rindfleisch, A. (2002): Materialism and Well-Being. A Conflicting Values Perspective, *Journal of Consumer Research*, 29(3): 348–370.
Butt, M.M.; de Run, E.C.; U-Din, A.; Mutum, D. (2018): Religious Symbolism in Islamic Financial Service Advertisements, *Journal of Islamic Marketing*, 9(2): 384–401.
Butt, M.M.; Rose, S.; Wilkins, S.; Haq, J.U. (2017): MNCs and Religious Influences in Global Markets. Drivers of Consumer-Based Halal Brand Equity, *International Marketing Review*, 34(6): 885–908.
Byrne, A.T.; Heiman, A.; Just, D.R. (2021): New Insights into Country of Origin Labeling (COOL). The Effects of Nationalism, Patriotism, and Xenophobia, *Marketing Science Institute Working Paper*, Report No. 21–125.
Cabano, F.G.; Minton, E.A. (2023): A Common Identity Intervention to Improve Service Quality for Consumers Experiencing Vulnerabilities. *Journal of Service Research*, 26(4), 597–613.
Cabano, F.G.; Minton, E.A. (2024): I Am Religious, Therefore I Am Good: The Influence of Consumer Religiosity on Purchase Intentions of Unethical Brands. Working Paper.
Cabano, F.G.; Minton, E.A. (2023): The Influence of Consumer Religiosity on Responses to Rational and Emotional Ad Appeals, *European Journal of Marketing*, 57(1): 185–201.
Cai, J.; Shi, G. (2019): Do Religious Norms Influence Corporate Debt Financing? *Journal of Business Ethics*, 157(1): 159–182.
Campbell, H.; Evolvi, G. (2019): Contextualizing Current Digital Religion Research on Emerging Technologies, *Human Behavior and Emerging Technologies*, 2(1): 5–17.
Cantrell, B.W.; Yust, C.G. (2018): The Relation between Religiosity and Private Bank Outcomes, *Journal of Banking & Finance*, 91(June): 86–105.
Carey, J.M.; Paulhus, D.L. (2013): Worldview Implications of Believing in Free Will and/or Determinism, *Journal of Personality*, 81(2): 130–141.
Carpenter, T.P.; Marshall, M.A. (2009): An Examination of Religious Priming and Intrinsic Religious Motivation in the Moral Hypocrisy Paradigm, *Journal for the Scientific Study of Religion*, 48(2): 386–393.
Carroll, A.B. (1979): A Three-Dimensional Conceptual Model of Corporate Performance, *Academy of Management Review*, 4(4): 497–505.
Carroll, A.B. (1999): Corporate Social Responsibility. Evolution of a Definitional Construct, *Business & Society*, 38(3): 268–295.
Carter, E.C.; McCullough, M.E.; Carver, C.S. (2012a): The Mediating Role of Monitoring in the Association of Religion with Self-control, *Social Psychological and Personality Science*, 3(6): 691–697.
Cartwright, S.; Schoenberg, R. (2006): Thirty Years of Mergers and Acquisitions Research. Recent Advances and Future Opportunities, *British Journal of Management*, 17(1): S1–S5.

Carver, C.S.; Scheier, M.F. (2012): *Attention and Self-Regulation. A Control-Theory Approach to Human Behavior*, New York: Springer.

Casidy, R.; Arli, D. (2018): Spirituality, Religion and Consumption, Introduction to a Special Issue, *International Journal of Consumer Studies*, 42(6): 583–585.

Casidy, R.; Duhachek, A.; Singh, V.; Tamaddoni, A. (2021): Religious Belief, Religious Priming, and Negative Word-of-Mouth, *Journal of Marketing Research*, 58(4): 762–781.

Casidy, R.; Phau, I.; Lwin, M. (2016): The Role of Religious Leaders on Digital Piracy Attitude and Intention, *Journal of* Retailing *and Consumer Services*, 32(September): 244–252.

Castro, E.; Hassan, M.K.; Rubio, J.F.; Halim, Z.A. (2020): Relative Performance of Religious and Ethical Investment Funds, *Journal of Islamic Accounting and Business Research*, 11(6): 1227–1244.

Cater, J.J.; Collins, L.A.; Beal, B.D. (2017): Ethics, Faith, and Profit. Exploring the Motives of the US Fair Trade Social Entrepreneurs, *Journal of Business Ethics*, 146(1): 185–201.

Cebula, R.J.; Rossi, F. (2021): Religiosity and Corporate Risk-Taking, *Journal of Economics and Finance*, 45(4): 751–763.

Central Hindu College (Ed.) (2010): *Sanatana Dharma. An Advanced Text Book of Hindu Religion and Ethics*. (Reprint 1903), Whitefish: Kessinger.

Chan, H.; Wan, L.C. (2008): Consumer Responses to Service Failures, *Journal of International Marketing*, 16(1): 72–97.

Chan, H.; Wan, L.C.; Sin, L.Y. (2007): Hospitality Service Failures. Who Will Be More Dissatisfied? *International Journal of Hospitality Management*, 26(3): 531–545.

Chan, H.; Wan, L.C.; Sin, L.Y. (2009): The Contrasting Effects of Culture on Consumer Tolerance. Interpersonal Face and Impersonal Fate, *Journal of Consumer Research*, 36(2): 292–304.

Chandon, J.L.; Laurent, G.; Valette-Florence, P. (2016): Pursuing the Concept of Luxury, *Journal of Business Research*, 69(1): 299–303.

Chang, H.H. (2021): Exploring Consumer Behavioral Predispositions toward Voluntary Simplicity, *Current Psychology*, 40(2): 731–743.

Charlton, J.P.; Soh, P.C.H.; Ang, P.H.; Chew K.W. (2013): Religiosity, Adolescent Internet Usage Motives and Addiction, *Information, Communication & Society*, 16(10): 1619–1638.

Chaves, M. (2010): Rain Dances in the Dry Season. Overcoming the Religious Congruence Fallacy, *Journal for the Scientific Study of Religion*, 49(1): 1–14.

Chintagunta, P.; Nair, H. (2011): Discrete-Choice Models of Consumer Demand in Marketing, *Marketing Science*, 30(6): 977–996.

Chiu, C.Y. (1991): Responses to Injustice in Popular Chinese Sayings and among Hong Kong Chinese Students, *Journal of Social Psychology*, 131(5): 655–665.

Choi, S.; Mattila, A.S. (2008): Perceived Controllability and Service Expectations. Influences on Customer Reactions Following Service Failure, *Journal of Business Research*, 61(1): 24–30.

Choi, Y. (2010): Religion, Religiosity, and South Korean Consumer Switching Behaviors, *Journal of Consumer Behavior*, 9(3): 157–171.

Choi, Y.; Kale, R.; Shin, J. (2010): Religiosity and Consumers' Use of Product Information Source among Korean Consumers, *International Journal of Consumer Studies*, 34(1): 61–68.

Choi, Y.; Paulraj, A.; Shin, J. (2013): Religion or Religiosity. Which Is the Culprit for Consumer Switching Behavior? *Journal of International Consumer Marketing*, 24(4): 262–280.

Chowdhury, R.M. (2018): Religiosity and Voluntary Simplicity, *Journal of Business Ethics*, 152(1): 149–174.

Chowdhury, R.M.; Arli, D.; Septianto, F. (2022): Consumers' Responses to Moral Controversies of Religiously Positioned Brands. The Effects of Religiosity on Brand Loyalty, *European Journal of Marketing*, 56(5), 1398–1433.

Chuah, S.H.; Gachter, S.; Hoffmann, R.; Tan, J.H.W. (2016): Religion, Discrimination, and Trust across Three Cultures, *European Economic Review*, 90: 280–301.

Chung, E.; Farrelly, F.; Beverland, M.B.; Karpen, I.O. (2018): Loyalty or Liability. Resolving the Consumer Fanaticism Paradox, *Marketing Theory*, 18(1): 3–30.

Chung, J.; Monroe, G.S. (2003): Exploring Social Desirability Bias, *Journal of Business Ethics*, 44(4): 291–302.

Churchill, S.A.; Appau, S.; Farrell, L. (2019): Religiosity, Income and Wellbeing in Developing Countries, *Empirical Economics*, 56(3): 959–985.

Clayton, R.R.; Gladden, J.W. (1974): The Five Dimensions of Religiosity. Toward Demythologizing a Sacred Artifact, *Journal for the Scientific Study of Religion*, 13(2): 135–143.

Cline, T.A. (2003): When Does Humor Enhance or Inhibit Ad Responses? *Journal of Advertising*, 32(3): 31–45.

Clobert, M.; Saroglou, V.; Hwang, K.K. (2015): Buddhist Concepts as Implicitly Reducing Prejudice and Increasing Prosociality, *Personality and Social Psychology Bulletin*, 41(4): 513–525.

Cohen, A.B.; Hill, P.C. (2007): Religion as Culture. Religious Individualism and Collectivism among American Catholics, Jews, and Protestants, *Journal of Personality*, 75(4): 709–742.

Collins-Kreiner, N. (2010): Researching Pilgrimage. Continuity and Transformations, *Annals of Tourism Research*, 37(2): 440–456.

Copeland, L.; Boulianne, S. (2020): Political Consumerism. A Meta-Analysis, *International Political Science Review*, 42(2): 1–16.

Cornwell, T.B. (2014): *Sponsorship in Marketing. Effective Communication through Sports, Arts, and Events*, London: Routledge.

Coşgel, M.M.; Minkler, L. (2004): Religious Identity and Consumption, *Review of Social Economy*, 62(3): 339–350.

Cottone, J.; Drucker, P.; Javier, R.A. (2007): Predictors of Moral Reasoning, *Journal for the Scientific Study of Religion*, 46(1): 37–53.

Cova, V.; Cova, B. (2019): Pain, Suffering and the Consumption of Spirituality. A Toe Story, *Journal of Marketing Management*, 35(5/6): 565–585.

Cowart, K.O.; Ramirez, E.; Brady, M.K. (2014): Religious Affiliation. Buffering Negative Reactions to Service Failures, *Journal of Services Marketing*, 28(1): 1–9.

Croucher, S.M.; Harris, T.M. (Eds.) (2012): *Religion and Communication*, New York: Peter Lang.

Cutler, B.D. (1991): Religion and Marketing. Important Research Area or a Footnote in the Literature? *Journal of Professional Services Marketing*, 8(1): 153–164.

Cutler, B.D.; Winans, W.A. (1998): What Do Religion Scholars Say about Marketing? *Journal of Professional Services Marketing*, 18(2): 133–145.

Dahl, D.W.; Frankerberger, K.D.; Manchanda, R.V. (2003): Does It Pay to Shock? Reactions to Shocking and Nonshocking Advertising Content among University Students, *Journal of Advertising Research*, 43(3): 268–280.

Dana, L.P. (2009): Religion as an Explanatory Variable for Entrepreneurship, *International Journal of Entrepreneurship and Innovation*, 10(2): 87–99.

Daniels, J.P.; von der Ruhr, M. (2005): God and the Global Economy. Religion and Attitudes toward Trade and Immigration in the United States, *Socio-Economic Review*, 3(3): 467–489.

Daniels, J.P.; von der Ruhr, M. (2010): Trust in Others. Does Religion Matter? *Review of Social Economy,* 68(2): 163–186.

Daniels, P.L. (2005): Economic Systems and the Buddhist World View. The 21st Century Nexus, *Journal of Socio-Economics*, 34: 245–268.

Davari, A.; Iyer, P.; Strutton, D. (2017): Investigating Moral Links between Religiosity, Altruism, and Green Consumption, *Journal of Nonprofit & Public Sector Marketing*, 29(4): 385–414.

Davidson, T.; Farquhar, L.K. (2014): Correlates of Social Anxiety, Religion, and Facebook, *Journal of Media and Religion*, 3(4): 208–225.

Davie, G. (2008): *The Sociology of Religion*, Los Angeles/CA: Sage.

Davis, D.E.; Worthington Jr, E.L.; Hook, J.N.; Hill, P.C. (2013): Research on Religion/Spirituality and Forgiveness. A Meta-Analytic Review, *Psychology of Religion and Spirituality*, 5(4): 233–241.

Davis, F.D. (1989): Perceived Usefulness, Perceived Ease of Use, and User Acceptance of Information Technology, *MIS Quarterly,* 13(3): 319–340.

Davis, F.D.; Bagozzi, R.P.; Warshaw, P.R. (1989): User Acceptance of Computer Technology, *Management Science*, 35(8): 982–1003.

Davis, J.H.; Schoorman, F.D.; Donaldson, L. (1997): Toward a Stewardship Theory of Management, *Academy of Management Review*, 22(1): 20–47.

Davis, L. (2016): Religiosity and Retail Store Choices. Exploring US Christian Consumers' Apparel Shopping Behavior, *International Journal of Business Anthropology*, 6(1): 47–72.

Davis, L.; Jai, C. (2014): Effects of Religiosity on Apparel Shopping Orientation. An Exploratory Study, *International Journal of Business Anthropology*, 5(2): 24–36.

Day, N.E. (2005): Religion in the Workplace. Correlates and Consequences of Individual Behavior, *Journal of Management, Spirituality & Religion*, 2(1): 104–135.

Dayton Jr, H.L. (2011): *Your Money Counts. The Biblical Guide to Earning, Spending, Saving, Investing, Giving, and Getting Out of Debt*, Carol Stream/IL: Tyndale House.

de Groot, M.; van den Born, R. (2007): Humans, Nature and God, *Worldviews: Global Religions, Culture, and Ecology*, 11(3): 324–351.

de Matos, C.A.; Henrique, J.L.; Rossi, C.A.V. (2007): Service Recovery Paradox. A Meta-Analysis, *Journal of Service Research*, 10(1): 60–77.

de Mooij, M. (2019): *Consumer Behavior and Culture. Consequences for Global Marketing*, 3rd ed., Thousand Oaks/CA: Sage.

de Noble, A.; Galbraith, C.S.; Singh, G.; Stiles, C.H. (2007): Market Justice, Religious Orientation, and Entrepreneurial Attitudes, *Journal of Enterprising Communities. People and Places in the Global Economy*, 1(2): 121–134.

de Pelsmacker, P.; Driesen, L.; Rayp, G. (2005): Do Consumers Care about Ethics? Willingness to Pay for Fair-Trade Coffee, *Journal of Consumer Affairs*, 39(2): 363–385.

de Pelsmacker, P.; Janssens, W. (2007): A Model for Fair Trade Buying Behavior, *Journal of Business Ethics*, 75(4): 361–380.

de Run, E.C.; Butt, M.M.; Fam, K.S.; Jong, H.Y. (2010): Attitudes toward Offensive Advertising. Malaysian Muslims' Views, *Journal of Islamic Marketing*, 1(1): 25–36.

Deitelhoff, N.; Ließmann, H.; Bauerochse, L.; Baumgart-Ochse, C.; Hofmeister, K.; Kösters, J.; Nembach, E. (2019): *Powerful Religion. Begleitbuch zum Funkkolleg Religion Macht Politik*, Frankfurt/Main: Wochenschau Verlag.

Dekhil, F.; Boulebech, H.; Bouslama, N. (2017a): Effect of Religiosity on Luxury Consumer Behavior. The Case of the Tunisian Muslim, *Journal of Islamic Marketing*, 8(1): 74–94.

Dekhil, F.; Jridi, H.; Farhat, H. (2017b): Effect of Religiosity on the Decision to Participate in a Boycott. The Case of Coca-Cola, *Journal of Islamic Marketing*, 8(2): 309–328.

Delener, N. (1989): Religious Differences in Cognitions Concerning External Information Search and Media Usage, 64–68, *Proceedings of the Southern Marketing Association*.

Delener, N. (1990a): The Effects of Religious Factors on Perceived Risk in Durable Goods Purchase Decisions, *Journal of Consumer Marketing*, 7(3): 27–38.

Delener, N. (1990b): An Examination of the Religious Influences as Predictors of Consumer Innovativeness, *Journal* of *Midwest Marketing*, 5: 167–178.

Delener, N. (1994): Religious Contrasts in Consumer Decision Behaviour Patterns. Their Dimensions and Marketing Implications, *European Journal of Marketing*, 28(5): 36–53.

Delhey, J.; Newton, K. (2005): Predicting Cross-National Levels of Social Trust. Global Pattern or Nordic Exceptionalism? *European Sociological Review*, 21(4): 311–327.

Demirguc-Kunt, A.; Klapper, L.; Randall, D. (2014): Islamic Finance and Financial Inclusion. Measuring Use of and Demand for Formal Financial Services among Muslim Adults, *Review of Middle East Economics and Finance*, 10(2): 177–218.

Deng, S.; Jivan, S.; Hassan, M.L. (1994): Advertising in Malaysia. A Cultural Perspective, *International Journal of Advertising*, 13(2): 153–166.

Diamantopoulos, A., Schlegelmilch, B. B., & Du Preez, J. P. (1995). Lessons for pan-European marketing? The role of consumerpreferences in fine-tuning the product-market fit. *International Marketing Review*, 12(2), 38–52.

Dietz, T.; Stern, P.C.; Guagnano, G.A. (1998): Social Structural and Social Psychological Bases of Environmental Concern, *Environment and Behavior*, 30(4): 450–471.

Dinh, H.P.; Van Nguyen, P.; Trinh, T.V.A.; Nguyen, M.H. (2022): Roles of Religiosity in Enhancing Life Satisfaction, Ethical Judgements and Consumer Loyalty, *Cogent Business & Management*, 9(1): 2010482.

Dion, D.; Borraz, S. (2015): Managing Heritage Brands. A Study of the Sacralization of Heritage Stores in the Luxury Industry, *Journal of Retailing and Consumer Services*, 22: 77–84.

Djupe, P.A. (2000): Religious Brand Loyalty and Political Loyalties, *Journal for the Scientific Study of Religion*, 39(1): 78–89.

Dockrill, D.W. (1971): TH Huxley and the Meaning of "Agnosticism", *Theology*, 74(616): 461–477.

Dolansky, E., & Alon, I. (2008). Religious freedom, religious diversity, and Japanese foreign direct investment. *Research in International Business and Finance*, 22(1), 29–39.

Dollinger, S.J. (2007): Creativity and Conservatism, *Personality and Individual Differences*, 43(5): 1025–1035.

Domínguez, A.D. (2013): Religión, Adversidad y Libre Comercio en América Latina, *Iberoforum, Revista de. Ciencias Sociales de la Universidad Iberoamericana*, 8(15): 131–155.

Donahue, M.J. (1985): Intrinsic and Extrinsic Religiousness. Review and Meta-Analysis, *Journal of Personality and Social Psychology*, 48(2): 400–419.

Doran, C.J. (2009): The Role of Personal Values in Fair Trade Consumption, *Journal of Business Ethics*, 84(4): 549–563.

Doran, C.J.; Natale, S.M. (2011): ἐμπάθεια (Empatheia) and Caritas. The Role of Religion in Fair Trade Consumption, *Journal of Business Ethics*, 98(1): 1–15.

Dotson, M.J.; Hyatt, E.M. (2000): Religious Symbols as Peripheral Cues in Advertising, *Journal of Business Research*, 48(1): 63–68.

Douglas, S.P & Craig, S.C. (1986). Global Marketing Myopia. *Journal of Marketing Management*, 2, 155–169.

Dow, D.; Cuypers, I.R.P.; Ertug, G. (2016): The Effects of Within-Country Linguistic and Religious Diversity on Foreign Acquisitions, *Journal of International Business Studies*, 47(3): 319–346.

Dow, D.; Karunaratna, A. (2006): Developing a Multidimensional Instrument to Measure Psychic Distance Stimuli, *Journal of International Business Studies*, 37(5): 578–602.

Doyle, K.O.; Doyle, M.R. (2001): Meanings of Wealth in European and Chinese Fairy Tales, *American Behavioral Scientist*, 45(2): 191–204.

Drane, J. W. (2000). *The McDonaldization of the church: Spirituality, creativity, and the future of the church* (p. 18). London: Darton Longman & Todd.

Draper, P. (2017), "Atheism and Agnosticism". Available at: https://plato.stanford.edu/entries/atheism-agnosticism/.

Drechsler, W. (2019): The Reality and Diversity of Buddhist Economics, *American Journal of Economics and Sociology*, 78(2): 523–560.

Drori, I.; Wrzesniewski, A.; Ellis, S. (2013): One Out of Many? Boundary Negotiation and Identity Formation in Postmerger Integration, *Organization Science*, 24(6): 1717–1741.

Dubé, J.P. (2019): Microeconometric Models of Consumer Demand, in: Dubé, J.P.; Rossi, P.E. (Eds.), *Handbook of the Economics of Marketing*, Vol. 1, 1–68, Amsterdam: North-Holland.

Dun, S. (2014): No Beer, No Way! Football Fan Identity Enactment Won't Mix with Muslim Beliefs in the Qatar 2022 World Cup, *Journal of Policy Research in Tourism, Leisure and Events*, 6(2): 186–199.

Duriez, B. (2003): Religiosity and Conservatism Revisited. Relating a New Religiosity Measure to the Two Main Conservative Political Ideologies, *Psychological Reports*, 92(2): 533–539.

Duriez, B.; Appel, C.; Hutsebaut, D. (2003): The German Post-critical Belief Scale. Internal and External Validity, *Journal of Social Psychology*, 34(4): 219–226.

Durkheim, E. (1912/1994): *The Elementary Forms of the Religious Life*, New York: Free Press.

Echchabi, A.; Olaniyi, H. (2012): Empirical Investigation of Customers' Perception and Adoption towards Islamic Banking Services in Morocco, *Middle-East Journal of Scientific Research*, 12(6): 849–858.

Eckberg, D.L.; Blocker, T.J. (1996): Christianity, Environmentalism, and the Theoretical Problem of Fundamentalism, *Journal for the Scientific Study of Religion*, 35(4): 343–355.

Effendi, I.; Murad, M.; Rafiki, A.; Lubis, M.M. (2020): The Application of the Theory of Reasoned Action on Services of Islamic Rural Banks in Indonesia, *Journal of Islamic Marketing*, 12(5): 951–976.

Eisinga, R.; Felling, A.; Peters, J. (1990): Religious Belief, Church Involvement, and Ethnocentrism in the Netherlands, *Journal for the Scientific Study of Religion*, 29(1): 54–75.

Eisinga, R.; Felling, A.; Peters, J. (1991): Christian Beliefs and Ethnocentrism in Dutch Society. A Test of Three Models, *Review of Religions Research*, 32(3): 305–320.

El-Bassiouny, N. (2016): Where Is "Islamic Marketing" Heading? A Commentary on Jafari and Sandikci's (2015): "Islamic" Consumers, Markets, and Marketing, *Journal of Business Research*, 69(2): 569–578.

El Ghoul, S.; Guedhami, O.; Ni, Y.; Pittman, J.; Saadi, S. (2012): Does Religion Matter to Equity Pricing? *Journal of Business Ethics*, 111(4): 491–518.

El Guindi, F. (1999): Veiling Resistance, *Fashion Theory*, 3(1): 51–80.

El-Gamal, M.A. (2006): *Islamic Finance. Law, Economics, and Practice*, Cambridge: Cambridge University Press.

Elhoushy, S.; Jang, S. (2021): Religiosity and Food Waste Reduction Intentions, *International Journal of Consumer Studies*, 45(2): 287–302.

Ellis, J.T. (1955): American Catholics and the Intellectual Life, *Thought: Fordham University Quarterly*, 30(3): 351–388.

Ellis, P.D. (2008): Does Psychic Distance Moderate the Market Size – Entry Sequence Relationship? *Journal of International Business Studies*, 39(3): 351–369.

Ellison, C.G.; Sherkat, D.E. (1993): Obedience and Autonomy. Religion and Parental Values Reconsidered, *Journal for the Scientific Study of Religion*, 32(4): 313–329.

El-Menouar, Y. (2014): The Five Dimensions of Muslim Religiosity, *Methods, Data, Analyses*, 8(1): 53–78.

Eom, K.; Saad, C.S.; Kim, H.S. (2021b): Religiosity Moderates the Link between Environmental Beliefs and Proenvironmental Support. The Role of Belief in a Controlling God, *Personality and Social Psychology Bulletin*, 47(6): 891–905.

Eom, K.; Tok, T.Q.H.; Saad, C.S.; Kim, H.S. (2021a): Religion, Environmental Guilt, and Pro-environmental Support, *Journal of Environmental Psychology*, 78: December (10171).

Erdem, O., & Tuncalp, S. (1998). Advertising agency scene in Saudi Arabia. *Management research news*, 21(1), 1–8.

Escalas, J.E.; Bettman, J.R. (2005): Self Construal, Reference Groups, and Brand Meaning, *Journal of Consumer Research*, 32(3): 378–389.

Escher, D. (2013): How Does Religion Promote Forgiveness? Linking Beliefs, Orientations, and Practices, *Journal for the Scientific Study of Religion*, 52(1): 100–119.

Essoo, N.; Dibb, S. (2004): Religious Influences on Shopping Behavior. An Exploratory Study, *Journal of Marketing Management*, 20(7/8): 683–712.

Evans, N.D.; Fetterman, A.K. (2021): It Doesn't Apply to Me, So It Isn't Real. People Are Likely to Deny Science If It Contradicts Their Personality, *Social Psychological and Personality Science*, 13(6): 1032–1046.

Faccio, M. (2006): Politically Connected Firms, *American Economic Review*, 96(1): 369–386.

Fam, K.S.; Waller, D.S.; Erdogan, B.Z. (2004): The Influence of Religion on Attitudes toward the Advertising of Controversial Products, *European Journal of Marketing*, 38(5/6): 537–555.

Fam, K.-S.; Yang, Z.; Hyman, Z. (2009): *A Handbook of Confucian/Chopsticks Marketing*, Wellington: Asia Business Research Corp.

Farah, M.F.; El Samad, L. (2014): The Effects of Religion and Religiosity on Advertisement Assessment among Lebanese Consumers, *Journal of International Consumer Marketing*, 26(4): 344–369.

Farah, M.F.; Newman, A.J. (2010): Exploring Consumer Boycott Intelligence Using a Socio-Cognitive Approach, *Journal of Business Research*, 63(4): 347–355.

Farías, P. (2020): The Use of Fear versus Hope in Health Advertisements, *International Journal of Environmental Research and Public Health*, 17(23): 1–15.

Farris, B.E.; Glenn, N.D. (1976): Fatalism and Familism among Anglos and Mexican Americans in San Antonio, *Sociology and Social Research*, 60(4): 393–402.

Fathi, E.; Zailani, S.; Iranmanesh, M.; Kanapathy, K. (2016): Drivers of Consumers' Willingness to Pay for Halal Logistics, *British Food Journal*, 118(2): 464–479.

Faulkner, J.E.; De Jong, G.F. (1966): Religiosity in 5-D. An Empirical Analysis, *Social Forces*, 45(2): 246–254.

Fawcett, B.G.; Francis, L.J.; Henderson, A.J.; Robbins, M.; Linkletter, J. (2013): Religiosity and Music Copyright. Theft among Canadian Baptist Youth, *Journal of Research on Christian Education*, 22(2): 153–164.

Felix, R.; Braunsberger, K. (2016): I Believe Therefore I Care. The Relationship between Religiosity, Environmental Attitudes, and Green Product Purchase in Mexico, *International Marketing Review*, 33(1): 137–155.

Felix, R.; Hinsch, C.; Rauschnabel, P.A.; Schlegelmilch, B.B. (2018): Religiousness and Environmental Concern. A Multilevel and Multi-country Analysis of the Role of Life Satisfaction and Indulgence, *Journal of Business Research*, 91(10): 304–312.

Figh, J. (2007): Weltreligionen und Weltethos, in: Bader, E. (Ed.), *Weltethos und Globalisierung*, Vienna: LIT.

Finnegan, F.R. Jr; Viswanath, K. (1998): Community Ties and the Use of Cable TV and Newspapers in a Midwest, *Suburb, Journalism Quarterly*, 65(4): 463–473.

Fiori, K.L.; Brown, E.E.; Cortina, K.; Antonucci, T.C. (2006): Locus of Control as a Mediator of the Relationship between Religiosity and Life Satisfaction, *Mental Health, Religion and Culture*, 9(3): 239–263.

Fishbein, M., & Ajzen, I. (1975). *Belief, Attitude, Intention, and Behavior: An Introduction to Theory and Research*. Reading, MA: Addison-Wesley.

Flood, G.D.; Flood, G.D.F. (1996): *An Introduction to Hinduism*, Cambridge: Cambridge University Press.

Floren, J.; Rasul, T.; Gani, A. (2019): Islamic Marketing and Consumer Behavior. A Systematic Literature Review, *Journal of Islamic Marketing*, 11(6): 1557–1578.

Folkes, V.S.; Kotsos, B. (1986): Buyers' and Sellers' Explanations for Product Failure, *Journal of Marketing*, 50(2): 74–80.

Fourie, J.; Rosselló, J.; Santana-Gallego, M. (2015): Religion, Religious Diversity and Tourism, *Kyklos*, 68(1): 51–64.

Fourie, J.; Rosselló, J.; Santana-Gallego, M. (2016): Which God Is Good for Tourism? *Tourism Economics*, 22(1):163–169.

Fox, A.; Thomas, T. (2008): Impact of Religious Affiliation and Religiosity on Forgiveness, *Australian Psychologist*, 43(3): 175–185.

Foxman, E.R.; Raven, P.V.; Stem, D. (1990): Locus of Control, Fatalism, and Responses to Dissatisfaction, *Journal of Consumer Satisfaction, Dissatisfaction, and Complaining Behavior*, 3: 21–28.

Frenkel-Brunswik, E. (1954): Further Exploration by a Contributor to "The Authoritarian Personality", in: Christie, R.; Jahoda, M. (Eds.), *Studies in the Scope and Method of "The Authoritarian Personality"*, 226–275, New York: Free Press.

Friedman, H.H. (2001): The Impact of Jewish Values on Marketing and Business Practices, *Journal of Macromarketing,* 21(1): 74–80.

Frise, N.R.; McMinn, M.R. (2010): Forgiveness and Reconciliation. The Differing Perspectives of Psychologists and Christian Theologians, *Journal of Psychology and Theology*, 38(2): 83–90.

Friske, W.; Cockrell, S.; King, R.A. (2021): Beliefs to Behaviors: How Religiosity Alters Perceptions of CSR. Initiatives and Retail Selection, *Journal of Macromarketing*, 42(1): 114–127.

Fromm, E. (1936): Sozialpsychologischer Teil, in: Horkheimer, M. (Ed.), *Studien über Autorität und Familie*, 77–135, Paris: Librairie Felix Alcan.

Furnham, A.; Valgeirsson, H. (2007): The Effect of Life Values and Materialism on Buying Counterfeit Products, *Journal of Socio-Economics*, 36(5): 677–685.

Gabor, A.; Granger, C.W. (1961): On the Price Consciousness of Consumers, *Journal of the Royal Statistical Society: Series C (Applied Statistics)*, 10(3): 170–188.

Galen, L.W. (2012): Does Religious Belief Promote Prosociality? A Critical Examination, *Psychological Bulletin*, 138(5): 876–906.

Ganesh, J.; Arnold, M.J.; Reynolds, K.E. (2000): Understanding the Customer Base of Service Providers. An Examination of the Differences between Switchers and Stayers, *Journal of Marketing*, 64(3): 65–87.

Gatersleben, B.; Murtagh, N.; Cherry, M.; Watkins, M. (2019): Moral, Wasteful, Frugal, or Thrifty? Identifying Consumer Identities to Understand and Manage Pro-environmental Behavior, *Environment and Behavior*, 51(1): 24–49.

Gavriilidis, K.; Kallinterakis, V.; Tsalavoutas, I. (2016): Investor Mood, Herding and the Ramadan Effect, *Journal of Economic Behavior & Organization*, 132(Supplement): 23–38.

Gayatri, G.; Chew, J. (2013): How Do Muslim Consumers Perceive Service Quality? *Asia Pacific Journal of Marketing and Logistics*, 25(3): 472–490.

Geiger-Oneto, S.; Minton, E.A. (2019): How Religiosity Influences the Consumption of Luxury Goods: Exploration of the Moral Halo Effect. *European Journal of Marketing*, 53(12), 2530–2555.

Gelb, B.D.; Pickett, C.M. (1983): Attitude-toward-the-Ad. Links to Humor and to Advertising Effectiveness, *Journal of Advertising*, 12(2): 34–42.

Gelbrich, K.; Müller, S. (2011): *Handbuch Internationales Management*, Munich: Oldenbourg.

Gelbrich, K.; Müller, S. (2023): Interreligiöses Marketing, Berlin: de Gruyter.

Gelbrich, K.; Müller, S. (2023): *Success Factors of Marketing*, 3rd ed, Munich: Vahlen.

Gelbrich, K.; Roschk, H. (2011): A Meta-Analysis of Organizational Complaint Handling and Customer Responses, *Journal of Service Research*, 14(1): 24–43.

Gelfand, M.J.; Shteynberg, G.; Lee, T.L.; Lun, J.; Lyons, S.; Bell, C.; Chiao J.Y. (2012): The Cultural Contagion of Conflict, *Philosophical Transactions of The Royal Society*, B367(1589): 692–703.

Ger, G. (2005): Special Session Summary Religion and Consumption. The Profane Sacred, in: Menon, G.; Rao, A.R. (Eds.), *Advances in Consumer Research*, Vol. 32, 79–81, Duluth/MN: Association for Consumer Research.

Gervais, W.M. (2011): Finding the Faithless, *Personality and Social Psychology Bulletin*, 37(4): 543–556.

Gervais, W.M.; Shariff, A.F.; Norenzayan, A. (2011): Do You Believe in Atheists? Distrust Is Central to Anti-Atheist Prejudice. *Journal of Personality and Social Psychology*, 101(6), 1189–1206.

Gervais, W.M.; Xygalatas, D.; McKay, R.T.; Van Elk, M.; Buchtel, E.E.; Aveyard, M.; Schiavone, S.R.; Dar-Nimrod, I.; Svedholm-Häkkinen, A.M.; Riekki, T.; Klocová, E.K. (2017): Global Evidence of Extreme Intuitive Moral Prejudice Against Atheists. *Nature Human Behaviour*, 1(8), 0151.

Geyer, A.L.; Baumeister, R.F. (2005): Religion, Morality, and Self-control. Values, Virtues, and Vices, in: Paloutzian, R.F.; Park, C.L. (Eds.), *Handbook of the Psychology of Religion and Spirituality*, 412–432, New York: Guilford.

Gibbs, J.O.; Crader, K.W. (1970): A Criticism of Two Recent Attempts to Scale Glock and Stark's Dimensions of Religiosity, *Sociology of Religion*, 31(2): 107–114.

Gilal, F.; Gadhi, A.; Gilal, R.; Gilal, N.; Zhang, N.; Gong, Z. (2020): Towards an Integrated Model of Customer Religiosity. A Self-determination Theory Perspective, *Central European Management Journal*, 28(2): 16–27.

Gilly, M.C. (1988): Sex Roles in Advertising. A Comparison of Television Advertisements in Australia, Mexico, and the United States, *Journal of Marketing*, 52(2): 75–85.

Gittelman, S.; Lange, V.; Cook, W.A.; Frede, S.M.; Lavrakas, P.J.; Pierce, C.; Thomas, R.K. (2015): Accounting for Social-Desirability Bias in Survey Sampling, *Journal of Advertising Research*, 55(3): 242–254.

Globerman, S.; Shapiro, D. (2003): Governance Infrastructure and US Foreign Direct Investment, *Journal of International Business Studies*, 34(1): 19–39.

Glock, C.Y.; Stark, R. (1965): *Religion and Society in Tension*, San Francisco/CA: Rand McNally.

Gokcekus, O.; Ekici, T. (2020): Religion, Religiosity, and Corruption, *Review of Religious Research*, 62(4): 563–581.

Golan, G.J.; Baker, S. (2012): Perceptions of Media Trust and Credibility among Mormon College Students, *Journal of Media and Religion*, 11(1): 31–43.

Golan, G.J.; Day, A.G. (2010): In God We Trust. Religiosity as a Predictor of Perceptions of Media Trust, Factuality, and Privacy Invasion, *American Behavioral Scientist*, 54(2): 120–136.

Göle, N. (1997): The Gendered Nature of the Public Sphere, *Public Culture*, 10(1): 61–81.

Goli, S.; Maurya, N.K.; Sharma, M.K. (2015): Continuing Caste Inequalities in Rural Uttar Pradesh, *International Journal of Sociology and Social Policy*, 35(3/4): 252–272.

Gore, R.; Zuckerman, P.; Galen, L.; Pollack, D.; LeRon Shults, F. (2019): Good Without God? Connecting Religiosity, Affiliation and Pro-sociality Using World Values Survey Data and Agent-Based Simulation, https://osf.io/preprints/socarxiv/jnpe9 (Dec. 16, 2022).

Gorski, P. S. (2000). Historicizing the secularization debate: Church, state, and society in late medieval and early modern Europe, ca. 1300 to 1700. *American sociological review*, 65(1), 138–167.

Graafland, J. (2017): Religiosity, Attitude, and the Demand for Socially Responsible Products, *Journal of Business Ethics*, 144(1): 121–138.
Grace, D.; Ross, M.; King, C. (2020): Brand Fidelity. Scale Development and Validation, *Journal of Retailing and Consumer Services*, 52(1): 1–12.
Gray, S.; Inglish, A.; Sodhi, T.S.; Lee, T.T. (2017): What Are They Really Selling? A Content Analysis of Advertisements during Religious Television Programming, *Journal of Media and Religion*, 16(3): 104–116.
Greenough, C. (2021): Profit over Prophet? A Critical Analysis of "Moses" in Advertising, *The Bible and Critical Theory*, 16(1): 218–237.
Grettenberger, D. (1996). *Environmental protection and environmental awareness: starting points for an efficient environmental policy*. Publisher Wiss. & Practice.
Grigg, R; Sharpe, M. (2011): In the Name of the Father. Understanding Monotheism and Fundamentalism, in: Oppy, G; Trakakis, N. (Eds.), *The Antipodean Philosopher*, Vol. 1, 81–87, Lanham/MD: Lexington Books.
Grimes, J.E.; Grimes, B.F. (Eds.) (1996): *Ethnologue Language Family Index*, Dallas/TX: Summer Institute of Linguistics.
Grönroos, C. (1988): Service Quality. The Six Criteria of Good Perceived Service Quality, *Review of Business*, 9(3): 10–13.
Grönroos, C. (2001): The Perceived Service Quality Concept. A Mistake? *Managing Service Quality*, 11(3): 150–152.
Gruber, J. (2004): Pay or Pray? The Impact of Charitable Subsidies on Religious Attendance, *Journal of Public Economics*, 88(12): 2635–2655.
Guimarães, M.O.; Paiva, P.C.P.; Paiva, H.N.; Lamounier, J.A.; Ferreira, E.F.; Zarzar, P.M.P.D.A. (2018): Religiosity as a Possible Protective Factor against "Binge Drinking" among 12-Year-Old Students. A Population-based Study, *Ciencia & Saude Coletiva*, 23(4): 1067–1076.
Guiso, L.; Sapienza, P.; Zingales, L. (2003): People's Opium? Religion and Economic Attitudes, *Journal of Monetary Economics*, 50(1): 225–282.
Guiso, L.; Sapienza, P.; Zingales, L. (2006): Does Culture affect Economic Outcomes? *Journal of Economic Perspectives*, 20(2): 23–48.
Guiso, L.; Sapienza, P.; Zingales, L. (2009): Cultural Biases in Economic Exchanges? *Quarterly Journal of Economics*, 124(3): 1095–1131.
Guo, R. (2004): How Culture Influences Foreign Trade. Evidence from the US and China, *Journal of Socio-Economics*, 33(6): 785–812.
Gürhan-Canli, Z.; Sarial-Abi, G.; Hayran, C. (2018): Consumers and Brands across the Globe. Research Synthesis and New Directions, *Journal of International Marketing*, 26(1): 96–117.
Guth, J. L., Green, J. C., Kellstedt, L. A., & Smidt, C. E. (1995). Faith and the environment: Religious beliefs and attitudes on environmental policy. *American Journal of Political Science*, 364–382.
Habib, D.G.; Donald, C.; Hutchinson, G. (2018): Religion and Life Satisfaction, *Journal of Religion and Health*, 57(4): 1567–1580.
Habib, M.D.; Bekun, F.V. (2021): Does Religiosity Matter in Impulsive Psychology Buying Behaviors? *Current Psychology*, 41(9): 1–13.
Hackensberger, A. (2005): Kulturkampf im Kinderzimmer, http://www.heise.de (05/11/2005).
Hahn, T. (2022): Die Macht der Religion, *Süddeutsche Zeitung*, 78(168): 10.

Halim, M.A.A.; Salleh, M.M.M. (2012): The Possibility of Uniformity on Halal Standards in Organization of Islamic Countries, *World Applied Sciences Journal*, 17(17): 6–10.

Hall, D.L.; Matz, D.C.; Wood, W. (2010): Why Don't We Practice What We Preach? A Meta-Analytic Review of Religious Racism, *Personality and Social Psychology Review*, 14(1): 126–139.

Halstead, D.; Haynes, P.J.; Taylor, V.A. (2009): Service Provider Use of Christian Religious Messages in Yellow Pages Advertising, *Advertising & Society Review*, 10(4). https://doi.org/10.1353/asr.0.0038

Hamilton, S.F.; Zilberman, D. (2006): Green Markets, Eco-certification, and Equilibrium Fraud, *Journal of Environmental Economics and Management*, 52(3): 627–644.

Hand, C. M., & Van Liere, K. D. (1984). Religion, mastery-over-nature, and environmental concern. *Social Forces*, 63(2), 555–570.

Hansen, R.A.; Deutscher, T. (1978): Empirical Investigation of Attribute Importance in Retail Store Selection, *Journal of Retailing*, 53(4): 59–72.

Hanudin, A.; Rahim, A.R.A.; Sondoh, S.L.; Liason, S.; Hwa, A.M.C. (2011): Determinants of Customers' Intention to Use Islamic Personal Financing, *Journal of Islamic Accounting and Business Research*, 2(1): 22–42.

Haque, A.; Anwar, N.; Sarwar, A. (2015a): The Effect of Country *of* Origin Image, Ethnocentrism, and Religiosity on Purchase Intentions, *Indian Journal of Marketing*, 45(10): 23–35.

Haque, A.; Anwar, N.; Yasmin, F.; Sarwar, A.; Ibrahim, Z.; Momen, A. (2015b): Purchase Intention of Foreign Products. A Study on Bangladeshi Consumer Perspective, *Sage Open*, 5(2), 1–12.

Hardy, S. A., & Carlo, G. (2005). Religiosity and prosocial behaviours in adolescence: The mediating role of prosocial values. *Journal of moral education*, 34(2), 231–249.

Hardy, S.A.; Nelson, J.M.; Moore, J.P.; King, P.E. (2019): Processes of Religious and Spiritual Influence in Adolescence. A Systematic Review of 30 Years of Research, *Journal of Research on Adolescence*, 29(2): 254–275.

Harjoto, M.A.; Rossi, F. (2019): Religiosity, Female Directors, and Corporate Social Responsibility for Italian Listed Companies, *Journal of Business Research*, 95(2): 338–346.

Harrison, L.E. (2011): Do Some Religions Do Better than Others? in: Berger, P.L.; Redding, G. (Eds.), *The Hidden Form of Capital. Spiritual Influences in Societal Progress*, 15–28, London: Anthem.

Harrison-Walker, L.J. (2019): The Critical Role *of* Customer Forgiveness in Successful Service Recovery, *Journal of Business Research*, 95(2): 376–391.

Harvey, P. (2012): *An Introduction to Buddhism. Teachings, History and Practices*, Cambridge: Cambridge University Press.

Hasan, R. (2017): *Religion and Development in the Global South*, Brighton: Palgrave Macmillan.

Hassan, K.; Lewis, M. (Eds.) (2009): *Handbook of Islamic Banking*, Cheltenham: Edward Elgar.

Hauser, M.; Singer, P. (2005), "Morality without Religion." Available at: https://www.qcc.cuny.edu/socialSciences/ppecorino/INTRO_TEXT/Chapter%208%20Ethics/CH8_HauserSingerMoralRelig.pdf.

Heiman, A.; Gordon, B.; Zilberman, D. (2019): Food Beliefs and Food Supply Chains. The Impact of Religion and Religiosity in Israel, *Food Policy*, 83(February): 363–369.

Heiman, A.; Just, D.R. (2021): How Political Support and Level of Religiosity Affect the Willingness to Pay for Foreign Products, *Marketing Science Institute Working Paper*, Report No. 21-109.

Helble, M. (2007): Is God Good for Trade? *Kyklos*, 60(3): 385–413.

Heller, E. (2004): Wie *Farben wirken*, 2nd ed., Reinbek: rororo.

Hendry, J. (2019): *Understanding Japanese Society*, 5th ed., London: Routledge.

Henley Jr, W.H.; Philhours, M.; Ranganathan, S.K.; Bush, A.J. (2009): The Effects of Symbol Product Relevance and Religiosity on Consumer Perceptions of Christian Symbols in Advertising, *Journal of Current Issues & Research in Advertising*, 31(1): 89–103.

Henningsgaard, J.M.; Arnau, R.C. (2008): Relationships between Religiosity, Spirituality, and Personality. A Multivariate Analysis, *Personality and Individual Differences*, 45(8): 703–708.

Henrich, J.; Ensminger, J.; McElreath, R.; Barr, A.; Barrett, C.; Bolyanatz, A.; ... Ziker, J. (2010): Markets, Religion, Community Size, and the Evolution of Fairness and Punishment, *Science*, 327(5972): 1480–1484.

Hergueux, J. (2011): How Does Religion Bias the Allocation of Foreign Direct Investment? The Role of Institutions, *International Economics*, 128(April): 53–76.

Hermann, A.L. (1991): *A Brief Introduction to Hinduism. Religion, Philosophy, and Ways of Liberation*, Boulder/CO: Westview.

Hilary, G.; Hui, K.W. (2009): Does Religion Matter in Corporate Decision Making in America? *Journal of Financial Economics*, 93(3): 455–473.

Hino, H. (2010): Antecedents of Supermarket Formats' Adoption and Usage, *Journal of Retailing and Consumer Services*, 17(1): 61–72.

Hirsch, J.S. (2008): Catholics Using Contraceptives. Religion, Family Planning, and Interpretive Agency in Rural Mexico, *Studies in Family Planning*, 39(2): 93–104.

Hirschman, E.C. (1981): American Jewish Ethnicity. It's Relationship to Some Selected Aspects of Consumer Behavior, *Journal of Marketing*, 45(3): 102–110.

Hirschman, E.C. (1982): Religious Differences in Cognitions Regarding Novelty Seeking and Information Transfer, in: Mitchell, A. (Ed.), *Advances in Consumer Research*, Vol. 9, 228–233, Ann Abor/MI: Association for Consumer Research.

Hirschman, E.C. (1983): Religious Affiliation and Consumption Processes, in: Sheth, J.W. (Ed.), *Research in Marketing*, Vol. 6, 131–170, Greenwich/CT: JAI.

Ho, D.Y.F. (1977): On the Concept *of* Face, *American Journal of Sociology*, 81(4): 72–78.

Hoetoro, A. (2020): The Relationship between Love of Money, Islamic Religiosity and Life Satisfaction. A Muslim‘s Perspective, *IQTISHADIA*, 13(1): 37–52.

Hoffmann, F.; Härle, M. (1992): Religion as a Strategic Success Factor, *Zeitschrift für Betriebswirtschaftslehre*, 62(Ergänzungsheft 1): 175–207.

Hoffmann, S.; Akbar, P. (2019): *Consumer Behavior*, 2nd ed., Wiesbaden: Springer Gabler.

Hofmann, C.; Schwaiger, N. (2020): Religion, Crime, and Financial Reporting, *Journal of Business Economics*, 90(5/6): 879–916.

Hofstede, G. (1980): *Culture's Consequences. International Differences in Work-Related Values*, Beverly Hills/CA: Sage.

Hofstede, G. (2001): *Culture's Consequences. Comparing Values, Behaviors, Institutions, and Organizations across Nations*, 2nd ed, Thousand Oaks/CA: Sage.

Holzmann, R. (2019): *Business Ethics*, 2nd ed. Wiesbaden: Springer Gabler.

Homburg, C.; Krohmer, H. (2017): *Fundamentals of Marketing Management*, Wiesbaden: Springer Fachmedien.

Hong, S.C. (2020): Digital Bible and Innovation Resistance, *Journal of Media and Religion*, 19(1): 24–34.
Hope, A.L.; Jones, C.R. (2014): The Impact of Religious Faith on Attitudes to Environmental Issues and Carbon. Capture and Storage (CCS) Technologies, *Technology in Society*, 38(August): 48–59.
Höpflinger, A.K.; Jeffers, A.; Pezzoli-Olgiati, D. (2008): *Handbuch Gender und Religion*, Stuttgart: UTB.
Hopkins, C.D.; Shanahan, K.J.; Raymond, M.A. (2014): The Moderating Role of Religiosity on Nonprofit Advertising, *Journal of Business Research*, 67(2): 23–31.
Hornik, J.; Miniero, G. (2010): *Ad Message Appeal Effectiveness. A Meta-Analysis*, Finanza, Marketing e Produzione. *Rivista di Economia d'Impresa dell' Università Bocconi*, 28: 88–98.
Hornik, J.; Ofir, C.; Rachamim, M. (2017): Advertising Appeals, Moderators, and Impact on Persuasion. A Quantitative Assessment Creates a Hierarchy of Appeals, *Journal of Advertising Research*, 57(3): 305–318.
Hornik, J.; Satchi, R.S.; Cesareo, L.; Pastore, A. (2015): Information Dissemination via Electronic Word-of-Mouth. Good News Travels Fast, Bad News Travels Faster! *Computers in Human Behavior*, 45: 273–280.
Hossain, K.A.; Basher, S.A.; Haque, A.E. (2018): Quantifying the Impact of Ramadan on Global Raw Sugar Prices, *International Journal of Islamic and Middle Eastern Finance and Management*, 11(4): 510–528.
Hossain, M.M.; Alam, M.; Islam, M.A.; Hecimovic, A. (2015): Do Stakeholders or Social Obligations Drive Corporate Social and Environmental Responsibility Reporting? *Qualitative Research in Accounting & Management*, 12(3): 287–314.
Hovland, C.I.; Janis, I.L.; Kelley, H.H. (1953): *Communication and Persuasion*, New Haven/CT: Yale University Press.
Hrynowski, Z. (2019): How Many Americans Believe in God, *Gallup News Service*.
Hu, J.; Yang, Y.; Jing, F.; Nguyen, B. (2018): Awe, Spirituality and Conspicuous Consumer Behavior. *International Journal of Consumer Studies*, 42(6), 829–839.
Huang, D.; Lu, D.; Luo, J.H. (2016): Corporate Innovation and Innovation Efficiency. Does Religion Matter? *Nankai Business Review International*, 7: 150–191.
Hubbard, R.C. (1993): Shock Advertising: The Benetton Case. *Studies in Popular Culture*, 16(1), 39–51.
Hui, M.K.; Au, K. (2001): Justice Perceptions of Complaint-Handling. A Cross-Cultural Comparison between PRC and Canadian Customers, *Journal of Business Research*, 52(2): 161–173.
Hunsberger, B.; Jackson, L.M. (2005): Religion, Meaning, and Prejudice, *Journal of Social Issues,* 61(4): 807–826.
Hunt, S.D.; Vitell, S. (1986): A General Theory of Marketing Ethics, *Journal of Macromarketing*, 6(1): 5–16.
Huntington, S.P. (1993): The Clash of Civilizations? *Foreign Affairs*, 72(3): 22–49.
Husemann, K.C.; Eckhardt, G.M. (2019a): Consumer deceleration, *Journal of Consumer Research*, 45(6): 1142–1163.
Husemann, K.C.; Eckhardt, G.M. (2019b): Consumer spirituality, *Journal of Marketing Management*, 35(5–6): 391–406.
Hwang, A.; Francesco, A.M.; Kessler, E. (2003): The Relationship between *Individualism-Collectivism*, Face, and Feedback and Learning Processes in Hong Kong, Singapore, and the United States, *Journal of Cross-Cultural Psychology*, 34(1): 72–91.

Hwang, H. (2018): Do Religion and Religiosity Affect Consumers' Intentions to Adopt Pro-environmental Behaviours? *International Journal of Consumer Studies*, 42(6): 664–674.

Hyodo, J.D.; Bolton, L.E. (2021): How Does Religion Affect Consumer Response to Failure and Recovery by Firms? *Journal of Consumer Research*, 47(5): 807–828.

Ibrahim, N.A.; Angelidis, J.A. (1993): Corporate Social Responsibility. A Comparative Analysis of Perceptions of Top Executives and Business Students, *Mid-Atlantic Journal of Business*, 29(3): 303–325.

Iftikhar, A.; Azam, F.; Ashraf, S.; Tahir, H.M. (2017): Exploring the Relationship between Religiosity, Brand Trust and Green Purchase Intention as a Catalyst of Attitude, *International Journal of Multidisciplinary and Current Research*, 5(Nov/Dec): 1485–1493.

Ingham, J.; Cadieux, J.; Berrada, A.M. (2015): e-Shopping Acceptance. A Qualitative and Meta-Analytic Review, *Information & Management*, 52(1): 44–60.

Inglehart, R. (1977): *The Silent Revolution. Changing Values and Political Styles among Western Publics*, Princeton: Princeton University Press.

Inglehart, R. (1997): *Modernization and Postmodernization. Cultural, Economic, and Political Change in 43 Societies*, Princeton: Princeton University Press.

Inglehart, R. (1998): *Modernization and Postmodernization. Cultural, Economic and Political Change in 43 Societies*, Frankfurt/Main: Campus.

Inglehart, R. (2001): Sociological Theories of Modernization, in: Smelser, N.J.; Baltes, P.B. (Eds.), *International Encyclopedia of the Social and Behavioral Sciences*, 9965–9971, Oxford: Elsevier Science.

Inglehart, R. (2020): *Religion's Sudden Decline: What's Causing It, and What Comes Next?*. Oxford: Oxford University Press.

Inglehart, R.; Baker, W.E. (2000): Modernization, Cultural Change, and the Persistence of Traditional Values, *American Sociological Review*, 65(1): 19–51.

Inglehart, R.; Haerpfer, C.; Moreno, A.; Welzel, C.; Kizilova, K.; Diez-Medrano, J.; et al. (Eds.) (2014): *World Values Survey. All Rounds – Country-Pooled Datafile Version*, Madrid: JD Systems Institute.

Inglehart, R.; Norris, P. (2003): The True Clash of Civilizations, *Foreign Policy*, 135(March/April): 62–70.

Iranmanesh, M.; Mirzaei, M.; Hosseini, S.M.P.; Zailani, S. (2019): Muslims' Willingness to Pay for Certified Halal Food, *Journal of Islamic Marketing*, 11(1): 14–30.

Islam, T.; Chandrasekaran, U. (2016): Religiosity and Ecologically Conscious Consumption Behavior, *Asian Journal of Business Research*, 5(2): 18–30.

Islam, T.; Chandrasekaran, U. (2019): Religiosity, Values and Consumer Behavior. A Study of Young Indian Muslim Consumers, *Journal of Consumer Marketing*, 36(7): 948–961.

Iyer, S. (2002): Religion and the Decision to Use Contraception in India, *Journal for the Scientific Study of Religion*, 41(4): 711–722.

Izberk-Bilgin, E. (2012): Infidel Brands. Unveiling Alternative Meanings of Global Brands at the Nexus of Globalization, Consumer Culture, and Islamism, *Journal of Consumer Research*, 39(4): 663–687.

Jack, A.; Friedman, J.; Boyatzis, R.; Taylor, S. (2016): Why Do You Believe in God? Relationships between Religious Belief, Analytic Thinking, Mentalizing and Moral Concern, *PLoS ONE*, 11, e0155283.

Jahandideh, B.; Golmohammadi, A.; Meng, F.; O'Gorman, K.D.; Taheri, B. (2014): Cross-Cultural Comparison of Chinese and Arab Consumer Complaint Behavior in the Hotel Context, *International Journal of Hospitality Management*, 41: 67–76.

Jamal, A.; Sharifuddin, J. (2015): Perceived Value and Perceived Usefulness of Halal Labeling. The Role of Religion and Culture, *Journal of Business Research*, 68(5): 933–941.

Jamal, A.A.; Milner, H.V. (2022): Islam and Mass Preferences toward Foreign Direct Investment in Tunisia, *Journal of Experimental Political Science*, 9(3): 314–325.

Jamshidi, D.; Hussin, N. (2016): Forecasting Patronage Factors of Islamic Credit Card as a New E-Commerce Banking Service. An Integration of TAM with Perceived Religiosity and Trust, *Journal of Islamic Marketing*, 7(4): 378–404.

Jelen, T.G. (1996): Catholicism, Conscience, and Censorship, in: Stout, D.A.; Buddenbaum, J.M. (Eds.), *Religion and Mass Media. Audiences and Adaptations*, 39–50, Thousand Oaks/CA: Sage.

Jensen, H.R. (2008): The Mohammed Cartoons Controversy and the Boycott of Danish Products in the Middle East, *European Business Review*, 20(2): 275–289.

Jha, S.; Balaji, M. (2015): Perceived Justice and Recovery Satisfaction. The Moderating Role of Customer-Perceived Quality, *Management & Marketing*, 10(2): 132–147.

Ji, C.H.C.; Pendergraft, L.; Perry, M. (2006): Religiosity, Altruism, and Altruistic Hypocrisy. Evidence from Protestant Adolescents, *Review of Religious Research*, 48(2): 156–178.

Joeckel, S. (2008): Funny as Hell. Christianity and Humor Reconsidered, *Humor: International Journal of Humor Research*, 21(4): 415–433.

Johan, Z.J.; Putit, L. (2016): Conceptualizing the Influences of Knowledge and Religiosity on Islamic Credit Card Compliance, *Procedia Economics and Finance*, 37: 480–487.

Johnson, C.; Mathews, B.P. (1997): The Influence of Experience on Service Expectations, *International Journal of Service Industry Management*, 8(4): 290–305.

Johnson, K.A.; Liu, R.L.; Minton, E.A.; Bartholomew, D.E.; Peterson, M.; Cohen, A.B.; & Kees, J. (2017): US Citizens' Representations of God and Support for Sustainability Policies. *Journal of Public Policy & Marketing*, 36(2), 362–378.

Johnson, K.A.; Minton, E.A.; McClernon, M.P. (2021): Recycling, Relatedness, and Reincarnation. Religious Beliefs about Nature and the Afterlife as Predictors of Sustainability Practices, *Psychology of Religion and Spirituality,* Advance online publication. doi:10.1037/rel0000407 (04/30/2022).

Johnson, M.K.; Rowatt, W.C.; LaBouff, J.P. (2012): Religiosity and Prejudice Revisited. In-Group Favoritism, Out-Group Derogation, or Both? *Psychology of Religion and Spirituality*, 4(2): 154–168.

Johnson, T.P.; Van de Vijver, F.J. (2003): Social Desirability in Cross-Cultural Research, in: Harness, J.; Van de Vijver, F.J.; Mohler, P. (Eds.), *Cross-Cultural Survey Methods*, 193–204, New York: Wiley.

Jones, A.E.; Elliott, M. (2017): Examining Social Desirability in Measures of Religion and Spirituality Using the Bogus Pipeline, *Review of Religious Research*, 59(1): 47–64.

Jones Jr, H. B., Furnham, A., & Deile, A. J. (2010). Religious orientation and the Protestant work ethic. *Mental Health, Religion & Culture*, 13(7-8), 697–706.

Jones, M.B. (1958): Religious Values and Authoritarian Tendency, *Journal of Social Psychology*, 48(1): 83–89.

Just, D.R.; Heiman, A.; Zilberman, D. (2007): The Interaction of Religion and Family Members' Influence on Food Decisions, *Food Quality and Preference*, 18(5): 786–794.

Juvan, E.; Dolnicar, S. (2014): The Attitude – Behavior Gap in Sustainable Tourism, *Annals of Tourism Research*, 48(September): 76–95.

Kadić-Maglajlić, S.; Arslanagić-Kalajdžić, M.; Micevski, M.; Michaelidou, N.; Nemkova, E. (2017): Controversial Advert Perceptions in SNS Advertising. The Role of Ethical Judgement and Religious Commitment, *Journal of Business Ethics*, 141(2): 249–265.

Kahane, B. (2012): Tikkun Olam. How a Jewish Ethos Drives Innovation, *Journal of Management Development*, 31(9): 938–947.

Kahneman, D.; Knetsch, J.L.; Thaler, R.H. (1991): Anomalies. The Endowment Effect, Loss Aversion, and Status Quo Bias, *Journal of Economic Perspectives*, 5(1): 193–206.

Kahoe, R.D. (1974): Personality and Achievement Correlates of Intrinsic and Extrinsic Religious Orientation, *Journal of Personality and Social Psychology*, 29(6): 812–818.

Kale, S. (2004): Spirituality, Religion, and Globalization, *Journal of Macromarketing*, 24(2): 92–107.

Kalliny, M.; Cruthirds, K.W.; Minor, M.S. (2006): Differences between American, Egyptian and Lebanese Humor Styles, *International Journal of Cross Cultural Management*, 6(1): 121–134.

Kalliny, M.; Hausman, A. (2007): The Impact of Cultural and Religious Values on Consumer's Adoption of Innovation, *Academy of Marketing Studies Journal*, 11(1): 125–137.

Kalliny, M.; Hausman, A.; Saran, A.; Ismaeil, D. (2017): The Cultural and Religious Animosity Model. Evidence from the United States, *Journal of Consumer Marketing*, 34(2): 169–179.

Kaltenbach, D.D. (2013): *At the table in the restaurant. Zwischenmenschliches auf einem Paradeplatz der Zivilisation*, Berlin: epubli.

Kamins, M.A.; Marks, L.J. (1991): The Perception of Kosher as a Third Party Certification Claim in Advertising for Familiar and Unfamiliar Brands, *Journal of the Academy of Marketing Science*, 19(3): 177–185.

Kanagaretnam, K.; Lobo, G.J.; Wang, C.; Whalen, D.J. (2015): Religiosity and Risk-Taking in International Banking, *Journal of Behavioral and Experimental Finance*, 7(September): 42–59.

Kanagy, C. L., & Willits, F. K. (1993). A" greening" of religion? Some evidence from a Pennsylvania sample. *Social Science Quarterly*.

Kang, Y.; Yang, K.C.C. (2019): The Relationship between Country Animosity and Consumption of Japanese Cultural Products, *Intercultural Communication Studies*, 28(2): 96–112.

Kanousi, A. (2005): An Empirical Investigation of the Role of Culture on Service Recovery Expectations, *Managing Service Quality: An International Journal*, 15(1): 57–69.

Kapferer, J.N.; Valette-Florence, P. (2019): How Self-success Drives Luxury Demand, *Journal of Business Research*, 102(9): 273–287.

Kapusuz, S.; Kimzan, H. (2016): The Role of Fair Trade Trust on the Relationship of Fair Trade Knowledge, Fair Trade Adhesion, and Willingness to Pay Fair Trade Premium. The Case of Turkey, *Turkish Journal of Business Ethics*, 9(1): 70–89.

Karani, K.G.; Fraccastoro, K.A. (2010): Resistance to Brand Switching. The Elderly Consumer, *Journal of Business & Economics Research*, 8(12): 77–83.
Karoui, S.; Khemakhem, R. (2019): Consumer Ethnocentrism in Developing Countries, *European Research on Management and Business Economics*, 25(2): 63–71.
Kasber, A.; El-Bassiouny, N.; Hamed, S. (2022): Can Religiosity Alter Luxury and Counterfeit Consumption? *Journal of Islamic Marketing*, 13, 1768–1792.
Kashif, M.; Jamal, K.F.; Rehman, M.A. (2018): The Dynamics of Zakat Donation Experience among Muslims, *Journal of Islamic Accounting and Business Research*, 9(1): 45–58.
Kasper, W. (2007). *A handbook of spiritual ecumenism*. New City Press.
Kaufer, E. (1998): *Spiegelungen wirtschaftlichen Denkens im Mittelalter*, Innsbruck: Studien-Verlag.
Kawata, Y.; Htay, S.N.N.; Salman, A.S. (2018): Non-Muslims' Acceptance of Imported Products with Halal Logo. A Case Study of Malaysia and Japan, *Journal of Islamic Marketing*, 9(1): 191–203.
Kay, A.C.; Gaucher, D.; McGregor, I.; Nash, K. (2010a): Religious Belief as Compensatory Control, *Personality and Social Psychology Review*, 14(1): 37–48.
Kay, A.C.; Shepherd, S.; Blatz, C.W.; Chua, S.N.; Galinsky, A.D. (2010b): For God (or) Country. The Hydraulic Relation between Government Instability and Belief in Religious Sources of Control, *Journal of Personality and Social Psychology*, 99(5): 725–739.
Keaveney, S.M.; Parthasarathy, M. (2001): Customer Switching Behavior in Online Services, *Journal of the Academy of Marketing Science*, 29(4): 374–390.
Keshkar, S.; Lawrence, I.; Dodds, M.; Morris, E.; Mahoney, T.; Heisey, K.; ... Santomier, J. (2019): The Role of Culture in Sports Sponsorship. An Update, *Annals of Applied Sport Science*, 7(1): 57–81.
Ketelaar, P.E.; Konig, R.; Smit, E.G.; Thorbjørnsen, H. (2015): In Ads We Trust. Religiousness as a Predictor of Advertising Trustworthiness and Avoidance, *Journal of Consumer Marketing*, 32(3): 190–198.
Khalil, M.A.; Surendran, S. (2006): Globalization Challenges in the Middle East, Religious Fundamentalism, *Competition Forum*, 4(2): 293–302.
Khan, A.; Azam, M.K.; Arafat, M.Y. (2019): Does Religiosity Really Matter in Purchase Intention of Halal Certified Packaged Food Products? *Pertanika Journal of Social Sciences and Humanities*, 27(4): 2383–2400.
Khan, R.; Misra, K.; Singh, V. (2013): Ideology and Brand Consumption, *Psychological Science*, 24(3): 326–333.
Khraim, H.S.; Khraim, A.S.; Al-Kaidah, F.M.; Al-Qurashi, D. (2011): Jordanian Consumer's Evaluation of Retail Store Attributes. The Influence of Consumer Religiosity, *International Journal of Marketing Studies*, 3(4): 105–116.
Kilian, K. (2009): Brand our. Branding zwischen höllisch gut und himmlisch verwegen, http://www.markenlexikon.com (28/07/2010).
Kiliçbay, B.; Binark, M. (2002): Consumer Culture, Islam, and the Politics of Lifestyle. Fashion for Veiling in Contemporary Turkey, *European Journal of Communication*, 17(4): 495–511.
Kilkon, K.; Seong-Gin, M. (2014): The Relationship between Religion and Corruption. Are the Proposed Causal Links Empirically Valid? *International Review of Public Administration*, 19(1): 44–62.
Kim, D.; Pan, Y.; Park, H.S. (1998): High- versus Low-Context Culture. A Comparison of Chinese, Korean, and American Cultures, *Psychology & Marketing*, 15(6): 507–521.

Kim, J.-H.; Kim, M.S. (2020): Consumer Animosity to Foreign Product Purchase, *Journal of Korea Trade*, 24(6): 61–81.

Kirk, C.M.; Lewis, R.K. (2013): The Impact of Religious Behaviors on the Health and Well-Being of Emerging Adults, *Mental Health, Religion & Culture*, 16(10): 1030–1043.

Klaschka, S. (2000): Happy Who Is a Civil Servant. China and Its Refined Art of Bureaucracy, www.zeit.de/ 2000/29/Gluecklich_wer_Beamter_ist/ (28/08/2021).

Klaschka, S. (2000): Glücklich, wer Beamter ist, Die Zeit, 55(29): https://www.zeit.de/2000/29/Gluecklich_wer_Beamter_ist/ (13/08/2024)

Klein, J.G.; Ettenson, R. (1999): Consumer Animosity and Consumer Ethnocentrism, *Journal of International Consumer Marketing*, 11(4): 5–24.

Klein, J.G.; Ettenson, R.; Morris, M.D. (1998): The Animosity Model of Foreign Product Purchase. An Empirical Test in the People's Republic of China, *Journal of Marketing*, 62(1): 89–100.

Kleinaltenkamp, M. (1998): Conceptual Definitions and Manifestations of Services, in: Bruhn, M.; Meffert, H. (Eds.), *Handbuch Dienstleistungsmanagement*, 29–52, Wiesbaden: Gabler.

Kluver, R.; Cheong, P.H. (2007): Technological Modernization, the Internet, and Religion in Singapore, *Journal of Computer-Mediated Communication*, 12(3): 1122–1142.

Knetsch, J.L.; Sinden, J.A. (1984): Willingness to Pay and Compensation Demanded. Experimental Evidence of an Unexpected Disparity in Measures of Value, *Quarterly Journal of Economics*, 99(3): 507–521.

Ko, K.; Moon, S.G. (2014): The Relationship between Religion and Corruption. Are the Proposed Causal Links Empirically Valid? *International Review of Public Administration*, 19(1): 44–62.

Kocas, C.; Bohlmann, J.D. (2008): Segmented Switchers and Retailer Pricing Strategies, *Journal of Marketing*, 72(3): 124–142.

Kogut, B.; Singh, H. (1988): The Effect of National Culture on the Choice of Entry Mode, *Journal of International Business Studies*, 19(3): 411–432.

Koopmans, R. (2020): *The Dilapidated House of Islam*, Munich: Beck.

Kopalle, P.K.; Lehmann, D.R.; Farley, J.U. (2010): Consumer Expectations and Culture. The Effect of Belief in Karma in India, *Journal of Consumer Research*, 37(2): 251–263.

Kortenkamp, K. V., & Moore, C. F. (2001). Ecocentrism and anthropocentrism: Moral reasoning about ecological commons dilemmas. *Journal of environmental psychology*, 21(3), 261–272.

Koydl, W. (2007): Fanatischer Hass aufs grüne Licht, http://www.sueddeutsche.de/panorama/grossbritannien-fanatischer-hass-aufs-gruene-licht-1.879795/ (12/08/2007).

Kraus, S.; Meier, F.; Eggers, F.; Bouncken, R.B.; Schuessler, F. (2016): Standardization vs. Adaptation. A Conjoint Experiment on the Influence of Psychic, Cultural and Geographical Distance on International Marketing Mix Decisions, *European Journal of International Management*, 10(2): 127–156.

Kreuser, G. (2002): *The Key to the Indian Market*, Wiesbaden: Gabler.

Krisjanous, J.; Allayarova, N.; Kadirov, D. (2021): Clothing of Righteousness. Exploring Tensions of Halal Maternity Wear on Online Apparel Websites, *Journal of Islamic Marketing*, 13(5): 1125–1142.

Kroeber-Riel, W.; Weinberg, P.; Gröppel-Klein, A. (2019): *Consumer Behavior*, 11th ed., Munich: Vahlen.

Kumar, A.; Page, J.K.; Spalt, O.G. (2011): Religious Beliefs, Gambling Attitudes, and Financial Market Outcomes, *Journal of Financial Economics*, 102(3): 671–708.

Kurpis, L.V.; Beqiri, M.S.; Helgeson, J.G. (2008): The Effects of Commitment to Moral Self-improvement and Religiosity on Ethics of Business Students, *Journal of Business Ethics*, 80(3): 447–463.

Kurt, D.; Inman, J.J.; Gino, F. (2018): Religious Shoppers Spend Less Money, *Journal of Experimental Social Psychology*, 78(September): 116–124.

Kurtulus, S.; Meltem Karakasoglu, M.; Baghirov, F. (2018): Role of Conservatism in Turkish Users' Instagram Behavior, *International Journal of Business & Information*, 13(2): 223–242.

Kusumawardani, K.A.; Yolanda, M. (2021): The Role of Animosity, Religiosity, and Allocentrism in Shaping Purchase Intention through Ethnocentrism and Brand Image, *Organizations and Markets in Emerging Economies*, 12(2): 503–525.

Kusumawati, A.; Listyorini, S.; Suharyono, S.; Yulianto, E. (2020): The Role of Religiosity on Fashion Store Patronage Intention of Muslim Consumers in Indonesia, *Sage Open*, 10(2): 1–15.

Kwok, D.W.; Meschi, P.X.; Bertrand, O. (2020): In CEOs We Trust. When Religion Matters in Cross-Border Acquisitions, *International Business Review*, 29(4): 101705.

La Barbera, P.A.; Gürhan, Z. (1997): The Role of Materialism, Religiosity, and Demographics in Subjective Well-being, *Psychology & Marketing*, 14(1): 71–97.

La Barre, W. (1970): *The Ghost Dance. Origins of Religion*, New York: Delta.

La Ferle, C.; Muralidharana, S.; Roth-Cohenb, O. (2022): Exploring the Differential Effects of Religious and Spiritual Cues in Online Advertising. A Study of U. S. Christians and the Nonreligious during COVID-19, *Journal of Advertising*, 51(1): 95–106.

La Porta, R.; Lopez-de-Silanes, F.; Shleifer, A.; Vishny, R.W. (1997): Trust in Large Organizations, *American Economic Association Papers and Proceedings*, 87(2): 333–338.

La, S.; Choi, B. (2019): Perceived Justice and CSR after Service Recovery, *Journal of Services Marketing*, 33(2): 206–219.

Lacy, T. (2018): Against and Beyond Hofstadter. Revising the Study of Anti-Intellectualism, in: Haberski, R.; Hartmann, A. (Eds.), *American Labyrinth*, 253–270, Ithaca/NY: Cornell University Press.

Lada, S.; Tanakinjal, G.H.; Amin, H. (2009): Predicting Intention to Choose Halal Products Using Theory of Reasoned Action, *International Journal of Islamic and Middle Eastern Finance and Management*, 2(1): 66–76.

Lam, D. (2006a): The Influence of Religiosity on Gambling Participation, *Journal of Gambling Studies*, 22(3): 305–320.

Lam, P. (2006b): Religion and Attitudes toward International Trade. Does Religiosity Increase Protectionism? *Unpublished Working Paper*,

Lambert, N.M.; Fincham, F.D.; Marks, L D.; Stillman, T.F. (2010): Invocations and Intoxication. Does Prayer Decrease Alcohol Consumption? *Psychology of Addictive Behaviors*, 24(2): 209–219.

Lämla, J.; Neckel, S. (Eds.) (2006): *Politisierter Konsum - konsumierte Politik*, Wiesbaden: VS Verlag für Sozial-Wissenschaften.

Landes, D.S. (1998): *The Wealth and Poverty of Nations. Why Some Are So Rich and Some Are So Poor*, New York: Norton.

Lasarov, W.; Hoffmann, S. (2020): Social Moral Licensing, *Journal of Business Ethics*, 165(1): 45–66.

Lascu, D.N.; Cotter, C.; Sato, M.; Wing, T. (2016): Indicators of Product Quality. Faith Labels as Branding Tools, *Innovative Marketing*, 12(2): 28–31.

Lastovicka, J.L.; Bettencourt, L.A.; Hughner, R.S.; Kuntze, R.J. (1999): Lifestyle of the Tight and Frugal. Theory and Measurement, *Journal of Consumer Research*, 26(1): 85–98.

LaTour, M.S.; Henthorne, T.L. (1994): Ethical Judgments of Sexual Appeals in Print Advertising, *Journal of Advertising*, 23(3): 81–90.

Laurin, K.; Shariff, A.F.; Henrich, J.; Kay, A.C. (2012): Outsourcing Punishment to God. Beliefs in Divine Control Reduce Earthly Punishment, *Proceedings of the Royal Society B: Biological Sciences*, 279(1741): 3272–3281.

Laux, B.; Bleyer, B. (2012): What Do YOU Buy? Basic Aspects of Consumer Ethics, *Regensburger RU-Notizen*, 32(1): 18–23.

Lavoie, D.; Chamlee-Wright, E. (2001): *Culture and Enterprise. The Development, Representation, and Morality of Business*, London: Routledge.

Leak, G.K.; Fish, S. (1989): Religious Orientation, Impression Management, and Self-deception. Toward a Clarification of the Link between Religiosity and Social Desirability, *Journal for the Scientific Study of Religion*, 28(3): 355–359.

Leary, R.B.; Minton, E.A.; Mittelstaedt, J.D. (2016): Thou Shall Not? The Influence of Religion on Beliefs of Stewardship and Dominion, Sustainable Behaviors, and Marketing Systems, *Journal of Macromarketing*, 36(4): 457–470.

Lee, C.W.; Park, S. (2016): Does Religious Similarity Matter in International Trade in Services? *The World Economy*, 39(3): 409–425.

Lee, E.J. (1995): Max Weber and Confucian Capitalism, *Leviathan*, 23(4): 517–529.

Lee, H.; Lalwani, A.K.; Wang, J.J. (2020): Price no Object! The Impact of Power Distance Belief on Consumers' Price Sensitivity, *Journal of Marketing*, 84(6): 113–129.

Lee, I. (2005): The Law and Culture of the Apology in Korean Dispute Settlement (with Japan and the United States in Mind), *Michigan Journal of International Law*, 27(1): 6–53.

Lehmann, H. (2004): *Secularization. Der europäische Sonderweg in Sachen Religion*, Göttingen: Walstein.

Leipold, H. (2022): Islamische Wirtschaftsethik, in: Aßländer, M.S. (Ed.), *Handbuch Wirtschaftsethik*, 2nd ed., 735–737, Berlin: Metzler.

Lemerise, E.A.; Arsenio, W.F. (2000): An Integrated Model of Emotion Processes and Cognition in Social Information Processing, *Child Development*, 71(1): 107–118.

Lemmergaard, J.; Muhr, S.L. (2011): Regarding Gifts. On Christmas Gift Exchange and Asymmetrical Business Relations, *Organization*, 1G(6): 763–777.

Lenski, G.E. (1963): *The Religious Factor. A Sociological Study of Religion's Impact on Politics, Economics, and Family Life*, Garden City/NY: Doubleday.

Lenski, G.E.; Smith, J.W.; Jamison, A.L. (1963): The Religious Factor, *Science and Society*, 27(3): 354–357.

Leventis, S.; Dedoulis, E.; Abdelsalam, O. (2018): The Impact of Religiosity on Audit Pricing, *Journal of Business Ethics*, 148(1): 53–78.

Levitt, T. (1983) 'The globalization of markets', *Harvard Business Review*, May–June(3): 92–102.

Lev-On, A.; Lissitsa, S. (2018): Facilitating Cross-Cleavage Communication Online. Findings from Interviews with Ultra-Orthodox, Religious, and Secular Participants, *Communication Review*, 21(3): 212–227.

Lewer, J.J.; Gerlick, R.N.; Lucas, D. (2008): The Impact of Christian Education and Curriculum on Illegal Media File Sharing Attitudes and Behavior, *Christian Business Academy Review*, 3(1): 70–79.

Li, F.; Zhou, N.; Kashyap, R.; Yang, Z. (2008): Brand Trust as a Second-Order Factor, *International Journal of Market Research*, 50(6): 817–839.

Li, N. (2008): Religion, Opportunism, and International Market Entry via Non-equity Alliances or Joint Ventures, *Journal of Business Ethics*, 80(4): 771–789.

Li, Y.; Sai, Q. (2020): The Effects of Language and Religion on Cross-Border Acquisition Completion, *Research in International Business and Finance*, 54(December): 101294.

Li, Y.J.; Johnson, K.A.; Cohen, A.B.; Williams, M.J.; Knowles, E.D.; Chen, Z. (2012): Fundamental (Is) Attribution Error. Protestants are Dispositionally Focused, *Journal of Personality and Social Psychology*, 102(2): 281–290.

Liang, M.Y. (2010): Confucianism and the East Asian Miracle, *American Economic Journal. Macroeconomics*, 2(3): 206–234.

Lim, C. (2015): Religion and Subjective Well-Being across Religious Traditions, *Journal for the Scientific Study of Religion*, 54(4): 684–701.

Lin, C.A. (1993): Cultural Differences in Message Strategies. A Comparison between American and Japanese TV Commercials, *Journal of Advertising Research*, 33(4): 40–48.

Lindridge, A. (2005): Religiosity and the Construction of a Cultural-Consumption Identity, *Journal of Consumer Marketing*, 22(3): 142–151.

Lindstrom, M. (2005): *Brand Sense. Build Powerful Brands Through Touch, Taste, Smell, Sight, and Sound*, New York: Free Press.

Lissitsa, S.; Cohen, O.R. (2018): The Decade of Online Shopping in the Jewish Ultra-Orthodox Community, *Journal of Media and Religion*, 17(2): 74–89.

Lissitsa, S.; Kol, O. (2016): Generation X vs. Generation Y. A Decade of Online Shopping, *Journal of Retailing and Consumer Services*, 31: 304–312.

Lissitsa, S.; Kol, O. (2021): Four Generational Cohorts and Hedonic M-Shopping. Association between Personality Traits and Purchase Intention, *Electronic Commerce Research*, 21(2): 545–570.

Lissitsa, S.; Madar, G. (2018): Do Disabilities Impede the Use of Information and Communication Technologies? Findings of a Repeated Cross-Sectional Study (2003–2015), *Israel Journal of Health Policy Research*, 7(1): 1–17.

Liu, R.L.; Minton, E.A. (2018): Faith-Filled Brands. The Interplay of Religious Branding and Brand Engagement in the Self-concept, *Journal of Retailing and Consumer Services*, 44(September): 305–314.

Liu, R.R.; McClure, P. (2001): Recognizing Cross-Cultural Differences in Consumer Complaint Behavior and Intentions, *Journal of Consumer Marketing*, 18(1): 54–75.

Liu, Z.; Guo, I.; Sun, P.; Wang, Z.; Wu, R. (2018): Does Religion Hinder Creativity? A National Level Study on the Roles of Religiosity and Different Denominations, *Frontiers in Psychology*, 9: 1–12.

Lord, K.R.; Putrevu, S. (2005): Religious Influence on Consumer Behavior. Classification and Measurement, in: Menon, G.; Rao, A.R. (Eds.), *Advances in Consumer Research*, Vol. 32, 651–652, Duluth/MN: Association for Consumer Research.

Loroz, P.S.; Helgeson, J.G. (2013): Boomers and Their Babies. An Exploratory Study Comparing Psychological Profiles and Advertising Appeal Effectiveness across Two Generations, *Journal of Marketing Theory and Practice*, 21(3): 289–306.

Lüchau, P. (2010): Atheism and Secularity: The Scandinavian Paradox. In *Atheism and Secularity: Volume 2: Global Expressions*, 177–196, Santa Barbara/CA: Praeger.

Luna-Arocas, R.; Tang, T.L.P. (2004): The Love of Money, Satisfaction, and the Protestant Work Ethic, *Journal of Business Ethics*, 50(4): 329–354.

Lütge, C.; Uhl, M. (2017): *Business Ethics*, Munich: Vahlen.

Ma, J.; Hong, J.; Yoo, B.; Yang, J. (2021): The Effect of Religious Commitment and Global Identity on Purchase Intention of Luxury Fashion Products. A Cross-Cultural Study, *Journal of Business Research*, 137(12): 244–254.

MacKenzie, S.B.; Lutz, R.J.; Belch, G.E. (1986): The Role of Attitude toward the Ad as a Mediator of Advertising Effectiveness. A Test of Competing Explanations, *Journal of Marketing Research*, 23(2): 130–143.

Mamun, M.A.A.; Strong, C.A.; Azad, M.A.K. (2021): Islamic Marketing. A Literature Review and Research Agenda, *International Journal of Consumer Studies*, 45(5): 964–984.

Mansori, S. (2012): Impact of Religion Affiliation and Religiosity on Consumer Innovativeness. The Evidence of Malaysia, *World Applied Sciences Journal*, 17(3): 301–307.

Mansori, S.; Sambasivan, M.; Md-Sidin, S. (2015): Acceptance of Novel Products. The Role of Religiosity, Ethnicity and Values, *Marketing Intelligence & Planning*, 33(1): 39–66.

Mansour, I.H.F.; Diab, D.M.E. (2016): The Relationship between Celebrities' Credibility and Advertising Effectiveness. The Mediation Role of Religiosity, *Journal of Islamic Marketing*, 7(2): 148–166.

Marks, M.L.; Mirvis, P.H. (2011): A Framework for the Human Resources Role in Managing Culture in Mergers and Acquisitions, *Human Resource Management*, 50(6): 859–877.

Martin, D.B. (2009): *Inventing Superstition. From the Hippocratics to the Christians*, Cambridge/MA: Harvard University Press.

Martín Martín, O.; Drogendijk, R. (2014): Country Distance (COD). Development and Validation of a New Objective Measure, *Journal of Small Business Management*, 52(1): 102–125.

Mathras, D.; Cohen, A.B.; Mandel, N.; Mick, D.G. (2016): The Effects of Religion on Consumer Behavior. A Conceptual Framework and Research Agenda, *Journal of Consumer Psychology*, 26(2): 298–311.

Mathwick, C. (2002): Understanding the Online Consumer. A Typology of Online Relational Norms and Behavior, *Journal of Interactive Marketing*, 16(1): 40–55.

Matikiti, R.; Roberts-Lombard, M.; Mpinganjira, M. (2018): The Influence of Perceived Justice on Recovery Satisfaction in the Airline Industry, *Journal of African Business*, 19(4): 512–530.

Mattila, A.; Patterson, P.G. (2004): Service Recovery and Fairness Perceptions in Collectivist and Individualist Contexts, *Journal of Service Research*, 6(4): 336–346.

Maung, M.; Tang, Z.; Wilson, C.; Xu, X. (2021): Religion, Risk Aversion, and Cross Border Mergers and Acquisitions, *Journal of International Financial Markets, Institutions and Money*, 70: 101262.

Maus, M. (1990): *The Gift. Form und Funktion des Austauschs in archaischen Gesellschaften*, Frankfurt/Main: Suhrkamp.

Mavor, K.I.; Ysseldyk, R. (2020): A Social Identity Approach to Religion, in: Mavor, K.I.; Ysseldyk, R. (Eds.), *The Science of Religion, Spirituality, and Existentialism*, 187–205, New York: Academic Press.

Mayer, A.J.; Sharp, H. (1962): Religious Preference and Worldly Success, *American Sociological Review*, 27(2): 218–227.

Mazar, N.; Zhong, C.B. (2010): Do Green Products Make us Better People? *ma*, 21(4): 494–498.

Mazereeuw, C.; Graafland, J.; Kaptein, M. (2014): Religiosity, CSR Attitudes, and CSR Behavior. An Empirical Study of Executives' Religiosity and CSR, *Journal of Business Ethics*, 123(3): 437–459.

Mazereeuw-van der Duijn Schouten, C.; Graafland, J.; Kaptein, M. (2014): Religiosity, CSR Attitudes, and CSR Behavior. An Empirical Study of Executives' Religiosity and CSR, *Journal of Business Ethics*, 123(3): 437–459.

McClure, P.K. (2020): The Buffered, Technological Self. Finding Associations between Internet Use and Religiosity, *Social Compass*, 67(3): 461–478.

McCollough, M.A. (2009): The Recovery Paradox. The Effect of Recovery Performance and Service Failure Severity on Post-recovery Customer Satisfaction, *Academy of Marketing Studies Journal*, 13(1): 89–104.

McCord, W. (1989): Explaining the East Asian "Miracle," *The National Interest*, 16(Summer): 74–82.

McCullough, M.E.; Worthington, Jr. E.L. (1999): Religion and the Forgiving Personality, *Journal of Personality*, 67(6): 1141–1164.

McCullough, M.E.; Bono, G.; Root, L.M. (2005): Religion and Forgiveness, in: Paloutzian; R.F.; Park, C.L. (Eds.), *Handbook of Psychology of Religion and Spirituality*, 394–411, New York: Guilford.

McCullough, M.E.; Willoughby, B.L. (2009): Religion, Self-regulation, and Self-control, *Psychological Bulletin*, 135(1): 69–93.

McDaniel, S.W.; Burnett, J.J. (1990): Consumer Religiosity and Retail Store Evaluation Criteria, *Journal of the Academy of Marketing Science*, 18(2): 101–112.

McDaniel, S.W.; Burnett, J.J. (1991): Targeting the Evangelical Market Segment, *Journal of Advertising Research*, 31(4): 26–33.

McGraw, P.A.; Schwartz, J.A.; Tetlock, P.E. (2012): From the Commercial to the Communal. Reframing Taboo Trade-Offs in Religious and Pharmaceutical Marketing, *Journal of Consumer Research*, 39(1): 157–173.

McGuire, S.T.; Newton, N.J.; Omer, T.C.; Sharp, N.Y. (2012): Does Local Religiosity Impact Corporate Social Responsibility? SSRN: https://ssrn.com/abstract=1926387 (03/25/2022).

McGuire, W.J. (1985): Attitudes and Attitude Change, in: Lindzey, G.; Aronson, E. (Eds.), *Handbook of Social Psychology*, Vol. 2, 233–346, New York: Random House.

McKinnon, A. (2002): Sociological Definitions, Language Games, and the "Essence" of Religion, *Method & Theory in the Study of Religion*, 14(1): 61–83.

McKelvey, S. M. (2004). The growth in marketing alliances between US professional sport and legalised gambling entities: Are we putting sport consumers at risk?. *Sport Management Review*, 7(2), 193–210.

McWilliams, P.B.; Heiman, A.; Zilberman, D. (2016): Religion, Religiosity, and the Consumption of Timesaving Foods, *Working Paper*, The Center for Research in Agricultural Economics, Rehovot: Israel.

Meerkerk, G.J.; Van den Eijnden, R.; Garretsen, H.F.L. (2006): Predicting Compulsive Internet Use, *Cyberpsychology & Behavior*, 9(1): 95–103.

Meffert, H. (2006): Marketing for Innovative Services, in: Bullinger, H.-J.; Scheer, A.-W. (Eds.), *Service Engineering*, 249–270, Heidelberg: Springer.

Meffert, H.; Burmann, C.; Kirchgeorg, M.; Eisenbeiß, M. (2019): *Marketing*, 13th ed. Wiesbaden: Springer Gabler.

Mehanna, R.A. (2003): International Trade, Religion, and Political Freedom, *Global Business and Economics Review*, 5(2): 284–296.

Mendl, H.; Sitzberger, R.; Lamberty, A. (2020): Identity Formation in Digital Worlds, *Austrian Religious Education Forum*, 28(1): 143–160.

Micheletti, M. (2003): *Political Virtue and Shopping*, New York: Palgrave Macmillan.

Micheletti, M.; Oral D. (2019): Problematic Political Consumerism, in: Boström, M.; Micheletti, M.; Oosterveer, P. (Eds.), *The Oxford Handbook of Political Consumerism*, 699–720, Oxford: Oxford University Press.

Michell, P.C.N.; Al-Mossawi, M. (1995): The Mediating Effect of Religiosity on Advertising Effectiveness, *Journal of Marketing Communications*, 1(3): 151–162.

Midgley, D.F.; Dowling, G.R. (1978): Innovativeness. The Concept and Its Measurement, *Journal of Consumer Research*, 4(4): 229–242.

Migdalis, N.I.; Tomlekova, N.; Serdaris, P.K.; Yordanov, Y.G. (2014): The Impact of Religion on Shopping Behavior, *International Journal of Management Research and Reviews*, 4(12): 1120–1128.

Mikolon, S.; Quaiser, B.; Wieseke, J. (2015): Don't Try Harder. Using Customer Inoculation to Build Resistance against Service Failures, *Journal of the Academy of Marketing Science*, 43(4): 512–527.

Miller, A.S.; Hoffmann, J.P. (1995): Risk and Religion. An Explanation of Gender Differences in Religiosity, *Journal for the Scientific Study of Religion*, 34(1): 63–75.

Minton, E. (2023): Sustainability and Religion: Consumption Insights from a Western vs. Eastern Comparison. *Religion and Consumer Behaviour*, Routledge, 1–19.

Minton, E.A. (2015): In Advertising We Trust. Religiosity's Inluence on Marketplace and Relational Trust, *Journal of Advertising*, 44(4): 403–414.

Minton, E.A. (2018): Affective and Cognitive Religiosity. Influences on Consumer Reactance and Self-control, *Journal of Consumer Behavior*, 17(2): 175–186.

Minton, E.A. (2019): Believing Is Buying. Religiosity, Advertising Skepticism, and Corporate Trust, *Journal of Management, Spirituality & Religion*, 16(1): 54–75.

Minton, E.A. (2020): When Open-Mindedness Lowers Product Evaluations. Influencers to Consumers' Response to Religious Cues in Advertising, *Psychology & Marketing*, 37(3): 369–383.

Minton, E.A.; Cabano, F.G. (2021): Religiosity's Influence on Stability-Seeking Consumption during Times of Great Uncertainty. The Case of the Coronavirus Pandemic, *Marketing Letters*, 32(2): 135–148.

Minton, E.A.; Cabano, F.G. (2022): Loving My Local Business as My Neighbor. Religiosity's Influence on Local Business Support during a Crisis, *International Journal of Consumer Studies*, 46(5): 1–14.

Minton, E.A.; Cabano, F.G.; Gardner, M.; Mathras, D.; Elliot, E.; Mandel, N. (2017): LGBTQ and Religious Identity Conflict in Service Settings, *Journal of Services Marketing*, 31(4/5): 351–361.

Minton, E.A.; Geiger-Oneto, S. (2020): Making One's Religious Self Feel Better about Luxury Use. The Role of Religiosity in Choice of Disposal Option for Luxury Goods, *Journal of Consumer Behavior*, 19(6): 581–593.

Minton, E.A.; Johnson, K.A.; Liu, R.L. (2019): Religiosity and Special Food Consumption. The Explanatory Effects of Moral Priorities, *Journal of Business Research*, 95(2): 442–454.

Minton, E.A.; Kahle, L.R. (2014): *Belief Systems, Religion, and Behavioral Economics. Marketing in Multicultural Environments*, Hampton/NJ: Business Expert Press.

Minton, E.A.; Kahle, L.R. (2016): Religion and Consumer Behavior, in: Jansson-Boyd, C.V.; Zawisza, M.J. (Eds.), *International Handbook of Consumer Psychology*, 292–311, New York: Routledge.

Minton, E.A.; Kahle, L.R.; Kim, C.H. (2015): Religion and Motives for Sustainable Behaviors, *Journal of Business Research*, 68(9): 1937–1944.

Minton, E.A.; Kaplan, B.; Cabano, F.G. (2022): The Influence of Religiosity on Consumers' Evaluations of Brands Using Artificial Intelligence, *Psychology & Marketing*, 39(11): 2055–2071.

Minton, E.A.; Leary, B.R.; Upadhyaya, S. (2018a): Religion's Influence on Consumer Response to Moral vs. Justice Message Appeals, *International Journal of Consumer Studies*, 42(6): 768–778.

Minton, E.A.; Liu, R.L. (2021): Religiosity and Consumer Belonging. Influences on Product Evaluations, *Journal of Consumer Behavior*, 20(1): 32–47.

Minton, E.A.; Tan, S.J.; Tambyah, S.K.; Liu, R.L. (2022): Drivers of Sustainability and Consumer Well-Being. An Ethically-Based Examination of Religious and Cultural Values, *Journal of Business Ethics*, 175(1): 167–190.

Minton, E.A.; Xie, H.J.; Gurel-Atay, E.; Kahle, L.R. (2018b): Greening Up because of God. The Relations among Religion, Sustainable Consumption and Subjective Well-Being, *International Journal of Consumer Studies*, 42(6): 655–663.

Miric, M.; Jeppesen, L.B. (2020): Does Piracy Lead to Product Abandonment or Stimulate New Product Development? Evidence from Mobile Platform-Based Developer FIFMs, *Strategic Management Journal*, 41(12): 2155–2184.

Moal-Ulvoas, G.; Taylor, V.A. (2014): The Spiritual Benefits of Travel for Senior Tourists. *Journal of Consumer Behaviour*, 13(6), 453–462.

Mochon, D.; Norton, M.I.; Ariely, D. (2011): Who Benefits from Religion? *Social Indicators Research*, 101(1): 1–15.

Mohrman, S.A.; O'Toole, J.; Lawler III, E.E. (Eds.) (2017): *Corporate Stewardship. Achieving Sustainable Effectiveness*, London: Routledge.

Mokhlis, S. (2006a): *The Influence of Religion on Retail Patronage Behavior in Malaysia*, Ph.D. Thesis, Stirling: University of Stirling.

Mokhlis, S. (2006b): The Effect of Religiosity on Shopping Orientation. An Exploratory Study in Malaysia, *Journal of American Academy of Business*, 9(1): 64–74.

Mokhlis, S. (2008): Consumer Religiosity and the Importance of Store Attributes, *Journal of Human Resources and Adult Learning*, 4(2): 122–133.

Mokhlis, S. (2009a): Religious Differences in Some Selected Aspects of Consumer Behavior. A Malaysian Study, *Journal of International Management Studies*, 4(1): 67–76.

Mokhlis, S. (2009b): Relevancy and Measurement of Religiosity in Consumer Behavior Research, *International Business Research*, 2(3): 75–84.

Mokhlis, S. (2010): Religious Contrasts in Consumer Shopping Styles, *Journal of Business Studies Quarterly*, 2(1): 52–64.

Montgomery, J.D. (2003): A Formalization and Test of the Religious Economies Model, *American Sociological Review*, 68(5): 782–809.

Moon, Y. (2003): Don't Blame the Computer. When Self-disclosure Moderates the Self-serving Bias, *Journal of Consumer Psychology*, 13(1–2): 125–137.

Moore, R.L. (1995): *Selling God. American Religion in the Marketplace of Culture*, Oxford: Oxford University Press.

Moraru, M. (2012): *Debt and Religion. Are Religious People More Debt Averse and Have High Willingness to Pay Their Debts Off?* Master's Thesis, University of Stavanger/Norway.

Morewedge, C.K.; Shu, L.L.; Gilbert, D.T.; Wilson, T.D. (2009): Bad Riddance or Good Rubbish? Ownership and Not Loss Aversion Causes the Endowment Effect, *Journal of Experimental Social Psychology*, 45(4): 947–951.

Morreall, J. (2008): Philosophy and Religion, in: Raskin, V. (Ed.), *The Primer of Humor Research*, 211–242, Berlin, New York: Mouton, de Gruyter.

Mortimer, G.; Fazal-e-Hasan, S.M.; Grimmer, M.; Grimmer, L. (2020): Explaining the Impact of Consumer Religiosity, Perceived Risk and Moral Potency on Purchase Intentions, *Journal of Retailing and Consumer Services*, 55(July): 102–115.

Moschis, G. P., & Ong, F. S. (2011). Religiosity and consumer behavior of older adults: A study of subcultural influences in Malaysia. *Journal of Consumer Behaviour, 10*(1), 8-17.Mostafa, M.M. (2019): Clustering Halal Food Consumers. A Twitter Sentiment Analysis, *International Journal of Market Research*, 61(3): 320–337.

Muhamad, N.; Leong, V.S.; Isa, N.M. (2017): Does the Country of Origin of a Halal Logo Matter? The Case of Packaged Food Purchases, *Review of International Business and Strategy*, 27(4): 484–500.

Muhamad, N.; Mizerski, D. (2013): The Effects of Following Islam in Decisions about Taboo Products, *Psychology & Marketing*, 30(4): 357–371.

Mukhtar, A.; Butt, M.M. (2012): Intention to Choose Halal Products. The Role of Religiosity, *Journal of Islamic Marketing*, 3(2): 108–120.

Müller, S.; Gelbrich, K. (2014): *Intercultural Communication*, Munich: Vahlen.

Müller, S.; Gelbrich, K. (2015): *Intercultural Marketing*, 2nd ed., Munich: Vahlen.

Müller, S.; Gelbrich, K. (2021): *Intercultural Consumer Behavior*, Munich: Vahlen.

Mullet, E.; Barros, J.; Usaï, V.; Frongia, L.; Neto, F.; Rivière Shafighi, S. (2003): Religious Involvement and the Forgiving Personality, *Journal of Personality*, 71(1): 1–19.

Muralidharan, S.; La Ferle, C. (2018): Religious Symbolism in the Digital Realm, *International Journal of Consumer Studies*, 42(6): 804–812.

Myers, S.D.; Deitz, G.D.; Huhmann, B.A.; Jha, S.; Tatara, J.H. (2020): An Eye-Tracking Study of Attention to Brand-Identifying Content and Recall of Taboo Advertising, *Journal of Business Research*, 111(4): 176–186.

Nadesan, M.H. (1999): The Discourses of Corporate Spiritualism and Evangelical Capitalism, *Management Communication Quarterly*, 13(1): 3–42.

Naseri, A.; Tamam, E. (2012): Impact of Islamic Religious Symbols in Producing Favorable Attitude toward Advertisement, *Revista de Administratie Publica si Politici Sociale*, 8(1): 61–78.

Nasution, M.D.T.P.; Rossanty, Y. (2018): Country of Origin as a Moderator of Halal Label and Purchase Behavior, *Journal of Business and Retail Management Research*, 12(2): 194–201.

Nelson, M.R.; Ham, C.D.; Haley, E. (2021): What Do We Know about Political Advertising? *Journal of Current Issues & Research in Advertising*, 42(4): 329–353.

Newholm, T.; Shaw, D. (2007): Studying the Ethical Consumer. A Review of Research, *Journal of Consumer Behavior*, 6(5): 253–270.

Newton, J.D.; Wong, J.; Casidy, R. (2018): Deck the Halls with Boughs of Holly to Soften Evaluations of Service Failure, *Journal of Service Research*, 21(4): 389–404.

Ngah, A.; Garbarre, S.; Jeevan, J.; Salleh, N.; Hanafiah, R. (2021): To Pay or Not to Pay. Measuring the Effect of Religiosity in the ABC Theory, *Management Science Letters*, 11(3): 795–806.

Ngai, E.W.; Heung, V.C.; Wong, Y.H.; Chan, F.K. (2007): Consumer Complaint Behavior of Asians and Non-Asians about Hotel Services, *European Journal of Marketing*, 41(11/12): 1375–1391.

Niazi, M.A.K.; Ghani, U.; Aziz, S. (2019): Impact of Islamic Religiosity on Consumers' Attitudes toward Islamic and Conventional Ways of Advertisements, Attitude toward Brands and Purchase Intentions, *Business and Economic Review*, 11(1): 1–29.

Nickerson, C.; Georgiadou, E.; Nandialath, A.M. (2023): Religious Affiliation and Religiosity. Do Islamic Appeals in Advertising Lead to Higher Purchase Intentions among Muslim Consumers in Dubai? *Journal of Islamic Marketing*, 14(4): 1128–1145.

Niebuhr, R. (1953): *Christian Realism and Political Problems*, New York: Scribners.

Nienhaus, V. (2004): Islam. Brake or Motor of Economic Development? in: von Hauff, M.; Vogt, U. (Eds.), *Islamic and Western World*, 227–253, Marburg: Metropolis.

Nix, T.W.; Gibson, J.G. (1989): Does a Hospital's Religious Affiliation Affect Choice of Hospital and Patient Satisfaction? *Journal of Health Care Marketing*, 9(2): 40–41.

***Nor Faiz Azizana, N.F.; Hafitb, N.I.A.; Zainudinc, A.; Mohdd, R.; Badrul Hisham Kamaruddine, B.H. (2022): Does only Religiosity Matter in Celebrity Endorsement and Advertising Effectiveness? *Journal of Emerging Economies & Islamic Research*, 10(2): 1–31.

Norenzayan, A.; Lee, A. (2010): It Was Meant to Happen. Explaining Cultural Variations in Fate Attributions, *Journal of Personality and Social Psychology*, 98(5): 702–720.

Norenzayan, A.; Shariff, A.F.; Gervais, W.M.; Willard, A.K.; McNamara, R.A.; Slingerland, E.; Henrich, J. (2016): The Cultural Evolution of Prosocial Religions, *Behavioral and Brain*, 39, e1 (19 pages). doi:10.1017/S0140525X14001356.

North, C.M.; Orman W.H.; Gwin C.R. (2013): Religion, Corruption, and the Rule of Law, *Journal of Money, Credit and Banking*, 45(5): 757–779.

Noussair, C.N.; Trautmann, S.T.; van de Kuilen, G.; Vellekoop, N. (2013): Risk Aversion and Religion, *Journal of Risk and Uncertainty*, 47(2): 165–183.

Nurhayati, T.; Hendar, H. (2019): Personal Intrinsic Religiosity and Product Knowledge on Halal Product Purchase Intention. Role of Halal Product Awareness, *Journal of Islamic Marketing*, 11(3): 603–620.

Nyland, R.; Near, C. (2007): Jesus Is My Friend. Religiosity as a Mediating Factor in Internet Social Networking Use, *AEJMC Midwinter Conference*, Reno/NV.

OAhluwalia, R.; Kaikati, A.M. (2010): Traveling the Paths to Brand Loyalty, in: Loken, B.; Ahluwalia, R.; Houston, M.J. (Eds.), *Brands and Brand Management*, 63–90, New York: Routledge.

O'Cass, A.; Lee, W.J.; Siahtiri, V. (2013): Can Islam and Status Consumption Live together in the House of Fashion Clothing? *Journal of Fashion Marketing and Management*, 17(4): 440–459.

Ockenfels, W. (1992): Catholic Church and Social Market Economy. Differences and Transitions, *The New Order*, 46(3): 184–194.

O'Guinn, T. C., & Belk, R. W. (1989). Heaven on earth: consumption at Heritage Village, USA. *Journal of Consumer Research*, 16(2), 227–238.

Oh, H.; Bae, J.; Currim, I.S.; Lim, J.; Zhang, Y. (2020): Influence of CEOs' Religious Affiliations on FIFMs' Advertising Spending and Shareholder Value, *European Journal of Marketing*, 55(5): 1440–1468.

Ohtsubo, Y.; Watanabe, E. (2009): Do Sincere Apologies Need to Be Costly? *Evolution and Human Behavior*, 30(2): 114–123.

Oliver, R.L. (1977): Effect of Expectation and DisconfIFMation on Postexposure Product Evaluations, *Journal of Applied Psychology*, 62(4): 480–486.

Oliver, R.L. (1997): *Satisfaction. A Behavioral Perspective on the Consumer*, Armonk/NY: Sharpe.

Orellano, A.; Valor, C.; Chuvieco, E. (2020): The Influence of Religion on Sustainable Consumption. A Systematic Review and Future Research Agenda, *Sustainability*, 12(19): 7901, doi:10.3390/su12197901 (04/05/2022).

Orr, R. (2003): Faith-Based Decisions. Parents Who Refuse Appropriate Care for Their Children, *AMA Journal of Ethics: Virtual Mentor*, 5(8): 223–225.

Osiri, J.; Houenou, B.; Stein, R. (2019): A Cross-Country Study of Innovation and Religiosity, *SSRN* 3451502.

o.V. (2004): New Religions, in: Lexikonredaktion des Verlags F.A. Brockhaus (Ed.), *Der Brockhaus. Religion*, 461–464, Mannheim: Brockhaus.

o.V. (2007): DJ Bobo verärgert Christen mit Vampirsong, https://www.spiegel.de/kultur/musik/grand-prix-stress-dj-bobo-veraergert-christen-mit-vampirsong-a-470409.html/ (13/08/2024)

o.V. (2022): What Is the Year-End Rally and How to Trade it? https://admiralmarkets.com/de/wissen/articles/trading-instruments/year-end-rally (12/21/2022).

Pace, S. (2013): Does Religion Affect the Materialism of Consumers? An Empirical Investigation of Buddhist Ethics and the Resistance of the Self, *Journal of Business Ethics*, 112(1): 25–46.

Pace, S. (2014): Effects of Intrinsic and Extrinsic Religiosity on Attitudes toward Products. Empirical Evidence of Value-Expressive and Social-Adjustive Functions, *Journal of Applied Business Research*, 30(4): 1227–1238.

Paldam, M. (2001): Corruption and Religion. Adding to the Economic Model, *Kyklos*, 54(2–3): 383–414.

Parasuraman, A.; Zeithaml, V.A.; Berry, L.L. (1988): SERVQUAL. A Multiple-Item Scale for Measuring Consumer Perceptions of Service Quality, *Journal of Retailing*, 64(1): 12–40.

Parboteeah, K.P.; Paik, Y.; Cullen, J.B. (2009): Religious Groups and Work Values. A Focus on Buddhism, Christianity, Hinduism, and Islam, *International Journal of Cross Cultural Management*, 9(1): 51–67.

Parry, S.; Jones, R.; Stern, P.; Robinson, M. (2013): Shockvertising. An Exploratory Investigation into Attitudinal Variations and Emotional Reactions to Shock Advertising, *Journal of Consumer Behavior*, 12(2): 112–121.

Patai, R. (1977): *The Jewish Mind*, New York: Charles Scribners and Sons.

Pearson, A.R.; Schuldt, J.P.; Romero-Canyas, R.; Ballew, M.T.; Larson-Konar, D. (2018): Diverse Segments of the US Public Underestimate the Environmental Concerns of Minority and Low-Income Americans, *Proceedings of the National Academy of Sciences*, 115(49): 12429–12434.

Pebri, P.; Bakti, S. (2022): The Influence of Brand Trust and Religiosity on the Mudharabah Deposit Product Selection Decision, *Journal of Social Science*, 3(1): 177–182.

Pennycook, G.; Ross, R.M.; Koehler, D.J.; Fugelsang, J.A. (2016): Atheists and Agnostics Are More Reflective than Religious Believers. Four Empirical Studies and a Meta-Analysis, *PLoS One*, 11(4), e0153039.

Penrose, J.; Weaver, D.H.; Cole, R.R.; Shaw, D.L. (1974): The Newspaper Reader 10 Years Later. A Partial Replication of Westley-Severin, *Journalism Quarterly*, 51(4): 631–638.

Pepper, M.; Jackson, T.; Uzzell, D. (2011): An Examination of Christianity and Socially Conscious and Frugal Consumer Behaviors, *Environment and Behavior*, 43(2): 274–290.

Perreault, S.; Bourhis, R.Y. (1999): Ethnocentrism, Social Identification, and Discrimination, *Personality and Social Psychology Bulletin*, 25(1): 92–103.

Perry, S.L. (2017): Spousal religiosity, religious bonding, and pornography consumption, *Archives of Sexual Behavior*, 46(2): 561–574.

Petty, R.E.; Cacioppo, J.T. (1986): The Elaboration Likelihood Model of Persuasion, in: Berkowitz, L. (Ed.), *Advances in Experimental Social Psychology*, Vol. 19, 123–205, New York: Academic Press.

Pew Research Center (2012): *The Global Religious Landscape. A Report on the Size and Distribution of the World's Major Religious Groups as of 2010*, https://www.pewresearch.org/religion/2012/12/18/global-religious-landscape-exec/

Pew Research Center (2020): *The Global God Divide*; https://www.pewresearch.org/religion/2020/07/20/the-global-god-divide/ (Oct. 12, 2021).

Pew Research Forum (2017): *The Changing Global Religious Landscape*, https://www.pewresearch.org/religion/2017/04/05/the-changing-global-religious-landscape/

Pfeiffer, H. (2001): Heikle Geschäfte in Allahs Namen, *Süddeutsche Zeitung*, 57(217): 23.

Pfister, S. (2002): Flattering the soul, *Dresdner Zeitung*, 44: 29.

Phillips, D.P.; Liu, G.C.; Kwok, K.; Jarvinen, J.R.; Zhang, W.; Abramson, I.S. (2001): The Hound of the Baskervilles Effect. Natural Experiment on the Influence of Psychological Stress on Timing of Death, *British Medical Journal*, 323(7327): 1443–1446.

Pícha, K.; Skořepa, L. (2018): Preference to Food with a Regional Brand, *Calitatea*, 19(162): 134–139.

Pickering, W.S.F. (Ed.) (1994): *Durkheim on Religion*, Atlanta/GA: Scholars.

Pinter, B.; Hakim, M.; Seidman, D.S.; Kubba, A.; Kishen, M.; Di Carlo, C. (2016): Religion and Family Planning, *European Journal of Contraception & Reproductive Health Care*, 21(6): 486–495.

Pinto de Oliveira, C.-J. (1980): Image de Dieu et Dignité Humaine, *Freiburger Zeitschrift für Philosophie und Theologie*, 3(27): 401–436.

Pleines, G. (1998): The Regions of Ukraine, *Eastern Europe*, 48(4): 365–372.

Pogačnik, A.; Črnič, A. (2014): iReligion. Religious Elements of the Apple Phenomenon, *Journal of Religion and Popular Culture*, 26(3): 353–364.

Pollmer, U.; Warmuth, S. (2001): *Lexikon der populären Ernährungsirrtümer. Misunderstandings, misinterpretations and half-truths*, 2nd ed.

Poon, P.S.; Hui, M.K.; Au, K. (2004): Attributions on Dissatisfying Service Encounters. A Cross-Cultural Comparison between Canadian and PRC Consumers, *European Journal of Marketing*, 38(11/12): 1527–1540.

Preko, A.; Mohammed, I.; Ameyibor, L.E.K. (2020): Muslim Tourist Religiosity, Perceived Values, Satisfaction, and Loyalty, *Tourism Review International*, 24(2–3): 109–125.

Prendergast, G.; Wong, C. (2003): Parental Influence on the Purchase of Luxury Brands of Infant Apparel. An Exploratory Study in Hong Kong, *Journal of Consumer Marketing*, 20(2): 157–169.

Preston, J.L.; Baimel, A. (2021): Towards a Psychology of Religion and the Environment, *Current Opinion in Psychology*, 40(August): 145–149.

Preston, J.L.; Ritter, R.S.; Hernandez, J.I. (2010): Principles of Religious Prosociality. A Review and Reformulation, *Social and Personality Compass*, 4: 574–590.

Price, C.R.; Sheremeta, R.M. (2015): Endowment Origin, Demographic Effects, and Individual Preferences in Contests, *Journal of Economics & Management Strategy*, 24(3): 597–619.

Pryor, F. L. (1990). A Buddhist economic system—in principle: Non-attachment to worldly things Is dominant but the way of the law is held profitable. *American Journal of Economics and Sociology*, 49(3), 339–349.

Purnomo, H. (2015): Analisis Pengaruh Citra Merek Produk Asli, Persepsian Nilai, Kualitas Produk, dan Kewa-jaran Harga Pada Niat Beli Produk Bajakan, *Focus Manajerial*, 13(1): 15–26.

Purwanto, H.; Fauzi, M.; Wijayanti, R.; Al Awwaly, K.U.; Jayanto, I.; Purwanto, A.; Hartuti, E.T.K. (2020): Developing Model of Halal Food Purchase Intention among Indonesian Non-muslim Consumers, *Systematic Reviews in Pharmacy*, 11(10): 396–407.

Purzycki, B.G.; Pisor, A.C.; Apicella, C.; Atkinson, Q.; Cohen, E.; Henrich, J.; ... Xygalatas, D. (2018): The Cognitive and Cultural Foundations of Moral Behavior, *Evolution and Human Behavior*, 39(5): 490–501.

Putnam, R.D.; Feldsten, L.M.; Cohen, D. (2003): *Better Together. Restoring the American Community*, New York: Simon & Schuster.

Putrevu, S.; Swimberghe, K.R. (2013): The Influence of Religiosity on Consumer Ethical Judgments and Responses toward Sexual Appeals, *Journal of Business Ethics*, 115(2): 351–365.

Qin, V.; Fitzsimons, G.J.; Staelin, R. (2017): The Price of Faith. Religion's Role in the Endowment Effect, in: Gneezy, A.; Griskevicius, V.; Williams, P. (Eds.), *Advances in Consumer Research*, Vol. 45, 107–111, Duluth/MN: Association for Consumer Research.

Raggiotto, F.; Mason, M.C.; Moretti, A. (2018): Religiosity, Materialism, Consumer Environmental Predisposition, *International Journal of Consumer Studies*, 42(6): 613–626.

Rahman, M.; Albaity, M.; Maruf, B. (2017): The Role of Religiosity on the Relationship between Materialism and Fashion Clothing Consumption among Malaysian Generation Y Consumers, *Social Indicators Research*, 132(2): 757–783.

Ramanujan, A.K. (1989): Is There an Indian Way of Thinking? *Contributions to Indian Sociology*, 23(1): 41–58.

Ramasamy, B.; Yeung, M.C.; Au, A.K. (2010): Consumer Support for Corporate Social Responsibility (CSR). The Role of Religion and Values, *Journal of Business Ethics*, 91(1): 61–72.

Rarick, C.; Falk, G.; Barczyk, C.; Feldman, L. (2012): Marketing to Muslims. The Growing Importance of Halal Products, *Journal of the International Academy for Case Studies*, 18(2): 101–106.

Rasmussen, K.R.; Grubbs, J.B.; Pargament, K.I.; Exline, J.J. (2018): Social Desirability Bias in Pornography-related Self-reports. The Role of Religion, *Journal of Sex* Research, 55(3): 381–394.

Ratnasari, R.T.; Ula, U.F.; Sukmana, R. (2020): Can Store Image Moderate the Influence of Religiosity Level on Shopping Orientation and Customers' Behavior in Indonesia? *Journal of Islamic Accounting and Business Research,* 12(1): 1759–1817.

Ratzinger, J. (2000): Europe's Culture and Its Crisis, *Die Zeit*, 55(50): 61–63.

Rauf, A.A.; Prasad, A.; Ahmed, A. (2019): How Does Religion Discipline the Consumer Subject? *Journal of Marketing Management*, 35(5/6): 491–513.

Rawwas, M. Y., Swaidan, Z., & Al-Khatib, J. (2006). Does religion matter? A comparison study of the ethical beliefs of marketing students of religious and secular universities in Japan. *Journal of Business ethics*, 65, 69–86.

Razmyar, S.; Reeve, C.L. (2013): Individual Differences in Religiosity as a Function of Cognitive Ability and Cognitive Style, *Intelligence*, 41(5): 667–673.

Recio-Román, A.; Recio-Menéndez, M.; Román-González, M.V. (2019): Religion and Innovation in Europe. Implications for Product Life-Cycle Management, *Religions*, 10(10): 589–624.

Recio-Román, A.; Recio-Menéndez, M.; Román-González, M.V. (2023): Religious Affiliation and Consumer Behavior toward Biodiversity Conservation in Europe, *Religions*, 14(7), 947–972.

Regenstein, J.M.; Chaudry, M.M.; Regenstein, C.E. (2003): The Kosher and Halal Food Laws, *Comprehensive Reviews in Food Science and Food Safety*, 2(3): 111–127.

Regnerus, M.D.; Uecker, J.E. (2007): Religious Influences on Sensitive Self-reported Behaviors. The Product of Social Desirability, Deceit, or Embarrassment? *Sociology of Religion*, 68(2): 145–163.

Rehman, A.; Shabbir, M.S. (2010): The Relationship between Religiosity and New Product Adoption, *Journal of Islamic Marketing*, 1(1): 63–69.

Reich, W. (1933): *Charakteranalyse*, Vienna: Selbstverlag.

Reinstein, D.; Song, J. (2012): Efficient Consumer Altruism and Fair Trade Products, *Journal of Economics & Management Strategy*, 21(1): 213–241.

Renfrew, C.; Boyd, M.J.; Morley, I. (Eds.) (2016): *Death Rituals and Social Order in the Ancient Wold*, Cambridge: Cambridge University Press.

Renneboog, L.; Spaenjers, C. (2012): Religion, Economic Attitudes, and Household Finance, *Oxford Economic Papers*, 64(1): 103–127.

Reutter, K.K.; Bigatti, S.M. (2014): Religiosity and Spirituality as Resiliency Resources. Moderation, Mediation, or Moderated Mediation? *Journal for the Scientific Study of Religion*, 53(1): 56–72.

Rice, G.; Al-Mossawi, M. (2002): The Implications of Islam for Advertising Messages, *Journal of Euromarketing*, 11(3): 1–16.

Richardson, C. (2014): FIFM Internationalization within the Muslim World, *Journal of World Business*, 49(3): 386–395.

Richardson, C.; Ariffin, S.K. (2019): A Leap of Faith? Managerial Religiosity and Market Entry Decisions, *Management International Review*, 59(2): 277–305.

Richardson, C.; Rammal, H.G. (2018): Religious Belief and International Business Negotiations. Does Faith Influence Negotiator Behavior? *International Business Review*, 27(2): 401–409.

Richins, M.L.; Dawson, S. (1992): A Consumer Values Orientation for Materialism and Its Measurement. Scale Development and Validation, *Journal of Consumer Research*, 19(3): 303–316.

Riefler, P.; Diamantopoulos, A. (2007): Consumer Animosity. A Literature Review and a Reconsideration of Its Measurement, *International Marketing Review*, 24(1): 87–119.

Rigney, D.; Hoffman, T.J. (1993): Is American Catholicism Anti-intellectual? *Journal for the Scientific Study of Religion*, 32(3): 211–222.

Rindfleisch, A.; Burroughs, J.E.; Wong, N. (2005): Religiosity and Brand Commitment, in: Ha, Y.-U.; Yi, Y. (Eds.), *Asia Pacific Advances in Consumer Research*, Vol. 6, 153–154, Duluth/MN: Association for Consumer Research.

Rindfleisch, A.; Burroughs, J.E.; Wong, N. (2009): The Safety of Objects. Materialism, Existential Insecurity, and Brand Connection, *Journal of Consumer Research*, 36(1): 1–16.

Ringberg, T.; Odekerken-Schröder, G.; Christensen, G.L. (2007): A Cultural Models Approach to Service Recovery, *Journal of Marketing*, 71(3): 194–214.

Rios, R.E.; Riquelme, H.E.; Abdelaziz, Y. (2014): Do Halal Certification, Country of Origin and Brand Name Familiarity Matter? *Asia Pacific Journal of Marketing and Logistics*, 26(5): 665–686.

Ritzer, G. (1998): The Weberian Theory of Rationalization and the McDonaldization of Contemporary Society, in: Kivisto, P. (Ed.), *Illuminating Social Life. Classical and Contemporary Theory Revisited*, 37–61, Los Angeles/CA: Sage.

Rizkitysha, T.L.; Hananto, A. (2020): Do Knowledge, Perceived Usefulness of Halal Label and Religiosity Affect Attitude and Intention to Buy Halal-Labeled Detergent? *Journal of Islamic Marketing*, 13(3): 649–670.

Roberts, C.L. (1983): Attitudes and Media Use of the Moral Majority, *Journal of Broadcasting*, 27(4): 403–410.

Roberts, J.A.; Manolis, C.; Tanner Jr, J.F. (2003): Family Structure, Materialism, and Compulsive Buying. A Reinquiry and Extension, *Journal of* the *Academy of Marketing Science*, 31(3): 300–311.

Roccas, S.; Elster, A. (2013): Values and Religiosity, in: Saroglou, V. (Ed.), *Religion, Personality, and Social Behavior*, 203–222, Hove/GB: Psychology Press.

Rodriguez-Rad, C.J.; Ramos-Hidalgo, E. (2018): Spirituality, Consumer Ethics, and Sustainability: The Mediating Role of Moral Identity. *Journal of Consumer Marketing*, 35(1), 51–63.

Rohe, M. (2022): *Islamic Law. History and present*, 4th ed., Munich: Beck.

Rokeach, M. (1968): *Beliefs, Attitudes, and Values. A Theory of Organization and Change*, San Francisco/CA: Jossey-Bass.

Rokeach, M. (1969): Value Systems in Religion, *Review of Religious Research*, 11(1): 3–23.

Romanelli, M.; Gazzola, P.; Grechi, D.; Pollice, F. (2021): Towards a Sustainability-Oriented Religious Tourism, *Systems Research and Behavioral Science*, 38(3): 386–396.

Root, F.R. (1994): *Entry Strategies for International Markets*, Lexington/MA: Lexington Books.

Rothlauf, J. (2012): *Interkulturelles Management*, 4th ed., Berlin: de Gruyter.

Rudski, J. (2004): The Illusion of Control, Superstitious Belief, and Optimism, *Current Psychology*, 22(4): 306–315.

Ruiu, G. (2013): The Origin of Fatalistic Tendencies. An Empirical Investigation, *Economics & Sociology*, 6(2): 103–125.

Rye, M.S.; Pargament, K.I.; Ali, M.A.; Beck, G.L.; Dorff, E.N.; Hallisey, C.; ... Williams, J. (2000): Religious Perspectives on Forgiveness, in: McCullough, M.E.; Pargament, K.I.; Thoresen, C.E. (Eds.), *Forgiveness*, 17–40, New York: Guilford.

Sabatier, C.; Mayer, B.; Friedlmeier, M.; Lubiewska, K.; Trommsdorff, G. (2011): Religiosity, Family Orientation, and Life Satisfaction of Adolescents in Four Countries, *Journal of Cross-Cultural Psychology*, 42(8): 1375–1393.

Sachsenmaier, S.; Guo, Y. (2019): Building Trust in Cross-Cultural Integration. A Study of Chinese Mergers and Acquisitions in Germany, *International Journal of Cross Cultural Management*, 19(2): 194–217.

Saeed, M.; Ahmed, Z.U.; Mukhtar, S.-M. (2001): International Marketing Ethics from an Islamic Perspective, *Journal of Business Ethics*, 32(2): 127–142.

Saeed, M.; Azmi, I.B.A.G. (2016): Brand Switching Behavior of Muslim Consumers, *International Journal of Research in Business and Social Science*, 5(4): 31–39.

Salvador, R.O.; Merchant, A.; Alexander, E.A. (2014): Faith and Fair Trade. The Moderating Role of Contextual Religious Salience, *Journal of Business Ethics*, 121(3): 353–371.

Samiee, S.; Leonidou, L.C.; Aykol, B.; Stöttinger, B.; Christodoulides, P. (2016): Fifty Years of Empirical Research on Country-of-Origin Effects on Consumer Behavior. A Meta-Analysis, in: Petruzzellis, L.; Winer, R. (Eds.), *Rediscovering the Essentiality of Marketing*, 505–510, Cham: Springer.

Sampson, E.E. (2000): Reinterpreting Individualism and Collectivism. Their Religious Roots and Monologic versus Dialogic Person-Other Relationship, *American Psychologist*, 55(12): 1425–1432.

Sanaie, A.; Ranjbarian, B. (1996): Marketing in Islamic Countries, *Journal of International Marketing and Marketing Research*, 21(3): 115–121.

Sanchez, Z.M.; Opaleye, E.S.; Chaves, T.V.; Noto, A.R.; Nappo, S.A. (2011): God Forbids or Mom Disapproves? Religious Beliefs that Prevent Drug Use among Youth, *Journal of Adolescent Research*, 26(5): 591–616.

Sandıkcı, Ö.; Rice, G. (Eds.) (2011): *Handbook of Islamic Marketing*, Cheltenham: Edgar Elgar.

Saptasari, K.; Aji, H.M. (2020): Factors Affecting Muslim Non-customers to Use Islamic Bank. Religiosity, Knowledge, and Perceived Quality, *Jurnal Ekonomi dan Keuangan Islam*, 6(2): 165–180.

Saracevic, S.; Schlegelmilch, B.B.; Wu, T. (2022): How Normative Appeals Influence Pro-environmental Behavior, *Journal of Cleaner Production*, 344: 131086.

Sardana, D.; Cavusgil, E.; Gupta, N. (2021): The Growing Popularity of Spiritual Brands. What Drives Purchase Intent? *International Business Review*, 30(4): 1–12.

Sarkar, A.; Sarkar, J.G. (2017): Sing Hosanna for the Brands. The Process of Substituting Religion with Brand, *Society and Business Review*, 12(1): 33–45.

Sarofim, S.; Cabano, F.G. (2018): In God We Hope, in Ads We Believe. The Influence of Religion on Hope, Perceived Ad Credibility, and Purchase Behavior, *Marketing Letters*, 29(3): 391–404P.

Sarofim, S.; Tolba, A.; Kalliny, M. (2022): The Effect of Religiosity on Customer's Response to Service Failure, *Journal of Consumer Affairs*, 56(1): 465–486.

Saroglou, V. (2002): Religion and Sense of Humor. An a Priori Incompatibility? *Humor*, 15(2): 191–214.

Saroglou, V.; Dupuis, J. (2006): Being Buddhist in Western Europe. Cognitive Needs, Prosocial Character, and Values, *International Journal for the Psychology of Religion*, 16(3): 163–179.

Saroglou, V.; Pichon, I.; Trompette, L.; Verschueren, M.; Dernelle, R. (2005): Prosocial Behavior and Religion, *Journal for the Scientific Study of Religion*, 44(3): 323–348.

Sarpal, R.; Saleh, R.; Teck, T.S.; Chia, K.M.; Yee, L.M. (2018): Literature Review on the Use of Sex Appeal vs Non-Sex Appeal Advertising in the Malaysian Context, *International Journal of Marketing Studies*, 10(2): 28–35.

Sasaki, M.; Suzuku, T. (1996): Changes in Religious Commitment in the United States, Holland, and Japan, in: Inkeles, A.; Sasaki, M. (Eds.), *Comparing Nations and Cultures*, 586–601, Englewood Cliffs/NJ: Prentice Hall.

Sayuti, K.M.; Amin, H. (2019): Integrating the Effects of Price Fairness and Islamic Altruism with the TPB Model. The Case of Islamic Mortgage Adoption, *International Journal of Housing Markets and Analysis*, 13(5): 791–807.

Schimmel, A. (2003): *The Signs of God*, 3rd ed. Munich: Beck.
Schirrmacher, T. (2005): Bribery and Corruption from a Biblical Perspective. Supplements to Ethics, *MBS Texts 49*.
Schjørring, J.H.; Hjelm, N.A. (Eds.) (2017): *History of global Christianity*, Stuttgart: Kohlhammer.
Schlegelmilch, B.B.; Khan, M.M.; Hair, J.F. (2016): Halal Endorsements. Stirring Controversy or Gaining New Customers? *International Marketing Review*, 33(1): 156–174.
Schmidt, R.; Sager, G.C.; Carney, G.T.; Muller, A.C.; Zanca, K.J.; Jackson, J.J.; Wayne Mayhall, C.; Burke, J.C. (2014): *Patterns of Religion*, 3rd ed., Boston/MA: Wadsworth.
Schmitt, D.P.; Realo, A.; Voracek, M.; Allik, J. (2008): Why Can't a Man Be More Like a Woman? Sex Differences in Big Five Personality Traits across 55 Cultures, *Journal of Personality and Social Psychology*, 94(1): 168–182.
Schnabel, U. (2008): The Path to Oneself. Wolf Singer, *Die Zeit*, 63(44): 45.
Schnädelbach, H. (2000): The Curse of Christianity, *Die Zeit*, 55(20): 41–42.
Schneider, H.; Krieger, J.; Bayraktar, A. (2011): The Impact of Intrinsic Religiousness on Consumers' Ethical Beliefs, *Journal of Business Ethics*, 102: 319–332.
Schoenberg, R. (2006): Measuring the Performance of Corporate Acquisitions, *British Journal of Management*, 17(4): 361–370.
Schouten, J.W.; McAlexander, J.H. (1995): Subcultures of Consumption. An Ethnography of the New Biker, *Journal of Consumer Research*, 22(1): 43–62.
Schwartz, S.H.; Bilsky, W. (1990): Toward a Theory of the Universal Content and Structure of Values. Extensions and Cross-Cultural Replications, *Journal of Personality and Social Psychology*, 58(5): 878–891.
Schwartz, S.H.; Huismans, S. (1995): Value Priorities and Religiosity in Four Western Religions, *Social Psychology Quarterly*, 58(2): 88–107.
Sedikides, C.; Gebauer, J.E. (2010): Religiosity as Self-enhancement. A Meta-Analysis of the Relation between Socially Desirable Responding and Religiosity, *Personality and Social Psychology Review*, 14(1): 17–36.
Self-con, G.P.; Ong, F.S. (2011): Religiosity and Consumer Behavior of Older Adults. A Study of Subcultural Influences in Malaysia, *Journal of Consumer Behavior*, 10(1): 8–17.
Severin, W.; Tankard, J. (Eds.) (2001): *Communication Theories. Origins, Methods, and Uses in the Mass Media*, 5th ed., New York/NY: Longman.
Shachar, R.; Erdem, T; Cutright, K.M.; Fitzsimons, G.J. (2011): Brands. The Opiate of the Nonreligious Masses? *Marketing Science*, 30(1): 92–110.
Shafiq, A. (2020): Non-Muslims' Beliefs about Islamic Advertising, *Jurnal Pengurusan*, 60. doi:10.17576/pengurusan-2020-60-02.
Shah, S.A.; Azhar, S.M.; Bhutto, N.A. (2019): Halal Marketing. A Marketing Strategy Perspective, *Journal of Islamic Marketing*, 11(6): 1641–1655.
Shaiko, R.G. (1987): Religion, Politics, and Environmental Concern, *Social Science Quarterly*, 68(2): 244–262.
Shariff, A.F.; Willard, A.K.; Andersen, T.; Norenzayan, A. (2016): Religious Priming. A Meta-Analysis with a Focus on Prosociality, *Personality and Social Psychology Review*, 20(1): 27–48.
Sharma, P.; Bharadhwaj, S.; Roger, M. (2010): Impulse Buying and Variety Seeking. A Trait-Correlates Perspective, *Journal of Business Research*, 63(3): 276–283.
Sharma, S.; Singh, G.; Gaur, L.; Sharma, R. (2022): Does Psychological Distance and Religiosity Influence Fraudulent Customer Behavior? *International Journal of Consumer Studies*, 46(4): 1468–1487.

Shatenstein, B.; Ghadirian, P.; Lambert, J. (1993): Influence of the Jewish Religion and Jewish Dietary Laws (Kashruth) on Family Food Habits in an Ultra-Orthodox Population in Montreal, *Ecology of Food and Nutrition*, 31(1–2): 27–44.

Shawchuck, N.; Kotler, P.; Wrenn, B.; Rath, G. (1992): *Marketing for Congregations*, Nashville/TN: Abingdon Press.

Shen, N.; Su, J. (2017): Religion and Succession Intention. Evidence from Chinese Family FIFMs, *Journal of Corporate Finance*, 45(August): 150–161.

Shenkar, O. (2001): Cultural Distance Revisited, *Journal of International Business Studies*, 32(3): 519–535.

Sheth, J.N. (1983): An Integrative Theory of Patronage Preference and Behavior, in: Darden, W.F.; Lusch R.F. (Eds.), *Patronage Behavior and Retail Management*, 9–28, New York: North-Holland.

Shimp, T.A.; Sharma, S. (1987): Consumer Ethnocentrism. Construction and Validation of the CETSCALE, *Journal of Marketing Research*, 24(3): 280–289.

Shin, J.; Park, M.; Moon, M.; Kim, M. (2010): *Does Religiosity Affect on Consumer's Socialization Agent and Shopping Orientation?* International Conference on E-Business, Management and Economics, 154–158, Hong Kong: IACSIT Press.

Shoham, A.; Brenčič, M.M. (2004): Value, Price Consciousness, and Consumption Frugality, *Journal of International Consumer Marketing*, 17(1): 55–69.

Shoham, A.; Davidow, M.; Klein, J.G.; Ruvio, A. (2006): Animosity on the Home Front. The Intifada in Israel and Its Impact on Consumer Behavior, *Journal of International Marketing*, 14(3): 92–114.

Shrivastava, P. (1986): Postmerger Integration, *Journal of Business Strategy*, 7(1): 65–76.

Shrivastava, P. (1987): Rigor and Practical Usefulness of Research in Strategic Management, *Strategic Management Journal*, 8(1): 79–97.

Shtudiner, Z.; Klein, G.; Zwilling, M.; Kantor, J. (2019): The Value of Souvenirs. Endowment Effect and Religion, *Annals of Tourism Research*, 74(January): 17–32.

Shuv-Ami, A.; Shalom, T. (2017): Demographic Differences of Perceived Service Quality in Emergency Rooms of Hospital Organizations, *International Journal of Organizational Analysis*, 25(2): 282–294.

Siala, H. (2013): Religious Influences on Consumers' High-Involvement Purchasing Decisions, *Journal of Services Marketing*, 27(2): 579–589.

Siala, H.; O'Keefe, R.M.; Hone, K.S. (2004): The Impact of Religious Affiliation on Trust in the Context of Electronic Commerce, *Interacting with Computers*, 16(1): 7–27.

Siamagka, N.T.; Balabanis, G. (2015): Revisiting Consumer Ethnocentrism. Review, Reconceptualization, and Empirical Testing, *Journal of International Marketing*, 23(3): 66–86.

Siegrist, M. (2008): Factors Influencing Public Acceptance of Innovative Food Technologies and Products, *Trends in Food Science & Technology*, 19(11): 603–608.

Siguaw, J.A.; Simpson, P.M. (1997): Effects of Religiousness on Sunday Shopping and Outshopping Behaviors, *International Review of Retail, Distribution and Consumer Research*, 7(1): 23–40.

Silalahi, S.A.F.; Fachrurazi, F.; Muchaddam Fahham, A. (2021): The Role of Perceived Religiosity in Strrengthening Celebrity Endorser's Credibility Dimensions, *Cogent Business & Management*, 8(1): 1956066.

Simbrunner, P.; Schlegelmilch, B.B. (2017): Moral Licensing. A Culture-Moderated Meta-Analysis, *Management Review Quarterly*, 67(4): 201–225.

Singh, J.; Singh, G.; Kumar, S.; Mathur, A.N. (2021): Religious Influences in Unrestrained Consumer Behavior, *Journal of Retailing and Consumer Services*, 58, 102262.

Singh, J.; Sirdeshmukh, D. (2000): Agency and Trust Mechanisms in Consumer Satisfaction and Loyalty Judgments, *Journal of the Academy of Marketing Science*, 28(1): 150–167.

Singhapakdi, A.; Salyachivin, S.; Virakul, B.; Veerayangkur, V. (2000): Some Important Factors Underlying Ethical Decision Making of Managers in Thailand, *Journal of Business Ethics*, 27(3): 271–284.

Singhapakdi, A.; Vitell, S.J.; Lee, D.J.; Nisius, A.M.; Yu, G.B. (2013): The Influence of Love of Money and Religiosity on Ethical Decision-Making in Marketing, *Journal of Business Ethics*, 114(1): 183–191.

Smith, A.M.; Chan, C.K. (1996): A Cross-Cultural Study of Students Expectations of Banking Services, *Working Paper Department of Management Studies*, Sheffield: University of Sheffield.

Smith, A.M.; Reynolds, N.L. (2001): Measuring Cross-Cultural Service Quality, *International Marketing Review*, 19(5): 450–480.

Smith, C.; Denton, M.L. (2005): *Soul Searching. The Religious and Spiritual Lives of American Teenagers*, New York: Oxford University Press.

Sobal, J.; Jackson-Beeck, M. (1981): Newspaper Nonreaders. A National Profile, *Journalism Quarterly*, 58(2): 9–13.

Sohaib, O.; Kang, K. (2014): The Impact of Religiosity on Interpersonal Trust in B2C Context. A Cross-Cultural Analysis, in: *Pacific Asia Conference on Information Systems*, AIS Electronic Library, https://opus.lib.uts.edu.au/handle/10453/33657 (01/12/2022).

Sohaib, O.; Kang, K. (2014): The Impact of Religiosity on Interpersonal Trust in B2C Context. A Cross-Cultural Analysis, in: The 18th Pacific Asia Conference on Information Systems (PACIS 2014 Proceedings), Chengdu/China. http://hdl.handle.net/10453/33657.

SOLOMON, M. R. 2011. Consumer behavior: buying,

Solomon, M.R. (2010): Consumer Behaviour: A European Perspective, Harlow: Pearson.

Soltani, E.; Syed, J.; Liao, Y.Y.; Iqbal, A. (2015): Managerial Mindsets toward Corporate Social Responsibility. The Case of Auto Industry in Iran, Journal of Business Ethics, 129(4): 795–810.

Sombart, W. (1911): *Die Juden und das Wirtschafsleben*, Leipzig: Duncker & Humblot.

Sood, J.; Nasu, Y. (1995): Religiosity and Nationality. An Exploratory Study of Their Effect on Consumer Behavior in Japan and the United States, *Journal of Business Research*, 34(1): 1–9.

Souiden, N.; Ladhari, R.; Zarrouk Amri, A. (2018): Is Buying Counterfeit Sinful? Investigation of Consumers' Attitudes and Purchase Intentions of Counterfeit Products in a Muslim Country, *International Journal of Consumer Studies*, 42(6): 687–703.

Souiden, N.; Rani, M. (2015): Consumer Attitudes and Purchase Intentions toward Islamic Banks. The Influence of Religiosity, *International Journal of Bank Marketing*, 33(2): 143–161.

Spiegel, P. (2010): *What Is kosher? Jüdischer Glaube - jüdisches Leben*, Berlin: Ullstein.

Spiegel, P. (2010): *Was ist kosher? Jüdischer Glaube - jüdisches Leben*, Berlin: Ullstein.

Spiro, M.E. (1966): Buddhism and Economic Action in Burma, *American Anthropologist*, 68(5): 1163–1173.

Stack, S.; Kposowa, A. (2006): The Effect of Religiosity on Tax Fraud Acceptability. A Cross-National Analysis, *Journal for the Scientific Study of Religion*, 45(3): 325–351.

Stark, R.; Glock, C.Y. (1968): *American Piety. The Nature of Religious Commitment*, Vol. 1, Berkeley/CA: University of California Press.

Starobin, S.; Weinthal, E. (2010): The Search for Credible Information in Social and Environmental Global Governance. The Kosher Label, *Business and Politics*, 12(3): 1–35.

Steger, M.F.; Kashdan, T.B.; Sullivan, B.A.; Lorentz, D. (2008): Understanding the Search for Meaning in Life, *Journal of Personality*, 76(2): 199–228.

Stiglitz, J.E. (1996): Some Lessons from the East Asian Miracle, *The World Bank Research Observer*, 11(2): 151–177.

Stillman, T.F.; Fincham, F.D.; Vohs, K.D.; Lambert, N.M.; Phillips, C.A. (2012): The Material and Immaterial in Conflict. Spirituality Reduces Conspicuous Consumption, *Journal of Economic Psychology*, 33(1): 1–7.

Stolle, D.; Micheletti, M. (2013): *Political Consumerism. Global Responsibility in Action*, Cambridge: Cambridge University Press.

Strieder, S. (2011): The Vedas, *Star Extra*, 2: 20–37.

Stulz, R.; Williamson, R. (2003): Culture Openness and Finance, *Journal of Financial Economics*, 70(3): 313–349.

Subrahmanyan, S.; Cheng, P.S. (2000): Perceptions and Attitudes of Singaporeans toward Genetically Modified Food, *Journal of Consumer Affairs*, 34(2): 269–290.

Sudbury-Riley, L.; Edgar, L. (2016): Why Older Adults Show Preference for Rational over Emotional Advertising Appeals, *Journal of Advertising Research*, 56(4): 441–455.

Sugden, C. (2001): Fair Trade as Christian Mission, in: Johnson, P.; Sugden, C. (Eds.), *Markets, Fair Trade, and the Kingdom of God*, 3–24, Oxford: Regnum Book International.

Sugiarto, C.; De Barnier, V. (2019): Are Religious Customers Skeptical toward Sexually Appealing Advertising? *Qualitative Market Research. An International Journal*, 22(5): 669–686.

Suhartanto, D.; Farhani, N.H.; Muflih, M. (2018): Loyalty Intention toward Islamic Bank. The Role of Religiosity, Image, and Trust, *International Journal of Economics & Management*, 12(1): 137–151.

Sumaedi, S.; Yarmen, M. (2015): Measuring Perceived Service Quality of Fast Food Restaurant in Islamic Country. A Conceptual Framework, *Procedia Food Science*, 3: 119–131.

Sun, S.; Goh, T.; Fam, K.S.; Xue, Y. (2012): The Influence of Religion on Islamic Mobile Phone Banking Services Adoption, *Journal of Islamic Marketing*, 3(1): 81–98.

Swatos, W.H. Jr; Olson, D.A. (Eds.) (2000): *The Secularization Debate*, Lanham: Rowman & Littlefield.

Swimberghe, K.R.; Wooldridge, B.R.; Ambort-Clark, K.A.; Rutherford, J. (2014): The Influence of Religious Commitment on Consumer Perceptions of Closed-on-Sunday Policies, *International Review of Retail, Distribution and Consumer Research*, 24(1): 14–29.

Swimberghe, K.R.; Sharma, D.; Flurry, L.A. (2011): Does a Consumer's Religion Really Matter in the Buyer-Seller Dyad? *Journal of Business Ethics*, 102(4): 581–598.

Swimberghe, K.R.; Sharma, D.; Flurry, L.A. (2009): An Exploratory Investigation of the Consumer Religious Commitment and Its Influence on Store Loyalty and Consumer Complaint Intentions, *Journal of Consumer Marketing*, 26(5): 340–347.

Tabassi, S.; Esmaeilzadeh, P.; Sambasivan, M. (2012): The Role of Animosity, Religiosity and Ethnocentrism on Consumer Purchase Intention. A Study in Malaysia towards European Brands, *African Journal of Business Management*, 6(23): 6890–6902.

Tajfel, H. (1974): Social Identity and Intergroup Behavior, *Social Science Information*, 13(2): 65–93.

Tajfel, H.; Turner, J.C. (1986): The Social Identity Theory of Intergroup Behavior, in: Austin, W.G.; Worchel, S. (Eds.), *Psychology of Intergroup Relations*, 2nd ed., 7–24, Chicago/MA: Nelson-Hall.

Talib, M.S.A.; Hamid, A.B.A.; Zulfakar, M.H.; Chin, T.A. (2015): Barriers to Halal Logistics Operation, *International Journal of Logistics Systems and Management*, 22(2): 193–209.

Tan, J.H. (2006): Religion and Social Preferences. An Experimental Study, *Economics Letters*, 90(1): 60–67.

Tan, J.H.; Vogel, C. (2008): Religion and Trust. An Experimental Study, *Journal of Economic Psychology*, 29(6):832–848.

Tang, T.L.P.; Chiu, R.K. (2003): Income, Money Ethic, Pay Satisfaction, Commitment, and Unethical Behavior, *Journal of Business Ethics*, 46(1): 13–30.

Tangney, J.P.; Baumeister, R.F.; Boone, A.L. (2004): High Self-control Predicts Good Adjustment, Less Pathology, Better Grades, and Interpersonal Success, *Journal of Personality*, 72(2): 271–324.

Tankard Jr, J.W.; Harris, M.C. (1980): A Discriminant Analysis of Television Viewers and Nonviewers, *Journal of Broadcasting & Electronic Media*, 24(3): 399–409.

Tansuhaj, P.; Gentry, J.W.; John, J.; Manzer, L.L.; Cho, B.J. (1991): A Cross-National Examination of Innovation Resistance, *International Marketing Review*, 8(3): 7–20.

Tao, M.; Lahuerta-Otero, E.; Alam, F.; Aldehayyat, J.S.; Farooqi, M.R.; Zhuoqun, P. (2022): Do Religiosity and Ethnocentrism Influence Indian Consumers' Unwillingness to Buy Halal-Made Products? The Role of Animosity toward Halal Products, *Frontiers in Psychology*, 13. doi:10.3389/fpsyg.2022.840515.

Tarhini, A.; Alalwan, A.A.; Al-Qirim, N.; Algharabat, R. (2018): An Analysis of the Factors Influencing the Adoption of Online Shopping, *International Journal of Technology Diffusion*, 9(3): 68–87.

Tariq, M.; Khan, M.A. (2017): Offensive Advertising. A Religion Based Indian Study, *Journal of Marketing*, 8(4): 656–668.

Taylor, C.R.; Raymond, M.A. (2000): An Analysis of Product Category Restrictions in Advertising in Four Major East Asian Markets, *International Marketing Review*, 17(3): 287–304.

Taylor, V.A.; Halstead, D. (2014): The Impact of Small Service Providers' Christian Identity on Consumer Perceptions, *Academy of Marketing Studies Journal*, 18(2): 203–237.

Taylor, V.A.; Halstead, D.; Haynes, P.J. (2010): Consumer Responses to Christian Religious Symbols in Advertising, *Journal of Advertising*, 39(2): 79–92.

Taylor, V.A.; Halstead, D.; Moal-Ulvoas, G. (2017): Millennial Consumer Responses to Christian Religious Symbols in Advertising. A Replication Study, *Journal of Empirical Generalizations in Marketing Science*, 17(1): 1–18.

Taylor, V.A.; Minton, E.A. (2021): Holiday Advertising versus Gift Cards. Influence of Religiosity on Retailer Evaluations, *International Journal of Consumer Studies*, 45(3): 409–422.

Terry, E. (2015): *How Asia Got Rich. Japan, China and the Asian Miracle*, London: Routledge.

Thaler, R. H.; Sunstein, C. R. (2008): *Nudge: Improving decisions about health, wealth, and happiness*, New Haven, CT: Yale University Press.

Thomsen, S.R.; Rekve, D. (2003): The Influence of Religiosity on Reaction to Alcohol Advertisements and Current Drinking among Seventh and Eight Graders, *Journal of Media and Religion*, 2(2): 93–107.

Tian, K.; Belk, R.W. (2005): Extended Self and Possessions in the Workplace, *Journal of Consumer Research*, 32(2): 297–310.

Tihanyi, L.; Griffith, D.A.; Russell, C.J. (2005): The Effect of Cultural Distance on Entry Mode Choice, International Diversification, and MNE Performance. A Meta-Analysis, *Journal of International Business Studies*, 36(3): 270–283.

Timothy, D.; Olsen, D. (2006): *Tourism, Religion and Spiritual Journeys*, London: Routledge.

Toprakyaran E. (2019): Does Religion Leave Room for Renewal? Islamic Images of God in History and the Present, in: Klußmann, J.; Kreutz, M.; Sarhan, A. (Eds.), *Reformation in Islam*, Wiesbaden: Springer VS.

Torvik, R. (2001): Learning by Doing and the Dutch Disease, *European Economic Review*, 45(2): 285–306.

Touzani, M.; Hirschman, E.C. (2008): Cultural Syncretism and Ramadan Observance. Consumer Research Visits Islam, in: Lee, A.Y.; Soman, D. (Eds.), *Advances in Consumer Research*, Vol. 35, 374–380, Duluth/MN: Association for Consumer Research.

Treisman, D. (2000): The Cause of Corruption. A Cross-National Comparison, *Journal of Public Economics*, 76(3): 399–457.

Trinitapoli, J. (2007): "I Know This Isn't PC, but...". Religious Exclusivism among US Adolescents, *Sociological Quarterly*, 48(3): 451–483.

Trudel, R.; Cote, J. (2009): Does It Pay to Be Good? *MIT Sloan Management Review*, 50(2): 61–68.

Truong, Y.; McColl, R.; Kitchen, P.J. (2010): Uncovering the Relationships between Aspirations and Luxury Brand Preference, *Journal of Product and Brand Management*, 19(5): 346–355.

Tsai, J.L.; Miao, F.F.; Seppala, E. (2007): Good Feelings in Christianity and Buddhism. Religious Differences in Ideal Affect, *Personality and Social Psychology Bulletin*, 33(3): 409–421.

Tsang, J.A.; McCullough, M.E.; Hoyt, W.T. (2005): Psychometric and Rationalization Accounts of the Religion-Forgiveness Discrepancy, *Journal of Social Issues*, 61(4): 785–805.

Tsarenko, Y.; Tojib, D. (2012): The Role of Personality Characteristics and Service Failure Severity in Consumer Forgiveness and Service Outcomes, *Journal of Marketing Management*, 28(9/10): 1217–1239.

Tscheulin, D.K.; Dietrich, M. (2001): Church Marketing, in: Tscheulin, D.K.; Helmig, B. (Eds.), *Industry-Specific Marketing*, 373–400, Wiesbaden: Gabler.

Tuttle, J.D.; Davis, S.N. (2015): Religion, Infidelity, and Divorce. Reexamining the Effect of Religious Behavior on Divorce among Long-Married Couples, *Journal of Divorce & Remarriage*, 56(6): 475–489.

Tylor, E.B. (1871): *Primitive Culture. Researches into the Development of Mythology, Philosophy, Religion, Art and Custom*, Vol. 2, London: Murray.

Ulvoas-Moal, G. (2010): Exploring the Influence of Spirituality: A New Perspective on Senior Consumers' Behavior. *Advances in Consumer Research*, 37(1), 917–919.

Uppal, J.S. (1986): Hinduism and Economic Development in South Asia, *International Journal of Social Economics*, 13(3): 20–33.

Usman, H.; Chairy, C.; Projo, N.W.K. (2021): Impact of Muslim Decision-Making Style and Religiosity on Intention to Purchasing Certified Halal Food, *Journal of Islamic Marketing*, 13(11): 2268–2289.

Usunier, J.C.; Stolz, J. (2016): *Religions as Brands. New Perspectives on the Marketization of Religion and Spirituality*, New York: Routledge.

Uysal, A.; Okumuş, A. (2019): Impact of Religiosity on Ethical Judgement. A Study on Preference of Retail Stores among Consumers, *Journal of Islamic Marketing*, 10(4): 1332–1350.

Vail, K.E.; Rothschild, Z.K.; Weise, D.R.; Solomon, S.; Pyszczynski, T.; Greenberg, J. (2010): A Terror Management Analysis of the Psychological Functions of Religion, *Personality and Social Psychology Review*, 14(1): 84–94.

van Assche, J.; Bahamondes, J.; Sibley, C. (2021): Religion and Prejudice across Cultures, *Social Psychological and Personality Science*, 12(3): 287–295.

van Cranenburgh, K.; Arenas, D.; Goodman, J.; Louche, C. (2014): Religious Organizations as Investors. A Christian Perspective on Shareholder Engagement, *Society and Business Review*, 9(2): 195–213.

van der Meer-Sanchez, Z.M.; De Oliveira, L.G.; Nappo, S.A. (2008): Religiosity as a Protective Factor against the Use of Drugs, *Substance Use & Misuse*, 43(10): 1476–1486.

van der Toorn, J.; Jost, J.T.; Packer, D.J.; Noorbaloochi, S.; van Bavel, J.J. (2017): In Defense of Tradition. Religiosity, Conservatism, and Opposition to Same-Sex Marriage in North America, *Personality and Social Psychology Bulletin*, 43(10): 1455–1468.

van Esch, P.; Overton, L.R.A.; van Esch, L.J. (2014): Mass Media Social Marketing Campaigns. A Review, *International Business Research*, 7(6): 1–17.

van Laer, T.; Izberk-Bilgin, E. (2019): A Discourse Analysis of Pilgrimage Reviews, *Journal of Marketing Management*, 35(5/6): 586–604.

Vasilenko, S.A.; Duntzee, C.I.; Zheng, Y.; Lefkowitz, E.S. (2013): Testing Two Process Models of Religiosity and Sexual Behavior, *Journal of Adolescence*, 36(4): 667–673.

Veer, E.; Shankar, A. (2011): Forgive Me, Father, for I Did Not Give Full Justification for My Sins. How Religious Consumers Justify the Acquisition of Material Wealth, *Journal of Marketing Management*, 27(5–6): 547–560.

Verbeke, W., Rutsaert, P., Bonne, K., & Vermeir, I. (2013). Credence quality coordination and consumers' willingness-to-pay for certified halal labelled meat. *Meat science*, 95(4), 790–797.

Verlegh, P.W.; Steenkamp, J.B.E. (1999): A Review and Meta-Analysis of Country-of-Origin Research, *Journal of Economic Psychology*, 20(5): 521–546.

Vietze, C. (2012): Cultural Effects on Inbound Tourism into the USA. A Gravity Approach, *Tourism Economics*, 18(1): 121–138.

Vigneron, F.; Johnson, L.W. (2004): Measuring Perceptions of Brand Luxury, *Journal of Brand Management*, 11(6): 484–506.

Vinod, H.D. (Ed.) (2013): *Handbook of Hindu Economics and Business*, Scotts Valey: CreateSpace.

Vinson, D.E.; Scott, J.E.; Lamont, L.M. (1977): The Role of Personal Values in Marketing and Consumer Behavior, *Journal of Marketing*, 41(2): 44–50.

Vitell, S.J. (2009): The Role of Religiosity in Business and Consumer Ethics. A Review of the Literature, *Journal of Business Ethics*, 90(2): 155–167.

Vitell, S.J.; Bing, M.N.; Davison, H.K.; Ammeter, A.P.; Garner, B.L.; Novicevic, M.M. (2009): Religiosity and Moral Identity. The Mediating Role of Self-control, *Journal of Business Ethics*, 88(4): 601–613.

Vitell, S.J.; King, R.A.; Howie, K.; Toti, J.F.; Albert, L.; Hidalgo, E.R.; Yacout, O. (2016): Spirituality, Moral Identity, and Consumer Ethics: A Multi-Cultural Study. *Journal of Business Ethics*, 139, 147–160.

Vitell, S.J.; Muncy, J. (2005): The Muncy-Vitell Consumer Ethics, Scale, *Journal of Business Ethics*, 62(3): 267–275.

Vitell, S.J.; Paolillo, J.G.; Singh, J.J. (2005): Religiosity and Consumer Ethics, *Journal of Business Ethics*, 57(2):175–181.

Vitell, S.J.; Paolillo, J.G.; Singh, J.J. (2006): The Role of Money and Religiosity in Determining Consumers' Ethical Beliefs, *Journal of Business Ethics*, 64(2): 117–124.

Vitell, S.J.; Singh, J.J.; Paolillo, J.G. (2007): Consumers' Ethical Beliefs. The Roles of Money, Religiosity and Attitude toward Business, *Journal of Business Ethics*, 73(4): 369–379.

Völckner, F.; Hofmann, J. (2007): The Price-Perceived Quality Relationship. A Meta-Analytic Review and Assessment of Its Determinants, *Marketing Letters*, 18(3): 181–196.

Wagner, U.; Jamsawang, J. (2014): Culture-Specific Number Symbolism in Restaurant Prices, *Global Economic Review*, 43(1): 58–72.

Wahyoedi, S.; Sudiro, A.; Sunaryo, S.; Sudjatno, S. (2021): The Effect of Religiosity and Service Quality on Customer Loyalty of Islamic Banks Mediated by Customer Trust and Satisfaction, *Management Science Letters*, 11: 187–194.

Walker, A.G.; Smither, J.W.; DeBode, J. (2012): The Effects of Religiosity on Ethical Judgments, *Journal of Business Ethics*, 106(4): 437–452.

Waller, D.S.; Casidy, R. (2021): Religion, Spirituality, and Advertising, *Journal of Advertising*, 50(4): 349–353.

Waller, D.S.; Fam, K.S. (2000): Cultural Values and Advertising in Malaysia, *Asia Pacific Journal of Marketing and. Logistics*, 12(1): 3–16.

Wang, C.L.; Sarkar, J.G.; Sarkar, A. (2019): Hallowed Be thy Brand. Measuring Perceived Brand Sacredness, *European Journal of Marketing*, 53(4): 733–757.

Wang, J.; Wang, C. (2021): Can Religions Explain Cross Country Differences in Innovative Activities? *Technovation*, 107(September): 1–16.

Wang, L.; Wong, P.P.W.; Elangkovan, N.A. (2020): The Influence of Religiosity on Consumer's Green Purchase Intention toward Green Hotel Selection in China, *Journal of China Tourism Research*, 16(3): 319–345.

Wang, L.; Zhang, Q. (2020): Marketing of Environmentally Friendly Hotels in China through Religious Segmentation, *International Journal of Tourism & Hotel Business Management*, 3(2): 405–425.

Wang, S.; Wang, J.; Li, J.; Zhou, K. (2020): How and When Does Religiosity Contribute to Tourists' Intention to Behave Pro-environmentally in Hotels? *Journal of Sustainable Tourism*, 28(8): 1120–1137.

Wang, S.W.; Scheinbaum, A.C. (2017): Trustworthiness Trumps Attractiveness and Expertise. Enhancing Brand Credibility through Celebrity Endorsement, *Journal of Advertising Research*, 58(1): 16–32.

Wang, Z.; Deshpande, S.; Waller, D.S.; Erdogan, B.Z. (2018): Religion and Perceptions of the Regulation of Controversial Advertising, *Journal of International Consumer Marketing*, 30(1): 29–44.

Watanabe, S.; Laurent, S.M. (2018): Past Its Prime? A Methodological Overview and Critique of Religious Priming Research in Social Psychology, *Journal for the Cognitive Science of Religion*, 6(1–2): 31–55.

Watson, P.J.; Jones, N.D.; Morris, R.J. (2004): Religious Orientation and Attitudes toward Money, *Mental Health*, 7(4): 277–288.

Watterson, K.; Giesler, B.R. (2012): Religiosity and Self-control, *Psychology of Religion and Spirituality*, 4(3): 193–205.

Weaver, A.J.; Flannelly, K.J.; Strock, A.L. (2005): A Review of Research on the Effects of Religion on Adolescent Tobacco Use Published between 1990 and 2003, *Adolescence*, 40(160): 761–775.

Webb, M.S.; Joseph, W.B.; Schimmel, K.; Moberg, C. (1998): Church Marketing. Strategies for Retaining and Attracting Members, *Journal of Professional Services Marketing*, 17(2): 1–16.

Weber, M. (1905): *The Protestant Ethic and the Spirit of Capitalism*, New York: Charles Scribner's Sons.

Weber, M. (1915): The Economic Ethics of the World's Religions. Sociological Sketches of Religion. Confucianism I/II, *Archives of Social Science and Social Policy*, 41(1): 1–87.

Weber, M. (1920): *Collected Essays on the Sociology of Religion*, Vol. 1, Tübingen: UTB.

Weber, M. (1988): *Collected Essays on the Sociology of Religion. The Economic Ethics of World Religions II – Hinduism and Buddhism*, Tübingen: Mohr.

Wei, S.; Ang, T.; Jancenelle, V.E. (2018): Willingness to Pay More for Green Products. The Interplay of Consumer Characteristics and Customer Participation, *Journal of Retailing and Consumer Services*, 45: 230–238.

Weller, L.; Levinbok, S.; Maimon, R.; Shaham, A. (1975): Religiosity and Authoritarianism, *Journal of Social Psychology*, 95(1): 11–18.

West, B.; Hillenbrand, C.; Money, K.; Ghobadian, A.; Ireland, R.D. (2016): Exploring the Impact of Social Axioms on FIFM Reputation, *British Journal of Management*, 27(2): 249–270.

Westley, B.H.; Severin, W.J. (1964): Some Correlates of Media Credibility, *Journalism Quarterly*, 41(3): 325–335.

White, K.; MacDonnell, R.; Ellard, J.H. (2012): Belief in a Just World. Consumer Intentions and Behaviors toward Ethical Products, *Journal of Marketing*, 76(1): 103–118.

White, L. (1967): The Historical Roots of Our Environmental Crisis, *Science*, 155(3767): 1203–1207.

Wicks, J.L.; Morimoto, S.; Wicks, R.H.; Schulte, S.R. (2017): Are Religious Factors Associated with Political Consumerism? *Journal of Media and Religion*, 16(3): 81–92.

Wiebe, K.F.; Fleck, J.R. (1980): Personality Correlates of Intrinsic, Extrinsic, and Nonreligious Orientations, *Journal of Psychology*, 105(2): 181–187.

Wilcox, K.; Kim, H.M.; Sen, S. (2009): Why Do Consumers Buy Counterfeit Luxury Brands? *Journal of Marketing Research*, 46(April): 247–259.

Wilkes, R.E.; Burnett, J.J.; Howell, R.D. (1986): On the Meaning and Measurement of Religiosity in Consumer Research, *Journal of the Academy of Marketing Science*, 14(1): 47–56.

Wilkins, S.; Butt, M.M.; Shams, F.; Pérez, A. (2019b): The Acceptance of Halal Food in Non-Muslim Countries, *Journal of Islamic Marketing*, 10(4): 1308–1331.

Williams, A.; Sharma, A. (2005): Building an Islamic Brand, *Brand Strategy*, 197: 52–53.

Williams, G.; Zinkin, J. (2010): Islam and CSR. A Study of the Compatibility between the Tenets of Islam and the UN Global Compact, *Journal of Business Ethics*, 91(4): 519–533.

Williams-Oerberg, E. (2021): The Economics of Buddhism, in: Barton, J. (Ed.), *Oxford Research Encyclopedia of Religion*, Oxford: Oxford University Press.

Wilson, D.S. (2002): *Darwin's Cathedral. Evolution, Religion, and the Nature of Society*, Chicago/IL: University of Chicago Press.

Wilson, D.S.; Wilson, E.O. (2007): Rethinking the Theoretical Foundation of Sociobiology, *Quarterly Review of Biology*, 82(4): 327–348.

Wilson, J.A.; Ayad, N.I. (2021): Religiosity and Egyptian Muslim Millennials' Views on Offensive Advertising, *Journal of Islamic Marketing*, 13(12): 2759–2777.

Wind, Y. (1986): The Myth of Globalization, *Journal of Consumer Marketing*, Vol. 3 No. 2, pp. 23–26. https://doi.org/10.1108/eb008160

Winram, S. (1984). The opportunity for world brands. International *Journal of Advertising*, 3(1), 17–26.

Wirtz, J.; Kum, D.; Lee, K.S. (2000): Should a Firm with a Reputation for Outstanding Service Quality Offer a Service Guarantee? *Journal of Services Marketing*, 14(6): 502–512.

Wirtz, J.G.; Sparks, J.V.; Zimbres, T.M. (2018): The Effect of Exposure to Sexual Appeals in Advertisements on Memory, Attitude, and Purchase Intention. A Meta-Analytic Review, *International Journal of Advertising*, 37(2): 168–198.

Wisker, Z.L. (2020): The Effect of Fake News in Marketing Halal Food. A Moderating Role *of* Religiosity, *Journal of Islamic Marketing*, 12(3): 558–575.

Wisker, Z.L.; McKie, R.N. (2021): The Effect of Fake News on Anger and Negative Word-of-Mouth. Moderating Roles of Religiosity and Conservatism, *Journal of Marketing Analytics*, 9(2): 144–153.

Wollschleger, J. (2017): The Rite Way. Integrating Emotion and Rationality in Religious Participation, *Rationality and Society*, 29(2): 179–202.

Wong, H.M. (2008): Religiousness, Love of Money, and Ethical Attitudes of Malaysian Evangelical Christians in Business, *Journal of Business Ethics*, 81(1): 169–191.

Wong, N.Y. (2004): The Role of Culture in the Perception of Service Recovery, *Journal of Business Research*, 57(9): 957–963.

Worsfold, K.; Worsfold, J.; Bradley, G. (2007): Interactive Effects of Proactive and Reactive Service Recovery Strategies, *Journal of Applied Social Psychology*, 37(11): 2496–2517.

Wu, E.C.; Cutright, K.M. (2018): In God's Hands. How Reminders of God Dampen the Effectiveness of Fear Appeals, *Journal of Marketing Research*, 55(1): 119–131.

Xu, A.J.; Olson, N.; Ahluwalia, R. (2016): Love It but Leave It. The Divergent Effects of Religiosity on Attitudinal versus Behavioral Brand Loyalty, in: Moreau, P.; Puntoni, S. (Eds.), *Advances in Consumer Research*, Vol. 44, 269–273, Duluth/MN: Association for Consumer Research.

Xygalatas, D. (2017), "Are Religious People More Moral?" Available at: https://theconversation.com/are-religious-peoplemore-moral-84560.

Yaakop, A.Y.; Hafeez, H.M.; Faisal, M.M.; Munir, M.; Ali, M. (2021): Impact of Religiosity on Purchase Intentions toward Counterfeit Products. Investigating the Mediating Role of Attitude and Moderating Role of Hedonic Benefits, *Heliyon*, 7(2): 1–7.

Yadav, S.; Kohli, N.; Kumar, V. (2016): Spiritual Intelligence and Ethics in Negotiation, *Journal of Psychosocial Research*, 11(1): 49–60.

Yao, X. (2000): *An Introduction to Confucianism*, Cambridge: Cambridge University Press.

Yau, O. H. (1988). Chinese cultural values: Their dimensions and marketing implications. *European Journal of marketing*, 22(5), 44–57.

Yau, O.H.M.; Lee, J.S.Y.; Raymond, P.M.C.; Leo, Y.M.; Tse, A.C.B. (2000): Relationship Marketing the Chinese Way, *Business Horizons*, 43(1): 16–24.

Yavas, U.; Tuncalp, S. (1984): Perceived Risk in Grocery Outlet Selection. A Case Study in Saudi Arabia, *European Journal of Marketing*, 18(3): 13–25.

Yousaf, S.; Malik, M.S. (2013): Evaluating the Influences of Religiosity and Product Involvement Level on the Consumers, *Journal of Islamic Marketing*, 4(2): 163–186.

Ysseldyk, R.; Matheson, K.; Anisman, H. (2010): Religiosity as Identity. Toward an Understanding of Religion from a Social Identity Perspective, *Personality and Social Psychology Review*, 14(1): 60–71.

Yun, Z.; Verma, S.; Pysarchik, D.T.; Yu, J.; Chowdhury, S. (2008): Cultural Influences on New Product Adoption of Affluent Consumers in India, *International Review of Retail, Distribution & Consumer Research*, 18(2): 203–220.

Yusuf, A.M.; Madichie, N.O. (2012): An Exploratory Enquiry into the Challenges of Modern Retailing on Muslim Consumers in Northern Nigeria, *African Journal of Business and Economic Research*, 7(1): 99–114.

Zaman, R.; Roudaki, J.; Nadeem, M. (2018): Religiosity and Corporate Social Responsibility Practices, *Social Responsibility Journal*, 14(2): 368–395.

Zehra, S.; Minton, E. (2020): Should Businesses Use Religious Cues in Advertising? *International Journal of Consumer Studies*, 44(5): 393–406.

Zhang, J.; Brown, E.; Xie, H. (2020): Effect of Religious Priming in Prosocial and Destructive Behavior, *Pacific. Economic Review*, 25(1): 47–68.

Zhou, W.; Lee, Y.F.L.; Hyman, M.R. (2017): When Old Meets New. How China's 'Double-Eleven' Day Challenges Confucianism, *Asian Journal of Business Research*, 7(1): 27–42.

Zuckerman, M.; Li, C.; Lin, S.; Hall, J.A. (2020): The Negative Intelligence – Religiosity Relation. New and ConfIFMing Evidence, *Personality and Social Psychology Bulletin*, 46(6): 856–868.

Zuckerman, M.; Silberman, J.; Hall, J.A. (2013): The Relation between Intelligence and Religiosity. A Meta-Analysis and Some Proposed Explanations, *Personality and Social Psychology Review*, 17(4): 325–354.

Index

adoption of innovative products 24, 111, 114
advertising: attitude 251–252; celebrities 254–255; Christmas 228; comparative 263; controversial 64, 261–263; design 252; effectiveness 265–266; emotional appeals 210, 255–257; fear-inducing appeals 252; icons 140; message 235–239; moral appeals 260; non-profit 98; personal 249; price 264–265; religious appeals 236, 259–260; subtle 67; symbols 237; testimonials 254–255; timing 243; trust 67, 69; word-of-mouth 232
ancestor worship 42
anger *see* emotions
animals 7, 144, 258–259
animism 40, 47–48
animistic beliefs 41–42
animosity 131–133
anti-intellectuality thesis 112
assortment policy 224–225
atheism 39
attention 236–239
attitudes: attitude/behavior gap 102–103; hypocrisy hypothesis 79, 145; interfaith attitudinal/behavioral model 18–20; toward advertising 251–252; toward money and possessions 179–181
attracting attention *see* attention
authoritarianism 52–53
awareness: brand awareness 64, 139; environmental awareness 100–103, 154; ethical awareness 74; fashion awareness 64; of living in the debt of God 60; quality awareness 118

backlash effect *see* risk
behavioral regulation 17–18
beliefs *see* animistic; ethical; fatalistic; folk; religious; spiritual
benefit: individual benefit 116, 173; material *vs.* immaterial *vs.* spiritual benefit 142; product benefit 193; spiritual benefit 75; types of benefits 107–108
bias: Cognitive Bias Codex 75; home 190; intergroup 210; judgment 75; response *see* comparative religion research; self-serving 75; social desirability 25, 75–76
brand loyalty: emotional brand loyalty 84; *see also* customer loyalty; loyalty
branding: brand awareness *see* awareness; brand communities 137; brand evangelism 137; brand love 137; brand loyalty 84 *see also* customer loyalty; brand philosophy 71; brand piracy 147; brand religiosity 137; brand trust *see* trust; brand types 135–136; religious brands 192; secular brands 191; substitute for religion 135
Buddhism 16–17, 31, 41–42, 44–47, 54, 68, 100, 102, 127, 179, 195, 236, 256, 258
business ethics: Buddhist 16–17; Catholic 11–12; Confucian 14–15; Hindu 15–16; Islamic 13–14; Jewish 10–11; Orthodox 13; Protestant 12–13
buyer types 66–69

caste system 16, 46
celebrities *see* advertising
Christian beliefs 126
Christianity 11–13, 19, 30, 42, 44, 47, 51, 63, 109, 127, 169, 204, 259; *see also* Christian beliefs
Christmas *see* advertising

color design *see* product policy
communication: communication policy 5, 233; of country of origin *see* country of origin; credibility 239, 245–248; face-to-face 166–167; goals 235–239; personal communication 249–250; target groups 240–242; timing 243
comparative religion research: methodological problems 21–25; moderation *vs.* mediation xviii
complaint: expectations 173–174; influence of confession 167; likelihood 81; management 171–173; satisfaction 174–175
conflict 167, 169, 172, 244
Confucianism 9, 14–15, 30–31, 47, 63, 127, 179, 188, 204, 236
consumer behavior *see* religion and religiosity
consumption: frugal consumption 122–123; luxury consumption 121–122
controversial products *see* product policy
convenience product *see* product policy
CoO *see* country of origin
Corporate Social Responsibility 87–89, 98, 229
corporate stewardship 98
corruption: business ethics 15; Corruption Perception Index 204; market entry 203–205; religion/corruption thesis 202–203
country distance *see* distance
country of origin: communication 130–134; effects 190–191
credibility *see* communication
CSR *see* Corporate Social Responsibility
cultural distance *see* distance
culture: corporate culture 213; country culture 5, 151–152; culture dimensions 205–206; national culture 4, 174; nature religions *vs.* culture religions 47; religion *vs.* culture 22–23
customer loyalty: brand loyalty 84, 134–137, 140–141; common religious identity 231; fair pricing 183; religiosity and customer loyalty 157–158, 230; shopping place loyalty 82–83; switching service provider *see* service
customer satisfaction *see* satisfaction

decision-making style 71–75
denomination 31, 42, 44
diaspora 23
dietary laws 6–7
differentiation 91–95
diffusion curve 114
direct investment 203, 207, 211–213
dissatisfaction *see* satisfaction
distance: country distance 208; cultural distance 208, 214; geographical distance 208, 220; linguistic distance 209; power distance 188, 205; religious distance 207–209, 214
distribution: brick-and-motar channels 217–219; distribution channels 216–217; distribution policy 5, 201; electronic channels 219–222
dogmatism 53–54, 61, 109, 132

effects: backlash *see* risk; economic, non-economic 265; interaction 68, 77, 119; vampire *see* risk
emotions: anger 167, 169, 171, 173, 250, 261; awe 36; brand love 137, 140; envy 128; fear 252; frustration 164; jealousy 128; love of one's own country 56; love thy neighbor commandment 79; mutual love 63; rage 171
endowment effect 181–182
environment: awareness 100–103, 146, 154; certificates 192–193; consciousness 39, 101 *see also* target group; environmentally conscious products *see* product policy; guilt 125; protection 24, 122–126
ethic: beliefs *see* ethical beliefs; business ethics 9–17; orientation 89; positioning 231–232; work ethic 59–63
ethical beliefs 39
ethnocentrism 54–56, 130–131, 144; ethnocentric beliefs 130
evening entertainment 153
eWoM *see* word of mouth
expected utility theory 6
experimental design *see* comparative religion research

fairness signaling 216; fairness of the market 215, 236
fairness: fair price 183; fairness toward other people 73; fair trade 193–195
fatalism 57–58, 81, 110–111, 166; *see* fatalistic beliefs

fatalistic beliefs 68
financial service 155–159, 260
five pillars of Islam 156
folk beliefs 41, 48
food laws 6–7, 120
forgiveness 81, 164, 169–171
frugal consumption *see* consumption
future orientation 63, 122, 205

geographical distance *see* distance
GLOBE Study 205
gratification theory 244

halal 7, 72, 78, 119–120, 131, 136, 143–144, 186, 192, 224, 230
health services 159–160
hinduism 9, 37, 44–47, 62, 68, 124–127, 146, 169, 172
Hofstede 205–207
holiday, religious 224
home bias *see* bias
hostility: animosity 131; different faith 207; outsiders 206–207; *see also* innovation
hypocrisy hypothesis *see* attitude

identity: theory of social identity 6, 8, 30–31, 135; *see also* customer loyalty; nation
information search 70
innovation: adoption 24; hostility to 14; innovation management 113–117; product innovation 109–113
intergroup bias *see* bias
Islam: basics 44–47; brand loyalty 84; Islamic business ethics 13–14; Islamic-compliant financial services 156–158; new religions 42; sacred color 126–127; Sufism 37; Zakāt 100
Islamic banking *see* Islam

joint ventures *see* market entry
Judaism 7, 11, 19, 22, 30, 37, 47–48, 51, 59, 109, 112, 142
judgment bias *see* bias

karma 61–62, 81
kosher 7, 65, 119, 136, 142, 184, 192

life satisfaction *see* satisfaction
lifestyle: ascetic 13; consumption-oriented 99; modest 74, 122; selfless 97; *see also* materialism
linguistic distance *see* distance
location: foreign investment 214; foreign production 130; headquarter 158; retail stores 223
long-term *vs.* short-term orientation *see* orientation
love of money 180
love *see* emotions
loyalty *see* customer loyalty
luxury consumption *see* consumption

magic 40
majority religion *see* religion
market entry: barriers 202; corruption 203–205; entry strategies 211; joint ventures 214–215; mergers and acquisition 213–214; religious distance 214; timing 114
market segmentation 92–95
marketing goals 87
materialism: consumers 99; hedonistic *vs.* utilitarian 141; lifestyle 99, 121, 180–181; personality 54, 79, 139; social status 107; *see also* satisfaction; target groups
media usage: credibility, trust 245; intensity 245; motives 244–245
mergers and acquisition 213–214
methodological problems *see* comparative religion research
minority religion *see* religion
mistrust *see* trust
moderation *vs.* mediation *see* comparative religion research
modesty 120–122
monotheism 46–47, 51, 98, 100, 109, 130, 147, 175
monotheistic religions *see* religion
moral: appeals 260–261; Confucian 14, 63; doctrines 30–31; duty 63; identity 90; licensing 74, 102–103; norms 40; self-improvement 88; socially responsibility 87; strictness 262
mysticism 36–37, 48, 53, 244

naming *see* product policy
nation: national culture 4, 22–23, 174; nationalism 56–57; national pride 56–78, 96, 130; national identity 144
natural religion *see* religion
nature religion 47
negotiations 187, 209–210; *see also* trust
New Testament 11
nudity 257–258

Old Testament 80, 169
online shopping *see* shopping
operationalization problems *see* comparative religion research
organizational buying behavior 195–196
orientation: control 175; ethical 89; future *see* future orientation; goal 173; long-term 73, 81; past *see* past orientation; performance 63; political 125; price *see* pricing policy; quality *see* quality; relationship 96, 216, 228; religious 159–160, 264; religious communities 92; value 96

past orientation 63
patriotism 55–57, 191
performance ethics *see* work ethic
phenomenology of religions *see* religion
pilgrimage 153–154, 224
political attitudes 103
polytheistic religions *see* religion
power distance *see* distance
price consciousness *see* pricing policy
price fairness *see* pricing policy
price interest *see* pricing policy
price orientation *see* pricing policy
price sensitivity *see* pricing policy
pricing policy: endowment effect 181–182; love of money 180; price advertising *see* advertising; price consciousness 185; price fairness 80, 183–184; price interest 186–187; price orientation 185–186; price satisfaction *see* satisfaction; price sensitivity 188; willingness to pay 71–72, 146, 188–197
product design *see* product policy
product ideas *see* product policy
product policy: color design 126–128; controversial products 261–262; convenience products 142; environmentally conscious products 144–146; naming 128–129; product benefit 193; product design 118–126; product ideas 113–114; product innovation 109–113; product quality 66–69; religious *vs.* sacralized products 143–144; taboo products 146–147
product: fair trade *see* fairness; risk 111
prophetic religions *see* religion
protectionism 206
Protestant beliefs 83, 165
purchase: decisions 70; family decisions 76–77; intention 77–78, 131, 139–140, 147, 237–239, 255–259; motives 87–89, 185–186; purchasing behavior 193; risk 71

quality: product quality 66–69, 118–119, 123, 130, 134, 217, 228; quality-oriented decision-making style 71–72; service quality 161–162
quality-orientation *see* quality

racism 41, 54–55
rage *see* emotions
Ramadan 18, 61, 156, 158, 196, 224–225, 243
religion/corruption thesis *see* corruption
religion: consumer behavior 64–79; definitions 29–31; majority and minority 23; monotheistic 47, 51, 98; mystical 48; natural 40–41; old and new 40, 42–43; personality 52; phenomenology 45–48; polytheistic 46–47, 53, 63; prophetic 48; religion *vs.* culture 22–23; salience 81; science 110; taboo subject 4; ubiquity 4; world religions 44–48
religiosity: acceptance of innovation 110–111; and customer loyalty 82–84; brand religiosity 137; consumer behavior 64–79; definition 31; environmental awareness 102; intrinsic *vs.* extrinsic religiosity 33; life satisfaction 102; measurement 32–35; national pride 58; personality 52–63; religious affiliation 35
religious affiliation 3, 6, 8, 10, 18–19, 21–22, 31, 32, 35, 54
religious beliefs 4, 6, 10, 19, 30–32, 36, 41, 46, 51, 64–65, 87, 90, 97, 122, 138, 159, 180, 228, 249; *see also* Christian beliefs; ethnocentrism; Protestant beliefs; superstition
religious distance *see* distance
religious symbols *see* symbols
reputation 165, 193, 223–224
response bias *see* comparative religion research
responsibility: attribution 172; consumer 73; individual 34, 61, 75; managerial 87–90; Zakat 156; *see also* business ethics; Corporate Social Responsibility
risk: acceptance 240–241; aversion 51, 65, 73, 84, 110–111, 211, 216, 222–223; backlash effect 238; decision-making style 72; functional

119; perception 58, 65, 110, 119; product 113, 118; psychological 119; purchase risk 71; quality 138; sensitivity 111, 241–242; social 118, 138; vampire effect 238, 257

sacralization 38, 137, 226
sacralized products *see* product policy
satisfaction: complaint satisfaction 174–175; customer satisfaction 81, 152, 162–164, 170; dissatisfaction 81, 152, 164–167; life satisfaction 102, 180, 229; materialism 54; patient satisfaction 160; price satisfaction 183
secularization 7, 34, 37–38, 92, 98–99, 136, 225, 244, 260
self-serving bias *see* bias
service: expectations of consumers 162–163; failure 165–166, 169–175, 250; financial *see* financial services; health *see* health services; importance 69; Islamic-compliant 156–158; quality 161–162; service businesses 153–160; service policy 149–152; transport *see* transport services
Shintoismus 17, 31, 42, 259
shopping: behavior 65, 110–111; frequency 230; location 226; online 219–222; shopping place preference 227–230; traditional 217–219; *see also* store
significance *vs.* relevance *see* comparative religion research
social desirability bias *see* bias
social identity *see* identity
spiritual beliefs 36, 97
spirituality: basics 36–37, 54, decision-making style 74–75, 171, 244; *see also* benefit; spiritual beliefs
sponsoring 264
standardization/differentiation debate: contribution to Interfaith Marketing 92; differentiated standardization 95; standardization thesis 91
stewardship 100, 122, 124–125; *see also* corporate stewardship
store: assortment policy 224–225; department 227–229, 230; evaluative criteria 216–217, 229; Islamic 231; loyalty 68, 82–83; management 223; neighborhood 218; online 221; opening hours 225; price level 186; shopping likelihood/frequency 229–230
strategic marketing 85–89
Sufism *see* Islam
superstition 41, 53; beliefs 130
sustainability 24, 100, 123–124, 184
switching service providers *see* service
symbols: luck 129; national 131; religious 41, 65, 118, 139–140, 166, 172, 236–238, 259–260; Tibetan 129

taboo: religion-specific 46 *see also* religion; product policy; sexuality 257–258, 261–263
target group: environmentally conscious 100–103; materialists 99–100; religious 31, 96–99
testimonials *see* advertising
timing: communication 243; market entry 114
tourism 153–154
traditional shopping *see* shopping
transport services 153–154, 192
trust: advertising 249; advertising success 240–241; artificial intelligence 115; brand trust 138, 195; cooperation 202–203, 218; emotional 220; fair trade 194; halal label 230; in other 155, 207, 215–216, 220–222; management 213–214; media 245; mistrust 202; mutual 207; negotiations 209; recommendations 167; religion 9; same religious community 231

value: added 226; caring 264; Catholic 12; conformity 252–254; financial 265; for money 188, 223; hedonistic 121; Islamic 88; religious 81; symbolic 241, 259; system 3, 135, 165; terminal 18, 64; typology (Vinson et al.) 18, 64
vampire effect *see* risk

willingness to pay *see* pricing policy
WoM *see* word of mouth
word of mouth: fake reviews 168; negative WoM 152, 164, 167–168, 249–250; positive WoM 83, 140
work ethic: Catholic 61; Confucian 62–63; Hindu 61–62; Islamic 61; Jewish 59; Protestant 59–60
world religions 44–47, 55, 74, 81, 92, 156, 169, 179, 248, 257–258
world religions *see* religion